Analyzing Linguistic Dat

A Practical Introduction to Statist

Statistical analysis is a useful skill for linguists and psychol ⌐
them to understand the quantitative structure of their data. This textbook provides a straightforward introduction to the statistical analysis of language data. Designed for linguists with a non-mathematical background, it clearly introduces the basic principles and methods of statistical analysis, using R, the leading computational statistics programming environment. The reader is guided step-by-step through a range of real data sets, allowing them to analyze phonetic data, construct phylogenetic trees, quantify register variation in corpus linguistics, and analyze experimental data using state-of-the-art models. The visualization of data plays a key role, both in the early stages of data exploration and later on when the reader is encouraged to criticize initial models fitted to the data. Containing over 40 exercises with model answers, this book will be welcomed by all linguists wishing to learn more about working with and presenting quantitative data.

The program R is available at http://cran.at.r-project.org/. The data sets and ancillary functions discussed in this book have been brought together in the language R package, which is available at the same URL.

R. H. BAAYEN is Professor of Quantitative Linguistics at the University of Alberta, Edmonton. He is author of *Word Frequency Distributions* (2001), co-editor of *Morphological Structure in Language Processing* (2003), and has published widely in linguistics and psycholinguistics journals.

To Jorn, Corine, Thera, and Tineke

Contents

Preface

This book provides an introduction to the statistical analysis of quantitative data for researchers studying aspects of language and language processing. The statistical analysis of quantitative data is often seen as an onerous task that we would rather leave to others. Statistical packages tend to be used as a kind of oracle, from which you elicit a verdict as to whether you have one or more significant effects in your data. In order to elicit a response from the oracle, you have to click your way through cascades of menus. After a magic button press, voluminous output tends to be produced that hides the p-values, the ultimate goal of the statistical pilgrimage, among lots of other numbers that are completely meaningless to the user, as befits a true oracle.

The approach to data analysis to which this book provides a guide is fundamentally different in several ways. First of all, we will make use of a radically different tool for doing statistics, the interactive programming environment known as R. R is an open source implementation of the (object-oriented) S language for statistical analysis originally developed at Bell Laboratories. It is the platform par excellence for research and development in computational statistics. It can be downloaded from the COMPREHENSIVE R ARCHIVE NETWORK (CRAN) at http://cran.r-project.org or one of the many mirror sites. Learning to work with R is in many ways similar to learning a new language. Once you have mastered its grammar, and once you have acquired some basic vocabulary, you will also have begun to acquire a new way of thinking about data analysis that is essential for understanding the structure in your data. The design of R is especially elegant in that it has a consistent uniform syntax for specifying statistical models, no matter which type of model is being fitted.

What is essential about working with R, and this brings us to the second difference in our approach, is that we will depend heavily on *visualization*. R has outstanding graphical facilities, which generally provide far more insight into the data than long lists of statistics that depend on often questionable simplifying assumptions. That is, this book provides an introduction to *exploratory data analysis*. Moreover, we will work *incrementally* and *interactively*. The process of understanding the structure in your data is almost always an iterative process involving graphical inspection, model building, more graphical inspection, updating and adjusting the model, etc. The flexibility of R is crucial for making this iterative process of coming to grips with your data both easy and in fact quite enjoyable.

A third, at first sight heretical aspect of this book is that I have avoided all formal mathematics. The focus of this introduction is on explaining the key concepts and on providing guidelines for the proper use of statistical techniques. A useful metaphor is learning to drive a car. In order to drive a car, you need to know the position and function of tools such as the steering wheel and the brake pedal. You also need to know that you should not drive with the handbrake on. And you need to know the traffic rules. Without these three kinds of knowledge, driving a car is extremely dangerous. What you do not need to know is how to construct a combustion engine, or how to drill for oil and refine it so that you can use it to fuel that combustion engine. The aim of this book is to provide you with a driving licence for exploratory data analysis. There is one caveat here. To stretch the metaphor to its limit: with R, you are receiving driving lessons in an all-powerful car, a combination of a racing car, a lorry, a family car, and a limousine. Consequently, you have to be a responsible driver, which means that you will find that you will need many additional driving lessons beyond those offered in this book. Moreover, it never hurts to consult professional drivers—statisticians with a solid background in mathematical statistics who know the ins and outs of the tools and techniques, and their advantages and disadvantages. Other introductions that you may want to consider are Dalgaard (2002), Verzani (2005), and Crawley (2002). The present book is written for readers with little or no programming experience. Readers interested in the R language itself should consult Becker *et al.* (1988) and Venables and Ripley (2002).

The approach I have taken in this course is to work with real data sets rather than with small artificial examples. Real data are often messy, and it is important to know how to proceed when the data display all kinds of problems that standard introductory textbooks hardly ever mention. Unless stated otherwise, data sets discussed in this book are available in the languageR package, which is available at the CRAN archives. You are encouraged to work through the examples with the actual data, to get a feeling for what the data look like and how to work with R's functions. To save typing, you can copy and paste the R code of the examples in this book into the R console (see the file examples.txt in languageR's scripts directory). The languageR package also makes available a series of functions. These convenience functions, some of which are still being developed, bear the extension .fnc to distinguish them from the well-tested functions of R and its standard packages.

An important reason for using R is that it is a carefully designed programming environment that allows you, in a very flexible way, to write your own code, or modify existing code, to tailor R to your specific needs. To see why this is useful, consider a researcher studying similarities in meaning and form for a large number of words. Suppose that a separate model needs to be fitted for each of 1000 words to the data of the other 999 words. If you are used to thinking about statistical questions as paths through cascaded menus, you will discard such an analysis as impractical almost immediately. When you work in R, you simply write the code for one word, and then cycle it through on all other words. Researchers are often unnecessarily limited in the questions they explore because they are thinking in a menu-driven language instead of in an interactive programming language like R. This is an area where language determines thought.

If you are new to working with a programming language, you will find that you will have to get used to getting your commands for R exactly right. R offers command line editing facilities, and you can also page through earlier commands with the up and down arrows of your keyboard. It is often useful to open a simple text editor (emacs, gvim, notepad), to prepare your commands in, and to copy and paste these commands into the R window, especially as more complex commands tend to be used more than once, and it is often much easier to make copies in the editor and modify these, than to try to edit multiple-line commands in the R window itself. Output from R that is worth remembering can be pasted back into the editor, which in this way comes to retain a detailed history both of your commands and of the relevant results. You might think that using a graphical user interface would work more quickly, in which case you may want to consider using the commercial software S-PLUS, which offers such an interface. However, as pointed out by Crawley (2002), "If you enjoy wasting time, you can pull down the menus and click in the dialog boxes to your heart's content. However, this takes about 5 to 10 times as long as writing in the command line. Life is short. Use the command line" (p. 11).

There are several ways in which you can use this book. If you use this book as an introduction to statistics, it is important to work through the examples, not only by reading them through, but by trying them out in R. Each chapter also comes with a set of problems, with worked-out solutions in Appendix A. If you use this book to learn how to apply in R particular techniques that you are already familiar with, then the quickest way to proceed is to study the structure of the relevant data files used to illustrate the technique. Once you have understood how the data are to be organized, you can load the data into R and try out the example. And once you have got this working, it should not be difficult to try out the same technique on your own data.

This book is organized as follows: Chapter 1 is an introduction to the basics of R. It explains how to load data into R, and how to work with data from the command line. Chapter 2 introduces a number of important visualization techniques. Chapter 3 discusses probability distributions, and Chapter 4 provides a guide to standard statistical tests for single random variables as well as for two random variables. Chapter 5 discusses methods for clustering and classification. Chapter 6 discusses regression modeling strategies, and Chapter 7 introduces mixed-effects models, the models required for analyzing data sets with nested or crossed repeated measures.

I am indebted to Carmel O'Shannessy for allowing me to use her data on Warlpiri, to Kors Perdijk for sharing his work on the reading skills of young children, to Joan Bresnan for her data on the dative alternation in English, to Maria Spassova for her data on Spanish authorial hands, to Karen Keune for her materials on social and geographical variation in the Netherlands and Flanders, to Laura de

Vaan for her experiments on Dutch derivational neologisms, to Mirjam Ernestus for her phonological data on final devoicing, to Wieke Tabak for her data on etymological age, to Jen Hay for the rating data sets, and to Michael Dunn for his data on the phylogenetic classification of Papuan and Oceanic languages. I am also grateful to Adrian Stenton for his careful copy-editing of the manuscript. Many students and colleagues have helped me with their comments and suggestions for improvement. I would like to mention by name Joan Bresnan, Mirjam Ernestus, Jen Hay, Reinhold Kliegl, Victor Kuperman, Petar Milin, Ingo Plag, Hedderik van Rijn, Stuart Robinson, Eva Smolka, and Fiona Tweedie. I am especially indebted to Douglas Bates for his detailed comments on Chapter 7, his advice for improving the `languageR` package, his help with the code for temporary ancillary functions for mixed-effects modeling, and the insights offered on mixed-effects modeling. In fact, I would like to thank Doug here for all the work he has put into developing the `lme4` package, which I believe is the most exciting tool discussed in this book for analyzing linguistic experimental data. Last but not least, I am grateful to Tineke for her friendship and support.

In this book, small capitals denote key concepts and technical terms. Typewriter font is used for R code and R objects. Linguistic examples are typeset with italics, as are statistical symbols.

1   An introduction to R

In order to learn to work with R, you have to learn to speak its language, the S language, developed originally at Bell Laboratories (Becker *et al.*, 1988). The grammar of this programming language is beautiful and easy to learn. It is important to master its basics, as this grammar is designed to guide you towards the appropriate way of thinking about your data and how you might want to carry out your analysis.

When you begin to use R on an Apple Macintosh or a Windows PC, you will start R either through a menu guiding you to applications, or by clicking on R's icon. As a result, a graphical user interface is started up, with as its central part a window with a prompt (>), the place where you type your commands. On UNIX or LINUX systems, the same window is obtained by opening a terminal and typing R at its prompt.

The sequence of commands in a given R session and the objects created are stored in files named .Rhistory and .RData when you quit R and respond positively to the question of whether you want to save your workspace. If you do so, then your results will be available to you the next time you start up R. If you are using a graphical user interface, this .RData file will be located by default in the folder where R has been installed. In UNIX and LINUX, the .RData file will be created in the same directory as where R was started up.

You will often want to use R for different projects, located in different directories on your computer. On UNIX and LINUX systems, simply open a terminal in the desired directory, and start R. When using a graphical user interface, you have to use the File drop-down menu. In order to change to another directory, select Change dir. You will also have to load the .RData and .Rhistory using the options Load Workspace and Load History.

Once R is up and running, you need to install a series of packages, including the package that comes with this book, languageR. This is accomplished with the following instruction, to be typed at the R prompt:

```
install.packages(c("rpart", "chron", "Hmisc", "Design",
"Matrix", "lme4", "coda", "e1071", "zipfR", "ape",
"languageR"), repos = "http://cran.r-project.org")
```

Packages are installed in a folder named library, which itself is located in R's home directory. On my system, R's home is /home/harald/R-2.4.0, so packages are found in /home/harald/R-2.4.0/library, and the code of the main examples in this book is located in `/home/harald/R-2.4.0/library/languageR/scripts`.

I recommend that you create a file named `.Rprofile` in your home directory. This file should contain the line,

```
library(languageR)
```

telling R that upon startup it should attach `languageR`. All data sets and functions defined in `languageR`, and some of the packages that we will need, will be automatically available. Alternatively, you can type `library(languageR)` at the R prompt yourself after you have started R. All examples in this book assume that the `languageR` package has been attached.

The way to learn a language is to start speaking it. The way to learn R, and the S language that it is built on, is to start using it. Reading through the examples in this chapter is not enough to become a confident user of R. For this, you need to actually try out the examples by typing them at the R prompt. You have to be very precise in your commands, which requires a discipline that you will master only if you learn from experience, from your mistakes and typos. Don't be put off if R complains about your initial attempts to use it, just carefully compare what you typed, letter by letter and bracket by bracket, with the code in the examples.

If you type a command that extends over separate lines, the standard prompt > will change into the special continuation prompt +. If you think your command is completed, but still have a continuation prompt, there is something wrong with your syntax. To cancel the command, use either the escape key, or hit CONTROL-C. Appendix B provides an overview of operators and functions, grouped by topic, that you may find useful as a complement to the example-by-example approach followed in the main text of this book.

1.1   R as a calculator

Once you have an R window, you can use R simply as a calculator. To add 1 and 2, type,

```
> 1 + 2
```

and hit the RETURN (ENTER) key, and R will display:

```
[1] 3
```

The `[1]` preceding the answer indicates that 3 is the first element of the answer. In this example, it is also the only element. Other examples of arithmetic operations are:

```
> 2 * 3            # multiplication
[1] 6
> 6 / 3            # division
[1] 2
> 2 ^ 3            # power
```

```
[1] 8
> 9 ^ 0.5                    # square root
[1] 3
```

The hash mark # indicates that the text to its right is a comment that should be ignored by R. Operators can be stacked, in which case it may be necessary to make explicit by means of parentheses the order in which the operations have to be carried out:

```
> 9 ^ 0.5 ^ 3
[1] 1.316074
> (9 ^ 0.5) ^ 3
[1] 27
> 9 ^ (0.5 ^ 3)
[1] 1.316074
```

Note that the evaluation of exponentiation proceeds from right to left, rather than from left to right. Use parentheses whenever you are not absolutely sure about the order in which R evaluates stacked operators.

The results of calculations can be saved and referenced by VARIABLES. For instance, we can store the result of adding 1 and 2 in a variable named x. There are three ways in which we can assign the result of our addition to x. We can use the equals sign as assignment operator,

```
> x = 1 + 2
> x
[1] 3
```

or we can use a left arrow (composed of < and -) or a right arrow (composed of - and >, as follows:

```
> x <- 1 + 2
> 1 + 2 -> x
```

The right arrow is especially useful in cases where you have typed a long expression and only then decide that you would like to save its output rather than have it displayed on your screen. Instead of having to go back to the beginning of the line, you can continue typing and use the right arrow as assignment operator. We can modify the value of x, for instance, by increasing its value by one:

```
> x = x + 1
```

Here we take x, add one, and assign the result (4) back to x. Without this explicit assignment, the value of x remains unchanged:

```
> x = 3
> x + 1    # result is displayed, not assigned to x
[1] 4
> x        # so x is unchanged
[1] 3
```

We can work with variables in the same way that we work with numbers:

```
> 4 ^ 3
[1] 64
> x = 4
```

```
> y = 3
> x ^ y
[1] 64
```

The more common mathematical operations are carried out with operators such as +, -, and *. For a range of standard operations, as well as for more complex mathematical calculations, a wide range of functions is available. Functions are commands that take some input, do something with that input, and return the result to the user. Above, we calculated the square root of 9 with the help of the ^ operator. Another way of obtaining the same result is by means of the sqrt() function:

```
> sqrt(9)
[1] 3
```

The argument of the square root function, 9, is enclosed between parentheses.

1.2   Getting data into and out of R

Bresnan *et al.* (2007) studied the dative alternation in English in the three-million-word Switchboard collection of recorded telephone conversations and in the Treebank *Wall Street Journal* collection of news and financial reportage. In English, the recipient can be realized either as an NP (*Mary gave John the book*) or as a PP (*Mary gave the book to John*). Bresnan and colleagues were interested in predicting the realization of the recipient (as NP or PP) from a wide range of potential explanatory variables, such as the animacy, the length in words, and the pronominality of the theme and the recipient. A subset of their data collected from the Treebank is available as the data set verbs. (Bresnan and colleagues studied many more variables, the full data set is available as dative, and we will study it in detail in later chapters.) You should have attached the languageR package at this point, otherwise verbs will not be available to you.

We display the first 10 rows of the verbs data with the help of the function head(). (Readers familiar with programming languages like C and Python should note that R numbering begins with 1 rather than with zero.)

```
> head(verbs, n = 10)
   RealizationOfRec Verb AnimacyOfRec AnimacyOfTheme LengthOfTheme
1                NP  feed      animate      inanimate     2.6390573
2                NP  give      animate      inanimate     1.0986123
3                NP  give      animate      inanimate     2.5649494
4                NP  give      animate      inanimate     1.6094379
5                NP offer      animate      inanimate     1.0986123
6                NP  give      animate      inanimate     1.3862944
7                NP   pay      animate      inanimate     1.3862944
8                NP bring      animate      inanimate     0.0000000
9                NP teach      animate      inanimate     2.3978953
10               NP  give      animate      inanimate     0.6931472
```

When the option *n* is left unspecified, the first 6 rows will be displayed by default. Tables such as exemplified by `verbs` are referred to in R as DATA FRAMES. Each line in this data frame represents a clause with a recipient, and specifies whether this recipient was realized as an NP or as a PP. Each line also lists the verb used, the animacy of the recipient, the animacy of the theme, and the logarithm of the length of the theme. Note that each elementary observation — here the realization of the recipient as NP or PP in a given clause — has its own line in the input file. This is referred to as the LONG DATA FORMAT, where *long* highlights that no attempt is made to store the data more economically.

It is good practice to spell out the elements in the columns of a data frame with sensible names. For instance, the first line with data specifies that the recipient was realized as an NP for the verb *to feed*, that the recipient was animate, and that the theme was inanimate. The length of the theme is listed in log units, for reasons that will become clear in later chapters. The actual length of the theme is 14, as shown when we undo the logarithmic transformation with its inverse, the exponential function `exp()`:

```
> exp(2.6390573)
[1] 14
> log(14)
[1] 2.639057
```

A data frame such as `verbs` can be saved outside R as an independent file with `write.table()`, enclosing the name of the file (including its path) between double quotes:

```
> write.table(verbs, file = "/home/harald/dativeS.txt")  # Linux
> write.table(verbs, file = "/users/harald/dativeS.txt") # MacOSX
> write.table(verbs, file = "c:stats/dativeS.txt")       # Windows
```

Users of Windows should note the use of the forward slash for path specification. Alternatively, on MacOS X or Windows, the function `file.choose()` may be used, replacing the file name, in which case a dialog box is provided.

External data in this tabular format can be loaded into R with `read.table()`. We tell this function that the file we just made has an initial line, its *header*, that specifies the column names:

```
> verbs = read.table("/home/harald/dativeS.txt", header = TRUE)
```

R handles various other data formats as well, including `sas.get()` (which converts SAS data sets), `read.csv()` (which handles comma-separated spreadsheet data), and `read.spss()` (for reading SPSS data files).

Data sets and functions in R come with extensive documentation, including examples. This documentation is accessed by means of the `help()` function. Many examples in the documentation can be also executed with the `example()` function:

```
> help(verbs)
> example(verbs)
```

1.3   Accessing information in data frames

When working with data frames, we often need to select or manipulate subsets of rows and columns. Rows and columns are selected by means of a mechanism referred to as subscripting. In its simplest form, subscripting can be achieved simply by specifying the row and column numbers between square brackets, separated by a comma. For instance, to extract the length of the theme for the first line in the data frame verbs, we type:

```
> verbs[1, 5]
[1] 2.639057
```

Whatever precedes the comma is interpreted as a restriction on the rows, and whatever follows the comma is a restriction on the columns. In this example, the restrictions are so narrow that only one element is selected, the one element that satisfies the restrictions that it should be on row 1 and in column 5. The other extreme is no restrictions whatsoever, as when we type the name of the data frame at the prompt, which is equivalent to typing:

```
> verbs[ , ]          # this will display all 903 rows of verbs!
```

When we leave the slot before the comma empty, we impose no restrictions on the rows:

```
> verbs[ , 5]                         # show the elements of column 5
 [1] 2.6390573 1.0986123 2.5649494 1.6094379 1.0986123
 [6] 1.3862944 1.3862944 0.0000000 2.3978953 0.6931472
 ...
```

As there are 903 rows in verbs, the request to display the fifth column results in an ordered sequence of 903 elements. In what follows, we refer to such an ordered sequence as a vector. Thanks to the numbers in square brackets in the output, we can easily see that 0.00 is the eighth element of the vector. Column vectors can also be extracted with the $ operator preceding the name of the relevant column:

```
> verbs$LengthOfTheme                  # same as verbs[, 5]
```

When we specify a row number but leave the slot after the comma empty, we impose no restrictions on the columns, and therefore obtain a row vector instead of a column vector:

```
> verbs[1, ]                           # show the elements of row 1
  RealizationOfRec Verb AnimacyOfRec AnimacyOfTheme LengthOfTheme
1               NP feed      animate      inanimate      2.639057
```

Note that the elements of this row vector are displayed together with the column names.

Row and column vectors can be extracted from a data frame and assigned to separate variables:

```
> row1 = verbs[1,]
> col5 = verbs[ , 5]
> head(col5, n = 5)
 [1] 2.6390573 1.0986123 2.5649494 1.6094379 1.0986123
```

Individual elements can be accessed from these vectors by the same subscripting mechanism, but simplified to just one index between the square brackets:

```
> row1[1]
  RealizationOfRec
1                NP
> col5[1]
 [1] 2.639057
```

Because the row vector has names, we can also address its elements by name, properly enclosed between double quotes:

```
> row1["RealizationOfRec"]
  RealizationOfRec
1                NP
```

You now know how to extract single elements, rows, and columns from data frames, and how to access individual elements from vectors. However, we often need to access more than one row or more than one column simultaneously. R makes this possible by placing vectors before or after the comma when subscripting the data frame, instead of single elements. (For R, single elements are actually vectors with only one element.) Therefore, it is useful to know how to create your own vectors from scratch. The simplest way of creating a vector is to combine elements with the concatenation operator c(). In the following example, we select some arbitrary row numbers that we save in the variable rs (shorthand for rows):

```
> rs = c(638, 799, 390, 569, 567)
> rs
 [1] 638 799 390 569 567
```

We can now use this vector of numbers to select precisely those rows from verbs that have the row numbers specified in rs. We do so by inserting rs before the comma:

```
> verbs[rs, ]
    RealizationOfRec Verb AnimacyOfRec AnimacyOfTheme LengthOfTheme
638               PP  pay      animate      inanimate     0.6931472
799               PP sell      animate      inanimate     1.3862944
390               NP lend      animate        animate     0.6931472
569               PP sell      animate      inanimate     1.6094379
567               PP send    inanimate      inanimate     1.3862944
```

Note that the appropriate rows of verbs appear in exactly the same order as specified in rs.

The combination operator c() is not the only function for creating vectors. Of the many other possibilities, the colon operator should be mentioned here. This operator brings into existence sequences of increasing or decreasing numbers with a stepsize of one:

```
> 1 : 5
[1] 1 2 3 4 5
> 5 : 1
[1] 5 4 3 2 1
```

In order to select from `verbs` the rows specified by `rs` and the first three columns, we specify the row condition before the comma and the column condition after the comma:

```
> verbs[rs, 1:3]
    RealizationOfRec   Verb AnimacyOfRec
638                PP  pay       animate
799                PP sell       animate
390                NP lend       animate
569                PP sell       animate
567                PP send     inanimate
```

Alternatively, we could have specified a vector of column names instead of column numbers:

```
> verbs[rs, c("RealizationOfRec", "Verb", "AnimacyOfRec")]
```

Note once more that when strings are brought together into a vector, they must be enclosed between quotes.

Thus far, we have selected rows by explicitly specifying their row numbers. Often, we do not have this information available. For instance, suppose we are interested in those observations for which the `AnimacyOfTheme` has the value `animate`. We do not know the row numbers of these observations. Fortunately, we do not need them either, because we can impose a condition on the rows of the data frame such that only those rows will be selected that meet that condition. The condition that we want to impose is that the value in the column of `AnimacyOfTheme` is `animate`. Since this is a condition on rows, it precedes the comma:

```
> verbs[verbs$AnimacyOfTheme == "animate", ]
    RealizationOfRec   Verb AnimacyOfRec AnimacyOfTheme LengthOfTheme
58                 NP  give      animate        animate     1.0986123
100                NP  give      animate        animate     2.8903718
143                NP  give    inanimate        animate     2.6390573
390                NP  lend      animate        animate     0.6931472
506                NP  give      animate        animate     1.9459101
736                PP trade      animate        animate     1.6094379
```

This is equivalent to:

```
> subset(verbs, AnimacyOfTheme == "animate")
```

It is important to note that the equality in the condition is expressed with a double equal sign. This is because the single equal sign is the assignment operator. The following example illustrates a more complex condition with the logical operator

AND (&) (the logical operator for OR is |):

```
> verbs[verbs$AnimacyOfTheme == "animate" & verbs$LengthOfTheme > 2, ]
    RealizationOfRec Verb AnimacyOfRec AnimacyOfTheme LengthOfTheme
100              NP give      animate        animate      2.890372
143              NP give    inanimate        animate      2.639057
```

Row and column names of a data frame can be extracted with the functions
rownames() and colnames():

```
> head(rownames(verbs))
 [1] "1"  "2"  "3"  "4"  "5"  "6"
> colnames(verbs)
[1] "RealizationOfRec" "Verb"  "AnimacyOfRec" "AnimacyOfTheme"
[5] "LengthOfTheme"
```

The vector of column names is a string vector. Perhaps surprisingly, the vector of
row names is also a string vector. To see why this is useful, we assign the subtable
of verbs obtained by subscripting the rows with the rs vector to a separate object
that we name verbs.rs:

```
> verbs.rs = verbs[rs, ]
```

We can extract the first line not only by row number,

```
> verbs.rs[1, ]
    RealizationOfRec Verb AnimacyOfRec AnimacyOfTheme LengthOfTheme
638              PP  pay      animate      inanimate     0.6931472
```

but also by row name:

```
> verbs.rs["638",]     # same output
```

The row name is a string that reminds us of the original row number in the data
frame from which verbs.rs was extracted:

```
> verbs[638, ]         # same output again
```

Let's finally extract a column that does not consist of numbers, such as the
column specifying the animacy of the recipient:

```
> verbs.rs$AnimacyOfRec
 [1] animate animate animate animate inanimate
Levels: animate inanimate
```

Two things are noteworthy. First, the words *animate* and *inanimate* are not enclosed between quotes. Second, the last line of the output mentions that there are
two LEVELS: animate and inanimate. Whereas the row and column names
are vectors of strings, non-numerical columns in a data frame are automatically converted by R into FACTORS. In statistics, a factor is a non-numerical
predictor or response. Its values are referred to as its levels. Here, the factor
AnimacyOfRec has as its only possible values animate and inanimate, hence
it has only two levels. Most statistical techniques don't work with string vectors, but with factors. This is the reason why R automatically converts non-
numerical columns into factors. If you really want to work with a string vector

instead of a factor, you have to do the back-conversion yourself with the function
`as.character()`:

```
> verbs.rs$AnimacyOfRec = as.character(verbs.rs$AnimacyOfRec)
> verbs.rs$AnimacyOfRec
 [1] "animate" "animate" "animate" "animate" "inanimate"
```

Now the elements of the vector are strings, and as such properly enclosed between
quotes. We can undo this conversion with `as.factor()`:

```
> verbs.rs$AnimacyOfRec = as.factor(verbs.rs$AnimacyOfRec)
```

If we repeat these steps, but with a smaller subset of the data in which `Anima-cyOfRec` is only realized as animate,

```
> verbs.rs2 = verbs[c(638, 390), ]
> verbs.rs2
    RealizationOfRec Verb AnimacyOfRec AnimacyOfTheme LengthOfTheme
638               PP  pay      animate      inanimate     0.6931472
390               NP lend      animate        animate     0.6931472
```

we observe that the original two levels of `AnimacyOfRec` are remembered:

```
> verbs.rs2$AnimacyOfRec
[1] animate animate
Levels: animate inanimate
```

In order to get rid of the uninstantiated factor level, we convert `AnimacyOfRec`
to a character vector, and then convert it back to a factor:

```
> as.factor(as.character(verbs.rs2$AnimacyOfRec))
[1] animate animate
Levels: animate
```

An alternative with the same result is:

```
> verbs.rs2$AnimacyOfRec[drop=TRUE]
```

1.4   Operations on data frames

1.4.1   Sorting a data frame by one or more columns

In the previous section, we created the data frame `verbs.rs`, the rows
of which appeared in the arbitrary order specified by our vector of row numbers
`rs`. It is often useful to sort the entries in a data frame by the values in one of the
columns, for instance, by the realization of the recipient,

```
> verbs.rs[order(verbs.rs$RealizationOfRec), ]
    RealizationOfRec Verb AnimacyOfRec AnimacyOfTheme LengthOfTheme
390               NP lend      animate        animate     0.6931472
638               PP  pay      animate      inanimate     0.6931472
799               PP sell      animate      inanimate     1.3862944
569               PP sell      animate      inanimate     1.6094379
567               PP send    inanimate      inanimate     1.3862944
```

or by verb and then by the length of the theme:

```
> verbs.rs[order(verbs.rs$Verb, verbs.rs$LengthOfTheme), ]
      RealizationOfRec Verb AnimacyOfRec AnimacyOfTheme LengthOfTheme
390                NP lend      animate       animate       0.6931472
638                PP  pay      animate     inanimate       0.6931472
799                PP sell      animate     inanimate       1.3862944
569                PP sell      animate     inanimate       1.6094379
567                PP send    inanimate     inanimate       1.3862944
```

The crucial work is done by `order()`. Its first argument is the primary column of the data frame by which the rows should be sorted (alphabetical or numerical depending on the column values). The second argument is the column that provides the sort key for those rows that have ties (identical values) according to the first column. Additional columns for sorting can be supplied as a third or fourth argument, and so on.

Note that the `order()` function occupies the slot in the subscript of the data frame that specifies the conditions on the rows. What `order()` actually does is supply a vector of row numbers, with the row number of the row that is to be listed first as first element, the row number that is to be listed second as second element, and so on. For instance, when we sort the rows by `Verb`, `order()` returns a vector of row numbers,

```
> order(verbs.rs$Verb)
 [1] 10  7  8  3  1  9  2  4  6  5
```

that will move the last row (for *cost*) to the first row, the seventh row (for *give*) to the second row, and so on.

The elements of a vector can be sorted in the same way. When sorting the vector,

```
> v = c("pay", "sell", "lend", "sell", "send",
+ "sell", "give",  "give", "pay", "cost")
```

(note that R changes the prompt from > to + when a command is not finished by the end of the line, so don't type the + symbol when defining this vector) we subscript it with `order()` applied to itself:

```
> v[order(v)]
 [1]  "cost" "give" "give" "lend" "pay"
 [6]  "pay"  "sell" "sell" "sell" "send"
```

However, a more straightforward function for sorting the elements of a vector is `sort()`:

```
> sort(v)
```

It is important to keep in mind that in all of the preceding examples we never assigned the output of the reordering operations, so `v` is still unsorted. In order to obtain sorted versions, simply assign the output to the original data object:

```
> v = sort(v)
```

1.4.2   Changing information in a data frame

Information in a data frame can be changed. For instance, we could manipulate the data in `verbs.rs` and change the realization of the recipient for the verb *to pay* (originally on line 638 in `verbs`) from PP into NP. (In what follows, I assume that this command is not actually carried out.)

```
> verbs.rs["638", ]$RealizationOfRec = "NP"
```

If many such changes have to be made, for instance in order to correct coding errors, then it may be more convenient to do this in a spreadsheet, save the result as a `.csv` file, and load the corrected data into R with `read.csv()`.

Changes that are easily carried out in R are changes that affect whole columns or subparts of the table. For instance, in order to reconstruct the length of the theme (in words) from the logarithmically transformed values listed in `verbs.rs`, all we have to do is apply the `exp()` function to the appropriate column. All values in the column will be changed accordingly:

```
> verbs.rs$LengthOfTheme
[1] 0.6931472 1.3862944 0.6931472 1.6094379 1.3862944
> exp(verbs.rs$LengthOfTheme)
[1] 2 4 2 5 4
```

We can also add new columns to a data frame. For instance, we might consider adding a column with the length of the verb (in letters). There is a function, `nchar()`, that conveniently reports the number of letters in its input, provided that its input is a character string or a vector of character strings. We illustrate `nchar()` for the longest word (without intervening spaces or hyphens) of English (Sproat, 1992) and the shortest word of English:

```
> nchar(c("antidisestablishmentarianism", "a"))
[1] 28  1
```

When applying `nchar()` to a column in a data frame, we have to keep in mind that non-numerical columns typically are not vectors of strings, but factors. So we must first convert the factor into a character vector with `as.character()` before applying `nchar()`. We add the result to `verbs.rs` with the `$` operator:

```
> verbs.rs$Length = nchar(as.character(verbs.rs$Verb))
```

We display only the first four rows of the result, and only the verb and its orthographic length:

```
> verbs.rs[1:4, c("Verb", "Length")]
     Verb Length
638   pay      3
799  sell      4
390  lend      4
569  sell      4
```

1.4.3   Extracting contingency tables from data frames

How many observations are characterized by animate recipients realized as an NP? Questions like this are easily addressed with the help of CONTINGENCY TABLES, tables that cross-tabulate counts for combinations of factor levels. Since the factors `RealizationOfRec` and `AnimacyOfRec` each have two levels, as shown by the function `levels()`,

```
> levels(verbs$RealizationOfRec)
[1] "NP" "PP"
> levels(verbs$AnimacyOfRec)
[1] "animate"   "inanimate"
```

a cross-tabulation of `RealizationOfRec` and `AnimacyOfRec` with `xtabs()` results in a table with four cells:

```
> xtabs( ~ RealizationOfRec + AnimacyOfRec, data = verbs)
                 AnimacyOfRec
RealizationOfRec animate inanimate
              NP     521        34
              PP     301        47
```

The first argument of `xtabs()` is a FORMULA. Formulas have the following general structure, with the tilde (∼) denoting "depends on" or "is a function of":

$$\text{dependent variable} \sim \text{predictor } 1 + \text{predictor } 2 + \ldots$$

A DEPENDENT VARIABLE is a variable the value of which we try to predict. The other variables are often referred to as INDEPENDENT VARIABLES. This terminology is somewhat misleading, however, because sets of predictors are often characterized by all kinds of interdependencies. A more appropriate term is simply PREDICTOR. In the study of Bresnan *et al.* (2007) that we are considering here, the dependent variable is the realization of the recipient. All other variables are predictor variables.

When we construct a contingency table, however, there is no dependent variable. A contingency table allows us to see how counts are distributed over conditions, without making any claim as to whether one variable might be explainable in terms of other variables. Therefore, the formula for `xtabs()` has nothing to the left of the tilde operator. We only have predictors, which we list to the right of the tilde, separated by plusses.

More than two factors can be cross-tabulated:

```
> verbs.xtabs =
+    xtabs( ~ AnimacyOfRec + AnimacyOfTheme + RealizationOfRec,
+    data = verbs)
> verbs.xtabs
, , RealizationOfRec = NP

             AnimacyOfTheme
AnimacyOfRec animate inanimate
   animate         4       517
   inanimate       1        33
```

```
, , RealizationOfRec = PP

                 AnimacyOfTheme
AnimacyOfRec animate inanimate
   animate          1       300
   inanimate        0        47
```

As three factors enter into this cross-classification, the result is a three-dimensional contingency table, that is displayed in the form of two 2 by 2 contingency tables. It is clear from this table that animate themes are extremely rare. It therefore makes sense to restrict our attention to the clauses with inanimate themes. We implement this restriction by conditioning on the rows of verbs:

```
> verbs.xtabs = xtabs( ~ AnimacyOfRec + RealizationOfRec,
+ data = verbs, subset = AnimacyOfTheme != "animate")
> verbs.xtabs            #!= denotes not equal to
            RealizationOfRec
AnimacyOfRec  NP  PP
   animate   517 300
   inanimate  33  47
```

It seems that recipients are somewhat more likely to be realized as an NP when animate and as a PP when inanimate.

This contingency table can be recast as a table of proportions by dividing each cell in the table by the sum of all cells, the total number of observations in the data frame with inanimate themes. We obtain this sum with the help of the function sum(), which returns the sum of the elements in a vector or table:

```
> sum(verbs.xtabs)
[1] 897
```

We verify that this is indeed equal to the number of rows in the data frame with inanimate themes only, with the help of the nrow() function:

```
> sum(verbs.xtabs) == nrow(verbs[verbs$AnimacyOfTheme != "animate",])
[1] TRUE
```

A table of proportions is obtained straightforwardly by dividing the contingency table by this sum:

```
> verbs.xtabs/sum(verbs.xtabs)
            RealizationOfRec
AnimacyOfRec         NP          PP
   animate   0.57636566 0.33444816
   inanimate 0.03678930 0.05239688
```

For percentages instead of proportions, we simply multiply by 100:

```
> 100 * verbs.xtabs/sum(verbs.xtabs)
            RealizationOfRec
AnimacyOfRec         NP         PP
   animate   57.636566 33.444816
   inanimate  3.678930  5.239688
```

It is often useful to recast counts as proportions (relative frequencies) with respect to row or column totals. Such proportions can be calculated with `prop.table()`. When its second argument is 1, `prop.table()` calculates relative frequencies with respect to the row totals,

```
> prop.table(verbs.xtabs, 1)   # rows sum to 1
            RealizationOfRec
AnimacyOfRec       NP        PP
   animate   0.6328029 0.3671971
   inanimate 0.4125000 0.5875000
```

when its second argument is 2, it produces proportions relative to column totals:

```
> prop.table(verbs.xtabs,2)    # columns sum to 1
            RealizationOfRec
AnimacyOfRec       NP        PP
   animate   0.9400000 0.8645533
   inanimate 0.0600000 0.1354467
```

These tables show that the row proportions are somewhat different for `animate` versus `inanimate` recipients, and that column proportions are slightly different for NP versus PP realizations of the recipient. Later we shall see that there is indeed reason for surprise: the observed asymmetry between rows and columns is unlikely to arise under chance conditions. For animate recipients, the NP realization is more likely than the PP realization. Inanimate recipients have a non-trivial preference for the PP realization.

1.4.4   Calculations on data frames

Another question that arises with respect to the data in `verbs` is to what extent the length of the theme, i.e. the complexity of the theme measured in terms of the number of words used to express it, covaries with the animacy of the recipient. Could it be that animate recipients show a preference for more complex themes, compared to inanimate recipients? To assess this possibility, we calculate the mean length of the theme for animate and inanimate recipients. We obtain these means with the help of the function `mean()`, which takes a numerical vector as input, and returns the arithmetic mean:

```
> mean(1:5)
[1] 3
```

We could use this function to calculate the means for the animate and inanimate recipients separately,

```
> mean(verbs[verbs$AnimacyOfRec == "animate", ]$LengthOfTheme)
[1] 1.540278
> mean(verbs[verbs$AnimacyOfRec != "animate", ]$LengthOfTheme)
[1] 1.071130
```

but a much more convenient way for obtaining these means simultaneously is to make use of the `tapply()` function. This function takes three arguments. The first argument specifies a numeric vector for which we want to calculate means. The second argument specifies how this numeric vector should be split into groups, namely, on the basis of its factor levels. The third argument specifies the function that is to be applied to these groups. The function that we want to apply to our data frame is `mean()`, but other functions (e.g. `sum()`, `sqrt()`) could also be specified:

```
> tapply(verbs$LengthOfTheme, verbs$AnimacyOfRec, mean)
  animate inanimate
 1.540278  1.071130
```

The output of `tapply()` is a table, here a table with two means labeled by the levels of the factor for which they were calculated. Later we shall see that the difference between these two group means is unlikely to be due to chance.

It is also possible to calculate means for subsets of data defined by the levels of more than one factor, in which case the second argument for `tapply()` should be a LIST of the relevant factors. Like vectors, lists are ordered sequences of elements, but unlike vectors, the elements of a list can themselves have more than one element. Thus we can have lists of vectors, lists of data frames, or lists containing a mixture of numbers, strings, vectors, data frames, and other lists. Lists are created with the `list()` function. For `tapply()`, all we have to do is specify the factors as arguments to the function `list()`. Here is an example for the means of the length of the theme cross-classified for the levels of `AnimacyOfRec` and `AnimacyOfTheme`, illustrating an alternative, slightly shorter way of using `tapply()` with the help of `with()`:

```
> with(verbs, tapply(LengthOfTheme,
+ list(AnimacyOfRec, AnimacyOfTheme), mean))
            animate inanimate
animate    1.647496  1.539622
inanimate  2.639057  1.051531
```

A final operation on data frames is best illustrated by means of a data set (`heid`) concerning reaction times RT in visual lexical decision elicited from Dutch subjects for neologisms ending in the suffix -*heid* ("-ness"):

```
> heid[1:5, ]
  Subject        Word   RT BaseFrequency
1     pp1    basaalheid 6.69          3.56
2     pp1   markantheid 6.81          5.16
3     pp1  ontroerdheid 6.51          5.55
4     pp1   contentheid 6.58          4.50
5     pp1     riantheid 6.86          4.53
```

This data frame comprises log reaction times for 26 subjects to 40 words. For each combination of subject and word, a reaction time (RT) was recorded. For each word, the frequency of its base word was extracted from the CELEX lexical database (Baayen *et al.*, 1995). Given what we know about frequency effects in lexical processing in general, we expect that neologisms with a higher base frequency elicit shorter reaction times.

Psycholinguistic studies often report two analyses, one for reaction times averaged over subjects, and one for reaction times averaged over words. The `aggregate()` function carries out these averaging procedures. Its syntax is similar to that of `tapply()`. Its first argument is the numerical vector for which we want averages according to the subsets defined by the list supplied by the second argument. Here is how we average over words:

```
> heid2 = aggregate(heid$RT, list(heid$Word), mean)
> heid2[1:5, ]
        Group.1        x
1    aftandsheid 6.705000
2    antiekheid 6.542353
3    banaalheid 6.587727
4    basaalheid 6.585714
5    bebrildheid 6.673333
```

As `aggregate()` does not retain the original names of our data frame, we change the column names so that the columns of `heid2` remain easily interpretable:

```
> colnames(heid2) = c("Word", "MeanRT")
```

In the averaging process, we lost the information about the base frequencies of the words. We add this information in two steps. We begin with creating a data frame with just the information pertaining to the words and their frequencies:

```
> items = heid[, c("Word", "BaseFrequency")]
```

Because each subject responded to each item, this data frame has multiple identical rows for each word. We remove these redundant rows with `unique()`:

```
> nrow(items)
[1] 832
> items = unique(items)
> nrow(items)
[1] 40
> items[1:4, ]
            Word BaseFrequency
1    basaalheid         3.56
2    markantheid        5.16
3  ontroerdheid         5.55
4   contentheid         4.50
```

The final step is to add the information in `items` to the information already available in `heid2`. We do this with `merge()`. As arguments to `merge()`, we first specify the receiving data frame (`heid2`), and then the donating data frame (`items`). We also specify the columns in the two data frames that provide the keys for the merging: `by.x` should point to the key in the receiving data frame and `by.y` should point to the key in the donating data frame. In the present example, the keys for both data frames have the same value, `Word`:

```
> heid2 = merge(heid2, items, by.x = "Word", by.y = "Word")
> head(heid2, n = 4)
          Word    MeanRT BaseFrequency
1 aftandsheid 6.705000          4.20
2  antiekheid 6.542353          6.75
3  banaalheid 6.587727          5.74
4  basaalheid 6.585714          3.56
```

Make sure you understand why the next sequence of steps leads to the same results:

```
> heid3 = aggregate(heid$RT, list(heid$Word, heid$BaseFrequency), mean)
> colnames(heid3) = c("Word", "BaseFrequency", "MeanRT")
> head(heid3[order(heid3$Word),], 4)
```

We shall see shortly that the MeanRT indeed tends to be shorter as BaseFrequency increases.

1.5   Session management

R stores the objects it creates during a session in a file named .RData, and it keeps track of the commands issued in a file named .Rhistory. These files are stored on your computer, except when you explicitly request R to delete these files when quitting. Since the names of these files begin with a period, they are invisible to file managers in Unix, Linux, and Mac OS X, except when these are explicitly instructed to show hidden files. In Windows, these files are visible, and an R session can be restored by double clicking on the icon for the .RData file. The data and history files can be moved around, copied, or deleted if so required. The history file is a text file that can be viewed with any editor or text processor. The contents of the .RData file, however, can only be viewed and manipulated within R.

When working in R, the current contents of the workspace can be viewed with the objects() function, which lists the objects that you have made:

```
> objects()
[1] "heid"    "heid2"    "heid3"    "verbs"    "verbs.rs"
```

Objects that are no longer necessary can be removed with rm():

```
> rm(verbs.rs)
> objects()
[1] "heid"    "heid2"    "heid3"    "verbs"
```

It is recommended that you allocate a different workspace to each project you are working on. This avoids your workspace becoming cluttered with objects that have nothing to do with your current project. It also helps to avoid your workspace becoming unmanageably large.

The proper way to exit from R from the console is to make use of the q() function, which then inquires whether the workspace should be saved.

```
> q()
Save workspace image? [y/n/c]:
y
```

Answering with no implies that whatever objects you created in R in your current session will not be available the next time you start up R in the same directory.

Note that we have to specify the opening and closing parentheses of the function, even when it is not supplied with an argument. If you type a function name at the prompt without the parentheses, R interprets this as a request to print the function's code on the screen:

```
> q
function (save = "default", status = 0, runLast = TRUE)
.Internal(quit(save, status, runLast))
<environment: namespace:base>
```

If you see unexpected code like this, you can be sure that you forgot your parentheses.

Workbook section

Exercises

The data set spanishMeta contains metadata about fifteen texts sampled from three Spanish authors. Each line in this file provides information on a single text. Later in this book we will consider whether these authors can be distinguished on the basis of the quantitative characteristics of their personal styles (gauged by the relative frequencies of function words and tag trigrams).

1. Display this data frame in the R terminal. Extract the column names from the data frame. Also extract the number of rows.

2. Calculate how many different texts are available in meta for each author. Also calculate the mean publication date of the texts sampled for each author.

3. Sort the rows in meta by year of birth (YearOfBirth) and the number of words sampled from the texts (Nwords).

4. Extract the vector of publication dates from meta. Sort this vector. Consult the help page for sort() and sort the vector in reverse numerical order. Also sort the row names of meta.

5. Extract from meta all rows with texts that were published before 1980.

6. Calculate the mean publication date for all texts. The arithmetic mean is defined as the sum of the observations in a vector divided by the number of elements in the vector. The length of a vector is provided by the function length(). Recalculate the mean year of publication by means of the functions sum() and length().

7. We create a new data frame with fictitious information on each author's favorite composer with the function data.frame():

```
> composer = data.frame(Author = c("Cela","Mendoza","VargasLLosa"),
+ Favorite = c("Stravinsky", "Bach", "Villa-Lobos"))
> composer
        Author    Favorite
1         Cela  Stravinsky
2      Mendoza        Bach
3 VargasLLosa Villa-Lobos
```

Add the information in this new data frame to meta with merge().

2   Graphical data exploration

2.1   Random variables

Chapter 1 introduced the data frame as the data structure for storing vectors of numbers as well as factors. Numerical vectors and factors represent in R what statisticians call RANDOM VARIABLES. A random variable is the outcome of an experiment. Here are some examples of experiments and their associated random variables:

tossing a coin Tossing a coin will result in either "head" or "tail." Hence, the toss of a coin is a random variable with two outcomes.

throwing a dice In this case, we are dealing with a random variable with six possible outcomes, $1, 2, \ldots, 6$.

counting words We can count the frequencies with which words occur in a given corpus or text. Word frequency is a random variable with, as possible values, $1, 2, 3, \ldots, N$, with N the size of the corpus.

familiarity rating Participants are asked to indicate on a seven-point scale how frequently they think words are used. The ratings elicited for a given word will vary from participant to participant, and constitute a random variable.

lexical decision Participants are asked to indicate, by means of button presses, whether a word presented visually or auditorily is an existing word of the language. There are two outcomes, and hence two random variables, for this type of experiment: the accuracy of a response (with levels "correct" and "incorrect") and the latency of the response (in milliseconds).

A random variable is random in the sense that the outcome of a given experiment is not known beforehand, and varies from measurement to measurement. A variable that always assumes exactly the same value is not a random variable but a constant. For instance, if an experiment consists of counting, with the same computer program, the number of words in the Brown corpus (Kučera and Francis, 1967), then you will always obtain exactly the same outcome. The size of the Brown corpus is a constant, and not a random variable.

Each random variable is associated with a PROBABILITY DISTRIBUTION that describes the likelihood of the different values that a random variable may assume. For a fair coin, the two outcomes (head and tail) are equally probable; for word frequencies, a minority of words has very high probabilities (for instance, the function words) while large numbers of words have very low probabilities. Knowledge of the probability distribution of a random variable is often crucial for statistical analysis, as we shall see in Chapter 3.

The present chapter addresses visualization. While numerical tables are hard to make sense of, data visualization often allows the main patterns to emerge remarkably well. In what follows, I therefore first discuss tools for visualizing properties of single random variables (in vectors and uni-dimensional tables). I then proceed with an overview of tools for graphing groups of random variables. In addition to introducing further statistical concepts, this chapter serves the purpose, as we go through the examples, of discussing the most commonly used options that R provides for plotting and visualization. Later chapters in this book depend heavily on these visualization techniques.

2.2   Visualizing single random variables

Bar plots and histograms are useful for obtaining visual summaries of the distributions of single random variables. We illustrate this by means of a data set (ratings) with several kinds of ratings collected for a set of 81 words for plants and animals:

```
> colnames(ratings)
 [1] "Word"            "Frequency"       "FamilySize"
 [4] "SynsetCount"     "Length"          "Class"
 [7] "FreqSingular"    "FreqPlural"      "DerivEntropy"
[10] "Complex"         "rInfl"           "meanWeightRating"
[13] "meanSizeRating"  "meanFamiliarity"
```

For each word, we have three ratings (averaged over subjects), one for the weight of the word's referent, one for its size, and one for the word's subjective familiarity. Class is a factor specifying whether the word's referent is an animal or a plant. Furthermore, we have variables specifying various linguistic properties, such as a word's frequency, its length in letters, the number of synsets (synonym sets) in which it is listed in WordNet (Miller, 1990), its morphological family size (the number of complex words in which the word occurs as a constituent), and its derivational entropy (an information theoretic variant of the family size measure). Figure 2.1 presents a bar plot and a number of histograms for these numeric variables. The upper left panel is a bar plot of the counts of word lengths, produced with the help of the function barplot():

```
> barplot(xtabs( ~ ratings$Length), xlab = "word length", col = "grey")
```

The option xlab (x-label) sets the label for the X axis, and with the option col we set the color for the bars to grey. We see that word lengths range from 3 to 10, and that the distribution is somewhat asymmetric, with a MODE (the value observed most often) at 5. The mean is 5.9, and the MEDIAN is 6. The median is obtained by ordering the observations from small to large, and then taking the central value (or

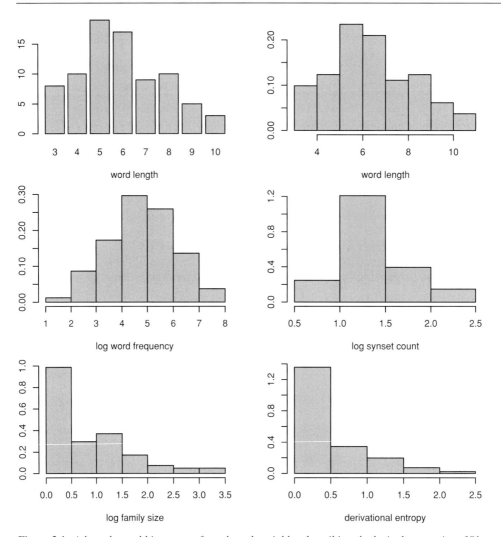

Figure 2.1. *A bar plot and histograms for selected variables describing the lexical properties of* 81 *words denoting plants and animals.*

the average of the two central values when the number of observations is even). Mean, median, and range are obtained with the functions `mean()`, `median()`, and `range()`:

```
> mean(ratings$Length)
[1] 5.91358
> median(ratings$Length)
[1] 6
> range(ratings$Length)
[1]    3 10
```

We can also extract the minimum and the maximum values separately with `min()` and `max()`:

```
> min(ratings$Length)
[1] 3
> max(ratings$Length)
[1] 10
```

The upper right panel of Figure 2.1 shows the histogram corresponding to the bar plot in the upper left panel. One difference between the bar plot and the histogram is that the bar plot is a natural choice for measures for discrete variables (such as word length) or factors (which have discrete levels). Another difference is that the histogram is scaled on the vertical axis in such a way that the total area of the bars is equal to 1. This allows us to see that the words of length 5 and 6 jointly already account for more than 40% of the data. This histogram was obtained with the truehist() function in the MASS package.

Packages are collections of functions, often written to facilitate a particular kind of statistical analysis. There are hundreds of packages, and every year more packages become available. When we start up R, the most important and central packages are loaded automatically. These packages make available the basic classical statistical tests and graphical tools. It does not make sense to load all available packages, as this would slow the performance of R considerably by having to allocate resources to a great many functions that a given user is not interested in at all. Packages that are installed but not loaded automatically can be made available by means of the library() function. Packages that are not yet installed can be added to your system with install.packages(), or through your graphical user interface.

The MASS package contains a wide range of functions discussed in Venables and Ripley (2003). We make the functions in this package available with:

```
> library(MASS)
```

All the functions in the MASS package will remain available to the end of your R session, unless the package is explicitly removed with detach():

```
> detach(package:MASS)
```

When you exit from R, all of the packages that you loaded are detached automatically. When you return to the same workspace, you will have to reload the packages that you used previously in order to have access again to the functions that they contain.

With the MASS package loaded, we can produce the histogram in the upper right panel of Figure 2.1 with truehist():

```
> truehist(ratings$Length, xlab="word length", col="grey")
```

The remaining panels of Figure 2.1 were made in the same way:

```
> truehist(ratings$Frequency,
+ xlab = "log word frequency", col = "grey")
> truehist(ratings$SynsetCount,
+ xlab = "log synset count", col = "grey")
> truehist(ratings$FamilySize,
```

```
+ xlab = "log family size", col = "grey")
> truehist(ratings$DerivEntropy,
+ xlab = "derivational entropy", col = "grey")
```

Note that the bottom panels show highly asymmetric, skewed distributions: most of the words in this data set have no morphological family members at all.

The bar plot and histograms in Figure 2.1 were brought together in one display. Such multipanel plots require changing the defaults for plotting. Normally, R will reserve the full graphics window for a single graph. However, we can divide the graphics plot window into a matrix of smaller plots by changing this default using a function that actually handles a wide range of graphical parameters, par(). The graphical parameter that we need to set here is mfrow, which should be a two-element vector specifying the number of rows and the number of columns for the matrix of plots:

```
> par(mfrow = c(3, 2))        # plots arranged in 3 rows and 2 columns
```

From this point onwards, any plot will be added to a grid of three rows and two columns, starting with the upper left panel, and filling a given row before starting on the next. After having filled all panels, we reset mfrow to its default value, so that the next plot will fill the full plot region instead of starting a new series of six small panels:

```
> par(mfrow = c(1, 1))
```

There are many other graphical parameters that can be set with par(), parameters for controlling color, font size, tick marks, margins, text in the margins, and so on. As we proceed through this book, many of these options will be introduced. A complete overview is available in the on-line help; type ?par or help(par) to see them all.

There are several ways in which plots can be saved as independent graphics files external to R. If you are using the graphical user interface for Mac OS X or Windows, you can right-click on the graphics window, and choose copy as or save as. R supports several graphics formats, including png, pdf, jpeg, and PostScript. Each format corresponds to a function that can be called from the command line: png(), pdf(), jpeg(), and postscript(). The command line functions offer many ways of fine-tuning how a figure is saved. For instance, a jpeg file with a width of 400 pixels and a height of 420 pixels is produced as follows:

```
> jpeg("barplot.jpeg", width = 400, height = 420)
> truehist(ratings$Frequency, xlab = "log word frequency")
> dev.off()
```

The jpeg() command opens the jpeg file. We then execute truehist(), the output of which is no longer shown on the standard graphics device, but redirected to the jpeg file. Finally, we close the jpeg file with dev.off(). The dev.off() command is crucial: if you forget to close your file, you will run into all sorts of trouble when you try to view the file outside R, or if you try to make a new figure in the graphics window of R. It is only after closing the file that further plot commands will be shown to you on your computer screen. Encapsulated PostScript files are produced in a similar way:

```
> postscript("barplot.ps", horizontal = FALSE,  height = 6, width = 6,
+ family = "Helvetica", paper = "special", onefile = FALSE)
> truehist(items$Frequency, xlab = "log word frequency")
> dev.off()
```

The first argument of `postscript()` is the name of the PostScript file. Whether the plot should be in portrait or landscape mode is controlled by the `horizontal` argument. If `horizontal = TRUE`, the plot will be produced in landscape mode, otherwise in portrait mode. The parameters `height` and `width` control the height and width of the plot in inches. In this example, we have set both height and width to six inches. The font to be used is specified by `family`, and with `paper="special"` the output will be an encapsulated PostScript file that can be easily incorporated in, for instance, a LATEX document. The final argument, `onefile`, is set to FALSE in order to indicate there is only a single plot in the file. (If you are going to add more than one plot to the file, set `onefile` to TRUE.)

The shape of a histogram depends, sometimes to a surprising extent, on the width of the bars and on the position of the left side of the first bar. The function `truehist()` that we used above has defaults that are chosen to minimize the risk of obtaining a rather arbitrarily shaped histogram (see also (Haerdle, 1991; Venables and Ripley, 2003)). Nevertheless, histograms for variables that represent real numbers remain somewhat unsatisfactory. The histogram suggests discrete jumps as you move from bar to bar, while the real distribution of probabilities that we try to approximate with the histogram is smooth.

We can avoid this problem with the function `density()`, which produces a "smoothed histogram." We illustrate the advantages of DENSITY ESTIMATION by means of the reaction times elicited in a visual lexical decision experiment using the same words as in the `ratings` data set. The reaction times for 79 of the 81 words used in the ratings data set are available as the data set `lexdec`. Details about the variables in this data set can be obtained with `?lexdec`. The left panel of Figure 2.2 shows the histogram as given by `truehist()` applied to the (logarithmically transformed) reaction times:

```
> truehist(lexdec$RT, col = "lightgrey", xlab = "log RT")
```

The distribution of the logged reaction times is somewhat skewed, with an extended right tail of long latencies.

The right panel of Figure 2.2 shows the histogram, together with the DENSITY curve, using the function `density()`. Below, we discuss in detail how exactly we made this plot. Here, we note that the histogram and the density curve have roughly the same shape, but that the density curve smoothes the discrete jumps

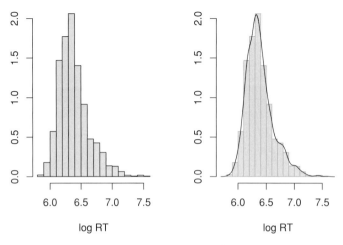

Figure 2.2. *Histograms and density function for the response latencies of* 21 *subjects to* 79 *nouns referring to animals and plants.*

of the histogram. As reaction time is a continuous variable, the density curve is both more appropriate and more accurate.

Plotting the right panel is not difficult, but it requires some special care and illustrates some more details of how plotting works in R. The problem that arises when superimposing one graph on another graph, as in Figure 2.2, is that we have to make sure that the ranges for the two axes are set appropriately. Otherwise R will set the ranges to accommodate the first graph, in which case the second graph may not fit properly. We begin with the standard function for making a histogram, hist(), which, unlike truehist(), can be instructed to produce a histogram object. As we don't want a plot at this point, we tell hist() to forget about producing a histogram in the graphics window by specifying plot = FALSE:

```
> h = hist(lexdec$RT, freq = FALSE, plot = FALSE)
```

(The option freq = FALSE ensures that the histogram has a total area of one.) A histogram object has many components, of which we need two: the locations of the edges of the bars, and the heights of the bars. These are available as components of our histogram object h, and accessible as h$breaks and h$density. As our next step, we make a density object,

```
> d = density(lexdec$RT)
```

which provides the x and y coordinates for the graph as d$x and d$y. We now have all the information we need for determining the smallest and largest values that should be displayed on the X and Y axes. We calculate these values with range(), which extracts the largest and smallest values from all its input vectors:

```
> xlimit = range(h$breaks, d$x)
> ylimit = range(0, h$density, d$y)
```

For the vertical axis, we include 0 when calculating the range in order to make sure that the origin will be included as the lowest value.

We can now proceed to plot the histogram, informing `hist()` about the limits for the axes through the options `xlim` and `ylim`:

```
> hist(lexdec$RT, freq=FALSE, xlim=xlimit, ylim=ylimit, main="",
+ xlab="log RT", ylab="", col="lightgrey", border="darkgrey",
+ breaks = seq(5.8, 7.6, by = 0.1))
```

With the option `col` we set the color of the bars to light grey, and with `border` we set the color of the borders of the bars to dark grey. We also prevent `hist()` from adding a title to the graph with `main = ""`. The `breaks` option is necessary for getting `hist()` to produce the same output as `truehist()` does for us by default. Finally, we add the curve for the density with the function `lines()`. The function `lines()` takes a vector of x coordinates and a vector of y coordinates, and connects the points specified by these coordinates with a line in the order specified by the input vectors:

```
> lines(d$x, d$y)
```

In this case, the command `lines(d$x, d$y)` is unnecessarily complex, as a density object such as d tells plotting functions like `lines()` where they can find the x and y coordinates. Therefore, all we actually have to specify is:

```
> lines(d)
```

You can plot a histogram or density object simply with the general plotting function `plot()`,

```
> plot(h)
> plot(d)
```

without having to specify the x and y values yourself. However, if you need those values, you can extract them from the objects, as we have seen when we calculated `xlimit` and `ylimit`. In other words, R provides sensible plotting defaults without giving up user control over the fine details.

There are several other ways in which you can visualize the distribution of a random variable. Figure 2.3 shows plots based on the values of the reaction times sorted from small to large. The upper left panel plots the index (or rank) of the reaction times on the horizontal axis, and the reaction times themselves on the vertical axis. This way of plotting the data reveals the range of values, as well as the presence of outliers. Outliers are data points with values that are surprisingly large or small given all data points considered jointly. There are a few outliers representing very short reaction times, and many more outliers representing very long reaction times. This difference between the head and the tail of the distribution corresponds to the asymmetry in the density curve shown in the right panel of Figure 2.2.

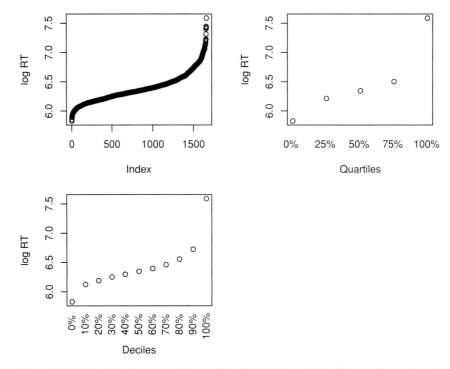

Figure 2.3. *Ordered values, quartiles, and deciles for logarithmically transformed reaction times in a visual lexical decision experiment.*

The upper left panel of Figure 2.3 was produced simply with:

```
> plot(sort(lexdec$RT), ylab = "log RT")
```

When `plot()` is supplied with only one vector of data, it assumes that this vector represents *Y*-values and generates a vector of *X*-values numbered from 1 to the number of elements in the input vector. As we provided a sorted vector of numbers, the automatically generated *X*-values represent the ranks of these numbers.

The upper right panel of Figure 2.3 shows the QUARTILES of the distribution of reaction times, and the lower panel the DECILES. The quartiles are the data points you get by dividing the sorted data into four equal parts. The 50% quartile is also known as the MEDIAN. The deciles are the data points dividing the sorted data into 10 equal parts. The function `quantile()` calculates the quantiles for its input vector; by default it produces the quartiles. By supplying a second vector with the required percentage points, the default can be changed.

Let's have a closer look at the code that produced the quantile plots in Figure 2.3, as this illustrates some further ways in which you can control what R plots. These quantile plots require special attention with respect to the labels on the horizontal axis. We do not want R to label the five points for the quartiles on the horizontal axis with five tick marks (the small vertical and horizontal lines marking the labeled values on the axes) and the numbers 1 through 5. What we want is sensibly labeled quartiles. We therefore instruct `plot()` to forget about tick marks and numbers labeling the horizontal axis, using the option `xaxt = "n"`:

```
> plot(quantile(lexdec$RT), xaxt = "n",
+ xlab = "Quartiles", ylab = "log RT")
```

The next step is to add the appropriate labels. We do this with the function `mtext()`, which adds text to a given margin of a plot. A plot margin is the white space between the edge of the graphics window and the plot itself. The margins are labeled 1 (bottom), 2 (left), 3 (top), and 4 (right). In other words, the first margin is the space between the X axis and the lower edge of the plotting region. We instruct `mtext()` to place the text vector `c("0%", "25%", "50%", "75%", "100%")` in the first margin (with the option `side = 1`), one line out (downwards) into the margin (with the option `line = 1`), with a font size reduced to 70% of the default font size (with the option `cex = 0.7`):

```
> mtext(c("0%", "25%", "50%", "75%", "100%"),
+ side = 1, at = 1:5, line = 1, cex = 0.7)
```

The option `at = 1:5` tells `mtext()` where to place the five elements of the text vector. Recall that we plotted the quartiles with `plot(quantile(lexdec$RT))`, i.e. without explicitly telling R about the X and Y coordinates. As there is only one vector of numbers, these numbers are taken to be Y coordinates. The X coordinates are the indexes of the input vector, the numbers 1, 2, ..., n, with n the length of the input vector (the total number of elements in the vector). As we have five elements in our input vector, we know that the X coordinates that `plot()` generated for us are the numbers 1 through 5. To get our labels at the appropriate location, we supply these positions to `mtext()` through the option `at`.

In the code that produced the lower panel of Figure 2.3,

```
> plot(quantile(lexdec$RT, seq(0, 1, 0.1)),
+ xaxt = "n", xlab = "Deciles", ylab = "log RT")
> mtext(paste(seq(0, 100, 10), rep("%", 11), sep = ""),
+ side = 1, at = 1:11, line = 1, cex = 0.7, las = 2)
```

the first argument to `plot()` is again the output of the quantile function. By default, `quantile()` outputs quartiles, but here we are interested in deciles. The second argument to `quantile()` specifies these deciles, created with the help of the function `seq()`:

```
> seq(0, 1, 0.1)
 [1] 0.0 0.1 0.2 0.3 0.4 0.5 0.6 0.7 0.8 0.9 1.0
```

The first argument of `seq()` specifies with which number a sequence should begin, its second argument specifies the number with which this sequence should end, and the third argument specifies the increment, here 0.1. This vector has eleven elements, hence the output of `quantile()` has eleven elements as well:

```
> quantile(lexdec$RT, seq(0, 1, 0.1))
      0%       10%       20%       30%       40%       50%       60%
5.828946 6.122493 6.188264 6.248816 6.297109 6.345636 6.395262
     70%       80%       90%      100%
6.459904 6.553933 6.721907 7.587311
```

As we are not interested in the *X* coordinates generated automatically by `plot()`, we suppress tick marks and labels for the tick marks by specifying `xaxt = "n"`. We now add our own tick marks. We could create a vector of strings by hand, but by combining `seq()` with another function, `paste()`, we save ourselves some typing. `paste()` takes two or more strings as input and glues them together so that they become one single string. The user has control over what character should separate the input strings. By default, the original arguments are separated by a space,

```
> paste("a", "b", "c")
[1] "a b c"
```

but we can remove the space by setting the separating character to the empty string:

```
> paste("a", "b", "c", sep = "")
```

When `paste()` is supplied with vectors of strings, it will glue the elements of these vectors together pairwise:

```
> paste(seq(0, 100, 10), rep("%", 11), sep = "")
 [1] "0%"   "10%"  "20%"  "30%"  "40%"  "50%"
 [7] "60%"  "70%"  "80%"  "90%" "100%"
```

This vector provides sensible labels for the horizontal axis of our plot. Above, we fed it to `mtext()`. We also instructed `mtext()` to place the strings perpendicular to the horizontal axis with `las=2`, as there are too many labels to fit together when placed horizontally along the axis.

Figure 2.4 plots the estimated density, the ordered values, and a new summary plot, a box and whiskers plot or boxplot, for the reaction times, with the untransformed RTs in milliseconds on the upper row of panels, and log RT on the lower row of panels. The rightmost panels show box and whiskers plots, produced with the function `boxplot()`, which provide useful graphical summaries of distributions:

```
> boxplot(exp(lexdec$RT))    # upper panel
> boxplot(lexdec$RT)         # lower panel
```

(For the upper panel, we use the exponential function `exp()` to undo the logarithmic transformation of the reaction times in the data frame `lexdec`.) The box in a box and whiskers plot shows the interquartile range, the range from the first to the third quartile. The whiskers in a boxplot extend to maximally 1.5 times the interquartile range. Points falling outside the whiskers are plotted individually; they are potential outliers. The horizontal line in the box represents the median. The large number of individual points extending above the upper whiskers in these boxplots highlight that we are dealing with a quite skewed, non-symmetrical distribution.

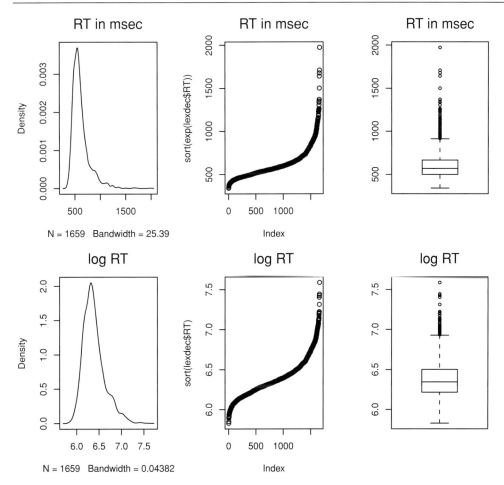

Figure 2.4. *Density, ordered values, and boxplots for reaction times and log reaction times in a visual lexical decision experiment.*

A comparison of the upper and lower panels in Figure 2.4 shows that the skewing is reduced, although not eliminated, by the logarithmic transformation. This is clearly visible in the boxplot in the lower right panel. There are still many marked outliers, but their number is smaller and the box has moved somewhat more towards the center of the graph.

The reason that many of the variables that we study in this book are logarithmically transformed is to eliminate or at least substantially reduce the skewing in their distribution. This reduction is necessary for most of the statistical techniques discussed in this book to work appropriately. Without the logarithmic transformation, just a few extreme outliers might dominate the outcome, partially or even completely obscuring the main trends characterizing the majority of data points.

The logarithmic transformation is not the only transformation that you might consider. An alternative that sometimes works well is the inverse transformation, 1/RT. In order to facilitate interpretation, it is useful to use as transformation $-1000/RT$. We multiply by 1000 to avoid very small values for the dependent

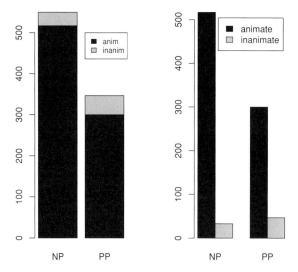

Figure 2.5. *Bar plots for the counts of clauses cross-classified by the realization of the recipient as* NP *or* PP *and the animacy of the recipient.*

variable, and we multiply by −1 to ensure that larger values of the original variable correspond to larger values of the transformed variable.

2.3   Visualizing two or more variables

In Chapter 1, we created a contingency table for the counts of clauses cross-classified by the animacy of the recipient and the realization of the recipient (NP versus PP), using the data analyzed by Bresnan *et al.* (2007). We recreate this contingency table,

```
> verbs.xtabs = xtabs( ~ AnimacyOfRec + RealizationOfRec,
+ data = verbs[verbs$AnimacyOfTheme != "animate", ])
> verbs.xtabs
            RealizationOfRec
AnimacyOfRec  NP   PP
   animate   517  300
   inanimate  33   47
```

and visualize it by means of a bar plot. We use the same `barplot()` function as above. However, as our input is not a vector but a table, we have to decide what kind of bar plot we want. Figure 2.5 illustrates the two options. The left panel shows two bars, each composed of subbars proportional to the two counts in the columns of `verbs.xtabs`. The right panel shows two pairs of bars, the first pair representing the counts for animacy within NP realizations, the second pair representing the same counts within the realizations of the recipient as a PP:

```
> par(mfrow = c(1, 2))
> barplot(verbs.xtabs, legend.text=c("anim", "inanim"))
> barplot(verbs.xtabs, beside = T, legend.text = rownames(verbs.xtabs))
> par(mfrow = c(1, 1))
```

In Chapter 1 we had a first look at the data of Bresnan and colleagues on the dative alternation in English. Let's consider their data once more, but now we make use of the full data set (`dative`), and cross-tabulate the realization of the recipient by its animacy and accessibility:

```
> verbs.xtabs =
+ xtabs( ~ AnimacyOfRec  + AccessOfRec + RealizationOfRecipient,
+ data = dative)
> verbs.xtabs
, , RealizationOfRecipient = NP

              AccessOfRec
AnimacyOfRec accessible  given   new
    animate         290   1931    78
    inanimate        11     99     5

, , RealizationOfRecipient = PP

              AccessOfRec
AnimacyOfRec accessible  given   new
    animate         259    239   227
    inanimate        55     33    36
```

Such a contingency table might be visualized with a bar plot, but twelve bars or smaller numbers of stacked bars quickly become rather complex to interpret. An attractive alternative is to make use of a mosaic plot, as shown in the left panel of Figure 2.6:

```
> mosaicplot(verbs.xtabs, main = "dative")
```

The areas of the twelve rectangles in the plot are proportional to the counts for the twelve cells of the contingency table. When there is no structure in the data, as in the mosaic plot in the right panel of Figure 2.6, each rectangle is approximately equally large. The many asymmetries in the left panel show, for instance, that in the actual data set given recipients are more likely to be realized as NP than new or accessible recipients, both for animate and inanimate recipients, irrespective of the overall preponderance of given recipients.

The relation between two numerical variables with many different values is often brought to light by means of a SCATTERPLOT. Figure 2.7 displays two versions of the same scatterplot for variables in the `ratings` data set. The upper panel was produced in two steps. The first step consisted of plotting the data points:

```
> plot(ratings$Frequency, ratings$FamilySize)
```

All we have to do is specify the vectors of X and Y values as arguments to `plot()`. By default, the names of the two input vectors are used as labels for the axes. You can see that words with a very high frequency tend to have a very high family size. In other words, the two variables are positively CORRELATED. At the same time, it is also clear that there is a lot of noise, and that the scatter (or variance) in family sizes is greater for lower frequencies. Such an uneven pattern is referred to as HETEROSKEDASTIC, and is endemic in lexical statistics.

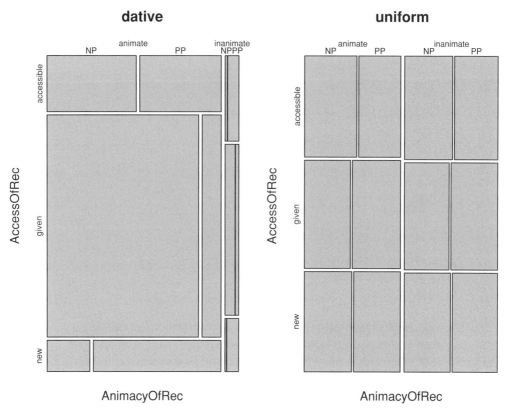

Figure 2.6. *A mosaic plot for observed counts of clauses cross-classified by the animacy of the recipient, the accessibility of the recipient, and the realization of the recipient (left panel), and for random counts (right).*

The second step consisted of adding the grey line to highlight the main trend:

```
> lines(lowess(ratings$Frequency, ratings$FamilySize), col="darkgrey")
```

This line shows that you have to proceed almost 2 log frequency units along the horizontal axis before you begin to see an increase in family size. For larger frequencies, the family size increases, slowly at first, but then faster and almost like a straight line. A curve like this is often referred to as a SCATTERPLOT SMOOTHER, as it smoothes away all the turbulence around the main trend in the data. The smoothing function that we used here is `lowess()`, which takes as input the X and Y coordinates of the data points and produces as output the X and Y coordinates of the smooth line. To plot this line, we fed its coordinates into `lines()`.

The basic idea underlying smoothers is to use the observations in a given span (or bin) of values of X to calculate the average increase in Y. You then move this span from left to right along the horizontal axis, each time calculating the new increase in y. There are many ways in which you can estimate these increases, and many ways in which you can combine all these estimated increases into a

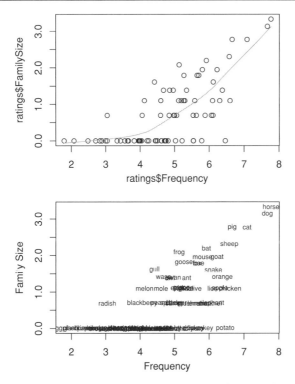

Figure 2.7. *Scatterplots for Family Size as a function of Frequency for* 81 *English nouns.*

line. Recall that Figure 2.2 illustrated that the smoothness of a histogram depends on the width of its bars. In a similar way, the smoothness of the line produced by `lowess()` is determined by the bin width used. As `lowess()` makes use of a sensible rule of thumb for calculating a reasonable bin width, we need not do anything ourselves. However, if you think that `lowess()` engages in too much smoothing (the line hides variation you suspect to be there) or too little smoothing (the line has too many idiosyncratic bumps) for your data, you can change the bin width manually, as documented in the on-line help. Venables and Ripley (2003:228–232) provide detailed information on various important smoothers that are available in R.

The lower panel of Figure 2.7 shows a different version of the same scatterplot. Data points are now labeled by the words they represent. It is now easy to see that *horse* and *dog* are the words with the highest frequency and family size in the sample. This scatterplot was also made in two steps. The first step consisted of setting up the axes, now with our own labels, specified with `xlab` and `ylab`. However, we instructed `plot()` not to add the data points by setting the plot type to "none" with `type = "n"`:

```
> plot(ratings$Frequency, ratings$FamilySize, type = "n",
+ xlab = "Frequency", ylab = "Family Size")
```

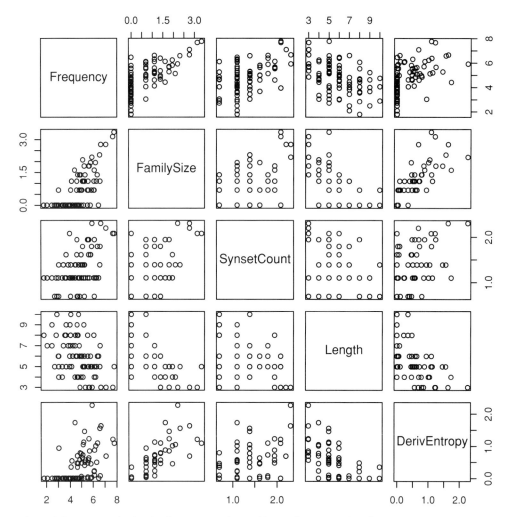

Figure 2.8. *A pairs plot for the five numerical variables in the ratings data frame.*

The second step consisted in adding the words to the plot with `text()`. Like `plot()`, it requires input vectors for the *X* and *Y* coordinates. Its third argument should be a vector with the strings that are to be placed in the plot. In the data frame `ratings`, the column labeled `Word` is a factor, so we first convert it into a vector of strings with `as.character()` before handing it over to `text()`. Finally, we set the font size to 0.7 of its default with `cex = 0.7`:

```
> text(ratings$Frequency, ratings$FamilySize,
+ as.character(ratings$Word), cex = 0.7)
```

Thus far, we have considered scatterplots involving two variables only. Many data sets have more than two variables, however, and although we might consider inspecting all possible pairwise combinations with a series of scatterplots, it is often more convenient and insightful to make a single multipanel figure that shows all pairwise scatterplots simultaneously. Figure 2.8 shows such a

SCATTERPLOT MATRIX for all two by two combinations of the five numerical variables in `ratings`. The panels on the main diagonal provide the labels for the axes of the panels. For instance, all the panels on the top row have Frequency on the vertical axis, and all the panels of the first column have Frequency on the horizontal axis. Each pair of variables is plotted twice, once with a given variable on the horizontal axis, and once with the same variable on the vertical axis. Such pairs of plots have coordinates that are mirrored in the main diagonal. Thus, panel (2, 1) is obtained by mirroring the points in panel (1, 2) across the main diagonal. Similarly, panel (5, 1) in the lower left has its opposite in the upper right corner at location (1, 5). The reason for having mirrored panels is that sometimes a pattern strikes the eye in one orientation, but not in the other.

Figure 2.8 was made with the `pairs()` plot function, which requires a data frame with numerical columns as input:

```
> pairs(ratings[ , -c(1, 6:8, 10:14)])
```

The condition on the columns has a minus sign, indicating that all columns specified to its right should be excluded instead of included. The columns that we exclude here are all factors. Factors cannot be visualized in scatterplots, hence we take them out before applying `pairs()`. Figure 2.8 reveals that a fair number of pairs of predictors enter into correlations, a phenomenon that is known as MULTICOLLINEARITY. Strong multicollinearity among a set of predictor variables may make it impossible to ascertain which predictor variables best explain the dependent variable. We will return to this issue in more detail when discussing multiple regression.

2.4   Trellis graphics

A trellis is a wooden grid for growing roses and other flowers that need vertical support. Trellis graphics are graphs in which data are visualized by many systematically organized graphs simultaneously. We have encountered one trellis graph already, the pairwise scatterplot matrix as illustrated in Figure 2.8, where each plot is a hole in the trellis. There are more advanced functions for more complex trellis plots, which are available in the `lattice` package:

```
> library(lattice)
```

Trellis graphics become important when you are dealing with different groups of data points. For instance, the words in the `ratings` data frame fall into two groups: animals on the one hand, and the produce of plants (fruits, vegetables, nuts) on the other hand. Therefore, the factor `Class` (with levels `animal` and `plant`) can be regarded as a GROUPING FACTOR for the words. Another possible grouping factor for this data is whether the word is morphologically complex (e.g. *woodpecker*) or morphologically simple (e.g. *snake*). With respect to the lexical

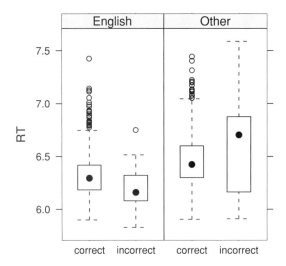

Figure 2.9. *Trellis box and whiskers plot for log reaction time by accuracy (correct versus incorrect response) grouped by the first language of the subject.*

decision data in `lexdec`, the factor `Subject` is a grouping factor: Each subject provided response latencies for the same 79 words.

A question that arises when running a lexical decision experiment with native and non-native speakers of English is whether there might be systematic differences in how these two groups of subjects perform. It is to be expected that non-native speakers require more time for a lexical decision. Furthermore, the conditions under which they make errors may differ as well. In order to explore this possibility, we make boxplots for the reaction times for correct and incorrect responses, and we do this for both the native speakers and the non-native speakers in the experiment. In other words, we use the factor `NativeLanguage` as a grouping factor. In order to make a grouped boxplot, we use the `bwplot()` function from the `lattice` package as follows:

```
> bwplot(RT ~ Correct | NativeLanguage, data = lexdec)
```

The result is shown in Figure 2.9. As you can see, `bwplot()` requires two arguments, a FORMULA and a data frame, `lexdec` in this example. The formula,

```
RT ~ Correct | NativeLanguage
```

considers `RT` as depending on the correctness of the response (`Correct`), grouped by the levels of `NativeLanguage`. In the formula, the vertical bar (|) is the GROUPING OPERATOR. Another way of reading this formula is as an instruction to create box and whiskers plots for the distribution of reaction times for the levels of `Correct` conditioned on the levels of `NativeLanguage`, the groups of native and non-native speakers. The result is a plot with two panels, one for each level of the grouping factor. Within each of these panels, we have two box and whiskers plots, one for each level of `Correct`.

    This trellis graph shows some remarkable differences between the native and non-native speakers of English (referenced as English and Other in Figure 2.9). First of all, we see that the boxes (and medians) for the non-native speakers are shifted upwards compared to those for the native speakers, indicating that they required more time for their decisions, as expected. Interestingly, we also see that the incorrect responses were associated with shorter decision latencies for the native speakers, but with longer latencies for the non-native speakers. Finally, note that there are many outliers only for the correct responses, for both groups of subjects. Later, we shall see how we can test whether what we see here is indeed reason for surprise. What is already clear at this point is that there is a pattern in the data that is worth examining in greater detail.

    There are many other kinds of trellis graphs, examples of which can be found in the on-line help for `xyplot()`. Here, we restrict ourselves to two important and easy ways to use trellis functions.

    It is often useful to explore data with scatterplots for each of the levels of a grouping factor. To make this more concrete, we consider the subjective estimates of weight elicited for the 81 words in the `ratings` data set that we examined previously. But now we inspect the individual ratings provided by the subjects to the different words, as available in the data set `weightRatings`:

```
> weightRatings[1:5, ]
  Subject Rating Trial Sex     Word Frequency   Class
1      A1      5     1   F    horse  7.771910  animal
2      A1      1     2   F  gherkin  2.079442   plant
3      A1      3     3   F hedgehog  3.637586  animal
4      A1      1     4   F      bee  5.700444  animal
5      A1      1     5   F   peanut  4.595120   plant
```

We inspect how weight ratings were influenced by frequency for each of the subjects separately by means of Figure 2.10. Each panel plots the data for one subject, the grouping factor in this trellis graph. Each panel is labeled with the relevant level of the grouping factor in the accompanying strip, here, an acronym for the subject. In each panel, the dependent variable (`Rating`) appears on the vertical axis, and the predictor (`Frequency`) on the horizontal axis.

    Figure 2.10 suggests that weight ratings increase with increasing (log) frequency, albeit only clearly so for the highest frequencies. There also seems to be some variation in how strong the effect is. To judge from the scatterplot smoothers, subject G does not seem to have much of a frequency effect, in contrast to, for instance, subject R5, for whom the effect seems quite large. This trellis display invites further research into whether these visual patterns are statistically robust.

    The code that produced Figure 2.10 is quite simple:

```
> xylowess.fnc(Rating ~ Frequency | Subject, data = weightRatings,
+ xlab = "log Frequency", ylab = "Weight Rating")
```

The same plot, but now without the lines for the scatterplot smoothers, is obtained with:

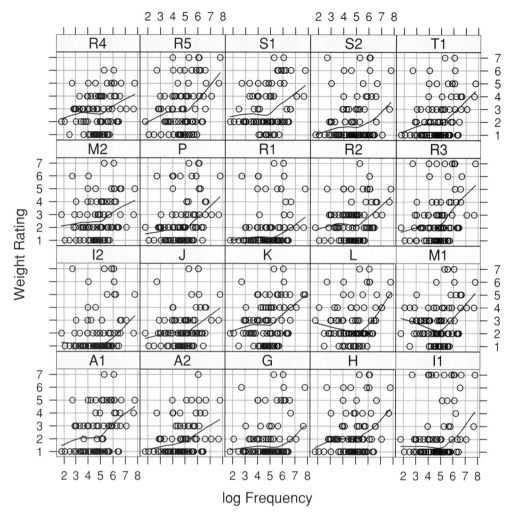

Figure 2.10. *Weight rating as a function of log word frequency grouped by subject.*

```
> xyplot(Rating   Frequency | Subject, data = weightRatings,
+ xlab = "log Frequency", ylab = "Weight Rating")
```

While `xyplot()` is part of the lattice package, `xylowess.fnc()` is not. It is a function that I wrote around `xyplot()` in order to make it easy to produce matrices with scatterplots and smoothers.

A second important trellis graph is the CONDITIONING PLOT. An example of a conditioning plot is Figure 2.11. It is based on a data set of 2284 English monomorphemic and monosyllabic words studied by Balota *et al.* (2004) and Baayen *et al.* (2006). The plot graphs morphological family size as a function of the number of complex synsets, conditioned on equal counts of written frequency. Recall that a word's morphological family size is the count of complex words in which it occurs as a constituent. The complex words on which this count is based

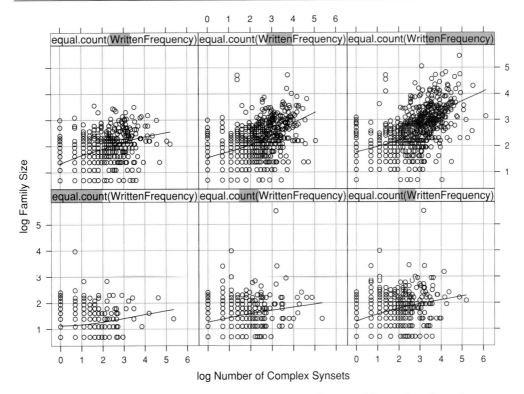

Figure 2.11. *A conditioning plot: morphological family size as a function of the number of complex synsets, for six overlapping ranges of written frequency (English monomorphemic and monosyllabic words).*

are words written without internal spaces. Hence, compounds such as *apple pie* are not included. By contrast, the count of complex synsets concerns the number of synonym sets in WordNet in which the word is listed as part of a compound with internal spaces. Therefore, the count of complex synsets is a complementary family size measure. Consequently, we may expect that, in general, words that have a high family size will also have a high value for the complex synsets measure. We also know that higher-frequency words tend to have more family members. The importance of a conditioning plot is that it allows us to inspect the joint correlational structure among three predictors in a single graphical display.

The conditioning plot shown in Figure 2.11 consists of six scatterplots, each with its own smoother, which graph log Family Size against log Number of Complex Synsets. The six panels are arranged by increasing intervals of Written Frequency. The lowest frequency band is found in the lower left plot, and the highest frequency band in the upper right plot. The shaded areas in the strips above the panels provide a visual indication of the frequency bands that characterize the data points in the scatterplots. As indicated by these shaded areas, written frequency increases as we move from the lower left to the lower right, and then from the upper left to the upper right. The six frequency bands are chosen such that there is an equal count of observations in each frequency band. What Figure 2.11

shows is that the correlation between the Family Size measure and the Number of Complex Synsets is present predominantly for the higher-frequency words. This may be due to a lexicographic bias favoring inclusion of compounds with internal spaces in dictionaries (and hence in WordNet) only if they are sufficiently frequent. Technically, the phenomenon illustrated here is referred to as an INTERACTION, in this example an interaction of Written Frequency by Number of Complex Synsets.

To reproduce Figure 2.11, we need the `english` data set (4568 rows), which provides mean reaction times to 2284 words for two subject populations. In order to obtain the characteristics of the items without duplicate entries, we restrict the data to the subset pertaining to the young subject population:

```
> english = english[english$AgeSubject == "young", ]
> nrow(english)
[1] 2284
```

This data frame provides a large number of quantitative lexical variables, among which are `WrittenFrequency`, `FamilySize`, and `NumberComplexSynsets`. A conditioning plot is useful here. Crucially, we do not condition on `Written-Frequency` as such—this would result in one panel for each distinct frequency. Instead, we use the function `equal.count()` to obtain what is referred to as a SHINGLE: six overlapping frequency bands with equal numbers of observations in each band:

```
> xylowess.fnc(FamilySize ~ NumberComplexSynsets |
+ equal.count(WrittenFrequency), data = english)
```

Workbook section

Exercises

1. The data set `warlpiri` (data courtesy Carmel O'Shannessy) provides information about the use of the ergative case in Lajamanu Warlpiri. Data were elicited for adults and children of various ages. The question of interest is to what extent the use of the ergative case marker is predictable from the animacy of the subject, word order, and the age of the speaker (adult versus child). Explore this data set with respect to this issue by means of a mosaic plot. (First construct a contingency table with `xtabs()`, then supply this contingency table as argument to `mosaicplot()`.)

2. In Chapter 1 we created a data frame with mean reaction times and mean base frequencies for neologisms in the Dutch suffix *-heid*. Reconstruct the data frame `heid2`. Both reaction times and frequencies are logarithmically transformed. Use `exp()` to undo these transformations and make a scatterplot of the averaged reaction times (`MeanRT`) against the frequency of the base (`BaseFrequency`). Compare this scatterplot with a scatterplot using the log-transformed values.

3. The data set `moby` is a character vector with the text of Melville's *Moby Dick*. In this exercise, we consider whether Zipf's law holds for *Moby Dick*. According to Zipf's law (Zipf, 1949),

the frequency of a word is inversely proportional to its rank in a numerically sorted list. The word with the highest frequency has rank 1, the word with the next highest frequency has rank 2, etc. If Zipf's law holds, a plot of log frequency against log rank should reveal a straight line. We make a table of word frequencies with `table()`—we cannot use `xtabs()`, because `words` is a vector and `xtabs()` expects a data frame—and sort the frequencies in reverse numerical order:

```
> moby.table = table(moby)
> moby.table = sort(moby.table, decreasing = TRUE)
> moby.table[1:5]
moby
   the     of    and      a     to
 13655   6488   5985   4534   4495
```

We now have the word frequencies. We use the colon operator and `length()`, which returns the length of a vector, to construct the corresponding ranks:

```
> ranks = 1 : length(moby.table)
> ranks[1:5]
[1] 1 2 3 4 5
```

Make a scatterplot of log frequency against log rank.

4. The column labeled `Trial` in the data set `lexdec` specifies, for each subject, the trial number of the responses. For a given subject, the first trial in the experiment has trial number 1, the second has trial number 2, etc. Use `xylowess.fnc()` to explore the possibility that the subjects proceeded through the experiment in different ways, some revealing effects of learning, and others effects of fatigue.

5. The data set `english` lists lexical decision and word naming latencies for two age groups. Inspect the distribution of the naming latencies (`RTnaming`). First plot a histogram for the naming latencies with `truehist()`. Then plot the density. The voicekey registering the naming responses is sensitive to the different acoustic properties of a word's initial phoneme. The column `Voice` specifies whether a word's initial phoneme was voiced or voiceless. Use `bwplot()` to make a trellis boxplot for the distribution of the naming latencies across voiced and voiceless phonemes with the age group of the subjects (`AgeSubject`) as grouping factor.

3   Probability distributions

Many statistical tests exploit the properties of the probability distributions of random variables. This chapter provides an introduction to some of the most important probability distributions, and lays the groundwork for the statistical tests introduced in Chapter 4.

3.1   Distributions

When we count how often a word is used, or when we measure the duration of a vowel, we carry out a statistical experiment. The outcome of such a statistical experiment varies each time it is carried out. For instance, the frequency of a word (the outcome of a counting experiment) will vary from text to text and from corpus to corpus, and similarly the length of a given vowel (the outcome of a measuring experiment) will vary from syllable to syllable and from word to word. For a given random variable, some outcomes may be more likely than others. The probability distribution of a random variable specifies the likelihood of the different outcomes. Random variables fall into two important categories. Random variables such as frequency counts are DISCRETE (with values that are integers), random variables such as durational measurements are CONTINUOUS (with values that are reals). We begin by introducing two discrete distributions.

3.2   Discrete distributions

The CELEX lexical database (Baayen *et al.*, 1995) lists the frequencies of a large number of English words in a corpus of 18.6 million words. Table 3.1 provides these frequencies for four words, the high-frequency definite article *the*, the medium-frequency word *president*, and two low-frequency words, *hare* and *harpsichord*. It also lists the RELATIVE FREQUENCIES of these words, which are obtained by dividing a word's frequency by the size of the corpus. These relative frequencies are estimates of the PROBABILITIES of these words in English.

Table 3.1. *Frequencies and relative frequencies of four words in the version of the Cobuild corpus underlying the* CELEX *frequency counts (corpus size:* 18580121 *tokens).*

	Frequency	Relative Frequency
the	1093547	0.05885575
president	2469	0.00013288
hare	153	0.00000823
harpsichord	16	0.00000086

In the simplest model for text generation, the selection of a word for inclusion in a text is similar to sampling marbles from a vase. The likelihood of sampling a red marble is given by the proportion of red marbles in that vase. Crucially, we sample with replacement, and we assume that the probabilities of words do not change over time. We also assume independence: the outcome of one trial does not affect the outcome of the next trial. It is obvious that these assumptions of what is known as the urn model involve substantial simplifications. The probability of observing *the*, a high-probability word, adjacent to another instance of *the* in real language is very small. In spoken language such sequences may occasionally occur, for instance, due to hesitations on the part of the speaker, but in carefully edited written texts a sequence of two instances of *the* is highly improbable. On the other hand, it is also clear that *the* is indeed very much more frequent than *hare* or *harpsichord*, and for questions at high aggregation levels, even simplifying assumptions can provide us with surprising leverage.

By way of example, consider the question of how the frequencies of these words compare to their frequencies observed in other, smaller, corpora of English such as the Brown corpus (Kučera and Francis, 1967) (1 million words). Table 3.2 lists the probabilities (relative frequencies) for the four words in Table 3.1, as well as the frequencies observed in the Brown corpus and the frequencies one would expect given CELEX. These expected frequencies are easy to calculate. For instance, if 0.05885575 is the proportion of word tokens in CELEX representing the word type *the*, then a similar proportion of tokens should represent this type in a 1 million corpus, i.e. $1000000 * 0.05885575 = 58856$ tokens. As shown in Table 3.2, the expected counts are smaller for *the* and *president*, larger for *hare*, and right on target for *harpsichord*.

Should we be surprised by the observed differences? In order to answer this question, we need to make some assumptions about the properties of the distribution of a word's frequency. There are 382 occurrences of the noun *president* in the Brown corpus, but the Brown corpus is only one sample from American English as spoken in the early 1960s. If additional corpora were compiled from the same kind of textual materials using the same sampling criteria, the number of occurrences of the noun *president* would still vary from corpus to corpus. In other

Table 3.2. *Probabilities (estimated from* CELEX*), expected frequencies and observed frequencies in the Brown corpus.*

	p	expected frequency	observed frequency
the	0.05885575	58856	69971
president	0.00013288	133	382
hare	0.00000823	8	1
harpsichord	0.00000086	1	1

words, the frequency of a word in a corpus is a random variable. The statistical experiment associated with this random variable involves creating a corpus of one million words, followed by counting how often *president* is used in this corpus. For repeated experiments sampling one million words, we expect this random variable to assume values similar to the 382 tokens observed in the Brown corpus. But what we really want to know is the magnitude of the fluctuations of the frequency of *president* across corpora.

At this point, we need some further terminology. Let's define two probabilities: the probability of observing a specific word and the probability of observing any other word. We call the former probability p the PROBABILITY OF SUCCESS, and the latter probability q the PROBABILITY OF FAILURE. The probability of failure is $1-$ probability of success. In the case of *hare*, these probabilities are $p = 0.0000082$ and $q = 0.9999918$. Furthermore, let the NUMBER OF TRIALS (n) denote the size of the corpus. Each token in the corpus is regarded as a trial which can result either in a success (*hare* is observed) or in a failure (some other word is observed). Given the previously mentioned simplifying assumption that words are used independently and randomly in text, it turns out that we can model the frequency of a word as a BINOMIALLY DISTRIBUTED RANDOM VARIABLE with PARAMETERS p and n. (The textbook example of a binomially distributed random variable is the count of heads observed when tossing a coin n times that has probability p of turning up heads.) The properties of the binomial distribution are well known, and make it possible to obtain better insight into how much variability we may expect for our word frequencies across corpora, given our simplifying assumptions.

There are two kinds of properties that we need to distinguish. On the one hand, there are the properties of the POPULATION, on the other hand, there are the properties of a given SAMPLE. When we consider the properties of the population, we consider what we expect to happen on average across an infinite series of experiments. When we consider the properties of a sample, we consider what has actually occurred in a finite, usually small, series of experiments. We need tools for both kinds of properties. For instance, we want to know whether an observed frequency of 382 is surprising for *president* given that $p = 0.000133$ according to the CELEX counts and $n = 1,000,000$. This is a question about the population. How often will we observe this frequency across an infinite series of samples of

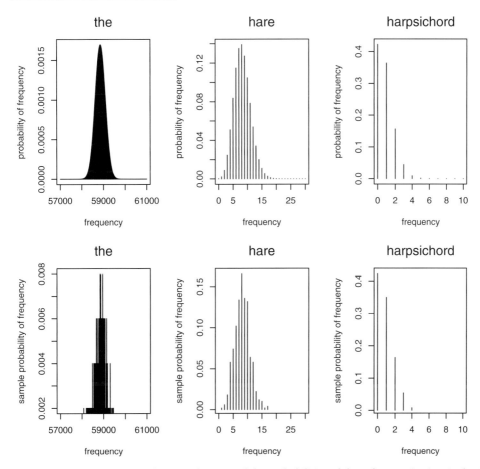

Figure 3.1. *The frequencies (horizontal axis) and the probabilities of these frequencies (vertical axis) for three words under the assumption that word frequencies are binomially distributed. Upper panels show the population distributions, lower panels the sample distributions for 500 random corpora.*

one million words? Is this close to what we would expect on average? In this book, we will mostly use properties of the population, but sometimes it is also useful to know what a sample of a given size might look like. R provides tools for both kinds of questions.

Consider the upper left panel of Figure 3.1. The horizontal axis graphs frequency, the vertical axis the probability of that frequency, given that the word *the* is binomially distributed with parameters $n = 1,000,000$ and $p = 0.059$. The tool that we use here is the dbinom() function, which is often referred to as the FREQUENCY FUNCTION and also as the PROBABILITY DENSITY FUNCTION. It requires three input values: a frequency (or a vector of frequencies), and values for the two parameters that define a binomial distribution, n, and p. dbinom() returns the probability of that frequency (or a vector of such probabilities in case a vector of frequencies was supplied). For instance, the expected probability of observing *the* exactly 59000 times averaged over an infinite series of corpora of one million words given the probability of success $p = 0.05885575$ is:

```
> dbinom(59000, 1000000, 0.05885575)
[1] 0.001403392
```

The upper panels of Figure 3.1 show, for each of the three words from Table 3.2, the probabilities of the frequencies with which these words are expected to occur. For each word and each frequency, we used `dbinom()` to calculate these probabilities given a sample size $n = 1,000,000$ and the word's population probability p as estimated by its relative frequency in CELEX.

The panel for *the* shows frequencies that are more or less centered around the mean frequency, 58856, the expected count listed in Table 3.2. We can see that the probability of observing values greater than 60000 are infinitesimally small, hence we have solid grounds to be surprised by the frequency of 69971 observed in the Brown corpus, given the CELEX counts. The next panel of Figure 3.1 shows the distribution of frequencies for *hare*. This is a low-frequency word, and we can now see the individual high-density lines for the individual frequencies. The pattern is one that is less symmetrical. The highest probability is 0.1391, which occurs for a frequency of 8, in conformity with the expected value we saw earlier in Table 3.2. The value actually observed in the Brown corpus, 1, is clearly atypically low. The upper right panel, finally, shows that for the very low-frequency word *harpsichord*, a frequency of zero is actually slightly more likely than the frequency of 1 listed in Table 3.2 (which rounded the expected frequency 0.86 to the nearest actually possible — discrete — number of occurrences).

The panels in the second row of Figure 3.1 correspond to those in the first row. The difference concerns the way in which the probabilities were obtained. The probabilities for the top row are those one would obtain for the frequencies observed across an infinite series of corpora (experiments) of one million words. They are population probabilities. The probabilities in the second row are those one might observe for a particular run of just 500 corpora (experiments) of one million words. They illustrate the kind of irregularities in the shape of a distribution that are typical for the actual samples with which we have to deal in practice. The irregularities that characterize sample distributions are most clearly visible in the lower left panel, but also to some extent in the lower central panel. Note that here the mode (the frequency with the highest sample probability) has an elevated value with respect to the immediately surrounding frequencies, compared to the upper central panel. Below, we discuss the tool for simulating random samples of a binomial random variable that we used to make these plots.

Figure 3.1 illustrates how the parameter p, the probability of success, affects the shape of the distribution. The other parameter, the number of trials (corpus size) n, likewise co-determines the shape of the distribution. Figure 3.2 illustrates this for the population, i.e. across an infinite series of corpora of $n = 1000$ (left) and $n = 50$ (right) word tokens. The left panel is still more or less symmetrical,

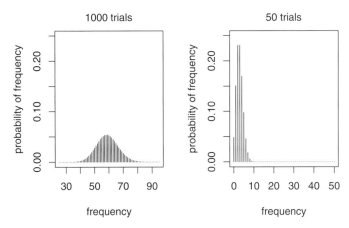

Figure 3.2. *The frequencies (horizontal axis) and the probabilities of these frequencies (vertical axis) for the assuming that its frequency is binomially distributed with p = 0.05885575 and n = 1000 (left panel) or n = 50 (right panel).*

but by the time that the corpus size is reduced to only 50 tokens, the symmetry is gone.

It is important to realize that the values that a binomially (n, p)-distributed random variable can assume are bounded by 0 and n. In the present example, this is intuitively obvious: a word need not occur in a corpus of size n, and so may have zero frequency. But a word can never occur more often than the corpus size. The upper bound, therefore, is n, for a boring but theoretically possible corpus consisting of just one word repeated n times. It is also useful to keep in mind that the EXPECTED (or mean) frequency is $n * p$, as p specifies the proportion of the n trials that are successful.

Let's now have a closer look at the tools that R provides for working with the binomial distribution. There are four such tools: the functions dbinom(), qbinom(), pbinom(), and rbinom(). R provides similar functions for a wide range of other random variables. Once you know how to use them for the binomial distribution, you know how to use the corresponding functions for any other distribution implemented in R.

First consider the observed frequency of 1 for *hare* where one would expect 8 given the counts in CELEX. What is the probability of observing such a low count under chance conditions? To answer this question, we use the function dbinom() that we have already introduced above. Given an observed value (its first argument), and given the parameters n and p (its second and third arguments), it returns the requested probability:

```
> dbinom(1, size = 1000000,  prob = 0.0000082)
[1] 0.002252102
```

In this example, I have spelled out the names of the second and third parameters, the size n and the probability p, in order to make it easier to interpret the function call, but the shorter version works just as well as long as the arguments are provided in exactly this order:

```
> dbinom(1, 1000000, 0.0000082)
[1] 0.002252102
```

Of course, if we think 1 is a low frequency, then 0 must also be a low frequency. So maybe we should ask what the probability is of observing a frequency of 1 or lower. Since the event of observing a count of 1 is independent of the event of observing a count of 0, we may add these two probabilities,

```
> dbinom(0, size = 1000000,  prob = 0.0000082) +
+ dbinom(1, size = 1000000,  prob = 0.0000082)
[1] 0.002526746
```

or, equivalently:

```
> sum(dbinom(0:1, size = 1000000,  prob = 0.0000082))
[1] 0.002526746
```

When dbinom() is supplied with a vector of frequencies, it returns a vector of probabilities, which we add using sum(). Another way to proceed is to make use of the pbinom() function, which immediately produces the sum of the probabilities for the supplied frequency as well as the probabilities of all smaller frequencies:

```
> pbinom(1, size = 1000000, prob = 0.0000082)
[1] 0.002526746
```

The low probability that we obtain here suggests that there is indeed reason for surprise about the low frequency of *hare* in the Brown corpus, at least, from the perspective of CELEX.

Recall that the Brown corpus mentions the word *president* 382 times, whereas we would expect only 133 occurrences given CELEX. In this case, we can ask what the probability is of observing a frequency of 382 or higher. This probability is the same as one minus the probability of observing a frequency of 381 or less:

```
> 1 - pbinom(381, size = 1000000, prob = 0.00013288)
[1] 0
```

The resulting probability is indistinguishable from zero given machine precision, and provides ample reason for surprise.

We used the function dbinom() to make the upper panels of Figure 3.1 and the panels of Figure 3.2. Here is the code producing the left panel of Figure 3.2:

```
> n = 1000
> p = 0.05885575
> frequencies = seq(25, 95, by = 1)  # 25, 26, 27, ..., 94, 95
> probabilities = dbinom(frequencies, n, p)
> plot(frequencies, probabilities, type = "h",
+ xlab = "frequency", ylab = "probability of frequency")
```

The first two lines define the parameters of the binomial distribution. The third line defines a range of frequencies for which the corresponding probabilities have to be provided. The fourth line calculates these probabilities. Since `frequencies` is a vector, `dbinom()` provides a probability for each frequency in this vector. The last two lines plot the probabilities against the frequencies, provide sensible labels, and specify, by means of `type = "h"`, that a vertical line (a "high-density line") should be drawn downwards from each point on the density curve.

Thus far, we have considered functions for using the population properties of the binomial distribution. But it is sometimes useful to know what a sample from a given distribution would look like. The lower panels of Figure 3.1, for instance, illustrated the variability that is typically observed in samples. The tool for investigating random samples from a binomial distribution is the function `rbinom()`. This function produces binomially distributed RANDOM NUMBERS. A random number is a number that simulates the outcome of a statistical experiment. A binomial random number simulates the number of successes one might observe given a success probability p and n trials. Technically, random numbers are never truly random, but for practical purposes they are a good approximation to randomness.

The following lines of code illustrate how to make the lower panel for *hare* in Figure 3.1. We first define the number of random numbers, the corpus size (the number of trials in one binomial experiment), and the probability of success:

```
> s = 500           # the number of random numbers
> n = 1000000       # number of trials in one experiment
> p = 0.0000082     # probability of success
```

Next, we use `rbinom()` to produce the random numbers representing the simulated frequencies of *hare* in the samples. This function takes three arguments: the number of random numbers required, and the two parameters of the binomial distribution, n and p. We feed the output of `rbinom()` into `xtabs()` to obtain a table listing for each simulated frequency how often that frequency occurs across the 500 simulation runs. We divide the resulting vector of counts by the number of simulation runs s to obtain the proportions (relative frequencies) of the simulated frequencies:

```
> x = xtabs( ~ rbinom(s, n, p) ) / s
> x
rbinom(s, n, p)
    2     3     4     5     6     7     8     9    10
0.012 0.028 0.062 0.086 0.126 0.118 0.138 0.132 0.084
   11    12    13    14    16    17    18    19
0.090 0.058 0.044 0.008 0.006 0.004 0.002 0.002
```

Note that in this simulation there are no instances where *hare* is observed not at all or only once. If you rerun this simulation, more extreme outcomes may be observed occasionally. This is because `rbinom()` simulates the randomness that is inherent in the sampling process. For plotting we convert the cell names in the table to numbers with `as.numeric()`:

```
> plot(as.numeric(names(x)), x, type = "h",  xlim = c(0, 30),
+ xlab = "frequency", ylab = "sample probability of frequency")
```

Recall that pbinom(x, n, p) produces the summed probability of values smaller than or equal to x, which is why it is referred to as the CUMULATIVE DISTRIBUTION FUNCTION. It has a mirror image (technically, its INVERSE function), qbinom(y, n, p), the QUANTILE FUNCTION, which takes this summed probability as input, and produces the corresponding count x:

```
> pbinom(4, size = 10, prob = 0.5)
[1] 0.3769531      # from count to cumulative probability
> qbinom(0.3769531, size = 10, prob = 0.5)
[1] 4              # from cumulative probability to count
```

Quantile functions are useful for checking whether a random variable is indeed binomially distributed. Consider, for example, the frequencies of the Dutch definite determiner for neuter nouns *het* in the consecutive stretches of 1000 words of a Dutch novel that gave its name to a fair trade brand in Europe, *Max Havelaar* (by Eduard Douwes Dekker, 1820–1887). The data set havelaar contains these counts for the 99 consecutive complete stretches of 1000 words in this novel:

```
> havelaar$Frequency
 [1] 13 19 19 14 20 18 16 16 17 32 25 10  9 12 15
[16] 22 26 16 23 10 12 11 16 13  8  4 16 13 13 11
[31] 11 18 12 16 10 18 10 11  9 18 15 36 22 10  7
[46] 20  5 13 12 14  9  6  8  7  9 11 14 16 10  9
[61] 12 11  6 20 11 12 12  1  9 11 11  7 13 13 10
[76]  9 13  7  8 16 11 15  8 16 26 23 13 11 15 12
[91]  7  9 18  8 21  5 16 11 13
```

Are these frequencies binomially distributed? As a first step, we estimate the probability of success from the sample, while noting that the number of trials n is 1000:

```
> n = 1000
> p = mean(havelaar$Frequency / n)
```

In order to see whether the observed frequencies indeed follow a binomial distribution, we plot the quantiles of an (n, p)-binomially distributed random variable against the sorted observed frequencies. Recall that the quantile for a given proportion p is the smallest observed value such that all observed values less than or equal to that value account for the proportion p of the data. If we plot the observed quantiles against the quantiles of a truly (n, p)-binomially distributed random variable, we should obtain a straight line if the observed frequencies are indeed binomially distributed. We therefore define a vector of proportions,

```
> qnts = seq(0.005, 0.995, by=0.01)
```

and use the quantile() function to obtain the corresponding expected and observed frequencies for these percentage points, which we then graph:

```
> plot(qbinom(qnts, n, p), quantile(havelaar$Frequency,qnts),
+ xlab = paste("quantiles of (", n, ",", round(p, 4),
+ ")-binomial", sep=""), ylab = "frequencies")
```

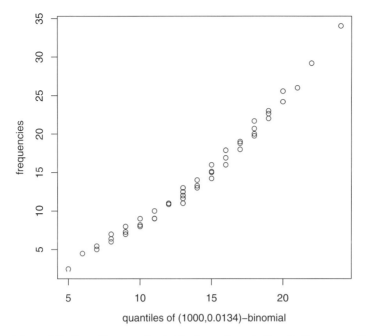

frequencies

quantiles of (1000,0.0134)–binomial

Figure 3.3. *Quantile-quantile plot for inspecting whether the frequency of the definite article* het *in the Dutch novel* Max Havelaar *is binomially distributed.*

As can be seen in Figure 3.3, the points in the resulting QUANTILE-QUANTILE PLOT do not follow a straight line. Especially the higher frequencies are too high for a binomially $(1000, 0.0134)$-distributed random variable.

To summarize, here is a short characterization of the four functions for working with the binomial distribution with n trials and success probability p:

dbinom(x, n, p) THE PROBABILITY DENSITY FUNCTION
  probability of the value x

qbinom(q, n, p) THE QUANTILE FUNCTION
  the largest value for the first $q\%$ of ranked data points

pbinom(x, n, p) THE CUMULATIVE DISTRIBUTION FUNCTION
  the proportion of values with a value less than or equal to x

rbinom(k, n, p) THE RANDOM NUMBER GENERATOR
  k binomially distributed random numbers

Thus far, we used the binomial distribution to gain some insight into the probabilities of the different frequencies with which *the* might occur in a corpus of one million words. We equated corpus size with the parameter n, and defined a success probability $p = 0.05885575$ of observing *the*. With a slight change in perspective, we can look at the frequency of *the* as specifying a rate of occurrence: *the* occurs (on average) 58856 times in a corpus of one million words. In other words, during a sampling time of one million tokens, we count (on average) 58856 tokens of *the*. This rate of occurrence is the (single) parameter (named λ) of

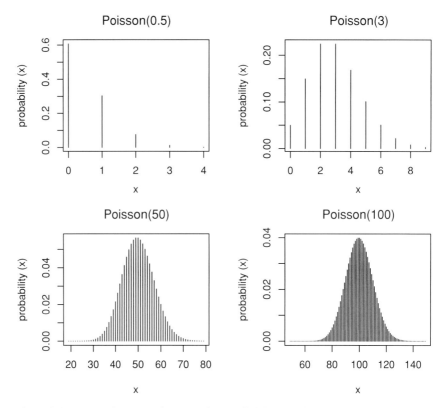

Figure 3.4. *Poisson frequency functions for* $\lambda = 0.5, 3, 50, 100$.

a second important discrete probability distribution, the POISSON DISTRIBUTION, named after the great French mathematician Siméon-Denis Poisson (1781–1840). If (and only if) n is large and p small, the binomial distribution is very similar to a Poisson distribution with λ taking as its value the product of n and p. Since the frequencies with which words occur in a corpus tend to be very small compared to the corpus size, and since the Poisson distribution has mathematical properties that are more convenient than those of the binomial distribution, it is useful for modeling word frequency distributions (Baayen, 2001).

The four functions for the Poisson distribution provided by R are `dpois()` for the frequency distribution, `rpois()` for random numbers, `qpois()` for the quantile function, and `ppois()` for the cumulative distribution function. Figure 3.4 shows the frequency function for four values of λ. Note that the frequency function becomes more and more symmetrical as we increase λ. For large λ, the (discrete) Poisson distribution becomes very similar to the continuous normal distribution that will be discussed in the next section.

Above, we observed that the frequency of the definite article *the* is not that well described by a binomial distribution. The same holds for the Poisson distribution. The average count of tokens of *het* in 1000 words is 0.0134. In terms of a binomial distribution, we therefore have $n = 1000$ trials with a probability of success $p =$

0.0134. In terms of a Poisson distribution, *het* appears at a rate $\lambda = 13.4$ per 1000 tokens. To get a sense of how similar the binomial and Poisson models are, and how they differ from the observed data, we inspect their frequency functions.

We begin by making a table listing for each frequency the number of text fragments in which *het* occurs with that frequency:

```
> havelaar.tab = xtabs( ~ havelaar$Frequency)
> havelaar.tab
 1  4  5  6  7  8  9 10 11 12 13 14 15 16 17 18 19 20 21 22 23
 1  1  2  2  5  5  8  7 12  8 10  3  4 10  1  5  2  3  1  2  2
25 26 32 36
 1  2  1  1
```

We divide these counts by the total number of text fragments in order to obtain the sample relative frequencies of the counts for *het*:

```
> havelaar.probs = xtabs( ~ havelaar$Frequency)/nrow(havelaar)
> round(havelaar.probs, 3)
    1     4     5     6     7     8     9    10    11    12
0.010 0.010 0.020 0.020 0.051 0.051 0.081 0.071 0.121 0.081
   13    14    15    16    17    18    19    20    21    22
0.101 0.030 0.040 0.101 0.010 0.051 0.020 0.030 0.010 0.020
   23    25    26    32    36
0.020 0.010 0.020 0.010 0.010
```

These proportions properly sum to 1:

```
> sum(havelaar.probs)
[1] 1
```

The upper left panel of Figure 3.5 displays the distribution of these proportions:

```
> plot(as.numeric(names(havelaar.probs)), havelaar.probs,
+ xlim=c(0, 40), type="h", xlab="counts", ylab="relative frequency")
> mtext("observed", 3, 1)
```

The upper right panel shows the corresponding binomial distribution. We first define the size n of the text fragments for which the occurrences of *het* were counted, and we also estimate the overall probability p as the average proportion of tokens of *het* for batches of 1000 tokens:

```
> n = 1000
> p = mean(havelaar$Frequency / n)
> p
[1] 0.0134
```

Counts are in the range 1–36. We choose a slightly broader range, 0–40, for plotting:

```
> counts = 0:40
> plot(counts, dbinom(counts, n, p),
+ type = "h", xlab = "counts", ylab = "probability")
+ mtext("binomial (1000, 0.013)", 3, 1)
```

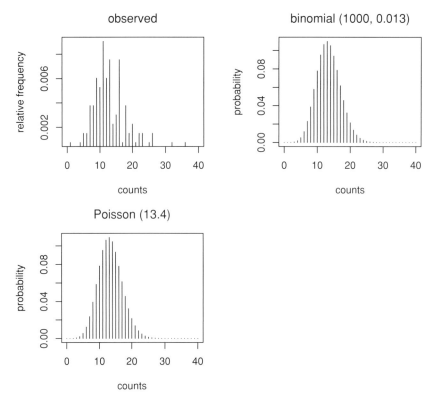

Figure 3.5. *Observed relative frequencies of the definite article* het *("the") in sequences of* 1000 *word tokens in the novel* Max Havelaar *and the corresponding binomial and Poisson distributions.*

The lower panel shows the corresponding Poisson distribution. We define λ,

```
> lambda = n * p
```

and now use dpois() instead of dbinom():

```
> plot(counts, dpois(counts, lambda),
+ type = "h", xlab="counts", ylab="probability")
> mtext("Poisson (13.4)", 3, 1)
```

Figure 3.5 illustrates, first of all, that the observed counts are much more erratic than the density functions for the binomial and Poisson distributions. This is to be expected, because the observed counts constitute a sample of how *het* was used in this particular sample of Dekker's writings. Second, it can be seen that the densities of the binomial and Poisson distributions are very similar, as expected for large *n* and small *p*. Third, there are obvious gaps in the distribution of observed counts, and their distribution seems to be somewhat less symmetrical, with more higher counts than one would expect on the basis of the binomial and Poisson distributions. This raises a question to which we will return below, namely, how to test more formally (instead of by visual inspection) whether the differences between what we observe in our data, and what we expect given binomial or Poisson models, should be attributed to chance, or whether there is reason to reject these models as inappropriate for this word.

As a final example, suppose a word occurs with a frequency of 100 tokens in a corpus of one million words. What is the probability that it will occur with at most 80 tokens in a second corpus of one million words? On the assumption that words are used independently, we obtain the desired probability with,

```
> sum(dpois(0:80, 100)) # sum of individual probabilities
[1] 0.02264918
```

or with:

```
> ppois(80, 100)        # joint probability of first 80
[1] 0.02264918
```

3.3   Continuous distributions

We now turn to consider some important distributions of continuous random variables. Examples of continuous random variables in language studies are acoustic measurements of segment durations, response latencies in chronometric experiments, evoked potentials measured at the scalp, grammaticality judgments measured on a gliding scale, and gaze durations in eye-tracking experiments. Just as there are many different discrete distributions, there are many continuous distributions. In this section, we focus on those continuous distributions that play a crucial role in many of the statistical tests that we will use in later chapters.

The basic concepts for continuous random variables are the same as for discrete random variables. As in the preceding section, we often need to know whether the value of a particular test statistic (which itself is a random variable) is extreme and surprising. If the distribution of the test statistic is known, such questions can be answered.

The key difference that sets continuous random variables apart from discrete random variables centers around a problem that arises when dealing with real numbers. Real numbers have the mathematical property that there are infinitely many of them in any interval. This has a far-reaching consequence for probabilities. Consider a random variable that assumes any real value in the interval [0, 1] with equal probability: a UNIFORM RANDOM VARIABLE. Since there is an infinite number of values in this interval, the probability of any specific value between 0 and 1 is infinitely small, i.e. zero. For a binomial (n, p) random variable, there are at most $n + 1$ values to be considered $(0, 1, 2, \ldots, n)$ so each value can be associated with its own probability. For a continuous random variable, this is not possible.

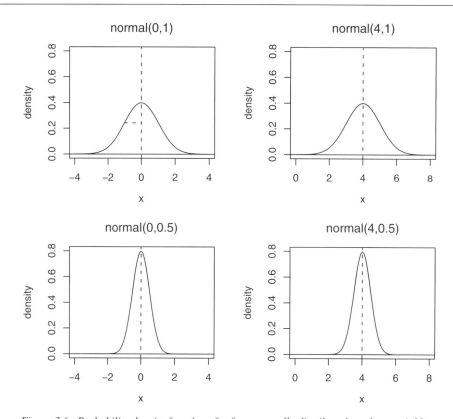

Figure 3.6. *Probability density functions for four normally distributed random variables.*

The solution to this technical problem is to consider the probability that a continuous variable assumes a value in a given interval of values. For instance, for the uniform random variable mentioned above, the probability of a value in the interval [0, 0.5] is equal to the probability of a value in the interval [0.5, 1], and both probabilities are equal to 0.5. Keep in mind that the probability of a value exactly equal to 0.5 is zero.

This property of continuous random variables has consequences for how we plot their density functions. For the discrete distributions in the preceding section, we were able to plot a vertical line representing the probability for each individual value of the random variable. This is not possible for continuous random variables, as the individual probabilities are all zero. Instead, we plot a continuous curve, as shown in Figure 3.6 for the most important continuous random variable, the NORMAL random variable.

3.3.1   The normal distribution

The upper left panel of Figure 3.6 shows the NORMAL DISTRIBUTION in its most simple form, the case in which its two parameters, the MEAN μ and the STANDARD DEVIATION σ, are 0 and 1 respectively. This specific form of the normal distribution is known as the STANDARD NORMAL DISTRIBUTION. The mean is represented by a vertical dashed line, and intersects the curve of the probability density function where it reaches its maximum. The dotted horizontal line segment represents the standard deviation, the parameter that controls the width of the curve. We can shift the curve to the left or right by changing the mean, as shown in the right panel, in which the mean is increased from 0 to 4. We can make the curve narrower or broader by changing the standard deviation, as shown in the bottom panels, where the standard deviation is 0.5 instead of 1.0. For all four panels, the area enclosed by the horizontal axis and the density curve is equal to 1. It represents the probability of observing any value. The density curves are symmetrical around the mean. Thus, the area to the left (or right) of the vertical dashed line that is enclosed by the curve and the horizontal axis represents a probability of 0.5. In other words, the probability that a random variable assumes a value less than the mean is 0.5. Similarly, the probability that its value will be greater than the mean is 0.5.

Plotting the density shown in the upper left panel of Figure 3.6 requires that we select a range of x-values to plot the density for. We select,

```
> x = seq(-4, 4, 0.1)
```

as values outside the interval $(-4, 4)$ have such an extremely low probability that we can ignore them for our plot. The y-values are obtained with the density function for the normal distribution, `dnorm()`:

```
> y = dnorm(x)
```

We called `dnorm()` without further arguments. If you do not specify mean and standard deviation explicitly, `dnorm()` (and also `pnorm()`, `qnorm()`, and `rnorm()`) assume that the mean is zero and the standard deviation is 1. Plotting the density is now straightforward:

```
> plot(x, y, xlab = "x", ylab = "density", ylim = c(0, 0.8),
+ type = "l")) # line type: the quoted character is lower case L
> mtext("normal(0, 1)", 3, 1)
```

We add two lines to the plot, a vertical line across all values represented on the vertical axis, and a horizontal line segment. The vertical line is easiest to produce with `abline()`, a function that takes an intercept as first argument and a slope as second argument, and adds the requested line to the plot. For horizontal or vertical lines, the argument `v` is set to specify where a vertical line intersects with the horizontal axis. Alternatively, the argument `h` is set to the point where a horizontal line is to intersect the vertical axis. Here, we set our vertical line to intersect at $X = 0$. We also request a dashed line with `lty` (line type):

```
> abline(v = 0, lty = 2) # the vertical dashed line
```

For line segments, we use `lines()`. This function connects the points specified by the vector of x coordinates (its first argument) and the vector of y coordinates

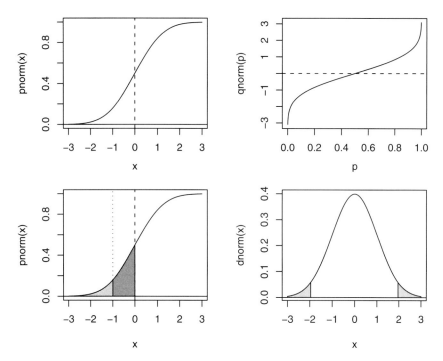

Figure 3.7. *Cumulative distribution function (left panels), quantile function (upper right panel), and probability density function (lower right panel) for the standard normal distribution.*

(its second argument). As X-coordinates, we have -1 and 0, as Y-coordinates, we have the density for $X = -1$ for both X-coordinates:

```
> lines(c(-1, 0), rep(dnorm(-1), 2), lty = 2)
```

For the remaining panels of Figure 3.6, the range of X-values and the parameters of dnorm() have to be adjusted. For instance, for the lower right panel, the density curve is obtained with:

```
> x = seq(0, 8, 0.1)
> y = dnorm(x, mean = 4, sd = 0.5)
```

Figure 3.7 shows the cumulative distribution function (upper left) and the quantile function (upper right) for a standard normal random variable. As for discrete random variables, these functions are each other's inverse:

```
> pnorm(-1.96)
[1] 0.02499790
> qnorm(0.02499790)
[1] -1.96
```

The lower left panel of Figure 3.7 illustrates how we calculate the probability that a standard normal random variable has a value between -1 and 0, using pnorm(). Since pnorm() plots the cumulative probability, the shaded area to the left of the dashed vertical line represents the probability of a value in the interval from minus infinity to zero. This area is too large, however. The appropriate area is highlighted with dark grey. The desired probability is obtained by subtracting the light grey area from the shaded area:

```
> pnorm(0) - pnorm(-1)
[1] 0.3413447
```

The final panel of Figure 3.7 (have a look at `shadenormal.fnc()` and its documentation for how this panel was produced) returns to the probability density function. The shaded areas in the tails of the distribution each represent a probability of 0.025. In other words, the shaded areas together highlight the 5% most extreme values in the distribution. The remaining area under the curve that is not shaded represents the 95% of values that are not extreme, given the rather arbitrary cutoff point of 5% for being extreme.

A fundamental property of the normal distribution is that it is possible to transform a normal random variable with mean $\mu \neq 0$ and $\sigma \neq 1$ into a standard normal random variable with mean $\mu = 0$ and $\sigma = 1$. This transformation is called STANDARDIZATION. Given a vector x, standardization amounts to subtracting the mean from each of its elements, followed by division by the standard deviation:

```
> x = rnorm(10, 3, 0.1)
> x
 [1] 2.985037 3.079029 2.895863 2.929407 2.841630 2.996799
 [7] 2.934391 3.125997 3.015932 3.072539
> x - mean(x)
 [1] -0.002625041  0.091366366 -0.091799655 -0.058255139
 [5] -0.146032681  0.009136216 -0.053271546  0.138334988
 [9]  0.028269929  0.084876563
> (x - mean(x)) / sd(x)
 [1] -0.02943848  1.02462691 -1.02948603 -0.65330150 -1.63768158
 [6]  0.10245798 -0.59741306  1.55135590  0.31703274  0.95184711
```

The function `sd()` provides our best guess of the standard deviation σ for the vector of sampled observations. By subtracting the mean, we move the density curve along the horizontal axis so that it is centered around zero. By subsequently dividing by the standard deviation, we reshape the curve to fit the curve of the standard normal. For example, a normal random variable with mean 3 and a small standard deviation of 0.1 is unlikely to have values below zero — in fact, it is highly unlikely to have values more than 3 standard deviations (0.3) away from the mean (3). After standardization, however, the new random numbers are nicely centered around the zero. The function in R for standardization is `scale()`. When its output is printed in the console, it also lists the mean and standard deviation as the object's attributes `scaled:center` and `scaled:scale`:

```
> scale(x)
             [,1]
 [1,] -0.02943848
 [2,]  1.02462691
 [3,] -1.02948603
 [4,] -0.65330150
  ...
[10,]  0.95184711
```

```
attr(,"scaled:center")
[1] 2.987662
attr(,"scaled:scale")
[1] 0.08917038
> mean(x) == attr(x, "scaled:center")
[1] TRUE
> sd(x) == attr(x1, "scaled:scale")
[1] TRUE
```

In the past, the standard normal distribution was especially important as it was only for the standard normal distribution that tables with probabilities for the cumulative distribution function were available. In order to use these tables, we had to standardize first. In R, this is no longer necessary. We can use pnorm() with the mean and standard deviation of our choice,

```
> pnorm(0, 1, 3) - pnorm(-1, 1, 3)
[1] 0.1169488
```

or we can standardize first, and then drop mean and standard deviation from pnorm():

```
> pnorm(-1/3) - pnorm(-2/3)
[1] 0.1169488
```

In both cases, the outcome is exactly the same.

The square of the standard deviation is known as the VARIANCE. The variance is calculated with the function var():

```
> v = rnorm(20, 4, 2)   # repeating this command
                        # will result in a different vector
                        # of random numbers
> sd(v)
[1] 2.113831            # sd of sample
> sqrt(var(v))          # square root of variance
[1] 2.113831
```

Like the standard deviation, the variance is a measure for how much the observations vary around the mean. At first glance, we might think a measure averaging divergences from the mean would do a sensible job, but this average is zero:[1]

```
> mean(v - mean(v))
[1] -5.32907e-16        # zero
```

This problem is avoided by the definition of the variance as a kind of average of the squared divergences from the mean,

```
> var(v)
[1] 4.46828
> sum( (v - mean(v))^2)/(length(v) - 1)
[1] 4.46828
```

---

[1] The number $-5.32907e-16$ is in scientific notation. The part $e-16$ specifies that the period should be shifted 16 positions to the left, yielding 0.0000000000000000532907 in standard notation.

where we divide, for technical reasons, not by the number of elements in the vector (returned by `length()`) but by that number minus one.

3.3.2   The t, F, and χ^2 distributions

Three other continuous distributions that we will make use of repeatedly in the remainder of this book are the t, F, and χ^2 distributions.

The t-DISTRIBUTION is closely related to the normal distribution. It has one parameter, known as its DEGREES OF FREEDOM (often abbreviated to df). Informally, degrees of freedom can be understood as a measure of how much precision an estimate has. This parameter controls the thickness of the tails of the distribution, as illustrated in the upper left panel of Figure 3.8. The solid grey line represents the standard normal distribution, the solid black line a t-distribution with 2 degrees of freedom, and the dashed black line a t-distribution with 5 degrees of freedom. As the degrees of freedom increase, the probability density function becomes more and more similar to that of the standard normal. For 30 or more degrees of freedom, the curves are already very similar, and for more than 100 degrees of freedom, they are virtually indistinguishable. The t-distribution plays an important role in many statistical tests, and we will use it frequently in the remainder of this book. R makes the by now familiar four functions available for this distribution: `dt()`, `pt()`, `qt()`, and `rt()`. Of these functions, the cumulative distribution function is the one we will use most. Here, we use it to illustrate the greater thickness of the tails of the t-distribution compared to the standard normal:

```
> pnorm(-3, 0, 1)
[1] 0.001349898
> pt(-3, 2)
[1] 0.04773298
```

The probability of observing extreme values (values less than -3 in this example) is greater for the t-distribution. This is what we mean when we say that the t-distribution has thicker tails.

There are many other continuous probability distributions besides the normal and t-distributions. We will often need two of these distributions: the F-DISTRIBUTION and the χ^2-DISTRIBUTION. The F-distribution has two parameters, referred to as DEGREES OF FREEDOM 1 and DEGREES OF FREEDOM 2. The upper right panel of Figure 3.8 shows the probability density function of the F-distribution for four different combinations of degrees of freedom. The ratio of two variances is F-distributed, and a question that often arises in statistical testing is whether the variance in the numerator is so much larger than the variance in the denominator that we have reason to be surprised.

For instance, if the F ratio is 6, then, depending on the degrees of freedom associated with the two ratios the probability of this value may be small (surprise) or large (no surprise):

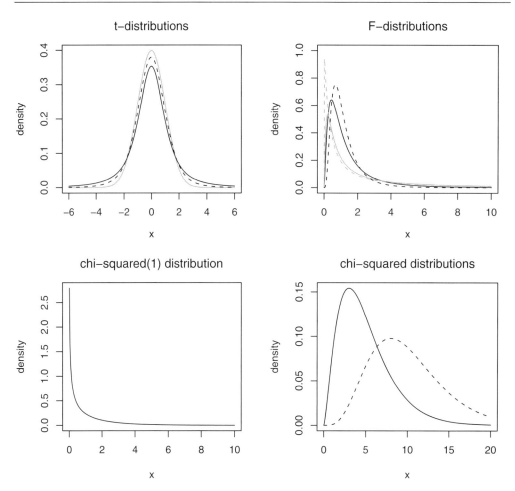

Figure 3.8. *Probability density functions. Upper left: t-distributions with 2 (solid black line) and 5 (dashed line) degrees of freedom, and the standard normal (grey line). Upper right: F-distributions with 5, 5 (black, solid line), 2, 1 (grey, dashed line), 5, 1 (grey, solid line) and 10, 10 (black, dashed line) degrees of freedom. Lower left: a χ^2-distribution with 1 degree of freedom. Lower right: χ^2-distributions with 5 (solid line) and 10 (dashed line) degrees of freedom.*

```
> 1 - pf(6, 1, 1)
[1] 0.2467517
> 1 - pf(6, 20, 8)
[1] 0.006905409
```

Here, pf() is the cumulative distribution function, which gives the probability of a ratio less than or equal to 6 (compare pt() for the t-distribution and ppois() and pbinom() for the Poisson and binomial distributions). To obtain the probability of a more extreme ratio, we take the complement probability.

The lower panels of Figure 3.8 show the probability density functions for three χ^2-distributions. The χ^2-distribution has a single parameter, which is also referred to as its degrees of freedom. The lower left panel shows the density function for a single degree of freedom; the lower right panel gives the densities for 5 (solid line) and 10 (dashed line) degrees of freedom.

The degree of non-homogeneity of a contingency table (see e.g. Figure 2.6 in Chapter 2) can be assessed by means of a statistic named chi-squared, which, unsurprisingly given its name, follows a χ^2-distribution. Given a chi-squared value and its associated degrees of freedom, we use the probability density function pchisq() to obtain the probability gauging the extent to which we have reason for surprise:

```
> 1 - pchisq(4, 1)
[1] 0.04550026
> 1 - pchisq(4, 5)
[1] 0.549416
> 1 - pchisq(4, 10)
[1] 0.947347
```

These examples illustrate that the *p*-values for one and the same chi-squared value (here 4) depends on the degrees of freedom. As the degrees of freedom increase, *p*-values increase. This is also evident in the lower panels of Figure 3.8. For 1 degree of freedom, 4 is already a rather extreme value. But for 5 degrees of freedom, 4 is more or less in the center of the distribution, and for 10 degrees, it is in fact a rather low value instead of a very high value.

Workbook section

Exercises

The text of Lewis Carroll's *Alice's Adventures in Wonderland* is available as the data set alice. The vector alice contains all words (defined as sequences of non-space characters) in this novel. Here, we convert all upper case letters to lower case with tolower ().

```
> alice = tolower(alice)
> alice[1:5]
[1] "alice"      "s"          "adventures" "in"         "wonderland"
```

In this exercise, we study the distribution of three words in this book, *Alice*, *very*, and *Hare* (the second noun of the collocation *March Hare*). Our goal is to partition this text into 40 equal-sized text chunks, and to study the frequencies with which our three target words occur in these 40 chunks.

A text with 27269 words cannot be divided into 40 equal-sized text chunks: We are left with a remainder of 22 tokens:

```
> 27269 %% 40    # %% is the remainder operator
[1] 29
```

We therefore restrict ourselves to the first 27240 tokens, and use cut() to partition the sequence of tokens into 40 equally sized chunks. The output of cut() is a factor with as levels the successive equal-sized chunks of data. For each element in its input vector, i.e. for each word, it specifies the chunk to which that word belongs. We combine the words and the information about their chunks into a data frame with the function data.frame():

```
> wonderland = data.frame(word = alice[1:27240],
+ chunk = cut(1:27240, breaks = 40, labels = F))
> wonderland[1:5, ]
        word chunk
1     alice     1
2         s     1
3 adventures     1
4        in     1
5 wonderland     1
```

We now add a vector of truth values to this data frame to indicate which rows contain the exact string `"alice"`:

```
> wonderland$alice = wonderland$word=="alice"
> wonderland[1:5, ]
        word chunk alice
1     alice     1  TRUE
2         s     1 FALSE
3 adventures     1 FALSE
4        in     1 FALSE
5 wonderland     1 FALSE
```

We count how often the word *Alice* (`alice`) occurs in each chunk:

```
> countOfAlice = tapply(wonderland$alice, wonderland$chunk, sum)
> countOfAlice
 1  2  3  4  5  6  7  8  9 10 11 12 13 14 15 16 17 18 19 20 21 22
10  7 10  9  4 10  8  8 12  6  9  8  8 14  9 11  6 11 11 15 13 13
23 24 25 26 27 28 29 30 31 32 33 34 35 36 37 38 39 40
18 10 10 13 12  9 15 14 17  9 13  7  8  3  7 10  4  7
```

Finally, we make a frequency table of these counts with `xtabs()`:

```
> countOfAlice.tab = xtabs(~countOfAlice)
countOfAlice
 3  4  6  7  8  9 10 11 12 13 14 15 17 18
 1  2  2  4  5  5  6  3  2  4  2  2  1  1
```

There is one chunk in which *Alice* appears only three times (chunk 36), and six chunks in which this word occurs ten times (e.g. chunks 1 and 6).

1. Create similar tables for the words *hare* and *very*.

2. Make a plot that displays by means of high-density lines how often *Alice* occurs in the successive chunks. Make similar plots for *very* and *hare*. What do you see?

3. Make a plot with the number of times *Alice* occurs in the chunks on the horizontal axis (i.e. `as.numeric(names(alice.tab))`), and with the proportion of chunks with that count on the vertical axis. Use high-density lines. Make similar sample density plots for *very* and for *hare*.

4. Also plot the corresponding densities under the assumption that these words follow a Poisson distribution with an estimated rate parameter λ equal to the mean of the counts in the chunks. Compare the Poisson densities with the sample densities.

5. Make quantile-quantile plots for graphical inspection of whether *Alice*, *very*, and *hare* might follow a Poisson distribution. First create the vector of theoretical quantiles for the X-coordinates, using as percentage points 5%, 10%, 15%, ..., 100%. Supply the percentage points as a vector of proportions as first argument to `qpois()`. The second argument is λ, estimated by the mean count. The sample quantiles are obtained with `quantile()`.

6. The mean count of *Alice* is 9.95. In chunk 39, *Alice* is observed only 4 times. Suppose we only have this chunk of text available. Calculate the likelihood of observing *Alice* more than 10 times in another chunk of similar size. Assume that *Alice* follows a Poisson distribution. Recalculate this probability on the basis of the mean count, and compare the expected number of chunks in which *Alice* occurs more than 10 times with the actual number of chunks.

4   Basic statistical methods

The logic underlying the statistical tests described in this book is simple. A statistical test produces a TEST STATISTIC of which the distribution is known.[1] What we want to know is whether the test statistic has a value that is extreme, so extreme that it is unlikely to be attributable to chance. In the traditional terminology, we pit a NULL-HYPOTHESIS, actually a straw man, that the test statistic does not have an extreme value, against an alternative hypothesis according to which its value is indeed extreme. Whether a test statistic has an extreme value is evaluated by calculating how far out it is in one of the tails of the distribution. Functions like `pt()`, `pf()`, and `pchisq()` tell us how far out we are in a tail by means of p-values, which assess what proportion of the population has even more extreme values. The smaller this proportion is, the more reason we have for surprise that our test statistic is as extreme as it actually is.

However, the fuzzy notion of what counts as extreme needs to be made more precise. It is generally assumed that a probability begins to count as extreme by the time it drops below 0.05. However, opinions differ with respect to how significance should be assessed.

One tradition holds that the researcher should begin by defining what counts as extreme, before gathering and analyzing data. The cutoff probability for considering a test statistic as extreme is referred to as the α LEVEL or SIGNIFICANCE LEVEL. The α level 0.05 is marked by one asterisk in R. More stringent α levels are 0.01 (marked by two asterisks) and 0.001 (marked by three asterisks). If the observed value of our test statistic is extreme given this pre-defined α level, i.e. if the associated p-value (obtained with, for instance, `pnorm()`) is less than α, then the outcome is declared to be statistically significant. If you fix α at 0.05, the α level enforced by most linguistic and psycholinguistic journals, then all you should do is report whether $p < 0.05$ or $p > 0.05$.

However, a cutoff point like 0.05 is quite arbitrary. This is why I have disabled significance stars in summary tables when the `languageR` package is attached (with `options(show.signif.stars=FALSE)`). If an experiment that required half a year's preparation results in a p-value of 0.052, it would have failed to reveal a statistically significant effect, whereas if it had produced a p-value of 0.048,

---

[1] This chapter introduces tests based on what is known as FREQUENTIST statistical inference. For an introduction to the alternative school in statistics known as BAYESIAN inference, see Bolstad (2004).

it would have succeeded in showing a statistically significant effect. Therefore, many researchers prefer to interpret p-values as a measure of surprise. Instead of reporting $p < 0.10$ or $p < 0.05$, they report $p = 0.052$ or $p = 0.048$. This allows you to make up your own mind about how surprising this really is. This is important, because assessing what counts as surprise often depends on many considerations that are difficult to quantify.

For instance, although most journals will accept a significance level of 0.05, no one in his right mind would want to cross a bridge that has a mere probability of 0.05 of collapsing. Nor would anyone like to use a medicine that has fatal side effects for one out of twenty patients, or even only one out of a thousand patients. When a paper with a result that is significant at the 5% level is accepted for publication, this is *only* because it opens new theoretical possibilities that have a fair chance of being replicated in further studies. Such replication experiments are crucial for establishing whether a given effect is really there. The smaller the p-value is, and the greater the POWER of the experiment (i.e. the greater the number of subjects, items, repetitions, etc.), the more likely it is that replication studies will also bear witness to the effect. Nevertheless, replication studies remain essential even when p-values are very small. We also have to keep in mind that a small p-value does not imply that an observed effect is significant in the more general sense of being important or applicable. We will return to this issue below.

In practice, our a priori assumptions about how difficult it is to find some hypothesized effect plays a crucial role in thinking about what counts as statistically significant. In physics, where it is often possible to bring a great many important factors under experimental control, p-values can be required to be very small. For an experiment to falsify an existing well-established theory, a p-value as small as 0.00001 may not be small enough. In the social sciences, where it is often difficult if not outright impossible to obtain full experimental control of the very diverse factors that play a potential role in an experiment, a p-value of 0.05 can sensibly count as statistically significant.

One assumption that is brought explicitly into the evaluation of p-values is the expected direction of an effect. Consider, for instance, the effect of frequency of use. A long series of experiments has documented that higher-frequency words tend to be recognized faster than lower-frequency words. If we run yet another experiment in which frequency is a predictor, we expect to observe shorter latencies for higher frequencies (facilitation) and not longer latencies (inhibition). In other words, previous experience, irrespective of whether previous experience has been formalized in the form of a theory, may give rise to expectations about the direction of an effect: inhibition or facilitation. Suppose that we examine our directional expectation by means of a test statistic t that follows the t-distribution. Facilitation then implies a negative t-value (the observed value of the test statistic is smaller than the value given by the null-hypothesis), and inhibition a positive t-value (the observed value is greater). Given a t-value of -2 for 10 degrees of freedom, and given that we expect facilitation, we calculate the probability of observing a t-value of -2 or lower using the left tail of the t-distribution:

```
> pt(-2, 10)
[1] 0.03669402
```

Since this probability is fairly small, there is reason to be surprised: the observed *t*-value is unlikely to be this small by chance. This kind of directional test, for which you should have very good independent reasons, is known as a ONE-TAILED test.

Now suppose that nothing is known about the effect of frequency, and that it might equally well be facilitatory or inhibitory. If the only thing we want to test is that frequency might matter, one way or another, then the *p*-value is twice as large:

```
> 2 * pt(-2, 10)
[1] 0.07338803
```

In this case, we reason that the *t*-value could just as well have been positive instead of negative, so we sum the probabilities in both tails of the distribution. This is known as a two-tailed test. Since the density curve of the *t*-distribution is symmetrical, the probability of *t* being less than -2 is the same as the probability that it is greater than 2. We sum the probabilities in both tails, and therefore obtain a *p*-value that is twice as large. Evidently, the present example now gives us less reason for surprise. Next suppose that we observed a *t*-value of 2 instead of -2. Our *p*-value is now obtained with:

```
> 2 * (1 - pt(2, 10))
[1] 0.07338803
```

Recall that `pt(2,10)` is the probability that the *t*-statistic assumes a value less than 2. We need the complementary probability, so we subtract from 1 to obtain the probability that *t* has a value exceeding 2. Again, we multiply the result by 2 in order to evaluate the likelihood that our *t*-value is either in the left tail or in the right tail of the distribution. We can merge the tests for negative and positive values into one generally applicable line of code by working with the absolute value of the *t*-value:

```
> 2 * (1 - pt(abs(-2), 10))
[1] 0.07338803
> 2 * (1 - pt(abs(2), 10))
[1] 0.07338803
```

Table 4.1 summarizes the different one and two-tailed tests that we will often use in the remainder of this book.

Any test that we run on a data set involves a statistical model, even the simplest of the standard tests described in this chapter. There are a number of basic properties of any statistical model that should be kept in mind at all times. As pointed out by Crawley (2002:17):

- *All models are wrong.*
- *Some models are better than others.*
- *The correct model can never be known with certainty.*
- *The simpler the model, the better it is.*

Table 4.1. *One-tailed and two-tailed tests in* R. df *denotes the number of degrees of freedom,* $\mathcal{N}$ *the normal distribution.*

$\mathcal{N}$	one-tailed	left tail	`pnorm(value, mean, sd)`
	one-tailed	right tail	`1 - pnorm(value, mean, sd)`
	two-tailed	either tail	`2 * (1 - pnorm(abs(value), mean, sd))`
t	one-tailed	left tail	`pt(value, df)`
	one-tailed	right tail	`1 - pt(value, df)`
	two-tailed	either tail	`2 * (1 - pt(abs(value), df))`
F			`1 - pf(value, df1, df2)`
χ^2			`1 - pchisq(value, df)`

As a consequence, it is important to check whether the model fits the data. This part of statistical analysis is known as MODEL CRITICISM. A test may yield a very small *p*-value, but if the assumptions on which the test is based are violated, the *p*-value is quite useless. In the remainder of this book, model criticism will therefore play an important role.

In what follows, we begin by discussing tests involving a single vector. We then proceed with tests addressing the broader range of questions that arise when you have two vectors of observations. Questions involving more than two vectors are briefly touched upon, but are discussed in detail in Chapters 5–7.

4.1   Tests for single vectors

4.1.1   Distribution tests

It is often useful to know what kind of distribution characterizes your data. For instance, since many statistical procedures assume that vectors are normally distributed, it is often necessary to ascertain whether a vector of values is indeed approximately normally distributed. Sometimes, the shape of a distribution is itself of theoretical interest.

By way of example, consider Baayen and Lieber (1997), who studied the frequency distributions of several Dutch derivational prefixes. The frequencies of 985 words with the prefix *ver-* are available in the data set ver. We plot the estimated density with:

```
> plot(density(ver$Frequency))
```

As can be seen in the left panel of Figure 4.1, we have a highly skewed distribution with a few high-frequency outliers and most of the probability mass squashed against the vertical axis. It makes sense, therefore, to logarithmically transform these frequencies, in order to remove at least some of the skewness:

```
> ver$Frequency = log(ver$Frequency)
> plot(density(ver$Frequency))
```

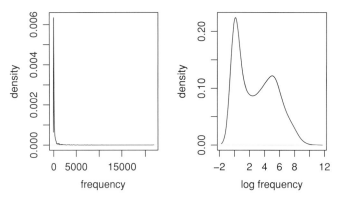

Figure 4.1. *Estimated probability density functions for the Dutch prefix* ver-.

The result is shown in the right panel of Figure 4.1. We now have a bimodal frequency distribution with two clear peaks. The question that arises here is what kind of distribution this might be. Could the logged frequencies follow a normal distribution that happens to have a second bump due to chance?

There are several ways to pursue this question. Let's first consider visualization by means of a quantile-quantile plot. We graph the quantiles of the standard normal distribution (displayed on the horizontal axis) against the quantiles of the empirical distribution (displayed on the vertical axis). If the empirical distribution is normal (irrespective of mean or variance), its quantiles should be identical to those of the standard normal, and the quantile-quantile plot should produce a straight line. The left panel of Figure 4.2 provides an example for 985 random numbers from a normal distribution with mean 4 and standard deviation 3:

```
> qqnorm(rnorm(length(ver$Frequency), 4, 3))
> abline(v = qnorm(0.025), col = "grey")
> abline(h = qnorm(0.025, 4, 3), col = "grey")
```

The theoretical and empirical values for the 2.5% percentage points are shown by means of grey lines. The horizontal axis shows the values of the standard normal, ordered from small to large. Around -1.96, 2.5% of the data points have been graphed, and around $+1.96$, 97.5% of the data points have been covered. The vertical axis shows the quantiles of the random numbers. In this case, 2.5% of the data points have been covered by the time you have reached the value -1.87. Whenever you compare the largest values observed for a given percentage of the ordered data, you will find that the points always lie very near the same line.

When we make a quantile-quantile plot for the logged frequencies of words with the Dutch prefix *ver-*, we obtain a weirdly shaped graph, as shown in the right panel of Figure 4.2:

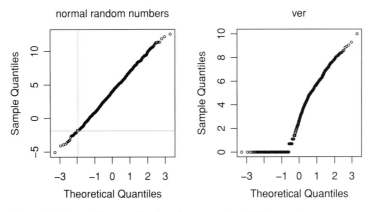

Figure 4.2. *Quantile-quantile plots for a sample of* 985 *normal*
(4, 3)-*distributed random numbers (left) and for the logged frequencies of* 985
Dutch derived words with the prefix ver-.

```
> qqnorm(ver$Frequency)
```

The lowest log frequency, zero, represents 27.8% of the words, and this shows up
as a horizontal bar of points in the graph. It is clear that we are not dealing with
a normal distribution.

Instead of visualizing the distribution, we can make use of two tests. The
simplest to use is the SHAPIRO-WILK TEST FOR NORMALITY:

```
> shapiro.test(ver$Frequency)
          Shapiro-Wilk normality test
data:   ver$Frequency
W = 0.9022, p-value = < 2.2e-16
```

This test makes use of a specific test statistic W, and the probability that W is as
large as it is under chance conditions for a normal distribution is vanishingly small.
We can safely reject the null-hypothesis that the log-transformed frequencies of
words with *ver-* follow a normal distribution.

A second test that can be used is the KOLMOGOROV-SMIRNOV ONE-SAMPLE
TEST. Its first argument is the observed vector of values; its second argument is
the name of the density function that we want to compare our observed vector
with. As we are considering a normal distribution here, this second argument is
pnorm. The remaining arguments are the corresponding parameters, in this case,
the mean and standard deviation which we estimate from the (log-transformed)
frequency vector:

```
> ks.test(ver$Frequency, "pnorm",
+ mean(ver$Frequency), sd(ver$Frequency))
          One-sample Kolmogorov-Smirnov test
data:   ver$Frequency
D = 0.1493, p-value < 2.2e-16
alternative hypothesis: two.sided

Warning message: cannot compute correct p-values with ties
```

This test produces a test statistic D that is so large that it is very unlikely to arise under the assumption that we would be dealing with a normal distribution.

The warning message arises because there are TIES (observations with the same value) in our data. This test presupposes that the input vector is continuous, and in a continuous distribution ties are, strictly speaking, impossible. The reason that we have ties in our data is that word frequency counts are discrete, even though the probabilities of words that we try to estimate with our frequency counts are continuous. A workaround to silence this warning is to add a little bit of noise to the frequency vector with the function `jitter()`, breaking the ties:

```
> ver$Frequency[1:5]
[1] 5.541264 5.993961 4.343805 0.000000 7.056175
> jitter(ver$Frequency[1:5])
[1] 5.5179064 6.0002591 4.2696683 0.0373808 6.9965528
> ks.test(jitter(ver$Frequency), "pnorm",
+ mean(ver$Frequency), sd(ver$Frequency))
        One-sample Kolmogorov-Smirnov test
data:  jitter(ver$Frequency)
D = 0.1493, p-value < 2.2e-16
alternative hypothesis: two.sided
```

When dealing with a vector of counts, we may face the question of whether the probabilities of the things counted are all essentially the same. For instance, the most frequent words in an earlier version of the introduction to this book are:

```
> intro = c(75, 68, 45, 40, 39, 39, 38, 33, 24, 24)
> names(intro) = c("the", "to", "of", "you", "is", "a",
+ "and", "in", "that", "data")
> the   to   of  you   is    a  and   in that data
   75   68   45   40   39   39   38   33   24   24
```

Are the probabilities of these words (as estimated by their frequencies) essentially the same? We can investigate this with a CHI-SQUARED TEST:

```
> chisq.test(intro)
        Chi-squared test for given probabilities
data:  intro
X-squared = 59.7294, df = 9, p-value = 1.512e-09
```

Unsurprisingly, the chi-squared test produces a test statistic named X-squared, that follows a χ^2-distribution, in this case with 9 degrees of freedom. (You can check that the p-value reported in this summary equals $1 - $ `pchisq(59.7294, 9)`). What this test shows is that the ten most frequent function words do not all have the same probability (frequency). The range of values is just too large. By contrast, the counts in the following vector,

```
> x = c(37, 21, 26, 30, 23, 26, 41, 26, 37, 33)
```

are much more similar, and the chi-squared test is no longer significant:

```
> chisq.test(x)
        Chi-squared test for given probabilities
data:  x
X-squared = 13.5333, df = 9, p-value = 0.1399
```

4.1.2   Tests for the mean

The question often arises as to whether the mean of a vector of observations has a particular value. By way of example, we examine the length in seconds of the *n* in the Dutch prefix *ont-*, available in the data set durationsOnt (Pluymaekers *et al.*, 2005). We calculate the mean length of the *n*:

```
> meanLengthN = mean(durationsOnt$DurationPrefixNasal)
> meanLengthN
[1] 0.04981508
```

Suppose that previous research of similar recordings had resulted in a mean of 0.053 seconds. Is the mean observed for the new sample, 0.0498, significantly different from 0.053? An answer can be obtained with a TWO-TAILED ONE-SAMPLE *t*-TEST, which requires as input the vector of lengths and the previously observed mean (mu):

```
> t.test(durationsOnt$DurationPrefixNasal, mu = 0.053)
            One Sample t-test
data:  ont$DurationPrefixNasal
t = -1.5038, df = 101, p-value = 0.1358
alternative hypothesis: true mean is not equal to 0.053
95 percent confidence interval:
 0.04561370 0.05401646
sample estimates:
 mean of x
0.04981508
```

The function t.test() carried out a one-sample *t*-test, as we supplied it with only one vector of data points, the sample of lengths of the *n* of the prefix *ont-*. The test statistic of the *t*-test is named *t*, and it follows a *t*-distribution with, in this case, 101 degrees of freedom (df). The *p*-value given in the summary is easily verified,

```
> 2 * (1 - pt(abs(-1.5038), 101))
[1] 0.1357535
```

and shows that the newly observed mean, 0.0498, is not significantly different from the old mean of 0.053.

R carries out a two-tailed test by default. It reports that the ALTERNATIVE HYPOTHESIS (alternative to the NULL-HYPOTHESIS that the mean is equal to 0.053) is that the true mean is not equal to 0.053. If you need a one-tailed test, you have to specify the direction of the test by adding the option alternative="less" or alternative="greater".

The next lines of the summary report the 95% CONFIDENCE INTERVAL. This is the interval of values, symmetrical around the observed sample mean 0.0498, where we expect 95% of the data points to be located. It is the range of values for which we accept that there is no significant difference with the previously observed mean. This range is highlighted in Figure 4.3. The 5% of data points that are extreme, and where we reject the idea that there might be no difference, fall outside this confidence interval. These REJECTION REGIONS are the white tails

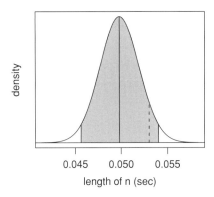

Figure 4.3. *95% confidence interval for the length (in seconds) of the nasal in the Dutch prefix* ont-. *The solid line represents the mean, the dashed line the tested mean, which falls within the acceptance region.*

in Figure 4.3. Since the mean previously observed, 0.053, falls well within the acceptance region, the *p*-value of the test is larger than 0.05. We therefore have no reason to suppose that the mean length in the new sample differs from that obtained in the previous sample.

The data frame `ont` also lists the length of the *t*, the mean of which is:

```
> mean(durationsOnt$DurationPrefixPlosive)
[1] 0.03633109
```

We could again use `t.test()` to test whether this mean is significantly different from, say, 0.044, and the resulting *p*-value, 0.008, would support this. Unfortunately, there is a problem here, as the distribution of the lengths of the *t* is not normal. Consider Figure 4.4, which shows the estimated densities for the lengths of the *t* and those of the *n*. In the case of the *n*, we have a reasonably symmetrical density, but in the case of the *t*, we have a bimodal density. The Shapiro-Wilk test,

```
> shapiro.test(durationsOnt$DurationPrefixPlosive)
        Shapiro-Wilk normality test
data:   ont$DurationPrefixPlosive
W = 0.9248, p-value = 2.145e-05
```

confirms that we are indeed dealing with a significant departure from normality.

The *t*-test is an excellent test for data that are more or less normally distributed. But it should not be used for variables with skewed distributions. For such variables, the ONE SAMPLE WILCOXON TEST, implemented in the function `wilcox.test()`, should be used instead. When we apply the Wilcoxon test, we obtain a *p*-value that is somewhat larger (although still small) compared to that of the *t*-test:

```
> wilcox.test(durationsOnt$DurationPrefixPlosive, mu = 0.044)
        Wilcoxon signed rank test with continuity correction
data:   ont$DurationPrefixPlosive
V = 1871, p-value = 0.01151
alternative hypothesis: true mu is not equal to 0.044
```

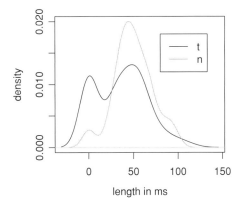

Figure 4.4. *Estimated probability density functions for the length in milliseconds of the* t *and* n *in the Dutch prefix* ont-.

This is usually the case when the *p*-values of these two tests are compared. The Wilcoxon test is slightly less good at detecting surprise for normal random variables than the *t*-test; it has reduced POWER, but it still does a good job when the *t*-test is inapplicable. The Wilcoxon test is a NON-PARAMETRIC test. It makes no assumptions about the distribution of the population from which a sample was drawn. The PARAMETRIC *t*-test has greater power because when its distributional assumptions are justified, it has access to more sophisticated mathematics to estimate probabilities.

4.2   Tests for two independent vectors

When you have two vectors of observations, it is important to distinguish between INDEPENDENT vectors (random variables) and PAIRED vectors (random variables). In the case of independent vectors, the observations in the one vector are not linked in a systematic way to the observations in the other vector. Consider, for instance, sampling 100 words at random from a frequency list compiled for Jane Austen's *Pride and Prejudice*, and then sampling another 100 words at random from a frequency list compiled for Herman Melville's *Moby Dick*. The two vectors of frequencies can be compared in various ways in order to address differences in general frequency of use between the two writers, and contain independent observations. As an example of paired observations, consider the case in which a specific list of 100 word types is compiled, with for each word type its frequency in *Pride and Prejudice* and its frequency in *Moby Dick*. The observations in the two vectors are now paired: the frequencies are tied, pairwise, to a given word. For such paired vectors, more powerful tests are available. In what follows, we first discuss tests for independent vectors. We then proceed to the case of paired vectors.

4.2.1   Are the distributions the same?

Recall that we observed a bimodal density for the Dutch prefix *ver-* in Figure 4.1. The presence of two modes for this distribution can be traced to two distributions having been mixed together, a distribution of semantically more opaque, non-compositional words, and a distribution of semantically more transparent, compositional words. The data frame `ver` with word frequencies also contains a column with information about semantic class (opaque versus transparent). Figure 4.5 plots the densities of the opaque and transparent words separately. The two distributions are quite dissimilar. There are many transparent and only a few opaque low-frequency words (recall that a log frequency of 0 represents a word with frequency 1, which explains the hump of probability mass above the zero in the graph for transparent formations).

Figure 4.5 requires the following steps. We first partition the words into the two classes:

```
> ver$Frequency = log(ver$Frequency)      # if not already logged
> ver.transp = ver[ver$SemanticClass == "transparent",]$Frequency
> ver.opaque = ver[ver$SemanticClass == "opaque", ]$Frequency
```

Next, we calculate the densities and store these, as we have to determine the limits for the horizontal and vertical axes before we can proceed with plotting:

```
> ver.transp.d = density(ver.transp)
> ver.opaque.d = density(ver.opaque)
> xlimit = range(ver.transp.d$x, ver.opaque.d$x)
> ylimit = range(ver.transp.d$y, ver.opaque.d$y)
> plot(ver.transp.d, lty = 1, col = "black",
+ xlab = "frequency", ylab = "density",
+ xlim = xlimit, ylim = ylimit, main = "")
> lines(ver.opaque.d, col = "darkgrey")
```

Before we make too much of the separation visible in our density plot, we should check whether this separation might have arisen by chance. To avoid complaints

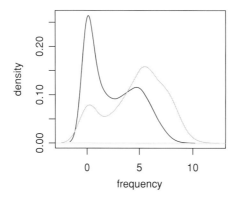

Figure 4.5. *Estimated probability density function of the transparent (black line) and opaque (grey line) words with the Dutch prefix* ver-.

about ties with the TWO-SAMPLE KOLMOGOROV-SMIRNOV TEST, we add some jitter:

```
> ks.test(jitter(ver.transp), jitter(ver.opaque))
        Two-sample Kolmogorov-Smirnov test
data:  jitter(ver.transp) and jitter(ver.opaque)
D = 0.3615, p-value = < 2.2e-16
alternative hypothesis: two.sided
```

The very small *p*-value provides support for the classification of these words into transparent and opaque subsets, each with its own probability density function.

4.2.2   Are the means the same?

In Chapter 2, we had a first look at the 81 English nouns for which several kinds of ratings as well as visual lexical decision latencies were collected. Here we visualize how the word frequencies are distributed for the subsets of simple and complex words cross-classified by class (plant versus animal) by means of a trellis boxplot:

```
> bwplot(Frequency ~ Class | Complex, data = ratings)
```

Figure 4.6 suggests that the distributions of frequencies for plants and animals differ for simplex words, with the animals having somewhat higher frequencies than the plants. We can ascertain whether we indeed have reason to be surprised by testing whether the means of these two distributions are different. The boxplots suggest reasonably symmetrical distributions, so we use the two-sample version of the *t*-test and apply it to the subset of morphologically simple words:

```
> simplex = ratings[ratings$Complex == "simplex", ]
> freqAnimals = simplex[simplex$Class == "animal", ]$Frequency
> freqPlants = simplex[simplex$Class == "plant", ]$Frequency
> t.test(freqAnimals, freqPlants)
        Welch Two Sample t-test
data:  freqAnimals and freqPlants
t = 2.674, df = 57.545, p-value = 0.009739
alternative hypothesis: true difference in means is not equal to 0
95 percent confidence interval:
 0.1931830 1.3443152
sample estimates:
mean of x mean of y
 5.208494  4.439745
```

The summary of the *t*-test begins with the statement that a WELCH TWO-SAMPLE *t*-TEST has been carried out. The *t*-test in its simplest form presupposes that its two input vectors are normally distributed with the same variance. Often, however, the variances of the two input vectors are not the same. The Welch two-sample *t*-test corrects for this difference by adjusting the degrees of freedom. Normally, degrees of freedom are integers. However, you can see in this example that the Welch adjustment led to a fractional number of degrees of freedom: 57.545.

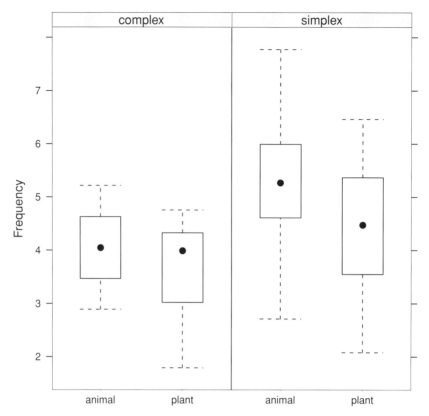

Figure 4.6. *Boxplots for frequency as a function of natural class (animal versus plant) grouped by morphological complexity for 81 English nouns.*

The next lines of the summary explain what the *t*-test did: it calculated the difference between the two means, and then tested whether this difference is not equal to 0. The 95% confidence interval around this difference in the means, 5.208494 − 4.439745 = 0.768749, does not include zero. As expected, the *p*-value is less than 0.05. If you need to know another confidence interval, for instance, the 99% confidence interval, this can be specified with the option `conf.level`:

```
> t.test(simplex[simplex$Class == "animal", ]$Frequency,
+        simplex[simplex$Class == "plant", ]$Frequency,
+        conf.level = 0.99)
t = 2.674, df = 57.545, p-value = 0.009739
alternative hypothesis: true difference in means is not equal to 0
99 percent confidence interval:
 0.002881662 1.534616532
```

It is important to keep in mind that the two-sample *t*-test is appropriate only for reasonably symmetrical distributions. For the opaque and transparent words with the prefix *ver-*, where we are dealing with bimodal, and markedly asymmetric distributions, we use the `wilcox.test`:

```
> wilcox.test(ver.opaque, ver.transp)
```

```
        Wilcoxon rank sum test with continuity correction
data:  ver.opaque and ver.transp
W = 113443.5, p-value = < 2.2e-16
alternative hypothesis: true mu is not equal to 0
```

This test confirms the conclusion reached above using the Kolmogorov-Smirnov test: we are dealing with two quite different distributions. These distributions differ in shape, and they differ in their medians, such that opaque words have the higher average frequency of use.

In Chapter 1 we started exploring the data set on the dative alternation in English studied by Bresnan *et al.* (2007). We calculated the mean length of the theme for clauses with animate and inanimate recipients with `tapply()`:

```
> tapply(verbs$LengthOfTheme, verbs$AnimacyOfRec, mean)
  animate inanimate
 1.540278  1.071130
```

We now use a Welch two-sample *t*-test to verify that the two means are significantly different:

```
> t.test(LengthOfTheme ~ AnimacyOfRec, data = verbs)
        Welch Two Sample t-test
data:  LengthOfTheme by AnimacyOfRec
t = 5.3168, df = 100.655, p-value = 6.381e-07
alternative hypothesis: true difference in means is not equal to 0
95 percent confidence interval:
 0.2941002 0.6441965
sample estimates:
  mean in group animate mean in group inanimate
               1.540278                1.071130
```

Inspection of the distributions by means of a boxplot suggests some asymmetry for the inanimate group, but, as you may verify for yourself, a Wilcoxon test also leaves no doubt that we have ample reason for surprise.

4.2.3   Are the variances the same?

It may be important to know whether the variances of two normal random variables are different. Here is an example from the R help for `var.test()`. Two vectors with standard normal random numbers with different means and standard deviations are defined first:

```
> x <- rnorm(50, mean = 0, sd = 2)
> y <- rnorm(30, mean = 1, sd = 1)
```

With `var.test()` we subsequently observe that, as expected, the two variances are not the same:

```
> var.test(x, y)
        F test to compare two variances
data:  x and y
F = 2.7485, num df = 49, denom df = 29, p-value = 0.004667
alternative hypothesis: true ratio of variances is not equal to 1
```

```
95 percent confidence interval:
 1.380908 5.171065
sample estimates:
ratio of variances
          2.748496
```

The F-value is the ratio of the two variances:

```
> var(x)/var(y)
[1] 2.748496
```

The degrees of freedom are one less than the numbers of observations in each vector, so we can just as well calculate the p-value directly without invoking var.test():

```
> 2 * (1 - pf(var(x)/var(y), 49, 29))
[1] 0.004666579
```

This test should be applied only to variances of normally distributed random variables. The help page for var.test() points to other functions that you should consider if this condition is not met.

4.3   Paired vectors

The tests described above for comparing the distributions of two dependent variables also apply to paired vectors; vectors with measurements or counts that are pairwise bound to the same experimental units. There are differences, however, in how we test for differences in the mean, and new questions arise as to the functional relation between the two vectors. We discuss these issues in turn.

4.3.1   Are the means or medians the same?

In order to test whether two paired vectors have the same mean or median, we again use t.test() and wilcox.test() respectively, but we now specify that we are dealing with PAIRED OBSERVATIONS. By way of example, we return to the average weight and size ratings elicited from English-speaking subjects for the 81 nouns denoting animals and plants. One question we may ask is whether weight ratings are smaller (or perhaps greater) than size ratings. We address this question using the mean ratings (averaged over participants) as available in the ratings data set. If we treat the two vectors of ratings (meanWeightRating and meanSizeRating) as independent, which they are not, then there is already some evidence that they are not identical in the mean:

```
> t.test(ratings$meanWeightRating, ratings$meanSizeRating)
       Welch Two Sample t-test
data:  ratings$meanWeightRating and ratings$meanSizeRating
```

```
t = -2.1421, df = 159.092, p-value = 0.0337
alternative hypothesis: true difference in means is not equal to 0
95 percent confidence interval:
 -0.64964319 -0.02637656
sample estimates:
mean of x mean of y
 2.570370   2.908380
```

When we apply the appropriate test, and take into account (by specifying `paired = T`) the important information that these ratings were elicited for the same set of 81 nouns, we obtain much stronger evidence that the two vectors differ in the mean:

```
> t.test(ratings$meanWeightRating, ratings$meanSizeRating, paired = T)
        Paired t-test
data:  ratings$meanWeightRating and ratings$meanSizeRating
t = -36.0408, df = 80, p-value < 2.2e-16
alternative hypothesis: true difference in means is not equal to 0
95 percent confidence interval:
 -0.3566737 -0.3193460
sample estimates:
mean of the differences
              -0.3380099
```

Note that the paired *t*-test reports the difference between the two means. In fact, you get exactly the same results by applying a one-sample *t*-test to the vector of paired differences:

```
> t.test(ratings$meanWeightRating - ratings$meanSizeRating)
        One Sample t-test
data:  ratings$meanWeightRating - ratings$meanSizeRating
t = -36.0408, df = 80, p-value < 2.2e-16
alternative hypothesis: true mean is not equal to 0
95 percent confidence interval:
 -0.3566737 -0.3193460
sample estimates:
 mean of x
-0.3380099
```

In this example, the paired differences are less than zero for all 81 words,

```
> sum(ratings$meanWeightRating - ratings$meanSizeRating < 0)
[1] 81
```

which explains why we get such an extremely small *p*-value.

Thus far, we have assumed that the two vectors of ratings are normally distributed. In order to check whether this assumption is justified, we inspect the boxplot shown in the left panel of Figure 4.7. There is some asymmetry here: the horizontal lines representing the medians are not located in the centers of the two boxes:

```
> par(mfrow=c(1,2))
> boxplot(ratings$meanWeightRating, ratings$meanSizeRating,
+ names=c("weight", "size"), ylab = "mean rating")
> boxplot(ratings$meanWeightRating - ratings$meanSizeRating,
```

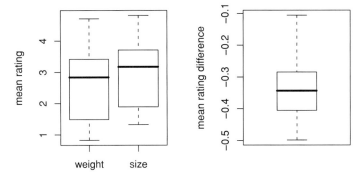

Figure 4.7. *Boxplots for the distributions of mean size and mean weight ratings (averaged over subjects; left panel) and their difference (right panel) for* 81 *English nouns denoting animals and plants.*

```
+ names="difference", ylab = "mean rating difference")
> par(mfrow=c(1,1))
```

Fortunately, most of this asymmetry is absent from the vector of paired differences, as witnessed by the mild *p*-value of the Shapiro-Wilk test and the boxplot shown in the right panel of Figure 4.7:

```
> shapiro.test(ratings$meanWeightRating-ratings$meanSizeRating)
        Shapiro-Wilk normality test
data:  ratings$meanWeightRating - ratings$meanSizeRating
W = 0.9644, p-value = 0.02374
```

Although we could rerun the test with the Wilcoxon signed rank test, with `paired = T`,

```
> wilcox.test(ratings$meanWeightRating, ratings$meanSizeRating,
+ paired = T)
        Wilcoxon signed rank test with continuity correction
data:  ratings$meanWeightRating and ratings$meanSizeRating
V = 0, p-value = 5.463e-15
alternative hypothesis: true mu is not equal to 0
```

the paired *t*-test is perfectly adequate.

4.3.2   Functional relations: linear regression

Instead of comparing just the means of the size and weight ratings, or comparing their distributions by means of boxplots, we can graph the individual data points in a scatterplot, as shown in the left panel of Figure 4.8:

```
> plot(ratings$meanWeightRating, ratings$meanSizeRating,
+ xlab = "mean weight rating", ylab = "mean size rating")
```

What this panel shows is that the data points pattern into a nearly straight line. In other words, we observe an exceptionally clear linear functional relation between estimated `size` and `weight`. This functional relation can be visualized by means

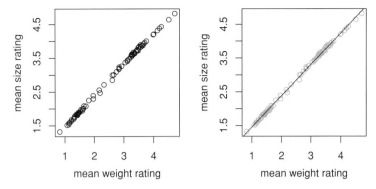

Figure 4.8. *Scatterplot for mean weight and size ratings (left), and the same data points with regression line (right).*

of a line drawn through the scatter of data points in such a way that the line is as close as possible to each of these data points. The question that arises here is how to obtain this regression line. In order to answer this question, we begin by recapitulating how a straight line is characterized.

4.3.2.1   Slope and intercept

Consider the two lines shown in Figure 4.9. For the dashed line, the INTERCEPT is 2 and the slope -2. For the dotted line, the intercept is -2 and the slope 1. It is easy to see that the intercept is the Y-coordinate of the line where it crosses the vertical axis. The slope of the line specifies the direction of the line in terms of how far you have to move along the horizontal axis for a unit change in the vertical direction. For the dashed line, two units down corresponds to one unit to the right. Using Δy and Δx to denote the change in y corresponding to a change in x, we find that we have a slope of $\Delta y / \Delta x = -2/1 = -2$. For the dotted line, moving two units up corresponds with moving two units to the right, so the slope is $\Delta y / \Delta x = 2/2 = 1$.

The function `abline()` adds parametrically specified lines to a plot. It takes two arguments, first the intercept, and then the slope. This is illustrated by the following code, which produces Figure 4.9:

```
> plot(c(-4, 4), c(-4, 4), xlab = "x", ylab = "y", type = "n")
                                      # set up the plot region
> abline(2, -2, lty = 2)                      # add the lines
> abline(-2, 1, lty = 3)
> abline(h = 0)                          # and add the axes
> abline(v = 0)
> abline(h = -2, col = "grey")   # and ancillary lines in grey
> abline(h = 2, col = "grey")
> abline(v = 1, col = "grey", lty = 2)
> abline(v = 2, col = "grey", lty = 2)
```

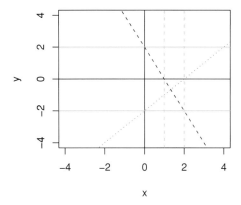

Figure 4.9. *Straight lines are defined by intercept and slope.*

The right panel of Figure 4.8 shows a straight line that has been drawn through the data points in such a way that all the data points are as close to the line as possible. Its intercept is 0.527 and its slope is 0.926:

```
> plot(ratings$meanWeightRating, ratings$meanSizeRating,
+ xlab = "mean weight rating", ylab = "mean size rating",
+ col = "darkgrey")
> abline(0.527, 0.926)
```

The question, of course, is how to determine this slope and intercept.

4.3.2.2   Estimating slope and intercept

We estimate slope and intercept with the help of the function for linear modeling, `lm()`. This function needs to be told what variable is the dependent variable (the variable on the *Y* axis) and what variable is the predictor (the variable on the *X* axis). We provide this information by means of a formula that we supply as the first argument to `lm()`:

```
> ratings.lm = lm(meanSizeRating ~ meanWeightRating, data = ratings)
```

The formula specifies that `meanSizeRating` is to be modeled as a function of, or depending on, `meanWeightRating`. The second argument tells R to look for these two variables in the data frame `ratings`. The output of `lm()` is a LINEAR MODEL object that we name after its input and the function that created it. By typing `ratings.lm` at the prompt, we get to see the coefficients of the desired LEAST SQUARES REGRESSION LINE. (The term LEAST SQUARES refers to the way in which slope and intercept are estimated, namely, by minimizing the squared vertical differences between the data points and the line.)

```
> ratings.lm
Call:
lm(formula = meanSizeRating ~ meanWeightRating, data = ratings)
Coefficients:
     (Intercept)    meanWeightRating
          0.5270              0.9265
```

We can extract from the model object a vector with just the intercept and slope with the function `coef()`, which returns the model's COEFFICIENTS:

```
> coef(ratings.lm)
    (Intercept) meanWeightRating
      0.5269981        0.9264743
```

In order to add this regression line to our scatterplot, we simply type,

```
> abline(ratings.lm)
```

as `abline()` is smart enough to extract slope and intercept from the linear model object by itself.

4.3.2.3 Correlation

You now know how to estimate the intercept and the slope of a regression line. There is much more to be learned from a linear model than just this. We illustrate this by looking in some more detail at scatterplots of paired standard normal random variables. Each panel of Figure 4.10 plots random samples of such paired vectors. The technical name for such paired distributions is a BIVARIATE STANDARD NORMAL DISTRIBUTION. The dashed line in these panels represents the line $Y = X$; the solid line the regression line. In the upper left panel, we have a scatter of points roughly in the form of a disc. Many points are far away from the regression line, which happens to have a negative slope. The upper right panel also shows a wide scatter, but here the regression line has a positive slope. The points in the lower left panel are somewhat more concentrated and closer to the regression line. The regression line itself is becoming more similar to the line $Y = X$. Finally, the lower right panel has a regression line that has crept even closer to the dashed line, and the data points are again much closer to the regression line.

The technical term for the degree to which the data points cluster around the regression line is CORRELATION. This degree of correlation is quantified by means of a CORRELATION COEFFICIENT. The correlation coefficient of a given population is denoted by ρ, and that of a sample from that population by r. The correlation coefficient is bounded by -1 (a perfect negative correlation) and $+1$ (a perfect positive correlation). When the correlation is -1 or $+1$, all the data points lie exactly on the regression line, and in that case the regression line is equal to the line $Y = -X$ and $Y = X$ respectively. This is a limiting case that never arises in practice.

The sample correlation r for each of the four scatterplots in Figure 4.10 is listed above each panel, and varies from -0.07 in the upper left to 0.89 in the lower right. You can regard r as a measure of how useful it is to fit a straight line to the data. If r is close to zero, the regression line does not help at all to predict where the data points will be for a given value of the predictor variable. This is easy to see by comparing the upper and lower panels. In the upper panels, the scatter along the Y axis is very large for almost all values of X. For a large majority of observed data points, the predicted value (somewhere on the regression line)

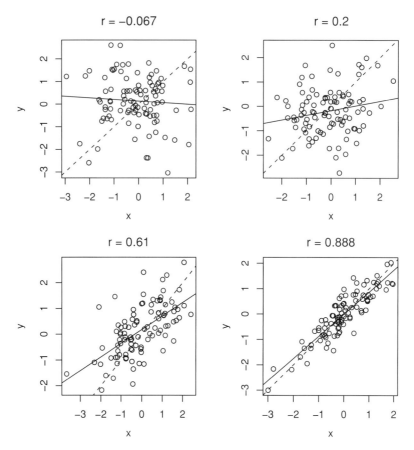

Figure 4.10. *Scatterplots for four paired standard normal random variables with different population correlations ($\rho = 0.0, 0.2, 0.5, 0.9$). The correlations shown above each panel are the sample correlations.*

is going to be way off. This changes in the lower panels, where the regression line starts to become predictive. Another way of thinking about r is that it tells us something about how much of the scatter we get a handle on. In fact, the appropriate measure for evaluating how much of the scatter is accounted for, or explained, by the model is not r itself, but r^2 (often denoted by R^2). More precisely, R^2 quantifies the proportion of the variance in the data that is captured and explained by the regression model.

Let's pause for a moment to think about what it means to explain variance. When we try to fit a model to a data set, the goal is to be able to predict what the value of the dependent variable is, given the predictors. The better we succeed in predicting, the better the predictors succeed in explaining the variability in the dependent variable. When you are in bad luck, with lousy predictors, there is little variability that your model explains. In that case, the values of the dependent variable jump around almost randomly. In this situation, R^2 will be close to zero.

The better the model, the smaller the random variation, the variation that we do not yet understand, will be, and the closer R^2 will be to one.

Scatterplots like those shown in the panels of Figure 4.10 can be obtained with the help of `mvrnormplot.fnc`,

```
> mvrnormplot.fnc(r = 0.9)
```

a convenience function defined in the `languageR` package. As we are dealing with random numbers, your output will be somewhat different each time you run this code, even for the same r. You should try out `mvrnormplot.fnc()` with different values of r to acquire some intuitions about what correlations of different strengths look like.

4.3.2.4   Summarizing a linear model object

We return to our running example of mean size and weight ratings. Recall that we created a linear model object, `ratings.lm`, and extracted the coefficients of the regression line from this object. If we summarize the model with `summary()`, we obtain much more detailed information, including information about R^2:

```
> summary(ratings.lm)
Call:
  lm(formula = meanSizeRating ~ meanWeightRating, data = ratings)
Residuals:
      Min       1Q    Median       3Q       Max
 -0.096368 -0.020285  0.002058  0.024490  0.075310
Coefficients:
                    Estimate Std. Error t value Pr(>|t|)
  (Intercept)       0.526998   0.010632   49.57   <2e-16
  meanWeightRating 0.926474   0.003837  241.45   <2e-16
Residual standard error: 0.03574 on 79 degrees of freedom
Multiple R-Squared: 0.9986,      Adjusted R-squared: 0.9986
F-statistic: 5.83e+04 on 1 and 79 DF,  p-value: < 2.2e-16
```

In what follows, we will walk through this summary line by line.

The first thing that the summary does is remind us of how the object was created. We then get a brief summary of the distribution of the residuals. We postpone to Chapter 6 the discussion of what the residuals are and why they are so important as to be mentioned in the summary of the model.

Next, we see a table with the coefficients of the model: a coefficient for the intercept (0.527) and a coefficient for the slope (0.926). Each coefficient comes with three other numbers: its standard error, a t-value, and a p-value. The p-value tells us whether the coefficient is significantly different from zero. If the coefficient for a predictor is zero, there is no relation at all between the predictor and the dependent variable, in which case it is worthless as a predictor. In order to ascertain whether a coefficient is significantly different from zero, and hence potentially useful, a two-tailed t-test is carried out, using the t-value and the associated degrees of freedom (79, this number is listed further down in the summary). The t-value itself is the value of the coefficient divided by its standard error. This standard error is a measure of how sure we are about the estimate of the coefficient. The smaller the standard error, the smaller the confidence interval around the estimate, the less likely it is that zero will be included in the acceptance region, and hence the smaller the probability that it might just as well be zero.

Sometimes, it is useful to be able to access the different parts of the summary. You can identify the components of the summary with `names(summary(ratings.lm))`, and we can extract these components from the summary with the help of the `$` operator. For instance, we obtain the table of coefficients with `$coef`:

```
> summary(ratings.lm)$coef
                  Estimate  Std. Error   t value      Pr(>|t|)
(Intercept)      0.5269981 0.010632282  49.56585  2.833717e-61
meanWeightRating 0.9264743 0.003837106 241.45129 4.380725e-115
```

Because this table is a matrix, we can access the t-values or the estimates of the coefficients themselves:

```
> summary(ratings.lm)$coef[ ,3]
    (Intercept) meanWeightRating
       49.56585        241.45129
> summary(ratings.lm)$coef[ ,1]
    (Intercept) meanWeightRating
      0.5269981        0.9264743
```

Since `summary(ratings.lm)$coef` is not a data frame, we cannot reference columns by name with the `$` operator, unfortunately. To do so, we first have to convert it explicitly into a data frame:

```
> data.frame(summary(ratings.lm)$coef)$Estimate
[1] 0.5269981 0.9264743
```

Let's return to the summary, and proceed to its last three lines. The RESIDUAL STANDARD ERROR is a measure of how unsuccessful the model is; it gauges the variability in the dependent variable that we can't handle through the predictor variables. The better a model is, the smaller its residual standard error will be. The next line states that the multiple R-squared equals 0.9986. This R-squared is the squared correlation coefficient, r^2, which quantifies, on a scale from 0 to 1, the proportion of the variance that the model explains. We get the value of the correlation coefficient r by taking the square root of 0.9986, which is 0.9993. This is a bit cumbersome, but, fortunately, there are quicker ways of calculating r. The function `cor()` returns the correlation coefficient,

```
> cor(ratings$meanSizeRating, ratings$meanWeightRating)
[1] 0.9993231
```

and `cor.test()` provides the correlation coefficient and also tests whether it is significantly different from zero. It also lists a 95% confidence interval:

```
> cor.test(ratings$meanSizeRating, ratings$meanWeightRating)
        Pearson's product-moment correlation
data:  ratings$meanSizeRating and ratings$meanWeightRating
```

```
t = 241.4513, df = 79, p-value < 2.2e-16
alternative hypothesis: true correlation is not equal to 0
95 percent confidence interval:
 0.9989452 0.9995657
sample estimates:
        cor
0.9993231
```

There is also a distribution-free, non-parametric correlation test, which does not depend on the input vectors being approximately normally distributed, the Spearman correlation test, which is based on the ranks of the observations in the two vectors. It is carried out by `cor.test()` when you specify the option `method="spearman"`:

```
> cor.test(ratings$meanSizeRating, ratings$meanWeightRating,
+ method = "spearman")
        Spearman's rank correlation rho
data:  ratings$meanSizeRating and ratings$meanWeightRating
S = 110, p value < 2.2e 16
alternative hypothesis: true rho is not equal to 0
sample estimates:
        rho
0.9986676
Warning message: p-values may be incorrect due to ties
```

We could have avoided the warning message by adding some jitter to the ratings, but given the very low *p*-value, this is superfluous. The Spearman correlation coefficient is often referenced as r_s.

Returning to the summary of `ratings.lm` and leaving the discussion of the adjusted *R*-squared to Chapter 6, we continue with the last line, which lists an *F*-value. This *F*-value goes with an overall test of whether the linear model as a whole succeeds in explaining a significant portion of the variance. Given the small *p*-value listed in the summary, there is no question about lack of statistical significance.

4.3.2.5   Problems and pitfalls of linear regression

Now that we have seen how to fit a linear model to a data set with paired vectors, we proceed to two more complex examples that illustrate some of the problems and pitfalls of linear regression. First consider the left panel of Figure 4.11, which plots the frequency of the plural against the frequency of the singular for the 81 nouns for animals and plants in the `ratings` data frame. The problem that we are confronted with here is that there is a cluster of observations near the origin combined with a handful of atypical points with very high values. The presence of such OUTLIERS may mislead the algorithm that estimates the coefficients of the linear model. If we fit a linear model to these data points, we obtain the solid line. But if we exclude just the four words with singular frequencies greater than 500, and then refit the model, we obtain the dashed line. The two lines tell a rather different story which suggests that these four words are

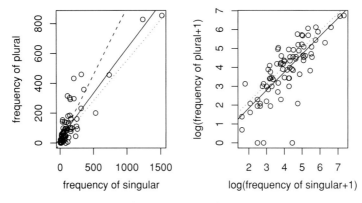

Figure 4.11. *Scatterplots for singular and plural frequency with regression lines. Solid lines represent ordinary least squares regression on all data points, the dashed line represents an ordinary least squares regression with four outliers excluded, and dotted lines represents robust regression lines obtained with* lmsreg().

atypical with respect to the lower-frequency words. There are various regression techniques that are more robust with respect to outliers than is lm(). The dotted line illustrates the lmsreg() function, which, unfortunately, does not tell us whether the predictors are significant. From the graph we can tell that it considers rather different words to be outliers, namely, the words with high plural frequency but singular frequency less than 500.

Before we move on to a better solution for this regression problem, let's first review the code for the left panel of Figure 4.11:

```
> plot(ratings$FreqSingular, ratings$FreqPlural)
> abline(lm(FreqPlural ~ FreqSingular, data = ratings), lty = 1)
> abline(lm(FreqPlural ~ FreqSingular,
+ data = ratings[ratings$FreqSingular < 500, ]), lty = 2)
```

In order to have access to lmsreg(), we must first load the MASS package:

```
> library(MASS)
> abline(lmsreg(FreqPlural ~ FreqSingular, data = ratings), lty = 3)
```

The problem illustrated in the left panel of Figure 4.11 is that word frequency distributions are severely skewed. There are many low-probability words and relatively few high-probability words. This skewness poses a technical problem to lm(). A few high-probability outliers become overly influential, and shift the slope and intercept to such an extent that it becomes suboptimal for the majority of data points. The technical solution is to apply a logarithmic transformation in order to remove at least a substantial amount of this skewness by bringing many straying outliers back into the fold. The right panel of Figure 4.11 visualizes these benefits of the logarithmic transforms. We now have a regression line that captures the main trend in the data quite well. The robust regression line has nearly the same slope, albeit a slightly higher intercept. It is influenced less by the four data points with exceptionally low plural frequencies given their singular frequencies, which have a small but apparently somewhat disproportionate effect on lm()'s estimate of the intercept. In Chapter 6, we will discuss in more detail how undue influence of potential outliers can be detected and what measures can be taken to protect your model against them.

The second example addresses the relation between the mean familiarity rating and mean size rating for our 81 nouns in the ratings data set. The question of interest is whether it is possible to predict how heavy people think an object is from how frequently they think the name for that object is used in the language. We address this question with lm(),

```
> ratings.lm = lm(meanSizeRating ~ meanFamiliarity, data = ratings)
```

extract the table of coefficients from the summary, and round it to four decimal digits:

```
> round(summary(ratings.lm)$coef, 4)
                Estimate Std. Error t value Pr(>|t|)
(Intercept)       3.7104     0.4143  8.9549   0.0000
meanFamiliarity  -0.2066     0.1032 -2.0014   0.0488
```

The summary presents a negative coefficient for meanFamiliarity that is just significant at the 5% level. This suggests that objects that participants judge to have more familiar names in the language receive somewhat lower size ratings.

This conclusion is, however, unwarranted as there are lots of things wrong with this analysis. But this becomes apparent only by graphical inspection of the data and of the predictions of the model. Let's make a scatterplot of the data, the first thing that we should have done anyway. The scatterplot smoother (lowess()) shown in the upper left panel of Figure 4.12 suggests a negative correlation, but what is worrying is that there are no points close to the line in the center of the graph. The same holds for the regression line for the model that we just fitted to the data with lm(), as shown in the upper right panel.

If you look carefully at the scatterplots, you can see that there seem to be two separate strands of data points, one with higher size ratings, and one with lower size ratings. This intuition is explored in the lower panels, where we link this difference to the two kinds of nouns in ratings. The nouns naming plants and those naming animals (as specified by the factor Class) now receive their own separate regression lines.

First consider the lower left panel of Figure 4.12. We set up the axes, their labels, and tick marks, but we prohibit displaying the data points with type = "n":

```
> plot(ratings$meanFamiliarity, ratings$meanSizeRating,
+ xlab = "mean familiarity", ylab = "mean size rating",
+ type = "n")
```

Since we want to consider the plants and animals by themselves, we create separate data frames,

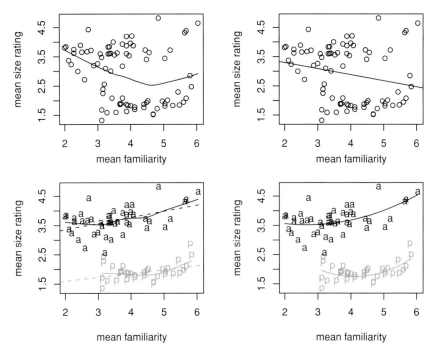

Figure 4.12. *Scatterplots for mean rated size as a function of mean familiarity, with scatterplot smoothers (left panels) and linear (upper right, lower left) and quadratic (lower right) fits. The upper panels show fits to all data points, the lower panels show fits to the words for plants (p) and animals (a) separately.*

```
> plants = ratings[ratings$Class == "plant", ]
> animals = ratings[ratings$Class == "animal", ]
```

add the points for the plants together with a scatterplot smoother,

```
> points(plants$meanFamiliarity, plants$meanSizeRating,
+ pch = 'p', col = "darkgrey")
> lines(lowess(plants$meanFamiliarity, plants$meanSizeRating),
+ col = "darkgrey")
```

and repeat the process for the animals:

```
> points(animals$meanFamiliarity, animals$meanSizeRating,
+ pch = 'a')
> lines(lowess(animals$meanFamiliarity, animals$meanSizeRating))
```

Finally, we fit separate models and add their regression lines as well:

```
> plants.lm = lm(meanSizeRating ~ meanFamiliarity, plants)
> abline(coef(plants.lm), col = "darkgrey", lty = 2)
> animals.lm = lm(meanSizeRating ~ meanFamiliarity, animals)
> abline(coef(animals.lm), lty = 2)
```

The pattern revealed in the lower left panel of Figure 4.12 makes a lot more sense. The plants and the animals received very different size ratings. Within each subset,

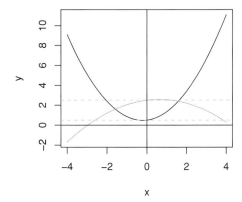

Figure 4.13. *Two parabola.*

there seems to be a positive correlation with mean familiarity, as shown by the smoothers (solid lines) and the linear regression lines (dashed).

However, we are still not there. If you inspect the two kinds of regression lines carefully, you will see that the smoother is slightly curved, both for the animals and also for the plants. Fitting a straight line through these data points may not be justified — after all, we have no theoretical reasons to suppose that this relation must be strictly linear. In the lower right panel of Figure 4.12, we have relaxed the linearity assumption by allowing for the possibility that the curve is part of a PARABOLA.

Figure 4.13 illustrates two parabola, one with a minimum (represented by the black line) and one with a maximum (represented by a grey line). Given a series of X-values,

```
> xvals = seq(-4, 4, 0.1)
```

we obtain the corresponding Y-values by summing an intercept, a weighted term with xvals, and a weighted term with xvals-squared:

```
> yvals1 = 0.5 + 0.25 * xvals + 0.6 * xvals^2
> yvals2 = 2.5 + 0.25 * xvals - 0.2 * xvals^2
```

We plot the points for the first parabola, connect them with a line (type = "l"), and add the line for the second parabola using a separate call to lines():

```
> plot(xvals, yvals1, xlab = "x", ylab = "y",
+ ylim = range(yvals1, yvals2), type = "l")
> lines(xvals, yvals2, col = "darkgrey")
```

Each parabola has an intercept, which determines where the parabola intersects with the Y-axis. It also has a slope, the number before xvals, just as do straight lines. But in addition, it has a second slope for xvals-squared. This is the QUADRATIC term that brings the curvature into the graph. If this second slope is positive, the curve is shaped like a cup, if it is negative, the curve is shaped like a cap.

In order to do justice to the curvature that we observed in the lower panels of Figure 4.12, we assume that the data points of, e.g. the nouns denoting plants, are close to part of the curve of a parabola. Instead of feeding `lm()` with a formula describing a straight line, we feed it a formula describing a parabola by adding a quadratic term, the square of `meanFamiliarity`. Because the $^\wedge$ operator has a different function in formulas (see Chapter 6), we include `meanFamiliarity^2` within the scope of the protective `I()` operator:

```
> plants.lm = lm(meanSizeRating ~ meanFamiliarity +
+ I(meanFamiliarity^2), data = plants)
> summary(plants.lm)$coef
                      Estimate Std. Error    t value      Pr(>|t|)
(Intercept)          5.1902476 1.28517759   4.038545 0.0003142449
meanFamiliarity     -1.6717053 0.59334724  -2.817415 0.0082290129
I(meanFamiliarity^2) 0.2030369 0.06659252   3.048944 0.0045826280
```

Instead of the familiar two coefficients, we now have three coefficients, one for the intercept, one for the LINEAR COMPONENT, and one for the QUADRATIC COMPONENT. Note that the linear and the quadratic components of `meanFamiliarity` are both significant, as you can tell by inspecting their p-values. Their joint effect is shown by the grey solid line in the lower right panel of Figure 4.12, where we use the function `predict()` to obtain the size ratings predicted by the model:

```
> plot(ratings$meanFamiliarity, ratings$meanSizeRating,
+ xlab = "mean familiarity", ylab = "mean size rating", type = "n")
> points(plants$meanFamiliarity, plants$meanSizeRating,
+ pch = 'p', col = "darkgrey")
> plants$predict = predict(plants.lm)
> plants = plants[order(plants$meanFamiliarity), ]
> lines(plants$meanFamiliarity, plants$predict, col = "darkgrey")
```

In a similar way, we can fit a quadratic function to the data points for the animals, extract the fitted values, and add these to the plot. What is unsatisfactory about this analysis, however, is that we have fitted two models to a single data set, instead of one. In section 4.4.1 we will return to this data set to show how to specify a model that can handle all data points simultaneously.

At this point, you may have started to wonder about the term "linear" in LINEAR MODEL, as we have just used a linear model to produce a curve and not a straight line. In fact, the term "linear" does not say anything about the relation between the dependent variable and the predictor(s). What "linear" denotes is that the dependent variable can be expressed as the sum of a series of weighted (possibly transformed) predictor variables. The technical term for this is that the dependent variable is a LINEAR COMBINATION of its predictors. The weights of the predictors are the coefficients that `lm()` estimates. Thus, in our model fit to the words for plants, the `meanSizeRating` is linear in `meanFamiliarity` and `I(meanFamiliarity^2)`. It may help to compare the formula that drives `lm()` and the resulting equation that tells us how to predict the mean size rating for a given word *i* from the mean familiarity rating of that word given the coefficients of the fitted model:

```
meanSizeRating ~ meanFamiliarity + I(meanFamiliarity^2)
```

$$\texttt{meanSizeRating}_i = 5.19 - 1.67 * \texttt{meanFamiliarity}_i +$$
$$+0.20 * \texttt{meanFamiliarity}_i^2$$

Note that we don't have to specify the intercept in the formula, as `lm()` adds an intercept term by default. The corresponding equation has the estimated intercept, followed by the same terms as in the formula, but now each term is preceded by its weight, its estimated coefficient that is listed in the summary.

Let's wrap up with a summary of four basic rules of conduct for the analysis of paired vectors:

1. **Visualize!** Make scatterplots, add non-parametric smoothers, look at your data.
2. **Beware of outliers!** If your distributions are skewed, transform them to bring the outliers back into the fold. Outliers due to experimental flaws should be removed from the data set.
3. **Do not impose linearity a priori!** Straight lines are often a convenient simplification at best: curves are ubiquitous in nature.
4. **Keep your model as simple as possible!** Don't add *unnecessary* quadratic terms.

4.3.3 What does the joint density look like?

When you have two vectors that are paired, the question arises of what their joint density looks like. Recall that when we are dealing with the density of a single random variable, the area enclosed by the density curve and the *X* axis is equal to 1. When we have two paired vectors, the density is a surface, and the volume between the density surface and the plane spanned by the *X* and *Y* axes is now equal to 1. The upper left panel of Figure 4.14 illustrates what the density of a random sample of 1000 bivariate standard normal variates might look like. In what follows, we go through the steps required to make this density plot. Along the way, some new functions and concepts will be introduced.

First of all, we need a function for bivariate normal random numbers. The function `rnorm()` is not useful here. We could use it to generate two vectors of random numbers, but these vectors will be uncorrelated. For a function for generating two or more correlated vectors (brought together in a matrix), we need to load the `MASS` package, so that the function `mvrnorm()` becomes available to us. We use `mvrnorm()` to generate a random sample of *n* = 1000 paired random numbers sampled from populations with means of 0, variances of 1, and a correlation of 0.8:

```
> library(MASS)
> x = mvrnorm(n = 1000, mu = c(0, 0),
```

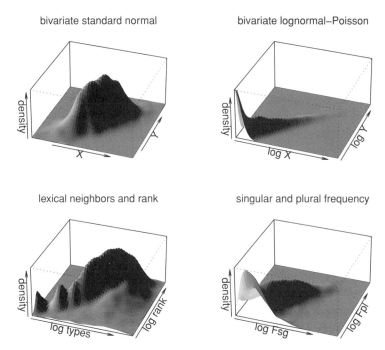

Figure 4.14. *Random samples of a bivariate standard normal and a lognormal-Poisson variate (upper panels). The lower left panel shows the joint distribution of phonological neighborhood size and rank in the neighborhood for four-phoneme Dutch word forms, the lower right panel shows the joint distribution for singular and plural frequency for monomorphemic Dutch nouns.*

```
+ Sigma = cbind(c(1, 0.8), c(0.8, 1)))
> head(x)
             [,1]         [,2]
[1,]   0.5694554   0.7122192
[2,]  -1.8851621  -2.2727134
[3,]  -1.7352253  -1.7685805
[4,]  -1.2654685  -0.1380204
[5,]  -0.2449445  -0.7448824
[6,]  -1.1241598  -1.0330096
```

We use `cor()` to check that the correlation between the two column vectors is indeed close to the population parameter (0.8) that we specified in the call to `mvrnorm()`:

```
> cor(x[,1], x[,2])
[1] 0.7940896
```

The third argument of `mvrnorm()`, `Sigma`,

```
> Sigma
     [,1] [,2]
[1,]  1.0  0.8
[2,]  0.8  1.0
```

created with cbind(), which binds vectors column-wise, is the VARIANCE-
COVARIANCE matrix of our bivariate standard normal sample x. The Sigma matrix
has the variances on the main diagonal, and the COVARIANCES on the subdiagonal.
The covariance is a measure that is closely related to the correlation. But whereas
the correlation is scaled so that its values are between -1 and $+1$, the value of
the covariance can range between $-\infty$ and $+\infty$, and depends on the scales of
its input vectors. We can illustrate the difference between the covariance and the
correlation by means of the output of mvrnorm(), which as we saw previously
is a two-column matrix. The correlation of the two-column vectors is the same,
irrespective of whether we scale any of the vectors up, or down:

```
> cor(x[, 1], x[, 2])
[1] 0.7940896
> cor(x[, 1], 100 * x[, 2])
[1] 0.7940896
> cor(0.001 * x[, 1], 100 * x[, 2])
[1] 0.7940896
```

In contrast, the covariance changes substantially by these changes in scale:

```
> cov(x[, 1], x[, 2])
[1] 0.7940896
> cov(x[, 1], 100 * x[, 2])
[1] 80.10768
> cov(0.003 * x[, 1], 100 * x[, 2])
[1] 0.2403230
```

It is only when the two variances are equal to 1, as in the above variance-covariance
matrix, that the covariance and the correlation are identical.

Now that we have seen how to create bivariate normal random numbers, we
proceed to estimate the corresponding density surface with the two-dimensional
analogue of density(), the function kde2d(). The output of kde2d() is a list
with X-coordinates, Y-coordinates, and the Z-coordinate for each combination
of the X and Y. The number of X-coordinates (and Y-coordinates) is specified
with the parameter n, which we set to 50. Jointly, the X-, Y-, and Z-coordinates
define the estimated density surface. We plot this surface with persp(), which
produces a PERSPECTIVE PLOT:

```
> persp(kde2d(x[, 1], x[, 2], n = 50),
+ phi = 30, theta = 20,    # angles  defining  viewing  direction
+ d = 10,                   # strength of perspective
+ col = "lightblue",        # color for the surface
+ shade = 0.75, ltheta = -100,  # shading for viewing direction
+ border = NA,              # we use shading, so we disable border
+ expand = 0.5,             # shrink the vertical direction by 0.5
+ xlab = "X", ylab = "Y", zlab = "density")     # add labels
+ mtext("bivariate standard normal", 3, 1)      # and add title
```

The wide range of options of persp() is described in detail on its help page. You
will also find the command demo(persp) useful, which gives some examples
of what persp() can do, including examples of the required code.

Paired vectors need not follow a bivariate normal distribution. The upper right panel of Figure 4.14 plots a bivariate density that is LOGNORMAL-POISSON DIS-TRIBUTED (cf. Baayen *et al.*, 2003). This is a distribution that provides a reasonable first approximation for paired word frequency counts obtained, e.g. by calculating the frequencies of a set of words in two equally sized text corpora. A LOGNORMAL RANDOM VARIABLE is a variate that is normally distributed after the logarithmic transformation. Given the (simplifying) assumption that word frequencies are lognormally distributed, we generate $n = 1000$ lognormally distributed random numbers with rlnorm() with which we model the Poisson rates λ at which 1000 words are used in texts. In other words, for a given word, we model its token frequency in a text corpus as being Poisson-distributed. In order to simulate the frequency of a given word in two corpora, we generate two random numbers with rpois() for that word, given its usage rate λ.

Let's make this more concrete by showing how this works in R. We begin with defining the number of words n, the corresponding vector of usage rates lambdas, and a two-column matrix of zeros in which we will store the two simulated frequencies of a given word:

```
> n = 1000                        # number of words
> lambdas = rlnorm(n, 1, 4)       # lognormal random numbers
> mat = matrix(nrow = n, ncol = 2)   # define matrix with zeros
```

We proceed with a FOR LOOP to store the two frequencies for each word i in mat. The variable i in the loop starts at 1, ends at n, and is incremented in steps of 1. For each value of i, we fill the i-th row of mat with two Poisson random numbers, both obtained for the same Poisson rate given by the i-th λ:

```
> for (i in 1:n) {                      # loop over each word index
+       mat[i,] = rpois(2, lambdas[i]) # store Poisson frequencies
+ }
> mat[1:10,]
        [,1] [,2]
 [1,]   319  328
 [2,]    22   18
 [3,]     0    0
 [4,]     3    2
 [5,]   307  287
 [6,]    29   29
 [7,]   240  223
 [8,]     2    1
 [9,]     1    0
[10,]   523  527
```

The first row of mat lists the frequencies for the first word, the second row those for the second word, and so on. Now that mat has been properly filled with simulated frequencies of occurrence, we use it as input to the density estimation function. Before we do so, it is essential to apply a logarithmic transformation to remove most of the skew. As there are zero frequencies in mat, and as the logarithm of zero is undefined, we back off from zero by adding 1 to all cells of mat before taking the log:

```
> mat = log(mat+1)
```

We now use the same code as previously for the bivariate normal density,

```
> persp(kde2d(mat[, 1], mat[, 2], n = 50),
+ phi = 30, theta = 20, d = 10, col = "lightblue",
+ shade = 0.75, box = T, border = NA, ltheta = -100, expand = 0.5,
+ xlab = "log X", ylab = "log Y", zlab = "density")
```

but change the accompanying text:

```
> mtext("bivariate lognormal-Poisson", 3, 1)
```

The lower panels of Figure 4.14 illustrate two empirical densities. The left panel concerns the phonological similarity space of 4171 Dutch word forms with four phonemes. For each of these words, we calculated the type count of four-phoneme words that differ in only one phoneme, its phonological neighborhood size. For each word, we also calculated the rank of that word in its neighborhood. (If the word was the most frequent word in its neighborhood, its rank was 1, etc.) After removal of words with no neighbors and log transforms, we obtain a density that is clearly not strictly bivariate normal, but that might perhaps be considered as sufficiently approximating a bivariate normal distribution when considering a regression model.

The lower right panel of Figure 4.14 presents the density for the (log) frequencies of 4633 Dutch monomorphemic nouns in the singular and plural form. This distribution has the same kind of shape as that of the lognormal-Poisson variate in the upper right.

4.4   A numerical vector and a factor: analysis of variance

Up till now, we have considered the functional relation between two numerical vectors. In this section, we consider how to analyze a numerical vector that is paired with a factor. Consider again mean familiarity ratings and the class of the words in the `ratings` data frame:

```
> ratings[1:5, c("Word", "meanFamiliarity", "Class")]
         Word meanFamiliarity  Class
23     almond            3.72  plant
70        ant            3.60 animal
12      apple            5.84  plant
76    apricot            4.40  plant
79 asparagus            3.68  plant
```

We can use the `lm()` function to test whether there is a difference in mean familiarity between nouns for plants and nouns for animals. This is known as a ONE-WAY ANALYSIS OF VARIANCE:

```
> summary(lm(meanFamiliarity ~ Class, data = ratings))
Coefficients:
            Estimate Std. Error t value Pr(>|t|)
(Intercept)   3.5122     0.1386  25.348  < 2e-16
Classplant    0.8547     0.2108   4.055 0.000117
```

The summary shows two highly significant *p*-values, so we may infer that the difference between the two group means must somehow be significant. But let's delve a little deeper into what is happening here. After all, `Class` is a factor and not a numerical variable representing a line for which a slope and an intercept make sense.

What `lm()` does for us with the factor `Class` is to recode its factor levels into one or more numerical vectors. Because `Class` has only two levels, one numerical vector suffices; a vector with zeros for the animals and with ones for the plants. This numerical vector is labeled as `Classplant`, and `lm()` carries out its standard calculations with this vector just as it would for any other numerical variable. Hence, it reports an intercept and a slope. However, intercept and slope receive a special interpretation that crucially depends on how the factor levels are recoded numerically.

The numerical recoding of factor levels is referred to as DUMMY CODING. There are many different algorithms for dummy coding. (The help page for `contr.treatment()` provides further information.) The kind of dummy coding used in this book is known as TREATMENT CODING. R handles dummy coding automatically for us, but by way of illustration we add treatment dummy codes to our data frame by hand. For convenience, we first make a copy of `ratings` with only the columns relevant for the current discussion included:

```
> dummy = ratings[,c("Word", "meanFamiliarity", "Class")]
```

We now add the dummy codes: a 1 for `plants`, and a 0 for animals, in a vector named `Classplant`, following R's naming conventions:

```
> dummy$Classplant = 1
> dummy[dummy$Class == "animal",]$Classplant = 0
> dummy[1:5, ]
        Word meanFamiliarity  Class Classplant
23    almond            3.72  plant          1
70       ant            3.60 animal          0
12     apple            5.84  plant          1
76   apricot            4.40  plant          1
79 asparagus            3.68  plant          1
```

It does not matter which factor level is assigned a 1 and which a 0. Some decision has to be made; R bases its decision on alphabetical order. Hence `animal` is singled out as the DEFAULT OR REFERENCE LEVEL that is contrasted with the level `plant`. R labels the dummy vector with the factor name followed by the non-default factor level, hence the name `Classplant`. If we now run `lm()` on `dummy` with `Classplant` as predictor instead of `Class`, we obtain exactly the same table of coefficients as above:

```
> summary(lm(meanFamiliarity ~ Classplant, data = dummy))
Coefficients:
            Estimate Std. Error t value Pr(>|t|)
(Intercept)   3.5122     0.1386  25.348  < 2e-16
Classplant    0.8547     0.2108   4.055 0.000117
```

Let's now study this table in some more detail. It lists two coefficients. First consider the coefficient labeled intercept. Since all we are doing is comparing the ratings for the two levels of the factor Class, the term "intercept" must have a more general interpretation than "the Y-value of a line when $X = 0$." What the intercept actually represents here is the group mean for the default level, animal. In other words, the intercept is nothing else but the mean familiarity for the subset of animals:

```
> mean(ratings[ratings$Class == "animal",]$meanFamiliarity)
[1] 3.512174
> coef(ratings.lm)[1]
 (Intercept)
    3.512174
```

The t-value and its corresponding p-value answer the question as to whether the group mean for the animals, 3.5122, is significantly different from zero. It clearly is, but this information is not that interesting to us as we are concerned with the difference between the two group means.

Consider therefore the second coefficient in the model, 0.8547. The value of this coefficient represents the contrast (i.e. the difference) between the group mean of the plants and that of the animals. When a word does not belong to the default class, i.e. it denotes a plant instead of an animal, then the mean has to be adjusted upwards by adding 0.8547 to the intercept, the group mean for the animals. In other words, the group mean for the nouns denoting plants is 4.3669 (3.5122 + 0.8547). What the t-test in the above table of coefficients tells us is that this adjustment of 0.8547 is statistically significant. In other words, we have ample reason to suppose that the two group means differ significantly.

The t-value and p-value obtained here are identical to those for a straight-forward t-test when we force t.test() to treat the variances of the familiarity ratings for plants and animals as identical:

```
> t.test(animals$meanFamiliarity, plants$meanFamiliarity,
+ var.equal = TRUE)
t = -4.0548, df = 79, p-value = 0.0001168
alternative hypothesis: true difference in means is not equal to 0
95 percent confidence interval:
 -1.2742408 -0.4351257
sample estimates:
mean of x mean of y
 3.512174  4.366857
```

Note once more that the mean for animals is identical to the coefficient for the intercept, and that the mean for plants is the sum of the intercept and the coefficient adjusting for the level plant of the factor Class.

Whereas the function `t.test()` is restricted to comparing two group means, the `lm()` function can be applied to a factor with more than two levels. By way of example, consider the `auxiliaries` data set, which provides information on 285 Dutch verbs:

```
> head(auxiliaries)
      Verb    Aux VerbalSynsets Regularity
1 blijken    zijn             1  irregular
2 gloeien  hebben             3    regular
3 glimmen  zijnheb            2  irregular
4  rijzen    zijn             4  irregular
5  werpen  hebben             3  irregular
6  delven  hebben             2  irregular
```

The column labeled `Aux` specifies what the appropriate auxiliary for the perfect tense is for the verb listed in the first column. Dutch has two auxiliaries for the perfect tense, *zijn* ("be") and *hebben* ("have"), and verbs subcategorize as to whether they select only *zijn*, only *hebben*, or both (depending on the aspect of the clause and the inherent aspect of the verb). The column `VerbalSynsets` specifies the number of verbal synsets in which a given verb appears in the Dutch WordNet. The final column categorizes the verbs as regular versus irregular.

We test whether the number of verbal synsets varies significantly with auxiliary by modeling `VerbalSynsets` as a function of `Aux`:

```
> auxiliaries.lm = lm(VerbalSynsets ~ Aux, data = auxiliaries)
```

Let's first consider the general question of whether `Aux` helps explain at least some of the variation in the number of verbal synsets. This question is answered with the help of the `anova()` function:

```
> anova(auxiliaries.lm)
Analysis of Variance Table

Response: VerbalSynsets
           Df  Sum Sq Mean Sq F value    Pr(>F)
Aux         2  117.80   58.90  7.6423 0.0005859
Residuals 282 2173.43    7.71
```

The `anova()` function reports an *F*-value of 7.64, which, for 2 and 282 degrees of freedom, is highly significant (compare `1-pf(7.6423, 2, 282)`). What this test tells us is that there are significant differences in the mean number of synsets for the three kinds of verbs. However, it does *not* specify which of the — in this case 3 — possible differences in the means might be involved: `hebben – zijn`, `hebben – zijnheb`, and `zijn – zijnheb`. Some information as to which of these means are really different can be gleaned from the summary:

```
> summary(auxiliaries.lm)
Coefficients:
            Estimate Std. Error t value Pr(>|t|)
(Intercept)   3.4670     0.1907  18.183  < 2e-16
Auxzijn       0.5997     0.7417   0.808 0.419488
Auxzijnheb    1.6020     0.4114   3.894 0.000123
```

From the summary we infer that the default or reference level is hebben: hebben precedes zijn and zijnheb in the alphabet. This explains why there is no row labeled with Auxhebben in the summary table. Since hebben is the default, the intercept (3.4670) represents the group mean for hebben. There are two additional coefficients, one for the contrast between the group mean of hebben versus zijn, represented by the vector of dummy contrasts labeled Auxzijn, and one for the contrast between the group mean for hebben and that of zijnheb, represented by the dummy vector Auxzijnheb. Hence, we can reconstruct the other two group means from the table of coefficients. The mean for zijn is $3.4670 + 0.5997$, and the mean for verbs allowing both auxiliaries is $3.4670 + 1.6020$. The t-test for the intercept tells us that 3.4670 is unlikely to be zero, which is not of interest to us here. The coefficient of 0.5997 (for the verbs taking zijn) is not significant ($p > 0.40$). This indicates that there is no reason to suppose that the means of the verbs taking hebben and those taking zijn are different. The coefficient for verbs taking both auxiliaries is significant, so we know that this mean is really different from the mean for verbs selecting only hebben.

There is one comparison that is left out in this example: (zijn versus zijn-heb). When a factor has more than three levels, there will be more comparisons that do not appear in the table of coefficients. This is because this table lists only those pairwise comparisons that involve the default level; the reference level that is mapped onto the intercept.

A question that often arises when a factor has more than two levels is which group means are actually different. In the present example, we might consider renaming the factor levels so that the missing comparison appears in the table of coefficients. This is not recommended, however, for two reasons. The first is that it is cumbersome to do so, the second is that there is a statistical snag when MULTIPLE COMPARISONS are carried out on the same data.

Recall that we accept the outcome of a statistical experiment as surprising when its p-value is extreme, for instance below $\alpha = 0.05$. When we are interested in the differences between, for instance, three group means, we have to be careful about how we define what we count as extreme. The proper definition of an extreme probability is, in this case, that at least one of the outcomes is truly surprising. Now, if we simply carry out three separate t-tests with $\alpha = 0.05$, the probability of surprise for at least one comparison increases from 0.05 to 0.143. To see this, we model our statistical experiment as a random variable with a probability of success equal to 0.05 and a probability of failure equal to 0.95. The probability of at least one success is the same as one minus the probability of no successes at all, hence:

```
> 1 - pbinom(0, 3, 0.05)
[1] 0.142625
```

In other words, the probability that at least one out of three experiments will be successful in producing a p-value less than 0.05 just by chance is 0.14. This example illustrates that when we carry out multiple comparison we run the risk of serious INFLATION IN SURPRISE. This is not what we want.

There are several remedies, of which I discuss two. The first is known as a BON-FERRONI CORRECTION. For n comparisons, simply divide α by n. Any comparison that produces a p-value less than α/n is sure to be significant at the α significance level. Applied to our example, we begin by noting that Aux has three levels and therefore three pairwise comparisons of two means are at issue. Since $n = 3$, any pairwise comparison that yields a p-value less than $0.05/3 = 0.0167$ can be accepted as significant. If Aux would have had four levels, the number of possible pairwise comparisons would be six, so $\alpha = 0.0083$ would have been appropriate.

The second remedy is to make use of TUKEY's HONESTLY SIGNIFICANT DIFFER-ENCE, available in R as TukeyHSD(). This method has greater power to detect significant differences than the Bonferroni method, but has the disadvantage that the means for each level of the factor should be based on equal numbers of ob-servations. The implementation of Tukey's HSD in R incorporates an adjustment for sample size that produces sensible results also for mildly unbalanced designs.

For the present example, the counts of verbs, cross-classified by the auxiliary they select, point to a very unbalanced design:

```
> xtabs(~ auxiliaries$Aux)
auxiliaries$Aux
 hebben    zijn zijnheb
    212      15      58
```

Hence, the Bonferroni adjustment is required. We could apply TukeyHSD() to these data, but the results would be meaningless. To illustrate how to carry out multiple comparisons using Tukey's honestly significant difference, consider the following (simplified) example from the help page of TukeyHSD(). From the built-in data sets in R, we select the data frame named warpbreaks, which gives the number of warp breaks per loom, where a loom corresponds to a fixed length of yarn. For more information on this data set, type ?warpbreaks. We run a one-way analysis of variance:

```
> warpbreaks.lm = lm(breaks ~ tension, data = warpbreaks)
> anova(warpbreaks.lm)
Analysis of Variance Table

Response: breaks
          Df Sum Sq Mean Sq F value   Pr(>F)
tension    2 2034.3  1017.1  7.2061 0.001753
Residuals 51 7198.6   141.1
> summary(warpbreaks.lm)
Coefficients:
            Estimate Std. Error t value Pr(>|t|)
(Intercept)    36.39       2.80  12.995  < 2e-16
tensionM      -10.00       3.96  -2.525 0.014717
tensionH      -14.72       3.96  -3.718 0.000501

Residual standard error: 11.88 on 51 degrees of freedom
Multiple R-Squared: 0.2203,    Adjusted R-squared: 0.1898
F-statistic: 7.206 on 2 and 51 DF,  p-value: 0.001753
```

The table of coefficients suggests that there are significant contrasts of medium and high tension compared to low tension. In order to make use of `TukeyHSD()`, we have to rerun this analysis using a function specialized for analysis of variance, `aov()`:

```
> warpbreaks.aov = aov(breaks ~ tension, data = warpbreaks)
```

The summary of the `aov` object gives exactly the same output as the `anova` function applied to the `lm` object:

```
> summary(warpbreaks.aov)
            Df Sum Sq Mean Sq F value  Pr(>F)
tension      2 2034.3  1017.1  7.2061 0.001753
Residuals   51 7198.6   141.1
```

The F-value is the ratio of the variance estimates in the third column of the table, $1017.1/141.1 = 7.21$. The F-test evaluates this ratio with the degrees of freedom listed in the first column:

```
> 1 - pf (7.206, 2, 51)
[1] 0.0017529
```

Also note that the F-test in this summary yields the same results as the F-test following the table of coefficients in the summary of `warpbreaks.lm`. Both F-values tell exactly the same story: there are statistically significant differences in the number of breaks as a function of the amount of tension. Let's now apply `TukeyHSD()`:

```
> TukeyHSD(warpbreaks.aov)
  Tukey multiple comparisons of means
    95% family-wise confidence level

Fit: aov(formula = breaks ~ tension, data = warpbreaks)

$tension
          diff        lwr        upr      p adj
M-L -10.000000 -19.55982 -0.4401756 0.0384598
H-L -14.722222 -24.28205 -5.1623978 0.0014315
H-M  -4.722222 -14.28205  4.8376022 0.4630831
```

This table lists the differences in the means, the lower and upper end points of the confidence intervals, and the adjusted p-value. A comparison of the adjusted p-values for the M-L and H-L comparisons with the p-values listed in the table of coefficients for `warpbreaks.lm` above shows that the adjusted p-values are more conservative. For visualization (see Figure 4.15) simply type:

```
> plot(TukeyHSD(warpbreaks.aov))
```

Above, we fitted a linear model to the auxiliary data using `lm()`. Alternatively, we could have used the `aov()` function. However, both methods, which are underlyingly identical, may be inappropriate. We have already seen that the numbers of observations for the three levels of `Aux` differ widely. More importantly, there are also substantial differences in their variances:

95% family–wise confidence level

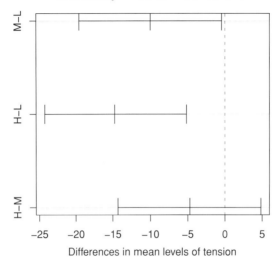

Figure 4.15. *Family-wise 95% confidence intervals for Tukey's honestly significant difference for the* warpbreaks *data. The significant differences are those for which the confidence intervals do not intersect the dashed zero line.*

```
> tapply(auxiliaries$VerbalSynsets, auxiliaries$Aux, var)
   hebben      zijn   zijnheb
 5.994165 18.066667 11.503932
```

It is crucial, therefore, to check whether a non-parametric test also provides support for differences in the number of synsets for verbs with different auxiliaries. The test we illustrate here is the KRUSKAL-WALLIS RANK SUM TEST:

```
> kruskal.test(auxiliaries$VerbalSynsets, auxiliaries$Aux)
        Kruskal-Wallis rank sum test
data:  auxiliaries$VerbalSynsets and auxiliaries$Aux
Kruskal-Wallis chi-squared = 11.7206, df = 2, p-value = 0.002850
```

The small *p*-value supports our intuition that the numbers of synsets are not uniformly distributed over the three kinds of verbs.

4.4.1   Two numerical vectors and a factor: analysis of covariance

In this section, we return to the analysis of the mean size ratings. What we have done thus far is to analyze these data either with linear regression (the first example in section 4.3.2) or with analysis of variance (section 4.4). In linear regression, we used a numerical vector as predictor; in analysis of variance, the predictor was a factor. The technical term for analyses with both numeric predictors and factorial predictors is ANALYSIS OF COVARIANCE. In R, the same function lm() is used for all three kinds of analyses (regression, analysis of variance, and analysis of covariance), as all three are built on the same fundamental principles.

Recall that we observed a nonlinear relation between familiarity and size rating, and that we fitted a linear model with a quadratic term to the subset of nouns denoting plants. We could fit a separate regression model to the subset of nouns denoting animals, but what we really need is a model that tailors the regression lines to both subsets of nouns simultaneously. This is accomplished in the following linear model, in which we include both `meanFamiliarity` and the factor `Class` as predictors:

```
> ratings.lm = lm(meanSizeRating ~ meanFamiliarity * Class +
+ I(meanFamiliarity^2), data = ratings)
> summary(ratings.lm)
Coefficients:
                               Estimate Std. Error t value Pr(>|t|)
(Intercept)                     4.42894    0.54787   8.084  7.6e-12
meanFamiliarity                -0.63131    0.29540  -2.137  0.03580
I(meanFamiliarity^2)            0.10971    0.03801   2.886  0.00508
Classplant                     -1.01248    0.41530  -2.438  0.01711
meanFamiliarity:Classplant     -0.21179    0.09779  -2.166  0.03346
---
Residual standard error: 0.3424 on 76 degrees of freedom
Multiple R-Squared: 0.8805,     Adjusted R-squared: 0.8742
F-statistic:    140 on 4 and 76 DF,  p-value: < 2.2e-16
```

Let's consider the elements of this model by working through the table of coefficients. As usual, there is an intercept, which represents a modified group mean for the subset of nouns denoting animals. We are dealing with a modified group mean because this mean is calibrated for words with zero `meanFamiliarity`. As familiarity ratings range between 1 and 7 in this experiment, this group mean is a theoretical construct. The next two coefficients define the nonlinear effect of `meanFamiliarity`, one for the linear term, and one for the quadratic term. These coefficients likewise concern the subset of nouns for animals.

The last two coefficients summarize how the preceding coefficients should be modified in order to make them more precise for the nouns that fall into the `plant` category. The coefficient of `Classplant` tells us that we should subtract -1.012 from the intercept in order to obtain the (modified) group mean for the plants. The final coefficient, `meanFamiliarity:Classplant`, tells us that the coefficient for `meanFamiliarity` should be decreased by -0.212 in order to make it precise for the plants. This last coefficient illustrates what is referred to as an INTERACTION, in this case an interaction between `meanFamiliarity` and `Class`. In the formula that we specified for `lm()`, this interaction was specified by means of the asterisk:

```
meanFamiliarity * Class
```

This is shorthand for

```
meanFamiliarity + Class + meanFamiliarity:Class
```

where the colon specifies the interaction of the predictors to its left and right. In the table of coefficients, all terms in the model are spelled out separately, including the interaction of `meanFamiliarity` by `Class`:

`meanFamiliarity:Classplant`

Since `meanFamiliarity` is a numeric vector, its name appears as such in the interaction. `Class`, by contrast, is a factor, and therefore the level to which the interaction applies is added to the factor name.

What the interaction tells us is that the linear coefficient of `meanFamiliarity` has to be adjusted downwards when dealing with plants rather than with animals. For animals, this coefficient is -0.631, for plants, we add the coefficient for the interaction of `meanFamiliarity` by `Class` to this coefficient: -0.631 $-0.212 = -0.843$. In other words, the linear term of `meanFamiliarity` differs for plants and animals. As there is no adjustment of the quadratic term in this model, the plants and animals share its coefficient (0.109).

Figure 4.16 shows what we have accomplished. We have a group difference between the plants and the animals (the plants have lower size ratings), we have a nonlinear functional relation between the ratings for familiarity and size, and we have fine-tuned the curves for plants and animals by adjusting the linear term only. It is left as an exercise to show that an adjustment to the squared term is not necessary. The present model is both parsimonious and adequate.

A first step for producing Figure 4.16 is to add the values for the mean size ratings that are predicted by the model to the data frame. These predicted values, often referred to as the FITTED values, are extracted from the model object with the function `fitted()`:

```
> ratings$fitted = fitted(ratings.lm)
```

As before, we set up the axes and plot the data points for plants and animals separately:

```
> plot(ratings$meanFamiliarity, ratings$meanSizeRating,
+ xlab = "mean familiarity", ylab = "mean size rating", type = "n")
> text(ratings$meanFamiliarity, ratings$meanSizeRating,
+ substr(as.character(ratings$Class), 1, 1), col = "darkgrey")
```

With `substr()` we extracted the first letter of the names of the factor levels. Its second argument specifies the first position of the substring that is to be extracted from the string (or vector of strings) supplied as first argument. Its third argument specifies the last position in the string that is to be extracted. We proceed with creating separate data frames for the plants and the animals,

```
> plants = ratings[ratings$Class == "plant", ]
> animals = ratings[ratings$Class == "animal", ]
```

which we sort by meanFamiliarity:

```
> plants = plants[order(plants$meanFamiliarity),]
> animals = animals[order(animals$meanFamiliarity),]
```

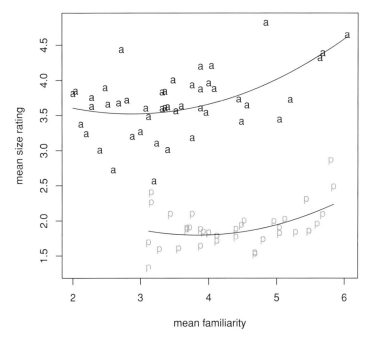

Figure 4.16. *Analysis of covariance for size rating as a function of Class (plant versus animal) and familiarity rating.*

As the vectors of the X and Y values are now in the appropriate order to serve as input to lines(), we finally add the regression curves to the plot:

```
> lines(plants$meanFamiliarity, plants$fitted)
> lines(animals$meanFamiliarity, animals$fitted)
```

4.5   Two vectors with counts

The examples in the preceding sections concerned various kinds of measurements resulting in real numbers. When you are dealing with counts (integers) instead of measurements, different techniques are called for. Continuing with the data set of Dutch verbs (auxiliaries), we cross-tabulate the verbs by regularity and auxiliary choice:

```
> xt = xtabs(~ Aux + Regularity, data = auxiliaries)
> xt
          Regularity
Aux         irregular regular
  hebben           94     118
  zijn             12       3
  zijnheb          36      22
```

Recall that tables with proportions by row or by column are obtained with prop.table(),

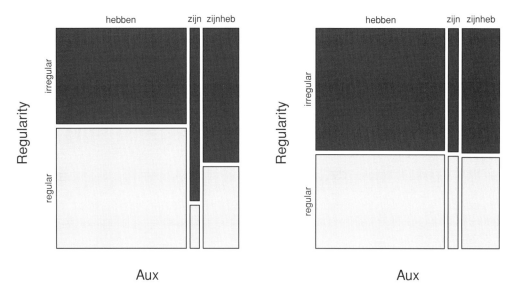

Figure 4.17. *Mosaic plots for Dutch verbs cross-classified by regularity and auxiliary (left panel) and a fictitious data set (right panel).*

```
> prop.table(xt, 1)        # rows add up to 1
          Regularity
Aux        irregular       regular
  hebben  0.4433962     0.5566038
  zijn    0.8000000     0.2000000
  zijnheb 0.6206897     0.3793103
> prop.table(xt, 2)        # columns add up to 1
          Regularity
Aux        irregular       regular
  hebben  0.6619718     0.8251748
  zijn    0.0845070     0.0209790
  zijnheb 0.2535211     0.1538462
```

and that the overall proportions are calculated by dividing the table by its sum:

```
> xt/sum(xt)
          Regularity
Aux        irregular    regular
  hebben  0.32982456 0.41403509
  zijn    0.04210526 0.01052632
  zijnheb 0.12631579 0.07719298
```

There are more regular verbs with `hebben` than irregular verbs, while there are more irregular verbs with `zijn` compared to regular verbs. This difference is clearly visible in the mosaic plot shown in the left panel of Figure 4.17:

```
> mosaicplot(xt, col=TRUE)
```

The mosaic plot shows very clearly that the smallest subset of verbs, those selecting *zijn* as auxiliary, are also the verbs with the greatest proportion of irregulars.

Suppose that we had observed the following fictitious counts:

```
> x = data.frame(irregular = c(100, 8, 30),
+ regular = c(77, 6, 22))
> rownames(x) = c("hebben", "zijn", "zijnheb")
> x
          irregular  regular
hebben          100       77
zijn              8        6
zijnheb          30       22
```

The mosaic plot of these counts, shown in the right panel of Figure 4.17, shows that the six blocks are divided by nearly straight horizontal and vertical lines. The proportions of verbs that are regular are approximately the same across all three classes of auxiliaries. Similarly, the proportions of verbs with a given auxiliary are very similar across regulars and irregulars. The counts in the various rows are nearly proportional, and the same holds for the columns.

The mosaic plots of Figure 4.17 suggest that there is reason for surprise for the actual data, but not for the artificial counts. Formal tests for the presence of non-proportionalities in contingency tables are the chi-squared test and Fisher's exact test of independence. The chi-squared test is carried out with chisq.test(), the same function that we encountered previously. It is also reported when the output of xtabs() is summarized:

```
> chisq.test(xt)
        Pearson's Chi-squared test
data:  xt
X-squared = 11.4929, df = 2, p-value = 0.003194
> summary(xt)
Call: xtabs(formula = ~Aux + Regularity, data = auxiliaries)
Number of cases in table: 285
Number of factors: 2
Test for independence of all factors:
        Chisq = 11.493, df = 2, p-value = 0.003194
```

The small *p*-value suggests that the counts in the two columns (or rows) are indeed not proportional given the total number of observations in each row (or column). Applied to the artificial data, we obtain a large *p*-value, as expected:

```
> chisq.test(x)
        Pearson's Chi-squared test
data:  x
X-squared = 0.0241, df = 2, p-value = 0.988
```

For tables with not too large counts, a test of independence of rows (or columns) that produces more precise *p*-values is FISHER'S EXACT TEST:

```
> fisher.test(xt)
        Fisher's Exact Test for Count Data
data:  xt
p-value = 0.002885
alternative hypothesis: two.sided
```

For this example, the exact probability (given the row and column totals) is slightly smaller than the probability as estimated using the chi-squared test.

4.6   A note on statistical significance

When a statistical test returns a statistically significant p-value, this does not imply that the tested effect is actually useful. The smaller the p-value is, the more likely it is that the effect is replicable. But the magnitude of the effect can be so small as to be useless for practical applications. By way of example, we simulate regression data, with $n = 100$ equally spaced x-coordinates, and y-coordinates that are one-third of the x-coordinates with substantial RANDOM NOISE superimposed. The random noise is obtained by adding, to each y-value, a random number from a normal distribution with mean 0 and a standard deviation of 80:

```
> n = 100
> x = seq(1, 100, length = n)
> y = 0.3 * x + rnorm(n, 0, 80)
```

A simulation run will typically produce non-significant results, such as:

```
> model100 = lm(y ~ x)
> summary(model100)$coef
               Estimate Std. Error    t value  Pr(>|t|)
(Intercept) -4.5578443 16.7875448 -0.2715015 0.7865764
x            0.4621986  0.2886052  1.6014910 0.1124869
```

Although there is a linear relation between y and x — we built it into the data set ourselves — the amount of noise that we superimposed is so large that we cannot detect it. A way around this is to increase the number of observations:

```
> n = 1000
> x = seq(1, 100, length = n)
> y = 0.3 * x + rnorm(n, 0, 80)
> model1000 = lm(y ~ x)
> summary(model1000)
Coefficients:
             Estimate Std. Error t value Pr(>|t|)
(Intercept) -2.30845    4.90536  -0.471 0.638031
x            0.30795    0.08452   3.644 0.000283

Residual standard error: 76.46 on 998 degrees of freedom
Multiple R-Squared: 0.01313,    Adjusted R-squared: 0.01214
F-statistic: 13.28 on 1 and 998 DF,  p-value: 0.0002827
```

The effect of x is now significant. However, even at this sample size it is virtually impossible to predict y from x. This is immediately evident from the scatterplot shown in Figure 4.18,

```
> plot(x, y)
> abline(lm(y ~ x))
```

and it is also indicated by the very small value of R^2: the regression model explains a mere 1% of the variance.

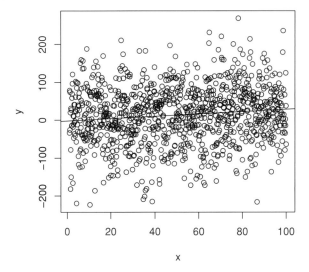

Figure 4.18. *Simulated regression data with significant p-value (p < 0.01) and no explanatory value (R² = 0.008).*

In order to assess the magnitude of an effect, *p*-values are clearly not appropriate. From a rather pessimistic point of view, a *p*-value merely reflects the sample size. To this, we should add that the null-hypothesis is often nothing more than a straw man. If we want to ascertain the effect of a given predictor that is worth running an experiment for, it is rather unlikely that we are truly interested in knowing whether its coefficient is *exactly* zero or *not* exactly zero. What we are more likely to be interested in is how close the predictor is to zero. Therefore, confidence intervals are at least as important as *p*-values, because they inform us straightforwardly about how different our estimated coefficient actually is from zero. For the above two regression models, we obtain the confidence intervals for the coefficients with the help of the function `confint()`:

```
> confint(model100)
                  2.5 %      97.5 %
(Intercept) -37.872181  28.756492
x            -0.110529   1.034926
> confint(model1000)
                   2.5 %     97.5 %
(Intercept) -11.9344605  7.317552
x             0.1420982  0.473801
```

For the model with 100 observations, we have a wide confidence interval that straddles zero. We can also see that the coefficient is more likely to be positive than negative. This is confirmed by the model with 1000 observations, which has a confidence interval that is much smaller and hence also more informative about the slope that we built into the model (0.3).

Whether a slope of 0.3 is meaningful and has any practical or theoretical significance remains an open question that can only be resolved given sufficient background information about the nature and the purposes of the experiment that is being evaluated statistically. For instance, Frauenfelder *et al.* (1993) showed that a word's frequency of use is a significant predictor for the density of its similarity neighborhood. For practical applications this result is pretty useless in the light of the very low R^2 of the regression model. However, from a certain theoretical perspective, the presence of this correlation is in fact expected, and the fact that the correlation is weak is not at all surprising. Similarly, in reaction time experiments, the amount of the total variance explained by linguistic predictors tends to be minute compared to the variance that is tied to the participants and their response execution, i.e. variance that is due to a very noisy measurement technique. Even though effects may be tiny, if they consistently replicate across experiments and laboratories, they may nevertheless be informative for theories of lexical representation and processing.

Workbook section

Exercises

1. In Chapter 1, we made a contingency table cross-tabulating the animacy of the recipient and the realization of the recipient for the subset of English verbs in the data set of Bresnan and colleagues that had inanimate themes. The following commands recreate this table:

   ```
   > verbs.xtabs = xtabs( ~ AnimacyOfRec + RealizationOfRec,
   + data = verbs[verbs$AnimacyOfTheme != "animate", ])
   > verbs.xtabs
                    RealizationOfRec
   AnimacyOfRec       NP  PP
       animate       517 300
       inanimate      33  47
   ```

   Animate recipients seem to have a slight preference for the NP realization, inanimate recipients for the PP realization. Evaluate whether this asymmetry is statistically significant.

2. In section 3.2, we visualized the density of the frequency of the determiner *het* in the Dutch novel *Max Havelaar* (see Figure 3.5). Are the frequencies in the vector `havelaar$Frequency` Poisson-distributed?

3. Pluymaekers *et al.* (2005) studied the acoustic durations of affixes in derived Dutch words. The data for the prefix *ge-* are available in the data set `durationsGe`. The `DurationOfPrefix` is the dependent variable, `Frequency` is the key predictor:

   ```
   > colnames(durationsGe, 3)
   [1] "Word"              "Frequency"         "Speaker"
   [4] "Sex"               "YearOfBirth"       "DurationOfPrefix"
   [7] "SpeechRate"        "NumberSegmentsOnset"
   ```

   The general question of interest is whether the frequency with which a word is used codetermines the durations of its constituent morphemes. Is the same morpheme, here *ge-*, shorter in higher-frequency words? Address this question by means of a regression model. Keep in mind that you should carefully check whether the distributions of the predictors are roughly symmetrical and take appropriate measures if not so before fitting the model to the data.

4. Show that an interaction of `Class` by the squared term of `meanFamiliarity` is superfluous for the covariance model discussed for the `ratings` data in section 4.4.1.

5. The exercise accompanying Chapter 3 addressed the frequency distributions for three words in *Alice's Adventures in Wonderland*: `alice`, `very`, and `hare`. Use the Kolmogorov-Smirnov test to test formally whether these words follow a Poisson distribution.

6. Run a one-way analysis of variance to ascertain whether naming latencies in the `english` data set differ for the young and old age groups in the data on English monomorphemic and monosyllabic nouns and verbs. Age group is labeled as `Age Subject`, the (log) naming latencies are labeled `RTnaming`. What is (in log units) the difference between the group means for the young and old subjects? What are the two group means?

7. The Dutch prefix *ont-* is subject to acoustic reduction in spontaneous speech. For instance, the plosive or the nasal may not be present in the speech signal. Pluymaekers *et al.* (2005) measured the acoustic durations of the vowel, the nasal, and the plosive of this prefix in derived words extracted from a corpus of spoken Dutch. Carry out an analysis of covariance to investigate whether the duration of the nasal is affected by the word's frequency and the presence of the plosive. Exclude the five outlier words for which the nasal was absent from the data in `durationsOnt`.

5   Clustering and classification

The previous chapter introduced various techniques for analyzing data with one or two vectors. The remaining chapters of this book discuss various ways of dealing with data sets with more than two vectors. Data sets with many vectors are typically brought together in matrices. These matrices list the observations on the rows, with the vectors (column variables) specifying the different properties of the observations. Data sets like this are referred to as multivariate data.

There are two approaches for discovering the structure in multivariate data sets that we discuss in this chapter. In one approach, we seek to find structure in the data in terms of groupings of observations. These techniques are UNSUPERVISED in the sense that we do not prescribe what groupings should be there. We discuss these techniques under the heading of CLUSTERING. In the other approach, we know what groups there are in theory, and the question is whether the data support these groups. This second group of techniques can be described as SUPERVISED, because the techniques work with a grouping that is imposed by the analyst on the data. We will refer to these techniques as methods for CLASSIFICATION.

5.1   Clustering

5.1.1   Tables with measurements: principal components analysis

Words such as *goodness* and *sharpness* can be analyzed as consisting of a stem, *good, sharp*, and an affix, the suffix *-ness*. Some affixes are used in many words, *-ness* is an example. Other affixes occur only in a limited number of words, for instance, the *-th* in *warmth* and *strength*. The extent to which affixes are used and available for the creation of new words is referred to as the productivity of the affix. Baayen (1994) addressed the question of the extent to which the productivity of an affix is codetermined by stylistic factors. Do different kinds of texts favor the use of different kinds of affixes?

The data set `affixProductivity` lists, for 44 texts with varying authors and genres, a productivity index for 27 derivational affixes. The 44 texts represent four different text types: religious texts (e.g. the *Book of Mormon*, coded B), books written for children (e.g. *Alice's Adventures in Wonderland*, coded C), literary texts (e.g. novels by Austen, Conrad, James, coded L), and other texts (including officialese from the US government accounting office), coded O. The classification codes are given in the column labeled `Registers`:

```
> affixProductivity[c("Mormon", "Austen", "Carroll", "Gao"), c(5:10, 29)]
            ian    ful      y   ness    able     ly Registers
Mormon     0 0.1887 0.5660 2.0755 0.0000 2.2642         B
Austen     0 1.2891 1.5654 1.6575 1.0129 6.2615         L
Carroll    0 0.2717 1.0870 0.2717 0.4076 6.3859         C
Gao        0 0.3306 1.9835 0.8264 0.8264 4.4628         O
```

The question of interest is whether there is any structure in this 44 by 27 table of numbers that sheds light on the relation between productivity and style. The tool that we will use here is PRINCIPAL COMPONENTS ANALYSIS.

In order to understand the main idea underlying principal components analysis, consider Figure 5.1. The upper left panel shows a cube, and the grey coloring of the cube indicates that data points are spread out everywhere in the cube. In order

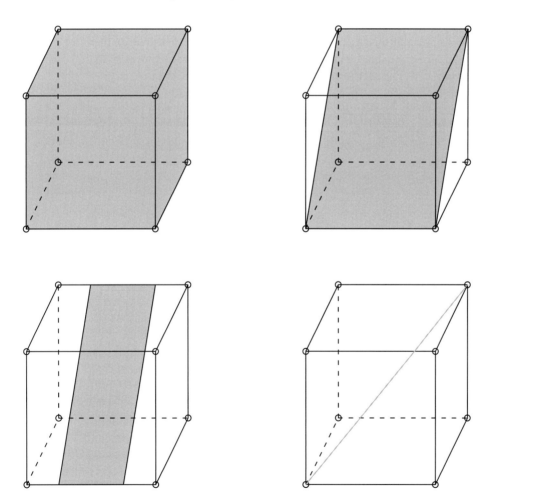

Figure 5.1. *Different distributions of points (highlighted in grey) in a cube.*

to describe a point in the cube, we need all three axes. The cube in the upper right describes the situation in which all the points are located on the grey plane. We could describe the location of a point on this plane using the three axes of the cube. But we can also choose new axes in this plane, in which case we can still describe each and every relevant point. This description is more economical, as it dispenses with the superfluous third dimension. The cube in the lower left panel also involves a plane, but now there is more variation (a greater range of values) in the Y and Z direction than in the X direction. The final cube depicts the case where all the points are located on a line. To describe the location of these points, a single axis (the line through these points) is sufficient. Here, we have only one dimension left.

What principal components analysis does is try to reduce the number of dimensions required for locating the approximate positions of the data points. For the upper left cube, this is impossible. For the upper right cube, this is possible: we can get rid of one dimension. The way in which principal components achieves this is by rotating the axes in such a way that you get two new axes in the diagonal plane of the original, unrotated, axes. If you imagine the points to be fixed in their location, while the cube itself can be moved around, then what happens is that the cube is rotated so that all the data points are lying on the bottom.

In the case of the lower left panel of Figure 5.1, principal components analysis will rotate the cube so that all the points are on its floor. It will then choose the dimension with most variation as its first axis (named principal component 1, henceforth PC1), in this example the axis going up and back. The second axis (PC2) will be, in this example, the original X axis. The third axis of the rotated cube (PC3) is one we don't need anymore, as it does not account for any variability in the data.

Of course, this example simplifies what happens in real data sets. It rarely happens that all data points are exactly on a plane, there is nearly always a little scatter around the plane. And instead of three dimensions, there may be many more dimensions, and the plane around which points cluster may be a hyperplane instead of a standard two-dimensional plane. But the key idea remains the same: we rotate our hypercube, and work with a reduced set of dimensions, ordered by how much variability they account for.

Returning to our data, we can regard the 44 texts as 44 points in a 27-dimensional space. Do we need all these 27 dimensions, or can we reduce the number of dimensions to a (much) smaller number? And do these new dimensions tell us something about how affixes are used in different kinds of texts?

Let's consider how we can address this question with the function `prcomp()`, which requires a matrix (or a data frame, but then only the numerical columns in that data frame) as input. As the last two columns of our data frame `affixes` contain descriptions of labels for authors and text types, we select only columns `1:27` as input:

```
> affixes.pr = prcomp(affixProductivity[, 1:(ncol(affixProductivity)-3)])
```

We now have created a principal components object that has several components, as shown when we request a list of the names of these components with the function names():

```
> names(affixes.pr)
[1] "sdev"      "rotation" "center"   "scale"     "x"
```

Let's consider these components step by step. The first component, sdev, is the standard deviation corresponding to each PC:

```
> round(affixes.pr$sdev, 4)
 [1] 1.8598 1.1068 0.5395 0.5320 0.4343 0.4095 0.3778
 [9] 0.3303 0.2952 0.2574 0.2270 0.2113 0.1893 0.1617 0.1503
[17] 0.1265 0.1126 0.1039 0.0870 0.0742 0.0674 0.0585 0.0429
[25] 0.0260 0.0098 0.0087
```

The summary() also lists these standard deviations (only part of the output is shown):

```
> summary(affixes.pr)
Importance of components:
                          PC1    PC2     PC3     PC4     PC5     PC6
Standard deviation      1.860  1.107 0.7044 0.5395 0.5320 0.4343
Proportion of Variance  0.512  0.181 0.0734 0.0431 0.0419 0.0279
Cumulative Proportion   0.512  0.693 0.7663 0.8094 0.8512 0.8791
  ...
                          PC23    PC24   PC25    PC26    PC27
Standard deviation      0.05853 0.04292 0.0260 0.00977 0.00872
Proportion of Variance  0.00051 0.00027 0.0001 0.00001 0.00001
Cumulative Proportion   0.99960 0.99987 1.0000 0.99999 1.00000
```

The proportions of variance are simply the squared standard deviations divided by the sum of the squared standard deviations, compare:

```
> props = round((affixes.pr$sdev^2/sum(affixes.pr$sdev^2)), 3)
> props[1:6]
[1] 0.512 0.181 0.073 0.043 0.042 0.028
```

The first principal component explains more than half of the variance; the last component has no explanatory value whatsoever. The question we now have to address is which dimensions are relevant, and which irrelevant. There is a rule of thumb stating that only those principal components are important that account for at least 5% of the variance. Figure 5.2 plots the proportions of variance accounted for by the principal components, the "significant" components are shown in black:

```
> barplot(props, col = as.numeric(props > 0.05),
+ xlab = "principal components",
+ ylab = "proportion of variance explained")
> abline(h = 0.05)
```

A very similar plot is obtained with:

```
> plot(affixes.pr)
```

Another rule of thumb is to locate the cutoff point where there is a clear discontinuity as you move from right to left. In the present example, the first

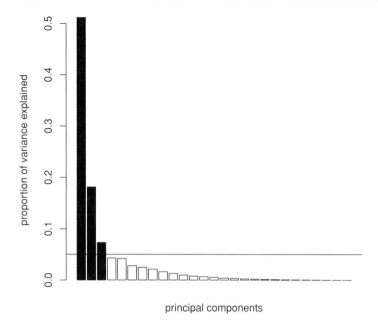

Figure 5.2. *Screeplot for the principal components analysis of texts in affix productivity space.*

minor discontinuity is at the fifth PC, and the first large discontinuity at the third PC. From the summary, we learn that we can reduce 27 dimensions to 3 dimensions without losing much of the structure in the data: the first three PCs jointly account for slightly more than three-quarters of the variance (76.6%). In other words, with just three dimensions, we can already get very close to the location of our 44 texts in the original 27-dimensional productivity space.

The coordinates of the texts in the new three-dimensional space spanned by the new axes, the first three principal components, are available in the component of affixes.pr labeled x. This component lists the coordinates on all 27 PCs; here we only need the first three:

```
> affixes.pr$x[c("Mormon", "Austen", "Carroll", "Gao"), 1:3]

                   PC1         PC2         PC3
  Mormon   -3.7613247   1.5552693   1.4117837
  Austen   -0.1745206  -1.5247233   0.3285241
  Carroll   0.3363524   1.5711792  -0.2937536
  Gao      -1.8250509  -0.8581186  -1.2897237
```

Figure 5.3 plots the texts in this three-dimensional space by means of a scatter-plot matrix displaying all three pairs of combinations of PCs. You can think of this as looking into a cube from three different sides: once from the top, once from the front, and once from the side. We can observe some clustering, especially in the panel for PC1 and PC2 (first panel of second row). The literary

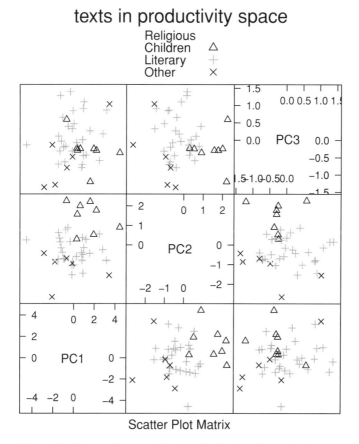

Figure 5.3. *Scatterplot matrix for the distribution of texts in the space spanned by the three first principal components of affix productivity scores.*

texts are in the center, the religious texts in the upper left, the texts for children are more to the lower right, and the officialese tends towards the bottom of the graph.

Visualization with scatterplot matrices is an important part of exploratory data analysis with principal components analysis. Figure 5.3 was made with a trellis function, `splom()` (for **scatterplot m**atrices). This is a powerful function with many options that are explained in the on-line help. We first load the `lattice` package:

```
> library(lattice)
```

The next line of code figures out about how points should be represented in terms of plot symbols and color coding. If you are using the R graphics window, it will figure out to use color coding. If you are saving the plot as PostScript or jpeg, it will use plotting symbols in black and white instead:

```
> super.sym = trellis.par.get("superpose.symbol")
```

The plot itself can now be produced with the following lines of code:

```
> splom(data.frame(affixes.pr$x[,1:3]),
+ groups = affixProductivity$Registers,
+  panel  = panel.superpose,
+  key    = list(
+     title  = "texts in productivity space",
+     text   = list(c("Religious", "Children",
+                     "Literary", "Other")),
+     points = list(pch = super.sym$pch[1:4],
+                   col = super.sym$col[1:4]))))
```

A third important component of a principal components object is the rotation matrix, which looks like this:

```
> dim(affixes.pr$rotation)
[1] 27 27
> affixes.pr$rotation[1:10, 1:3]
              PC1           PC2           PC3           PC4
semi  0.0018753121 -0.001359615  0.003074151 -0.0033841237
anti -0.0003107270 -0.002017771 -0.002695399  0.0005929162
ee   -0.0019930399  0.001106277 -0.017102260 -0.0033997410
ism   0.0087251807 -0.046360929  0.046553003  0.0300832267
ian  -0.0459376905 -0.008605163 -0.010271978 -0.0937441773
ful   0.0334764289  0.013734791  0.010000845 -0.0966573851
y     0.1113180755 -0.043908360 -0.276324337 -0.5719405630
ness  0.0297280626 -0.112768134  0.700249340 -0.1374734621
able  0.0084568997 -0.124364821  0.012313097  0.1119376764
ly    0.9729027985 -0.111160032 -0.020500850  0.1585457448
```

This matrix lists the LOADINGS of the affixes on each principal component. These loadings are proportional to the correlation of the original productivity values of an affix with the PC. Therefore, you can get some idea of what a PC might indicate by looking at which affixes have large positive or negative loadings. For instance, the suffix *-ly* (as in *badly*) has a very high positive loading on PC1 compared to the other affixes shown above.

What makes principal components analysis attractive is the insights offered when we plot affixes and texts together in a BIPLOT. As you can see in Figure 5.4, the variation on PC1 is dominated by the suffix *-ly*, which seems to have been favored especially in the Barrie novel. There is somewhat more diversification on PC2. Comparatives and superlatives are somewhat more characteristic for texts with high values on PC2, such as Kipling, Carroll, and Grimm. On the other hand, *-ation* emerges as characteristic for the Federalist papers and also the texts by James and Austen.

The biplot shown in Figure 5.4 is obtained with the `biplot()` function, which in its simplest form simply takes the principal components object as input. Here, we make use of a number of options to fine-tune the plot:

```
> biplot(affixes.pr,  scale = 0, var.axes = F,
+ col = c("darkgrey", "black"),  cex = c(0.9, 1.2))
```

By default, `biplot()` rescales the principal components and the loadings. This rescaling is disabled with `scale = 0`. I have also disabled the displaying of

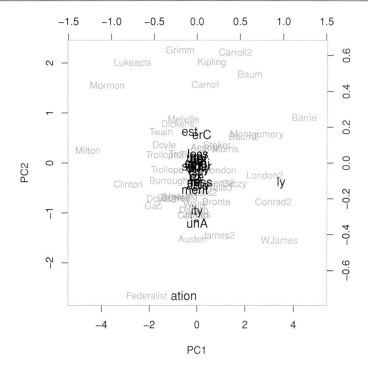

Figure 5.4. *Biplot with principal components* 1 *and* 2 *for authors in productivity space, and the loadings of the affixes on these principal components.*

arrows pointing to the affixes with `var.axes = F`. The parameter `col` controls the colors for the texts (dark grey) and the affixes (black), and the parameter `cex` controls the font sizes. Note that the primary coordinate system (bottom and left axes) represents the principal compononts, and that the secondary coordinate system (upper and right axes) represents the corresponding loadings.

When carrying out a principal components analysis, there are two things that should be kept in mind. First, the variables should have reasonably symmetrical distributions. Second, and more importantly, it is almost always advisable to scale the columns. If the columns contain variables with very different ranges, then the columns with the greatest ranges may dominate the results. We have seen for the present data that two affixes dominate the first two principal components, *-ly* on PC1 and *-ation* on PC2. This lopsided effect of a few variables is avoided by running the `prcomp()` function with the option `scale = TRUE`. Technically, this amounts to running the analysis not on the covariance matrix, but on the correlation matrix. The upper panel of Figure 5.5 shows the biplot for a principal components analysis when the correlation matrix is used:

```
> affixes.pr = prcomp(affixProductivity[ ,1:27], scale = T, center = T)
> biplot(affixes.pr, var.axes = F, col = c("darkgrey", "black"),
+ cex = c(0.6, 1), xlim = c(-0.42, 0.38))
```

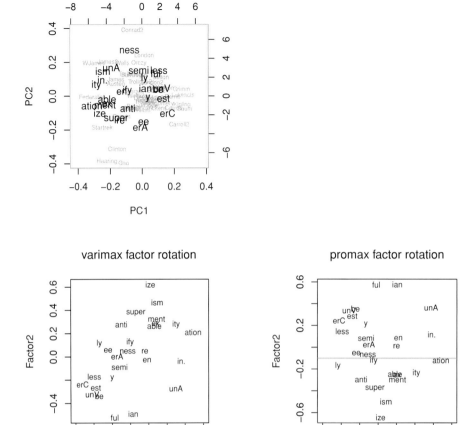

Figure 5.5. *Upper panel: Biplot for the principal components analysis of texts and affixes based on productivity scores, now using the correlation matrix instead of the covariance matrix. Lower panel: The loadings of the affixes on the first two factors in a factor analysis using varimax (left) and promax factor rotation.*

The loadings of the affixes now reveal more interesting structure. Native affixes (e.g. *-ness*, *-less*, *-er*) tend to occur more in the upper and right parts of the plot. Non-native affixes (e.g. *-ation, super-, anti-*) tend to occur in the lower left of the biplot. The use of non-native affixes is more typical for officialese (e.g. congress hearings (Hearing)) and formal texts such as the Federalist papers. Native affixes are more typical for, for instance, the stories for children by Carroll and Baum. In other words, non-native affixes are more productive in more formal and educated registers.

5.1.2   Tables with measurements: factor analysis

An extension of principal components analysis is EXPLORATORY FACTOR ANALYSIS. Factor analysis has been used extensively by Biber (1988, 1995) to study register variation. Factor analysis also plays a key role in an important technique for corpus-based computational semantics, latent semantic analysis (Landauer and Dumais, 1997).

In principal components analysis, the total variance is partitioned among the PCs. Therefore, the proportion of variance explained by a PC is given by that PC's variance divided by the summed variance of all PCs, as we saw above. In factor analysis, however, an error term is added to the model in order to do justice to the possibility that there is noise in the data. As a consequence, there is no unique set of principal components (now called factors) and loadings. Instead, various alternative factors (and loadings) are available thanks to a technique called FACTOR ROTATION. Factor rotation serves the purpose of making the interpretation of the factor model as simple as possible. Interpretation becomes more straightforward if the variables have high loadings on only a few factors, and if the loadings on a given dimension are either large or near zero.

To make this more concrete, we carry out a factor analysis on the productivity data with the function factanal(). This function expects the user to specify how many factors are required. We choose three, and summarize the resulting object by typing its name at the R prompt:

```
> affixes.fac = factanal(affixProductivity[ ,1:27], factors = 3)
> affixes.fac

Call:
factanal(x = affixes[, 1:27], factors = 3)

Uniquenesses:
 semi  anti    ee   ism   ian   ful     y  ness ...
0.865 0.909 0.934 0.244 0.705 0.688 0.964 0.633 ...

Loadings:
        Factor1 Factor2 Factor3
semi                     0.348
anti             0.278
ee                      -0.246
ism      0.493   0.467   0.543
ian      0.229  -0.490
ful             -0.522   0.196
y               -0.184
...
est     -0.180  -0.266  -0.126
ment     0.486   0.324  -0.139
ify      0.196   0.126
re       0.359          -0.372
ation    0.888   0.211  -0.269
in       0.758           0.134
ex       0.476   0.284  -0.108
en       0.382          -0.127
be      -0.142  -0.336   0.107

                Factor1 Factor2 Factor3
SS loadings       4.186   2.242   1.853
Proportion Var    0.155   0.083   0.069
```

```
Cumulative Var     0.155     0.238     0.307

Test of the hypothesis that 3 factors are sufficient.
The chi square statistic is 308.11 on 273 degrees of freedom.
The p-value is 0.0707
```

The summary repeats the original function call, and then reports the uniquenesses for the affixes, the by-affix amounts of error variance. Next, the factor loadings are listed. Loadings that are too close to zero are not shown. The table of loadings is followed by a table reporting the proportions of variance explained by the factors. Finally, a test is reporting for whether three factors are sufficient for this data. As the associated p-value is greater than 0.05, we conclude that we do not need more factors for this data set.

The lower left panel of Figure 5.5 plots the loadings of the affixes on the first two factors:

```
> loadings = loadings(affixes.fac)
> plot(loadings, type = "n", xlim = c(-0.4, 1))
> text(loadings, rownames(loadings), cex = 0.8)
```

From this plot, the distinction between native and non-native affixes emerges perhaps more clearly than from the biplot in the upper panel. Non-native affixes tend to the upper right part of the plot, native affixes cluster more to the lower left. In other words, nativeness is a hidden, LATENT, variable determining affixal productivity, but thus far it is expressed by means of two factors. By choosing a different factor rotation, promax, we can rearrange the affixes such that nativeness is expressed primarily by the second factor, as shown in the lower right panel of Figure 5.5:

```
> affixes.fac2 = factanal(affixProductivity[ ,1:27], factors = 3,
+ rotation = "promax")
> loadings2 = loadings(affixes.fac2)
> plot(loadings2, type = "n", xlim = c(-0.4, 1))
> text(loadings2, rownames(loadings))
> abline(h = -0.1, col = "darkgrey")
```

Most non-native affixes are located below the horizontal grey line; most native affixes are found above this line.

There are no hard and fast rules for choosing a particular kind of rotation. The varimax rotation builds on the assumption that the rotated factors are uncorrelated. It is preferentially used when we are interested primarily in the generalizability of the results. The promax rotation allows the factors to be correlated, and tends to be selected when the primary concern is to obtain a factor model that provides a close fit to the data.

5.1.3   Tables with counts: correspondence analysis

In the preceding sections we used principal components analysis and factor analysis for analyzing a two-way table of measurements (i.e. real-valued numbers). For two-way contingency tables, correspondence analysis provides an attractive alternative. Like principal components analysis, correspondence analysis seeks to provide a low-dimensional map of the data.

The correspondence map is made in two steps. First, two matrices of distances are calculated, one for the distances between columns, and one for the distances between rows. In daily life, you may have encountered distance matrices for geographical distances between major cities. The cities are listed in both margins of the table. Hence, a distance matrix is always a square matrix. The distances on the main diagonal are zero, as the distance of a city to itself is zero. Furthermore, the distances above the main diagonal are the flip image of the distances below the main diagonal: A distance matrix is symmetrical. Hence, some distance tables for cities show only the upper or the lower triangle of the distance matrix.

In correspondence analysis, we regard row vectors (or column vectors) as profiles of "cities," and calculate the distances between them. There are many different ways in which distances (or dissimilarities) between vectors can be computed, the on-line help pages for `dist()` document a range of options. The distance measure that is used in correspondence analysis is the so-called chi-squared distance. Given a contingency table with 20 rows and 5 columns, correspondence analysis constructs two distance matrices, a 20 by 20 matrix specifying the distances between the rows, and a 5 by 5 matrix specifying the distances between the columns.

The second step in correspondence analysis is to represent these distances as faithfully as possible in a two-dimensional scatterplot; a low-dimensional map. The larger the distance between two rows, the further these two rows should be apart in the map for rows. Likewise, dissimilar columns should be far apart, while similar columns should be near to each other in the map for columns. In correspondence analysis, we superimpose the row and column maps, analogous to the superposition of the PC scores and the loadings on these PCs in the biplot. Thanks to the chi-squared distance measure, we ensure that proximity between rows and columns in the merged map is as good an approximation as possible of the correlation between rows and columns. The set of functions illustrated in the following examples extend the code of Murtagh (2005).

Ernestus *et al.* (2007) studied register variation and diachronic variation in the use of syntactic constructions in Medieval French. For 29 authors (some of whom are anonymous), and often for several manuscript versions of the same text, the counts of the 35 most frequent tag trigrams (tag triplets) were calculated. Texts with more than 2000 words were subdivided into chunks of 2000 words.

The data of this study are available in the form of two data frames. The `oldFrench` data frame contains the counts of tag trigrams (columns) for 342 texts (rows). The `oldFrench Meta` data frame provides metadata on these texts, including information on author, region of origin, date of composition, register, and topic:

```
> oldFrench[1:3, 1:4]
      T30.16.00 T00.31.51 T16.00.31 T00.60.31
Abe.2        11         2         1         6
Abe.3        13         4         6         5
Abe.4         7         1         4         2
> oldFrenchMeta[1:3, ]
  Textlabels Codes Author Topic Genre Region Year
1        Abe Abe.2   Meun    12 prose     R2 1325
2        Abe Abe.3   Meun    12 prose     R2 1325
3        Abe Abe.4   Meun    12 prose     R2 1325
```

In both data frames, rows represent text fragments. Rows are ordered alphabetically by the codes for the fragments. As a consequence, the information in the two data frames is perfectly aligned. As will become apparent below, this alignment allows us to select subsets of rows from oldFrench using information in oldFrenchMeta with R's subscripting mechanism.

The columns of oldFrench represent the frequencies of the tag trigrams in the text fragments. What we would like to know is whether there are systematic differences in the frequencies of these tag trigrams as a function of author, topic, genre, region, and time. As a first step, we make use of the function corres.fnc(), which takes a data frame with counts as input and produces as output a correspondence analysis object. This object can subsequently be summarized and plotted:

```
> oldFrench.ca = corres.fnc(oldFrench)
```

Let's first inspect the summary. As its output is rather voluminous, we specify head = TRUE, so that only the first six lines of relevant tables are shown:

```
> summary(oldFrench.ca, head = TRUE)

Call:
corres.fnc(oldFrench)

Eigenvalue rates:

    0.1704139 0.1326913 0.06854973 0.05852097 0.05394474  ...

Factor 1

          coordinates correlations contributions
T30.16.00      -0.113        0.074         0.012
T00.31.51      -0.560        0.464         0.103
T16.00.31      -0.139        0.053         0.006
T00.60.31      -0.122        0.050         0.006
T16.00.33      -0.085        0.020         0.003
T02.00.30       0.293        0.227         0.027
...

Factor 2

          coordinates correlations contributions
T30.16.00       0.119        0.082         0.017
T00.31.51       0.205        0.062         0.018
T16.00.31       0.255        0.179         0.024
```

```
    T00.60.31        0.162        0.090        0.014
    T16.00.33       -0.220        0.139        0.029
    T02.00.30        0.166        0.073        0.011
    ...
```

The summary of `oldFrench.ca` begins with listing EIGENVALUE RATES. These rates have a similar interpretation to the proportions of the variance explained by the principal components in principal components analysis. The larger the rate, the more successful a factor is in accounting for differences among the distances between the texts. The first rate pertains to the first factor, the X axis in a correspondence map, the second rate to the second factor, the Y axis in the map. Higher dimensions are seldom considered in correspondence analysis. (For inspection of higher dimensions, specify `n=a` and the summary will display the first a dimensions.)

The summary then proceeds with two tables that specify, for the first two factors, how the distances between the columns relate to the distances between the rows. As we called `summary()` with `head=T`, only the first six tag trigrams are shown. For each tag trigram, its coordinate on the relevant axis is listed first, followed by its correlation with that axis. These correlations, however, are not standard correlations. They are more comparable to the loadings in principal components analysis, and as such they provide an important guide to the interpretation of the dimensions. The final column provides a measure for the extent to which a row (tag trigram) contributes to the explanatory value of the factor.

The attractiveness of correspondence analysis resides in the possibilities it offers for visualization. For instance, we can query whether the difference between prose and poetry is reflected in the frequencies with which particular tag trigrams are used. Figure 5.6 shows that there is a clear separation of prose and poetry on the first factor, which is carried primarily by the tag trigrams `T00.30.01`, `T00.31.51`, and `T51.10.00`.

This correspondence plot has a number of features that are controlled by a range of options. First, the texts of the two genres are shown with different colors. Second, tags are represented with their own font size, and also with another color. Third, we have not shown all 35 tags, which would clutter the center of the plot, but only those tags that drive the separation of the genres. Although,

```
> plot(oldFrench.ca)
```

is sufficient to obtain a correspondence plot, the result, with 342 texts and 35 tag trigrams, is an extremely cluttered scatterplot. We therefore consider the plot method for correspondence objects in some more detail.

It is often useful to plot text properties as specified in the metadata rather than the identifiers of the texts themselves: by default, `plot()` uses the row names of the data frame serving as input to `corres.fnc()` for labeling the row data points in the scatterplot. We override this default with the option for row labels, which we set to point to, for instance, the genre labels in `oldFrenchMeta` by setting `rlabels = oldFrenchMeta$Genre`.

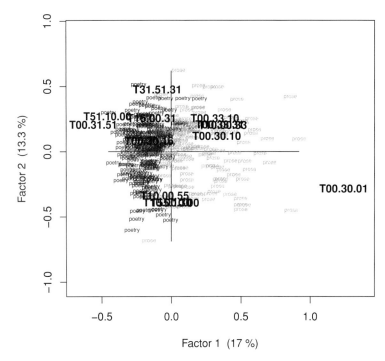

Figure 5.6. *Correspondence analysis of the frequencies of* 35 *tag trigrams in*
342 *Medieval French text fragments. Text fragments are labeled by register
(prose versus poetry); only highly predictive tag trigrams are displayed.*

The option for row colors, `rcol`, allows us to specify different colors for the
levels of `Genre`. This option should point to a vector that specifies, for each row
(text), the color with which it is to be displayed. For instance, we can convert the
factor `oldFrenchMeta$Genre` into a numerical vector with `as.numeric()`.
The first factor level will now be paired with a 1, the second factor level with a 2,
and so on. We then use these numbers as identifiers of colors by setting `rcol =
as.numeric(oldFrenchMeta$Genre)`.

We scale down the row font size with `rcex = 0.5`. As it makes no sense to
add 35 column names to the plot, we restrict the tag trigrams to be shown to those
that have extreme values in the first or last decile on either axis with `extreme =
0.1`. Finally, we set the color for the column names to blue (`ccol = "blue"`).
This completes our plot instructions:

```
> plot(oldFrench.ca, rlabels = oldFrenchMeta$Genre,
+ rcol = as.numeric(oldFrenchMeta$Genre), rcex = 0.5,
+ extreme = 0.1, ccol = "blue")
```

In Figure 5.6, colors have been changed to greyscales, the colors will be shown
on your computer screen when the preceding lines of code are used.

When we zoom in on the prose, we find indications of diachronic change. As a
first step, we exclude those texts for which the approximate date of composition

is not known. Because the rows of `oldFrench` and `oldFrenchMeta` are synchronized, we subscript `oldFrench` with information in `oldFrenchMeta`:

```
> prose = oldFrench[oldFrenchMeta$Genre == "prose" &
+ !is.na(oldFrenchMeta$Year),]
```

Texts for which we have no information on their approximate date of origin are labeled as missing data with NA. The function `is.na()` returns TRUE for those cells in its input vector that contain missing data. By negating this vector of truth values, we obtain a condition on the rows that allows only non-missing information into the new data frame. We likewise create a version of `oldFrenchMeta` that is synchronized with `prose`,

```
> proseinfo = oldFrenchMeta[oldFrenchMeta$Genre=="prose" &
+ !is.na(oldFrenchMeta$Year),]
```

and because the chronological information is coarse, we set a major boundary at the year 1250·

```
> proseinfo$Period = as.factor(proseinfo$Year <= 1250)
```

We apply `corres.fnc()` and plot the result, disabling the addition of the column names with `addcol = F`:

```
> prose.ca = corres.fnc(prose)
> plot(prose.ca, addcol = F, rcol = as.numeric(proseinfo$Period) + 1,
+ rlabels = proseinfo$Year, rcex = 0.7)
```

As can be seen in Figure 5.7, the texts from 1250 or before, shown in light grey (or green on the computer screen), reveal some separation from texts dated after 1250, shown in dark grey (or red on the computer screen).

Let's now consider the prose text for which the approximate date of composition is unknown—labeled as NA in `oldFrenchMeta$Year`. Can anything be said about their date of composition? To address this issue, we first select the relevant texts and store them in a separate data frame:

```
> proseSup = oldFrench[oldFrenchMeta$Genre == "prose" &
+ is.na(oldFrenchMeta$Year),]
```

We add these additional data to the correspondence plot with `corsup.fnc()`, a function for adding so-called SUPPLEMENTARY ROWS or SUPPLEMENTARY COLUMNS:

```
> corsup.fnc(prose.ca, bycol = F, supp = proseSup, font = 2,
+ cex = 0.8, labels = substr(rownames(proseSup), 1, 4))
```

By default, `corsup.fnc()` proceeds on the assumption that we add supplementary columns. In the present example, we are dealing with supplementary rows, so we change the default by specifying `bycol = F`. The supplementary rows themselves are specified with `supp = proseSup`, and we label them with the manuscript identifiers provided by the row names, after stripping off the fragment numbers with `substr()`. Figure 5.7 locates the fragments more or less

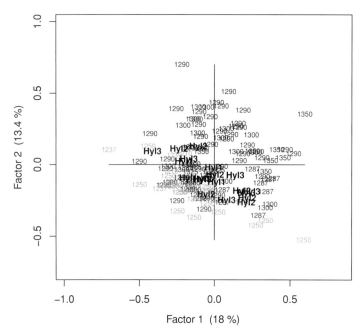

Figure 5.7. *Correspondence analysis of the frequencies of* 35 *tag trigrams in*
125 *Medieval French prose fragments. Text fragments are labeled by*
approximate date of origin, texts dating from 1250 *or earlier are shown in light*
grey, texts located later in time are shown in dark grey. The texts in black
represent supplementary rows representing texts of unknown date.

at the transition area of the early and late texts, perhaps with a slight bias towards the late texts. The advantage of not including the undated texts from the
beginning in the correspondence analysis is that we establish a correspondence
map on the basis of known data, against which we pit unknown supplementary
data.

Finally consider a sociolinguistic data set, `variationLijk`, which provides
the frequency counts in eight subcorpora of spoken Dutch for 32 words ending
in the Dutch suffix *-lijk* (similar to English *-ly* and *-like*) (Keune *et al.* 2005).
The subcorpora are constructed with contrasts along three dimensions: country
(Flanders versus the Netherlands), sex (male versus female), and education level
(high versus mid). We load the data, and display the first four columns for the
first five lines:

```
> variationLijk[1:5, 1:4]
            nlfemaleHigh nlfemaleMid nlmaleHigh nlmaleMid
afhankelijk            1           1          3         4
belachelijk            7           4          7         3
dadelijk              8          13          6        10
degelijk              1           1          1         1
duidelijk            11           6         14         8
```

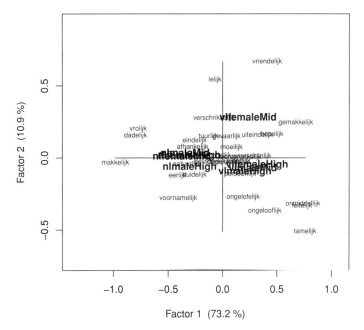

Figure 5.8. *Correspondence analysis of the frequencies of 32 words ending in the Dutch suffix -lijk in eight subcorpora of spoken conversational Dutch.*

The full set of column names,

```
> colnames(variationLijk)
[1] "nlfemaleHigh" "nlfemaleMid"  "nlmaleHigh"   "nlmaleMid"
[5] "vlfemaleHigh" "vlfemaleMid"  "vlmaleHigh"   "vlmaleMid"
```

reflects the design of this data set, with nl representing the Netherlands, and vl representing Flanders. A chi-squared test shows that the words in *-lijk* are not uniformly distributed over the subcorpora:

```
> chisq.test(variationLijk)
...
X-squared = 575.3482, df = 217, p-value < 2.2e-16
...
```

This chi-squared test is rather uninformative, however. We have lots and lots of data points, so it is unlikely a priori that the test will report a non-significant *p*-value. Furthermore, all that this test tells us is that the counts are not proportionally distributed in the table. The correspondence plot shown in Figure 5.8 is much more revealing:

```
> variationLijk.ca = corres.fnc(variationLijk)
> plot(variationLijk.ca)
```

The subcorpora from the Netherlands (labels beginning with nl) cluster at the left hand side of the plot, and those from Flanders (vl) cluster at the right hand side of the plot. *Vriendelijk* ("friendly") emerges from this plot as characteristic for female speakers from Flanders with a medium education level.

5.1.4   Tables with distances: multidimensional scaling

Multidimensional scaling is a technique for tracing structure in a matrix of distances. Like principal components analysis, it is a technique for dimension reduction, usually to two or three dimensions. As in correspondence analysis, which is in fact a special case of multidimensional scaling, the idea is to create a representation in, for instance, a plane, such that the distances between the points in that plane mirror as best as possible the distances between the points in the original multidimensional space.

By way of example, we consider the similarities in conversational Dutch between 165 speakers as available in a corpus of spoken Dutch. We are interested in whether the age and sex of the speaker are reflected in a quantitative measure of textual dissimilarity based on the notion of cross-entropy of two texts (Juola, 2003), a measure that gauges the extent to which the one text can be predicted from the other. Metadata on the speakers are available as `dutchSpeakersDistMeta`; `dutchSpeakersDist` provides the matrix of between-speaker cross-entropy distances. We convert this matrix of distances into a distance object with `as.dist()`,

```
> dutchSpeakersDist.d = as.dist(dutchSpeakersDist)
```

and supply it as input to `cmdscale()`, the function that carries out standard multidimensional scaling. We request a reduction to three dimensions with $k = 3$:

```
> dutchSpeakersDist.mds = cmdscale(dutchSpeakersDist.d, k = 3)
```

The result is a matrix with 3 columns and 165 rows: the coordinates of the speakers in the reduced three-dimensional space that we requested:

```
> head(dutchSpeakersDist.mds)
        [,1]         [,2]        [,3]
1 -0.68954160 -0.10911462  0.5577156
2 -0.40487679 -0.16424549 -0.3747578
3 -0.25708988  0.06313037  0.2857530
4 -0.37567012 -0.10035375 -0.1644606
5 -0.39665853 -0.08165329 -0.1193554
6  0.02534566  0.09426173 -0.4670765
```

Do these dimensions reflect differences in the age and sex of the speakers? Before addressing this question, we first convert this matrix into a data frame and add speaker information:

```
> dat = data.frame(dutchSpeakersDist.mds,
+ Sex = dutchSpeakersDistMeta$Sex,
+ Year = dutchSpeakersDistMeta$AgeYear,
+ EduLevel = dutchSpeakersDistMeta$EduLevel)
> dat = dat[!is.na(dat$Year),]
> dat[1:2, ]
```

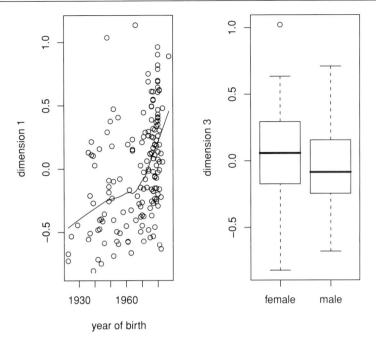

Figure 5.9. *Year of birth and sex as reflected in the first and third dimension of a multidimensional scaling of string-based cross-entropies for the spontaneous spoken Dutch of 165 speakers.*

```
          X1           X2          X3     Sex Year EduLevel
1 -0.6895416 -0.10911462  0.5577156 female 1952     high
2 -0.4048768 -0.16424549 -0.3747578   male 1952     high
```

Two exploratory plots, shown in Figure 5.9, are now straightforward to make:

```
> par(mfrow=c(1,2))
> plot(dat$Year, dat$X1, xlab="year of birth",
+ ylab = "dimension 1", type = "p")
> lines(lowess(dat$Year, dat$X1))
> boxplot(dat$X3 ~ dat$Sex, ylab = "dimension 3")
> par(mfrow=c(1,1))
```

These plots suggest that there is indeed some interpretable structure in the dimensions obtained with multidimensional scaling. The first dimension seems to capture an effect of age: younger speakers tend to have somewhat higher scores on the first dimension. Furthermore, the sex of the speaker seems to be represented to some extent on the third dimension. These visual impressions are supported by formal tests of significance, a Spearman rank-correlation test for Year,

```
> cor.test(dat$X1, dat$Year, method="sp")

        Spearman's rank correlation rho

data:  dat$X1 and dat$Year
S = 392556.7, p-value = 9.435e-10
```

```
alternative hypothesis: true rho is not equal to 0
sample estimates:
      rho
0.4561149
```

and a *t*-test for the speaker's Sex:

```
> t.test(dat$X3~dat$Sex)

        Welch Two Sample t-test

data:  dat$X3 by dat$Sex
t = 2.1384, df = 155.156, p-value = 0.03405
alternative hypothesis: true difference in means is not equal to 0
95 percent confidence interval:
 0.008260503 0.208387229
sample estimates:
mean in group female   mean in group male
          0.04567817          -0.06264569
```

5.1.5   Tables with distances: hierarchical cluster analysis

The final technique for tracing groups in numerical tables that we consider in this chapter is hierarchical cluster analysis. Hierarchical cluster analysis is the name for a family of techniques for clustering data and displaying them in a tree-like format. Just as with multidimensional scaling, these techniques require a distance object as input.

There are many different ways to form clusters. One way is to begin with an initial cluster containing all data points, and then to proceed with successively PARTITIONING clusters into smaller clusters. One of the functions in R that uses this DIVISIVE CLUSTERING approach is diana(). This method is reported to have difficulties finding optimal divisions for smaller clusters. However, when the goal is to find a few large clusters, it is an attractive method.

More commonly, clustering begins small, with single points, which are then agglomerated into groups, and these groups into larger groups, and so on. AGGLOMERATIVE CLUSTERING is implemented in the function hclust(). The clustering depends to a considerable extent on the criteria used for combining points and groups of points into larger clusters. Which criteria hclust() should use is specified by means of the option method. The default in R is complete, which evaluates the dissimilarity between two clusters as the maximum of the dissimilarities between the individual members of these clusters.

By way of example, we consider 23 lexical measures characterizing 2233 monomorphemic and monosyllabic English words as available in the english data set. For convenience, the information pertaining to just the words and their associated measures are available separately as the data set lexicalMeasures. Brief information on these measures can be obtained with ?lexicalMeasures or help(lexicalMeasures):

```
> lexicalMeasures[1:5, 1:6]
    Word     CelS      Fdif       Vf    Dent    Ient
1    doe 3.912023  1.0216510 1.386294 0.14144 0.02114
2  whore 4.521789  0.3504830 1.386294 0.42706 0.94198
3 stress 6.505784  2.0893560 1.609438 0.06197 1.44339
4   pork 5.017280 -0.5263339 1.945910 0.43035 0.00000
5   plug 4.890349 -1.0445450 2.197225 0.35920 1.75393
```

All these measures are correlated to some extent. A matrix listing all pairwise correlations between these variables, the CORRELATION MATRIX of this data set, is obtained simply with cor() applied to measures after excluding the first column, which is not numeric:

```
> lexicalMeasures.cor = cor(lexicalMeasures[, -1])
> lexicalMeasures.cor[1:5, 1:5]
            CelS        Fdif          Vf        Dent        Ient
CelS  1.00000000  0.04553879  0.66481876  0.25211726 -0.04662943
Fdif  0.04553879  1.00000000 -0.13101020 -0.02376464 -0.12678869
Vf    0.66481876 -0.13101020  1.00000000  0.68828793  0.08484806
Dent  0.25211726 -0.02376464  0.68828793  1.00000000 -0.06582160
Ient -0.04662943 -0.12678869  0.08484806 -0.06582160  1.00000000
```

Even correlations that seem quite small, such as the correlation of CelS (frequency) and Ient (inflectional entropy) are significant, thanks to the large number of words in this data set:

```
> cor.test(lexicalMeasures$CelS, lexicalMeasures$Ient)
        Pearson's product-moment correlation
data:  measures$CelS and measures$Ient
t = -2.2049, df = 2231, p-value = 0.02757
alternative hypothesis: true correlation is not equal to 0
95 percent confidence interval:
 -0.087940061 -0.005158676
sample estimates:
       cor
-0.04662943
```

The question of interest to Baayen *et al.* (2006) was whether word frequency (CelS) enters into stronger correlations with measures of a word's form (such as its length) or with measures of its meaning (such as its morphological family size or its number of synsets in WordNet). The answer to this question may contribute to understanding the role of frequency in lexical processing. The ubiquitous effect of word frequency in reaction time experiments has often been interpreted as reflecting the processing load of a word's form. But if word frequency happens to be more tightly correlated with semantic measures, this would suggest that it might be useful to reconceptualize frequency as a measure of one's familiarity with a word's meaning. In an experimental task such as lexical decision, it might then be thought of as gauging, at least in part, semantic processing load.

A hierarchical cluster analysis is ideal for exploring the correlational structure of these 23 measures. However, the above correlation matrix is not the best starting point for a cluster analysis. Correlations can be both positive and negative. For a matrix of distances, it is desirable to have only non-negative values. This requirement is easy to satisfy by squaring the correlation matrix. (When we square the matrix, each of its elements is squared.)

```
> (lexicalMeasures.cor^2)[1:5, 1:5]
          CelS         Fdif          Vf         Dent         Ient
CelS 1.000000000 0.002073781 0.441983979 0.063563114 0.002174303
Fdif 0.002073781 1.000000000 0.017163673 0.000564758 0.016075372
Vf   0.441983979 0.017163673 1.000000000 0.473740272 0.007199192
Dent 0.063563114 0.000564758 0.473740272 1.000000000 0.004332483
Ient 0.002174303 0.016075372 0.007199192 0.004332483 1.000000000
```

Another consideration is that cor() works best for reasonably symmetrical vectors. However, many of the present measures have skewed distributions or distributions with more than one peak (MULTIMODALITY). Therefore, it makes sense to make use of Spearman correlations:

```
> lexicalMeasures.cor = cor(lexicalMeasures[,-1], method="spearman")^2
> lexicalMeasures.cor[1:5, 1:5]
           CelS          Fdif          Vf         Dent         Ient
CelS 1.0000000000 0.0004464715 0.44529233 0.097394824 0.003643291
Fdif 0.0004464715 1.0000000000 0.02163948 0.001183269 0.017550778
Vf   0.4452923284 0.0216394843 1.00000000 0.533855660 0.011743931
Dent 0.0973948244 0.0011832693 0.53385566 1.000000000 0.001875520
Ient 0.0036432911 0.0175507780 0.01174393 0.001875520 1.000000000
```

The last preparatory step is to convert this matrix into a distance object:

```
> lexicalMeasures.dist = dist(lexicalMeasures.cor)
```

The cluster analysis itself is straightforward. First consider agglomerative clustering, for which we use hclust() to carry out the cluster analysis, and plclust() to plot the dendrogram:

```
> lexicalMeasures.clust = hclust(lexicalMeasures.dist)
> plclust(lexicalMeasures.clust)
```

Figure 5.10 shows that the highest split separates three measures of orthographic consistency from all other measures. The next split isolates another four measures of orthographic consistency, and the same holds for the next split as well. The fourth split starts to become interesting, in that its left branch groups together four semantic measures: family size (Vf), derivational entropy (Dent), and two synset counts (NsyS, NsyC). It also contains frequency (CelS). The right branch dominates various measures of form such as the count of neighbors (Ncou) and word length (Len). But this right branch also contains two measures that are not measures of form: inflectional entropy (Ient, a measure of the complexity of a word's inflectional paradigm) and the ratio of the word's frequency as a noun and as a verb (NVratio). In other words, the clustering algorithm that we used shows some structure, but a clear separation of measures of form and measures of meaning is not obtained.

Let's now consider divisive clustering with the diana() function from the cluster package. We feed the output of diana() into pltree(), which handles the graphics. The result is shown in Figure 5.11:

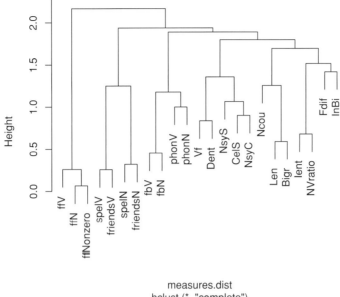

Figure 5.10. *Agglomerative hierarchical cluster analysis of 23 lexical variables.*

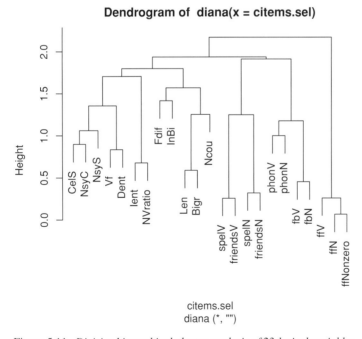

Figure 5.11. *Divisive hierarchical cluster analysis of 23 lexical variables.*

```
> library(cluster)
> pltree(diana(lexicalMeasures.dist))
```

Divisive clustering succeeds in bringing all measures that do not pertain to meaning together in one cluster at the left of the dendrogram, the left branch of the third main split. Again, frequency (CelS) does not side with the measures of word form.

If you want to know to which clusters the variables are assigned, you first have to decide how many clusters you think you need, and use this number as the second argument for cutree(). Here, we opt for five clusters:

```
> cutree(diana(lexicalMeasures.dist), 5)
 [1] 1 2 1 1 1 1 1 2 2 2 2 2 3 3 4 4 3 3 5 5 4 4 5 1
```

When combined with the names of the measures, and with the classification of these measures in the data set lexicalMeasuresClasses, we obtain a very close correspondence between the class of the variable and cluster number, with as the only exception the Fdif measure, which gauges the difference between a word's frequency in speech versus writing:

```
> x = data.frame(measure = rownames(lexicalMeasures.cor),
+ cluster = cutree(diana(lexicalMeasures.dist), 5),
+ class = lexicalMeasuresClasses$Class)
> x = x[order(x$cluster), ]
> x
       measure cluster    class
1         CelS       1 Meaning
3           Vf       1 Meaning
4         Dent       1 Meaning
5         Ient       1 Meaning
6         NsyS       1 Meaning
7         NsyC       1 Meaning
23     NVratio       1 Meaning
2         Fdif       2 Meaning
8          Len       2    Form
9         Ncou       2    Form
10        Bigr       2    Form
11        InBi       2    Form
12       spelV       3    Form
13       spelN       3    Form
16     friendsV       3    Form
17     friendsN       3    Form
14       phonV       4    Form
15       phonN       4    Form
20         fbV       4    Form
21         fbN       4    Form
18         ffV       5    Form
19         ffN       5    Form
22   ffNonzero       5    Form
```

As a second example of cluster analysis, we consider data published by Dunn *et al.* (2005) on the phylogenetic classification of Papuan and Oceanic languages using grammatical features. The vocabularies of Papuan languages are so different that classification based on the amount of lexical overlap using basic word lists is bound to fail. Dunn and colleagues showed that it is possible to probe the classification of Papuan languages in an interesting and revealing way using non-lexical, grammatical traits. Their data set, available as `phylogeny`, contains a great many binary features for 15 Papuan and 16 Oceanic languages (columns). The first column specifies the language, the second the language family, and the remaining 125 columns the grammatical properties, such as whether a language has prenasalized stops. Presence is coded by 1, absence by 0:

```
> phylogeny[1:5, 1:5]
    Language Family Frics PrenasalizedStops PhonDistBetweenLAndR
1    Motuna Papuan     1                 0                    0
2       Kol Papuan     1                 0                    1
3    Rotokas Papuan    1                 0                    0
4       Ata Papuan     1                 0                    0
5      Kuot Papuan     1                 0                    1
```

The left panel of Figure 5.12 shows the dendrogram obtained by applying divisive clustering using `diana()`. We first create a distance object appropriate for binary data,

```
> phylogeny.dist = dist(phylogeny[ ,3:ncol(phylogeny)], method="binary")
```

and we also create a vector of language names with the names for Papuan languages in upper case with `toupper()`:

```
> plotnames = as.character(phylogeny$Language)
> plotnames[phylogeny$Family=="Papuan"] =
+   toupper(plotnames[phylogeny$Family=="Papuan"])
```

Divisive clustering and visualization is now straightforward:

```
> library(cluster)
> plot(diana(dist(phylogeny[, 3:ncol(phylogeny)],
+ method = "binary")), labels = plotnames, cex = 0.8,
+ main = " ", xlab= " ", which.plot = 2)
```

We note a fairly clear separation of Papuan and Oceanic languages.

The right panel of Figure 5.12 shows an unrooted tree obtained with an algorithm known as neighbor-joining that is often used for phylogeny estimation. In what follows, we use the `ape` package developed by Paradis and described in detail, together with other packages for phylogenetic analysis, in Paradis (2006). We load the `ape` package. We then apply the `nj()` function to obtain a phylogenetic tree object:

```
> library(ape)
> phylogeny.dist.tr = nj(phylogeny.dist)
```

The plot method for phylogenetic tree objects has a wide variety of options. One option, illustrated in the right panel of Figure 5.12, is to use different fonts to highlight subsets of observations. Since the leaf nodes (or tips) of the tree are labeled by default with the row numbers of the observations in the input distance matrix, we need to do some extra preparatory work to get the names of the languages into the plot. We begin with the row numbers, which are available in

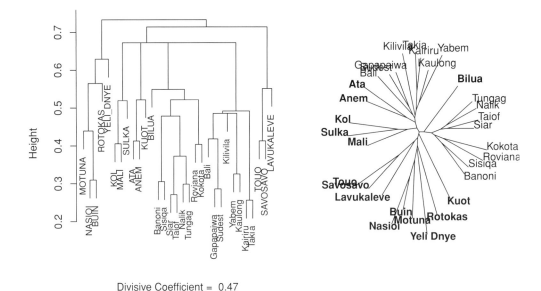

Divisive Coefficient = 0.47

Figure 5.12. *Divisive clustering with* diana() *(in the* cluster *package) and the corresponding unrooted tree obtained with the neighbor-joining algorithm* nj() *(in the* ape *package) of* 16 *Oceanic and* 15 *Papuan languages using* 125 *grammatical traits (Dunn* et al., *2005).*

the form of a character vector in the tree object as tip.label. We then use these row numbers to reconstruct the names of the language families,

```
> families = as.character(
+ phylogeny$Family[as.numeric(phylogeny.dist.tr$tip.label)])
```

and also the names of the languages themselves:

```
> languages = as.character(
+ phylogeny$Language[as.numeric(phylogeny.dist.tr$tip.label)])
```

We substitute the language names for the row names in the tree object,

```
> phylogeny.dist.tr$tip.label = languages
```

and plot the tree:

```
> plot(phylogeny.dist.tr, type="u",
+ font = as.numeric(as.factor(families)))
```

The option type="u" requests an unrooted tree. In unrooted trees, all nodes have at least three connecting branches, and there is no longer a single root node that can be considered as the common ancestor of all tip nodes. It is easy to see that the two dendrograms shown in Figure 5.12 point to basically the same topology.

As mentioned above, the focus of the study of Dunn and colleagues was the internal classification of the Papuan languages, as it is here that traditional word-based classification fails most dramatically. The tree presented in the upper left

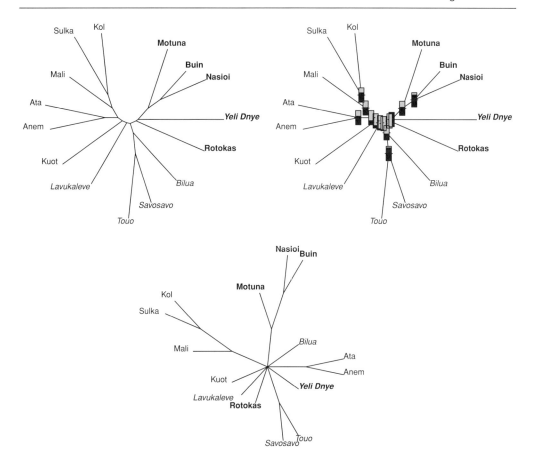

Figure 5.13. *Unrooted phylogenetic trees for the subset of Papuan languages in the data of Dunn* et al. *(2005), obtained with the node-joining algorithm. The fonts represent geographical areas (plain: Bismarck Archipelago; bold: Bougainville; italic: Central Solomons; bold italic: Louisiade Archipelago). The upper right tree adds thermometers for bootstrap support to the tree in the upper left. The lower tree is a consensus tree across* 200 *bootstrap trees.*

of Figure 5.13 shows that the unrooted phylogenetic tree groups languages according to geographical region, as indicated by different fonts (plain: Bismarck Archipelago; bold: Bougainville; italic: Central Solomons; bold italic: Louisiade Archipelago). This striking result is reproduced as follows:

```
> papuan = phylogeny[phylogeny$Family == "Papuan",]
> papuan$Language = as.factor(as.character(papuan$Language))
> papuan.meta = papuan[ ,1:2]
> papuan.mat = papuan[, 3:ncol(papuan)]
> papuan.meta$Geography = c(
+    "Bougainville", "Bismarck Archipelago", "Bougainville",
+    "Bismarck Archipelago", "Bismarck Archipelago", "Central Solomons",
+    "Bougainville", "Louisiade Archipelago", "Bougainville",
+    "Bismarck Archipelago", "Bismarck Archipelago",
+    "Bismarck Archipelago", "Central Solomons", "Central Solomons",
```

```
+    "Central Solomons")
> papuan.dist = dist(papuan.mat, method = "binary")
> papuan.dist.tr = nj(papuan.dist)
> fonts = as.character(papuan.meta$Geography[as.numeric(
+    papuan.dist.tr$tip.label)])
> papuan.dist.tr$tip.label =
+    as.character(papuan.meta$Language[as.numeric(
+    papuan.dist.tr$tip.label)])
> plot(papuan.dist.tr, type = "u", font = as.numeric(as.factor(fonts)))
```

The clustering techniques that we have considered in this section are not based on a formal model, but on reasonable but nevertheless heuristic procedures. As a consequence, there are no hard and fast criteria to help decide what kind of clustering (agglomerative or divisive) is optimal for a given data set. When a cluster analysis is reported, only one dendrogram tends to be shown, even though the authors may have tried out a variety of clustering techniques. Typically, the dendrogram shown is the one that best fits the authors' hypothesis about the data. This is fine, as long as you keep in mind that the dendrogram probably depicts an optimal solution.

A technique that provides a means for validating a cluster analysis is the BOOT-STRAP. The bootstrap is a general technique that we will also use in the chapters on regression modeling. The basic idea of the bootstrap as applied to the present data is that we sample (with replacement) from the columns of our data matrix. For each sample, we construct the distance matrix and grow the corresponding unrooted tree with the node-joining algorithm. Finally, we compare our original dendrogram with the dendrograms for the bootstrap samples, and calculate the proportions of bootstrapped dendrograms that support the groupings (subtrees, or clades in the terminology of phylogenetics) in the original trees. In this way, we obtain insight into the extent to which the clustering depends on the idiosyncracies of the set of grammatical traits that happened to be selected for analysis.

The proportion of support for the different subtrees is shown in the upper right panel of Figure 5.13 by means of thermometers: the higher the temperature, the greater the proportional support for a subtree. The bootstrap analysis underlying this panel closely follows the example of Paradis, 2006:117. We begin by defining the number of bootstrap runs, and prepare a list in which we save the bootstrap trees:

```
> B = 200
> btr = list()
> length(btr) = B
```

We now create 200 bootstrap trees, sampling with replacement from the columns of our data matrix:

```
> for (i in 1:B) {
+   trB = nj(dist(papuan.mat[ ,sample(ncol(papuan.mat), replace = TRUE)],
+       method = "binary"))
+   trB$tip.label = as.character(papuan.meta$Language[as.numeric(
+       trB$tip.label)])
+   btr[[i]] = trB
+ }
```

The proportions of bootstrap trees that support the subtrees of our original tree
are obtained with the help of prop.clades():

```
> props = prop.clades(papuan.dist.tr, btr)/B
> props
 [1] 1.000 0.600 0.865 0.050 0.100 0.115 0.200 0.315 0.555 0.680 0.625
[12] 0.445 0.920
```

We plot the original tree,

```
> plot(papuan.dist.tr, type = "u", font = as.numeric(as.factor(fonts)))
```

and add the thermometers with nodelabels():

```
> nodelabels(thermo = props, piecol = c("black", "grey"))
```

The proportion of bootstrap support decreases as one moves to the center of the
graph. This points to a lack of consensus with respect to how subtrees should be
linked. A different way of bringing this uncertainty out into the open is to plot
a CONSENSUS TREE. In a consensus tree, subgroups that are not observed in all
bootstrap trees (strict consensus) or in a majority of all bootstrap trees (majority-
rule consensus) will be collapsed. The result is a tree with multichotomies. The
lower left tree of Figure 5.13 shows such a multichotomy in the center, where nine
branches come together. The ape package provides the function consensus()
for constructing a consensus tree for a list of trees, given a proportion p specifying
the required level of consensus:

```
> btr.consensus = consensus(btr, p = 0.5)
```

Consensus trees come with a plot method, and can be visualized straightforwardly
with plot(). Some extra steps are required to plot the tree with fonts representing
geographical areas:

```
> x = btr.consensus$tip.label
> x
 [1] "Anem"       "Ata"        "Bilua"      "Buin"      "Nasioi"
 [6] "Motuna"     "Kol"        "Sulka"      "Mali"      "Kuot"
[11] "Lavukaleve" "Rotokas"    "Savosavo"   "Touo"      "Yeli Dnye"
> x = data.frame(Language = x, Node = 1:length(x))
> x = merge(x, papuan.meta, by.x = "Language", by.y = "Language")
> head(x)
  Language Node Family          Geography
1     Anem    1 Papuan Bismarck Archipelago
2      Ata    2 Papuan Bismarck Archipelago
3    Bilua    3 Papuan     Central Solomons
4     Buin    4 Papuan         Bougainville
5      Kol    7 Papuan Bismarck Archipelago
6     Kuot   10 Papuan Bismarck Archipelago
> x = x[order(x$Node),]
> x$Geography = as.factor(x$Geography)
> plot(btr.consensus, type = "u", font = as.numeric(x$Geography))
```

The consensus tree shows that the grouping of Bilua, Kuot, Lavukaleve, Rotokas,
and Yeli Dnye is inconsistent across bootstrap runs. We should at the same time

keep in mind that a given bootstrap run will make use of roughly 80 of the 125 available grammatical traits. A loss of about a third of the available grammatical markers may have had severe adverse consequences for the goodness of the clustering. Therefore, replication studies with a larger set of languages and an even broader range of grammatical traits may well support the interesting similarity in geographical and grammatical topology indicated by the original tree constructed with all 125 traits currently available.

5.2   Classification

In the previous section, we have been concerned with discerning clusters and groupings for data points described by the rows of numerical matrices. When we visualized data, we often used color coding or changes in font size to distinguish subsets of data points. But information on these subsets was never used in the calculations. We only added it to our plots afterwards. In this section, we change our perspective from CLUSTERING to CLASSIFICATION, and take information on subsets (classes) of data points as our point of departure. Our aim is now to ascertain whether the class of a data point can be predicted.

5.2.1   Classification trees

In Chapters 1 and 2 we started exploring data on the dative alternation in English (Bresnan *et al.*, 2007). The dependent variable in this study is a factor with levels NP (the dative is realized as an NP, as in *John gave Mary the book*) and PP (the dative is realized as a PP, as in *John gave the book to Mary*). For 3263 verb tokens in corpora of written and spoken English, the values of a total of 12 variables were determined, in addition to the realization of the dative, coded as `RealizationOfRecipient` in the data set `dative`:

```
> colnames(dative)
 [1] "Speaker"               "Modality"
 [3] "Verb"                  "SemanticClass"
 [5] "LengthOfRecipient"     "AnimacyOfRec"
 [7] "DefinOfRec"            "PronomOfRec"
 [9] "LengthOfTheme"         "AnimacyOfTheme"
[11] "DefinOfTheme"          "PronomOfTheme"
[13] "RealizationOfRecipient" "AccessOfRec"
[15] "AccessOfTheme"
```

Short descriptions of these variables are available with `?dative`. The question that we address here is whether the realization of the recipient as NP or PP can be predicted from the other variables. The technique that we introduce here is CART analysis, an acronym for Classification And Regression Trees. This section restricts itself to discussing classification trees. (When the dependent variable is not a factor but a numerical variable, the same principles apply and the result is a regression tree.)

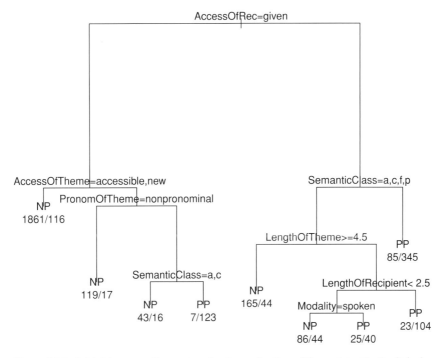

Figure 5.14. *Initial (unpruned)* CART *tree for the realization of the recipient in English clauses* (NP *or* PP) *in written and spoken English.*

An initial classification tree for the dative alternation is shown in Figure 5.14. The tree outlines a decision procedure for determining the realization of the recipient as NP or PP. Each split in the tree is labeled with a decision rule. The decision rule at the root, the top node of the tree, asks whether or not the factor Access-OfRec has the level given. If so, follow the left branch, otherwise, follow the right branch. At each next branch a new decision rule is considered that directs us to a new branch in its subtree. This process is repeated until a leaf node, a node with no further splits, is reached. A data point for which the accessibility of the recipient is given, for which the accessibility of the theme is given, and for which the pronominality of the theme is nonpronominal, we go left, right, and left at which point we reach a leaf node for which the predicted outcome is NP. This outcome is supported by 119 observations and contradicted by only 17 observations.

The leaf nodes of the tree specify a partition of the data, i.e. a division of the data set into a series of non-overlapping subsets that jointly comprise the full data set. Hence, CART analysis is often referred to as RECURSIVE PARTITIONING. For any node, the algorithm for growing a tree inspects all predictors and selects the one that is most useful. The algorithm begins with the root node, which represents the full data set, and creates two subsets. For each of these subsets, it creates two new subsets, for which in turn new subsets are created, and so on. Without a stopping criterion, the tree would keep growing until its leaves would contain single observations only. Such leaves would be *pure*, in the sense that only one level of the dependent variable would be represented at any leaf node. But such leaf nodes would also be *trivially* pure, and would not allow generalization: the tree would severely overfit the data. Therefore, the tree-growing algorithm stops when there are too few observations at a node, by default 20. In addition, the tree-growing algorithm refuses to implement useless splits. For a split to be useful, the daughter nodes should be purer than the mother node, in the sense that the ratio of NP to PP realizations in the daughter nodes should be more extreme (i.e. closer to 1 or to 0) than in the mother node. How exactly NODE IMPURITY is assessed is a technical issue that need not concern us here. What is important is that the usefulness of a predictor is assessed by its success in reducing the impurity in the mother node, and its success in creating purer daughter nodes. The vertical parts of the branches in the tree diagram are proportional to the achieved reduction in node heterogeneity, and provide a graphical representation of the explanatory value of a split.

The tree shown in Figure 5.14 was grown by the function `rpart()` from the `rpart` package:

```
> library(rpart)
> dative.rp = rpart(RealizationOfRecipient ~ .,
+ data = dative[ ,-c(1, 3)]) # exclude the columns with subjects, verbs
```

In this formula, the dot following the equation is shorthand for all variables in the data frame with the exception of the dependent variable. The tree object `dative.rp` is visualized with `plot()` and labeled with `text()`:

```
> plot(dative.rp, compress = T, branch = 1, margin = 0.1)
> text(dative.rp, use.n = T, pretty = 0)
```

The plot options are explained in detail in the help for `plot.rpart()`, and the options for labeling in the help for `text.rpart()`. When the option `use.n` is set to TRUE, counts are added to the leaf nodes. By setting `pretty` to zero, we force the use of the full names of the factor levels, instead of the codes that `rpart()` produces by default.

The problem with this initial tree is that it still overfits the data. It implements too many splits that have no predictive value for new data. To increase the prediction accuracy of the tree, we have to prune it by snipping off useless branches. This is done with the help of an algorithm known as COST-COMPLEXITY PRUNING. Cost-complexity pruning pits the size of the tree (in terms of its number of leaf nodes) against its success in reducing the impurity in the tree by means of a cost-complexity parameter `cp`. The larger the value of `cp`, the greater the number of branches that are pruned. For very large `cp`, all that remains of the tree is its root stump. When `cp` is very low, it is too small to induce any pruning.

How should we evaluate the balance between success in classification accuracy on the one hand and the complexity of our theory (gauged by its number of leaf nodes) on the other hand? The answer to this question is 10-fold cross-validation.

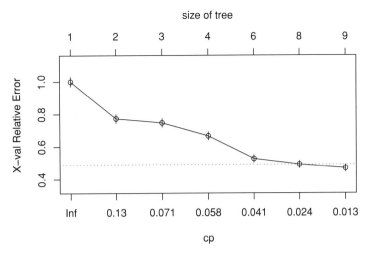

Figure 5.15. *Cost-complexity cross-validation plot for the unpruned* CART *tree (Figure 5.14) for the realization of the recipient in English.*

For successive values of cp, and hence for successive tree sizes, we take the data and randomly divide it into ten equally sized parts. We then select the first part, put it aside, and build a tree for the remaining nine parts lumped together. Next, we evaluate how well this tree predicts the realization of the recipient for the held-out part by comparing its misclassification rate with the misclassification rate for the root model, the simplest possible model without any predictors. The result is a relative error score. We repeat this process for each of the nine remaining parts. What we end up with is, for each tree size, ten relative error scores that inform us how well the model generalizes to unseen data. Of course, it would be better to evaluate the model against new data, but in the absence of a second equivalent data set, cross-validation provides a way of assessing predictivity anyway.

Figure 5.15, obtained with `plotcp()`, plots the means of these error scores:

```
> plotcp(dative.rp)
```

The horizontal axis displays the values of the cost-complexity parameter cp at which branches are pruned. The corresponding sizes of the pruned tree are shown at the top of the plot. The vertical axis represents the cross-validation error. The small vertical lines for each point mark one standard error above and below the mean. The dotted line represents one standard error above the mean for the lowest point in the graph. A common selection rule for the cost-complexity parameter is to select the leftmost point that is still under this dotted line. In this example, this leftmost point would also be the rightmost point. To be a little conservative, we prune the tree (with `prune()`) for cp = 0.041, and obtain a tree with six leaves, as shown in Figure 5.16:

```
> dative.rp1 = prune(dative.rp, cp = 0.041)
> plot(dative.rp1, compress = T, branch = 1, margin = 0.1)
> text(dative.rp1, use.n = T, pretty = 0)
```

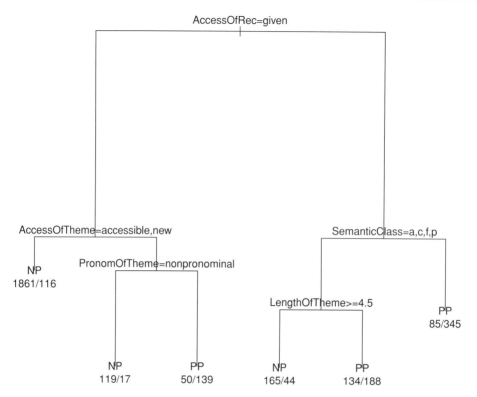

Figure 5.16. *Cost-complexity pruned* CART *tree for the realization of the recipient in English.*

We accept the predictors in this tree as statistically significant, and note that here cross-validation has taken over the function of the *p*-values associated with classical statistics associated with the *t*, *F*, or chi-squared distributions.

A verbal summary of the model is obtained by typing the object name at the prompt:

```
> dative.rp1
n= 3263

node), split, n, loss, yval, (yprob)
      * denotes terminal node

 1) root 3263 849 NP (0.74 0.26)
   2) AccessOfRec=given 2302 272 NP (0.88 0.12)
     4) AccessOfTheme=accessible,new 1977 116 NP (0.94 0.06) *
     5) AccessOfTheme=given 325 156 NP (0.52 0.48)
      10) PronomOfTheme=nonpronominal 136  17 NP (0.88 0.12) *
      11) PronomOfTheme=pronominal 189  50 PP (0.26 0.74) *
   3) AccessOfRec=accessible,new 961 384 PP (0.40 0.60)
     6) SemanticClass=a,c,f,p 531 232 NP (0.56 0.44)
      12) LengthOfTheme>=4.5 209  44 NP (0.79 0.21) *
      13) LengthOfTheme< 4.5 322 134 PP (0.42 0.58) *
     7) SemanticClass=t 430  85 PP (0.20 0.80) *
```

The first line mentions the number of data points. The second line provides a legend for the remainder, each line of which consists of a node number, the splitting criterion, the number of observations in the subtree dominated by the node, a measure of the reduction in node impurity effected by the split, and the probabilities of the NP and PP realizations.

How successful is the model in predicting the realization of the recipient? To answer this question, we pit the predictions of the CART tree against the actually observed realizations. We extract the predictions from the model with `predict()`:

```
> head(predict(dative.rp1))
            NP         PP
[1,] 0.9413252 0.05867476
[2,] 0.9413252 0.05867476
[3,] 0.9413252 0.05867476
[4,] 0.9413252 0.05867476
[5,] 0.9413252 0.05867476
[6,] 0.9413252 0.05867476
```

Each row of the input data frame is paired with probabilities, one for each level of the dependent variable. In the present example, we have a probability for the realization as NP and one for the realization as PP. We choose the realization with the largest probability (see section 7.4 for a more precise evaluation method using the `somers2()` function). Our choice is therefore NP if the first column has a value greater than or equal to 0.5, and PP otherwise:

```
> choiceIsNP = predict(dative.rp1)[,1] >= 0.5
> choiceIsNP[1:6]
[1] TRUE TRUE TRUE TRUE TRUE TRUE
```

We combine this vector with the original observations,

```
> preds = data.frame(obs = dative$RealizationOfRecipient, choiceIsNP)
> head(preds)
  obs choiceIsNP
1  NP       TRUE
2  NP       TRUE
3  NP       TRUE
4  NP       TRUE
5  NP       TRUE
6  NP       TRUE
```

and cross-tabulate:

```
> xtabs( ~ obs + choiceIsNP, data = preds)
    choiceIsNP
obs FALSE TRUE
 NP   269 2145
 PP   672  177
```

On a total of 3263 data points, only $269 + 177 = 446$ are misclassified; 13.7%. This compares favorably to a baseline classifier that simply predicts the most likely realization for all data points, and therefore is in error for all and only all data points with PP as realization:

```
> xtabs( ~ RealizationOfRecipient, dative)
RealizationOfRecipient
  NP   PP
2414  849
```

The misclassification rate for this baseline model is $849/3263 = 26\%$.

An important property of CART trees is that they deal very elegantly with interactions. Interactions arise when the effects of two predictors are not independent, i.e. when the effect of one predictor is codetermined by the value of another predictor. Figure 5.16 illustrates many interactions. For instance, SemanticClass appears only in the right branch of the tree, hence it is relevant only for clauses in which the accessibility of the recipient is not given. Hence, we have here an interaction of SemanticClass by AccessOfRec. The other three predictors in the model also interact with AccessOfRec. Furthermore, LengthOfTheme interacts with SemanticClass, and PronomOfTheme with AccessOfTheme. Whereas such complex interactions can be quite difficult to understand in regression models, they are transparent and easy to grasp in classification and regression trees.

5.2.2   Discriminant analysis

Discriminant analysis is used to predict an item's class on the basis of a set of numerical predictors. As in principal components analysis, the idea is to represent the items in a low-dimensional space, typically a plane that can be inspected with the help of a scatterplot. Instead of principal components, the analysis produces LINEAR DISCRIMINANTS. In both principal components analysis (PCA) and discriminant analysis, the new axes are linear combinations of the original variables. But in discriminant analysis, the idea is to choose the linear discriminants such that the means of the groups are as different as possible while the variance around these means within the groups is as small as possible. We illustrate the use of discriminant analysis by a study in authorship attribution (Spassova, 2006).

Five texts from each of three Spanish writers were selected for analysis. Metadata on the texts are given in spanishMeta:

```
> spanishMeta = spanishMeta[order(spanishMeta$TextName),]
> spanishMeta
    Author YearOfBirth  TextName PubDate Nwords    FullName
1        C        1916  X14458gll    1983   2972        Cela
2        C        1916  X14459gll    1951   3040        Cela
3        C        1916  X14460gll    1956   3066        Cela
4        C        1916  X14461gll    1948   3044        Cela
5        C        1916  X14462gll    1942   3053        Cela
6        M        1943  X14463gll    1986   3013     Mendoza
7        M        1943  X14464gll    1992   3049     Mendoza
8        M        1943  X14465gll    1989   3042     Mendoza
9        M        1943  X14466gll    1982   3039     Mendoza
```

```
10       M       1943 X14467g11    2002   3045       Mendoza
11       V       1936 X14472g11    1965   3037 VargasLLosa
12       V       1936 X14473g11    1963   3067 VargasLLosa
13       V       1936 X14474g11    1977   3020 VargasLLosa
14       V       1936 X14475g11    1987   3016 VargasLLosa
15       V       1936 X14476g11    1981   3054 VargasLLosa
```

From each text, fragments of approximately 3000 words were extracted. These text fragments were tagged, and the relative frequencies of tag trigrams were obtained. These relative frequencies are available as the data set `spanish`, rows represent tag trigrams and columns represent text fragments:

```
> dim(spanish)
[1] 120   15
> spanish[1:5, 1:5]
         X14461g11 X14473g11 X14466g11 X14459g11 X14462g11
P.A.N4    0.027494  0.006757  0.000814  0.024116  0.009658
VDA.J6.N5 0.000786  0.010135  0.003257  0.001608  0.005268
C.P.N5    0.008641  0.001126  0.001629  0.003215  0.001756
P.A.N5    0.118617  0.118243  0.102606  0.131833  0.118525
A.N5.JQ   0.011783  0.006757  0.014658  0.008039  0.000878
```

As we are interested in differences and similarities between texts, we transpose this matrix, so that we can consider the texts to be points in tag space:

```
> spanish.t = t(spanish)
```

It is instructive to begin with an unsupervised exploration of these data, for instance with principal components analysis:

```
> spanish.pca = prcomp(spanish.t, center = T, scale = T)
> spanish.x = data.frame(spanish.pca$x)
> spanish.x = spanish.x[order(rownames(spanish.x)), ]
> library(lattice)
> super.sym = trellis.par.get("superpose.symbol")
> splom(~spanish.x[ , 1:3], groups = spanishMeta$Author,
+ panel = panel.superpose,
+ key=list(
+     title=" ",
+     text=list(levels(spanishMeta$FullName)),
+     points = list(pch  = super.sym$pch[1:3],
+                   col  = super.sym$col[1:3])
+     )
+ )
```

Figure 5.17 suggests some authorial structure: `Cela` and `Mendoza` occupy different regions in the plane spanned by PC1 and PC2. `VargasLLosa`, however, seems to be indistinguishable from the other two authors.

Let's now replace unsupervised clustering by supervised classification. We order the rows of `spanish.t` so that they are synchronized with the author information in `spanishMeta`, and load the `MASS` package in order to have access to the function for linear discriminant analysis, `lda()`:

```
> spanish.t = spanish.t[order(rownames(spanish.t)),]
> library(MASS)
```

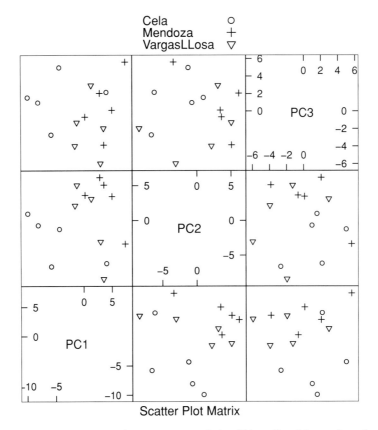

Figure 5.17. *Principal components analysis of fifteen Spanish texts from three authors.*

lda() takes two arguments, the matrix of numerical predictors and a vector with class labels. A first attempt comes with a warning about collinearity:

```
> spanish.lda = lda(spanish.t, spanishMeta$Author)
Warning message:
variables are collinear in: lda.default(x, grouping, ...)
```

The columns in spanish.t are too correlated for lda() to work properly. We therefore continue our analysis with the first eight principal components, which, as revealed by the summary (not shown) of the PCA objects, capture almost 80% of the variance in the data. These principal components are, by definition, uncorrelated, so the warning message should disappear:

```
> spanish.pca.lda = lda(spanish.x[ , 1:8], spanishMeta$Author)
> plot(spanish.pca.lda)
```

Figure 5.18 shows a clear separation of the texts by author. We can query the model for the probability with which it assigns texts to authors with predict(), supplied with the model object as first argument, and the input data as second

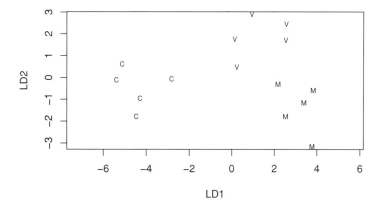

Figure 5.18. *Linear discriminant analysis of* 15 *Spanish texts by author.*

argument. A table with the desired probabilities is available under the name
posterior, which we round to four decimal digits for ease of interpretation:

```
> round(predict(spanish.pca.lda,
+ spanish.x[ ,1:8])$posterior, 4)
                 C      M      V
X14458g11 1.0000 0.0000 0.0000
X14459g11 1.0000 0.0000 0.0000
X14460g11 1.0000 0.0000 0.0000
X14461g11 1.0000 0.0000 0.0000
X14462g11 0.9999 0.0000 0.0001
X14463g11 0.0000 0.9988 0.0012
X14464g11 0.0000 1.0000 0.0000
X14465g11 0.0000 0.9965 0.0035
X14466g11 0.0000 0.9992 0.0008
X14467g11 0.0000 0.8416 0.1584
X14472g11 0.0000 0.0001 0.9998
X14473g11 0.0000 0.0000 1.0000
X14474g11 0.0000 0.0014 0.9986
X14475g11 0.0000 0.0150 0.9850
X14476g11 0.0001 0.0112 0.9887
```

It is clear that each text is assigned to its own author with a very high probability.

Unfortunately, this table is rather misleading because the model seriously overfits the data. It has done its utmost to find a representation of the data that separates
the groups as best as possible. This is fine as a solution for this particular sample of texts, but it does not guarantee that prediction will be accurate for unseen
text fragments as well. The existence of a problem lurking in the background
is indicated by scrutinizing the group means, as provided by a summary of the
discriminant object, abbreviated here for convenience:

```
> spanish.pca.lda
...
Group means:
          PC1        PC2        PC3         PC4        PC5
C -4.820024 -2.7560056  1.3985890 -0.94026140  0.2141179
M  3.801425  2.9890677  0.6494555 -0.01748498  0.4472681
```

```
V  1.018598 -0.2330621 -2.0480445  0.95774638 -0.6613860
            PC6         PC7         PC8
C -0.02702131 -0.5425466  0.86906543
M  1.75549883 -0.6416654  0.09646039
V -1.72847752  1.1842120 -0.96552582
...
```

There are differences among these group means, but they are not that large, and we may wonder whether any are actually significant. A statistical test appropriate for answering this question is a MULTIVARIATE ANALYSIS OF VARIANCE, available in R as the function manova(). It considers a group of numerical vectors as the dependent variable, and takes one or more factors as predictors. We use it to ascertain whether there are significant differences in the mean among the dependent variables. (Running a series of separate one-way analyses of variance, one for each PC, would run into the same problem of inflated p-values as discussed in Chapter 4 for a series of t-tests where a one-way analysis of variance is appropriate.)

```
> spanish.manova =
+ manova(cbind(PC1, PC2, PC3, PC4, PC5, PC6, PC7, PC8) ~
+ spanishMeta$Author, data = spanish.x)
```

There are several methods for evaluating the output of manova(); we use R's default, which makes use of the Pillai-Bartlett statistic, which approximately follows an F-distribution:

```
          Df Pillai approx F num Df den Df  Pr(>F)
Author     2 1.6283   3.2854     16     12 0.02134
Residuals 12
```

The p-value is sufficiently small to suggest that there are indeed significant differences among the group means. On the other hand, the evidence for such differences is not that exciting, and certainly not strong enough to inspire confidence in the perfect classification by authors obtained with lda().

In order to gauge the extent to which our results might generalize, we carry out a leave-one-out cross-validation. We run fifteen different discriminant analyses, each of which is trained on fourteen texts and is used to predict the author of the remaining held-out text. The proportion of correct attributions will give us improved insight into how well the model would perform when confronted with new texts by one of these three authors. Although lda() has an option for carrying out leave-one-out cross-validation (CV=TRUE), we cannot use this option here because the orthogonalization of our input (resulting in spanish.x) takes the data from all authors and all texts into account. We therefore implement cross-validation ourselves, and begin by making sure that the texts in spanish.t and spanishMeta are in sync. We then set the number of PCs to be considered to 8 and define a vector with 15 empty strings to store the predicted authors:

```
> spanish.t = spanish.t[order(rownames(spanish.t)), ]
> n = 8
> predictedClasses = rep("", 15)
```

Next, we loop over the fifteen texts. In each pass through the loop, we create a training data set and a vector with the corresponding information on the author by omitting the *i*-th text. Following orthogonalization, we make sure that the texts remain in sync with the vector of authors, and then apply `lda()`. Finally, we obtain the predicted authors for the full data set on the basis of the model for the training data, but select only the *i*-th element and store it in the *i*-th cell of `predictedClasses`:

```
> for (i in 1:15) {
+   training = spanish.t[-i,]
+   trainingAuthor = spanishMeta[-i,]$Author
+   training.pca = prcomp(training, center=T, scale=T)
+   training.x = data.frame(training.pca$x)
+   training.x = training.x[order(rownames(training.x)), ]
+   training.pca.lda = lda(training[ , 1:n], trainingAuthor)
+   predictedClasses[i] =
+   as.character(predict(training.pca.lda, spanish.t[ , 1:n])$class[i])
+ }
```

Finally, we compare the observed and predicted authors:

```
> data.frame(obs = as.character(spanishMeta$Author),
+ pred = predictedClasses)
   obs pred
1    C    V
2    C    C
3    C    C
4    C    C
5    C    V
6    M    M
7    M    M
8    M    M
9    M    M
10   M    V
11   V    M
12   V    V
13   V    V
14   V    M
15   V    M
```

The number of correct attributions is,

```
> sum(predictedClasses==as.character(spanishMeta$Author))
[1] 9
```

which reaches significance according to a binomial test: The likelihood of observing 9 or more successes in 15 trials is 0.03:

```
> sum(dbinom(9:15, 15, 1/3))
[1] 0.03082792
```

We conclude that there is significant authorial structure, albeit not as crisp and clear as Figure 5.18 suggested at first. We may therefore expect our discriminant model to achieve some success at predicting the authorial hand of unseen texts from one of these three authors.

5.2.3   Support vector machines

Support vector machines are a relatively recent development in classification, and their performance is often excellent. A support vector machine for a binary classification problem tries to find a hyperplane in multidimensional space such that ideally all elements of a given class are on one side of that hyperplane, and all the other elements are on the other side. Furthermore, it allocates a margin around that hyperplane, and points that are exactly the margin distance away from the hyperplane are called its support vectors. In other words, whereas discriminant analysis tries to separate groups by focusing on the group means, support vector machines target the border area where the groups meet, and seeks to set up a boundary there.

Let's re-examine the Medieval French texts studied previously with the help of correspondence analysis. Instead of clustering (unsupervised), we apply classification (supervised) with the `svm()` function from the `e1071` package:

```
> library(e1071)
```

Correspondence analysis revealed a clear difference in the use of tag trigrams across prose and poetry. We give `svm()` the reverse task of determining the amount of support that our a priori classification into prose versus poetry receives from the use of tag trigrams across our texts. The first argument that we supply to `svm()` is the data frame with counts; the second argument is the vector specifying the genre for each row in the data frame:

```
> genre.svm = svm(oldFrench, oldFrenchMeta$Genre)
```

Typing the object name at the prompt results in a brief summary of the parameters used for the classification (many possibilities are offered, we have simply used the defaults), and the number of support vectors:

```
> genre.svm
Call:
svm.default(x = oldFrench, y = oldFrenchMeta$Genre, cross = 10)

Parameters:
SVM-Type:  C-classification
SVM-Kernel:  radial
cost:  1
gamma:  0.02857143

Number of Support Vectors:  158
```

There is no straightforward way to visualize the classification. Some intuitions about the support vectors can be gleaned by means of multidimensional scaling, with special plot symbols for the observations that are chosen as support vectors, in Figure 5.19 the plus symbol. Note that the plus symbols are especially dense in the border area between the two (color-coded) genres:

```
> plot(cmdscale(dist(oldFrench)),
+ col = c("black", "darkgrey")[as.integer(oldFrenchMeta$Genre)],
+ pch = c("o", "+")[1:nrow(oldFrenchMeta) %in% genre.svm$index + 1])
```

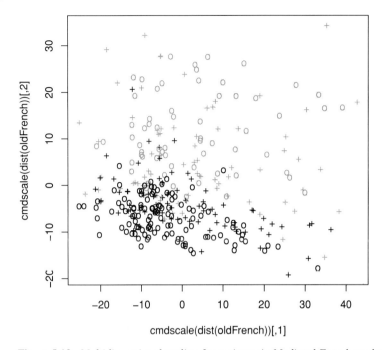

Figure 5.19. *Multidimensional scaling for registers in Medieval French on the basis of tag trigram frequencies, with support vectors highlighted by the plus symbol. Black points represent poetry, grey points represent prose.*

The second and third lines of this plot command illustrate a feature of subscripting that has not yet been explained, namely, that a vector can be subscripted for more elements as it is long, provided that these elements refer to legitimate indices in the vector:

```
> c("black", "darkgrey")[c(1, 2, 1, 2, 2, 1)]
[1] "black"    "darkgrey" "black"    "darkgrey" "darkgrey" "black"
```

In the second line of the plot command, `as.integer(oldFrenchMeta$ Genre)` is a vector with ones and twos, corresponding to the levels `poetry` and `prose`. This vector is mapped onto a vector with `blue` representing poetry and `red` representing `prose`. The same mechanism is at work for the third line. The vector between the square brackets is dissected as follows. The index extracted from the model object,

```
> genre.svm$index
[1]    2    3    6   13   14   15   16   17
```

refers to the row numbers in `oldFrench` of the support vectors. The vector

```
1:nrow(oldFrenchMeta)
```

is the vector of all row numbers. The `%in%` operator checks for set membership. The result is a vector that is TRUE for the support vectors and FALSE for all other rows. When 1 is added to this vector, TRUE first converts to 1 and FALSE to zero, so the result is a vector with ones and twos, which are in turn mapped onto the o and + symbols.

A comparison of the predicted classes with the actual classes shows that only a single text is misclassified:

```
> xtabs( ~ oldFrenchMeta$Genre + predict(genre.svm))
                  predict(genre.svm)
oldFrenchMeta$Genre poetry prose
          poetry    198    0
          prose      1    143
```

However, the model might be overfitting the data, so we carry out ten-fold cross-validation by running svm() with the option cross (by default 0) set to 10:

```
> genre.svm = svm(oldFrench, oldFrenchMeta$Genre, cross = 10)
```

The summary specifies the average accuracy as well as the accuracy in each separate cross-validation run:

```
> summary(genre.svm)
10-fold cross-validation on training data:

Total Accuracy: 96.78363
Single Accuracies:
  97.05882 97.05882 97.05882 94.11765 97.14286 97.05882
  97.05882 97.05882 100 94.28571
```

An average success rate of 0.97 (so roughly eight misclassifications) shows that genre is indeed very predictable from the authors' syntactic habits.

Classification by Region, by contrast, poses a more serious challenge:

```
> region.svm = svm(oldFrench, oldFrenchMeta$Region, cross = 10)
> xtab = xtabs(~oldFrenchMeta$Region + predict(region.svm))
> xtab
                    predict(region.svm)
oldFrenchMeta$Region  R1   R2   R3
                R1    86   32   1
                R2     1  152   0
                R3     6   18   46
```

To calculate the proportion of the correct classifications, we extract the diagonal elements,

```
> diag(xtab)
R1   R2   R3
86  152   46
```

take their sum and divide by the total number of observations:

```
> sum(diag(xtab))/sum(xtab)
[1] 0.8304094
```

Unfortunately, this success rate is severely inflated due to overfitting, as shown by ten-fold cross-validation:

```
> summary(region.svm)
10-fold cross-validation on training data:
```

```
Total Accuracy: 61.9883
Single Accuracies:
   64.70588 67.64706 67.64706 50 57.14286 64.70588
   44.11765 70.58824 73.52941 60
```

However, a success rate of 62% still compares favorably with a baseline classifier that would always assign the majority class, R2:

```
> max(xtabs( ~ oldFrenchMeta$Region))/nrow(oldFrench)
[1] 0.4473684
```

This success rate differs significantly from the cross-validated success rate. To see this, we bring together the number of successes and failures for both classifiers into a contingency table,

```
> cbind(c(153, 342-153), c(212, 342-212))
      [,1] [,2]
[1,]  153  212
[2,]  189  130
```

and apply a chi-squared test:

```
> chisq.test(cbind(c(153, 342-153), c(212, 342-212)))

     Pearson's Chi-squared test with Yates' continuity correction

data:  cbind(c(153, 342 - 153), c(212, 342 - 212))
X-squared = 19.7619, df = 1, p-value = 8.771e-06
```

An alternative test that produces the same low *p*-value is the proportions test:

```
> prop.test(c(153, 212), c(342, 342))
...
data:  c(153, 212) out of rep(342, 2)
X-squared = 19.7619, df = 1, p-value = 8.771e-06
alternative hypothesis: two.sided
95 percent confidence interval:
-0.2490838 -0.0959454
sample estimates:
   prop 1    prop 2
0.4473684 0.6198830
```

In summary, support vector machines are excellent classifiers and probably our best choice if the goal is to achieve optimal classification performance for an application. Their disadvantage is that they are difficult to interpret and provide little insight into what factors drive the classification.

Workbook section

Exercises

1. Burrows (1992), in a study using principal components analysis of English authorial hands, observed that one of his principal components represented time. Burrows' study was based on a careful selection of texts from the same register (novels written in the first person

singular). Explore for the `affixProductivity` data whether time is a latent variable for productivity for the subset of literary texts (labeled with `L` in the column `Registers`), using the year of birth as specified in the last column of the data frame (`Birth`). Run a principal components analysis using the correlation matrix. Make sure to exclude the last three columns from the data frame before running `prcomp`. Then use `pairscor.fnc()` (available if you have attached the `languageR` package), that, like `pairs()`, creates a scatterplot matrix. Unlike `pairs()`, it lists correlations in the lower triangle of the matrix. Use the output of `pairscor.fnc()` to determine whether there is a principal component that represents time. Finally use a biplot to investigate which affixes were used most productively by the early authors and which by the late authors.

2. Consider the lexical measures for English monosyllabic monomorphemic words in the data set `lexicalMeasures`. Calculate the correlation matrix (exclude the first column, which lists the words) using the Spearman correlation. Square the correlation matrix, and use multidimensional scaling to study whether the measures `CelS,NsyC,NsyS,Vf,Dent,Ient,NVratio`, and `Fdif` form a cluster.

3. Ernestus and Baayen (2003) studied if it is predictable whether a stem-final obstruent in Dutch alternates with respect to its voice specification. The data set `finalDevoicing` is a data frame with 1697 monomorphemic Dutch words, together with the properties of their onsets, vowels, codas, etc. The dependent variable is `Voice`, which specifies whether the final obstruent is voiced instead of voiceless when it is syllable-initial (as, for instance, in the plural of *muis*: *mui-zen* ("mice"). Use a classification tree to trace the probabilistic grammar underlying voice alternation in Dutch. Calculate the classification accuracy, and compare it with a baseline model that always selects `voiceless`. Details on the factors and their levels are available in the description of the data set—type `?finalDevoicing` at the R prompt.

4. The data set `spanishFunctionWords` provides the relative frequencies of the most common function words in the Spanish texts studied above using the frequencies of tag trigrams. Analyze this data set with linear discriminant analysis with cross-validation. As in the analysis of tag trigrams, first orthogonalize the data with principal components analysis. Which measure is a better predictor for authorship attribution: tag trigram frequency or function word frequency?

5. The data set `regularity` specifies for 700 Dutch verbs whether or not they are regular or irregular, along with numeric predictors such as frequency and family size, and a categorical predictor, the auxiliary selected by the verb for the past perfect. Investigate whether a verb's regularity is predictable from these variables using support vector machines. After loading the data, we convert the factor `Auxiliary` into a numeric predictor as support vector machines cannot handle factors:

```
> regularity$AuxNum = as.numeric(regularity$Auxiliary)
```

Exclude columns 1, 8, 10 (the columns labeling the verbs, their regularity, and the auxiliary) from the data frame when supplied as first argument to `svm()`. Use 10-fold cross-validation and formally test whether the cross-validated accuracy is superior to the baseline model that always selects regularity.

6 Regression modeling

Sections 4.3 and 4.4 introduced the basics of linear regression and analysis of covariance. This chapter begins with a recapitulation of the central concepts and ideas introduced in Chapter 4. It then broadens the horizon on linear regression in several ways. Section 6.2 discusses multiple linear regression and various analytical strategies for dealing with multiple predictors simultaneously. Section 6.3 introduces the GENERALIZED LINEAR MODEL, which extends the linear modeling approach to binary dependent variables (successes versus failures, correct versus incorrect responses, NP or PP realizations of the dative, etc.) and factors with ordered levels (e.g. low, mid, and high education level). (The VARBRUL program used widely in sociolinguistics implements the general linear model for binary variables.) Finally, section 6.4 outlines a method for dealing with breakpoints, and section 6.5 discusses the special care required for dealing with word frequency distributions.

6.1   Introduction

Consider again the *ratings* data set that we studied in Chapter 4. We are interested in whether the rated size (averaged over subjects) of the referents of 81 English nouns can be predicted from the subjective estimates of these words' familiarity and from the class of their referents (`plant` versus `animal`). We begin by fitting a model of covariance with `meanFamiliarity` as nonlinear numeric predictor and `Class` as factorial predictor. The SIMPLE MAIN EFFECTS, i.e. main effects that are not involved in any interactions, are separated by plus symbols in the formula for `lm()`:

```
> ratings.lm = lm(meanSizeRating ~ meanFamiliarity +
+ I(meanFamiliarity^2) + Class, data = ratings)
> summary(ratings.lm)
Coefficients:
                        Estimate Std. Error t value Pr(>|t|)
(Intercept)              4.09872    0.53870    7.609 5.75e-11
meanFamiliarity         -0.38880    0.27983   -1.389   0.1687
I(meanFamiliarity^2)     0.07056    0.03423    2.061   0.0427
Classplant              -1.89252    0.08788  -21.536  < 2e-16
```

This model has four coefficients: a coefficient for the intercept, coefficients for the linear and quadratic terms of `meanFamiliarity`, and a coefficient for the contrast between the levels of the factor `Class`: the group mean for the subset of plants is -1.89 units lower than that for the animals, the reference level mapped onto the intercept. Although we want our model to be as simple as possible, we leave the non-significant coefficient for the linear effect of `meanFamiliarity` in the model, for technical reasons, given that the quadratic term is significant.

The model that we ended up with in Chapter 4 was more complex, in that it contained an INTERACTION term for `Class` by `meanFamiliarity`:

```
> ratings.lm = lm(meanSizeRating ~ meanFamiliarity * Class +
+ I(meanFamiliarity^2), data = ratings)
> summary(ratings.lm)
Coefficients:
                           Estimate Std. Error t value Pr(>|t|)
(Intercept)                 4.42894    0.54787   8.084  7.6e-12
meanFamiliarity            -0.63131    0.29540  -2.137  0.03580
I(meanFamiliarity^2)        0.10971    0.03801   2.886  0.00508
Classplant                 -1.01248    0.41530  -2.438  0.01711
meanFamiliarity:Classplant -0.21179    0.09779  -2.166  0.03346
```

This model has three main effects and one interaction. The interpretation of this main effect, which is no longer a *simple* main effect because of the presence of an interaction in which it is involved, is not as straightforward as in the previous model. In that model, the effect of `Class` is very similar to the difference in the group means for animals and plants. (It is not identical to this difference because `meanFamiliarity` is also in the model.) In the new model with the interaction, everything is recalibrated, and the main effect by itself is no longer very informative. In fact, a main effect need not be significant as long as it is involved in interactions that are significant, in which case it normally has to be retained in the model.

Thus far, we have inspected this model with `summary()`, which tells us whether the coefficients are significantly different from zero. There is another way to look at these data, using `anova()`:

```
> anova(ratings.lm)
Analysis of Variance Table
Response: meanSizeRating
                     Df Sum Sq Mean Sq  F value    Pr(>F)
meanFamiliarity       1  3.599   3.599  30.6945 4.162e-07
Class                 1 60.993  60.993 520.2307 < 2.2e-16
I(meanFamiliarity^2)  1  0.522   0.522   4.4520   0.03815
meanFamiliarity:Class 1  0.550   0.550   4.6907   0.03346
Residuals            76  8.910   0.117
```

This summary tells us, by means of F-tests, whether a predictor contributes significantly to explaining the variance in the dependent variable. It does so in a sequential way, by ascertaining whether a predictor further down the list has anything to contribute over and above the predictors higher up the list. Hence the output of `anova()` for a model fit with `lm()` is referred to as a SEQUENTIAL

ANALYSIS OF VARIANCE TABLE. A sequential ANOVA table answers different questions than the `summary()` function. To see why, we fit a series of separate models, each with one additional predictor:

```
> ratings.lm1 = lm(meanSizeRating ~ meanFamiliarity, ratings)
> ratings.lm2 = lm(meanSizeRating ~ meanFamiliarity + Class, ratings)
> ratings.lm3 = lm(meanSizeRating ~ meanFamiliarity + Class +
+ I(meanFamiliarity^2), ratings)
> ratings.lm4 = lm(meanSizeRating ~ meanFamiliarity * Class +
+ I(meanFamiliarity^2), ratings)
```

We compare the first and the second model to test whether `Class` is predictive given that `meanFamiliarity` is in the model. In the same way, we compare the second and the third model to ascertain whether we need the quadratic term, and the third and the fourth model to verify that we need the interaction. We carry out all these comparisons simultaneously with,

```
> anova(ratings.lm1, ratings.lm2, ratings.lm3, ratings.lm4)
Analysis of Variance Table
Model 1: meanSizeRating ~ meanFamiliarity
Model 2: meanSizeRating ~ meanFamiliarity + Class
Model 3: meanSizeRating ~ meanFamiliarity + Class + I(meanFamiliarity^2)
Model 4: meanSizeRating ~ meanFamiliarity * Class + I(meanFamiliarity^2)
  Res.Df    RSS Df Sum of Sq        F  Pr(>F)
1     79 70.975
2     78  9.982  1    60.993 520.2307 < 2e-16
3     77  9.460  1     0.522   4.4520 0.03815
4     76  8.910  1     0.550   4.6907 0.03346
```

and obtain the same results as produced with `anova(ratings.lm)`. Each successive row in a sequential ANOVA table evaluates whether adding a new predictor is justified, given the other predictors in the preceding rows. By contrast, the `summary()` function evaluates whether the coefficients are significantly different from zero in a model containing all other predictors. This is a different question, that often results in different p-values.

An interaction of `Class` by the quadratic term for `meanFamiliarity` turns out not to be necessary:

```
> ratings.lm5 = lm(meanSizeRating ~ meanFamiliarity * Class +
+ I(meanFamiliarity^2) * Class, data = ratings)
> anova(ratings.lm5)
Analysis of Variance Table
Response: meanSizeRating
                         Df Sum Sq Mean Sq F value    Pr(>F)
meanFamiliarity           1  3.599   3.599 30.7934 4.128e-07
Class                     1 60.993  60.993 521.9068 < 2.2e-16
I(meanFamiliarity^2)      1  0.522   0.522  4.4663   0.03790
meanFamiliarity:Class     1  0.550   0.550  4.7058   0.03323
Class:I(meanFamiliarity^2) 1  0.145   0.145  1.2449   0.26810
Residuals                75  8.765   0.117
```

With a minimal change in the specification of the model, the replacement of the second asterisk in the model formula by a colon, we obtain a very different result:

```
> ratings.lm6 = lm(meanSizeRating ~ meanFamiliarity * Class +
+ I(meanFamiliarity^2) : Class, data = ratings)
> anova(ratings.lm5)
Analysis of Variance Table
Response: meanSizeRating
                          Df Sum Sq Mean Sq  F value    Pr(>F)
meanFamiliarity            1  3.599   3.599  30.7934 4.128e-07
Class                      1 60.993  60.993 521.9068 < 2.2e-16
meanFamiliarity:Class      1  0.095   0.095   0.8166   0.36906
Class:I(meanFamiliarity^2) 2  1.122   0.561   4.8002   0.01092
Residuals                 75  8.765   0.117
```

It would now seem as if the interaction is significant after all. In order to understand what is going on, we inspect the table of coefficients:

```
> summary(ratings.lm6)
Coefficients:
                                   Estimate Std. Error t value Pr(>|t|)
(Intercept)                         4.16838    0.59476   7.008 8.95e-10
meanFamiliarity                    -0.48424    0.32304  -1.499   0.1381
Classplant                          1.02187    1.86988   0.546   0.5864
meanFamiliarity:Classplant         -1.18747    0.87990  -1.350   0.1812
Classanimal:I(meanFamiliarity^2)    0.09049    0.04168   2.171   0.0331
Classplant:I(meanFamiliarity^2)     0.20304    0.09186   2.210   0.0301
```

Note that the coefficients for `meanFamiliarity`, `Classplant`, and their interaction are no longer significant. This may happen when a complex interaction is added to a model. The last two lines show that we have two quadratic coefficients, one for the animals (0.09) and one for the plants (0.20). This is what we asked for when we specified the interaction (`I(meanFamiliarity^2) : Class`) without including a main effect for `meanFamiliarity` in the formula for `ratings.lm6`. The question, however, is whether we need these two coefficients. At first glance, the two coefficients look fairly different, but the standard error of the second coefficient is quite large, 0.09. A quick and dirty estimate of the confidence interval for the second coefficient is $0.20 \pm 2 * 0.09$, which includes the value of the first coefficient. Clearly, these two coefficients are not significantly different. This is why the `anova()` and `summary()` functions reported a nonsignificant effect for model `ratings.lm5`. What we are asking with the formula of `ratings.lm6` is whether the individual coefficients of the quadratic terms of `meanFamiliarity` for the plants and the animals are different from zero. This they are. We are not asking whether we need two different coefficients. This we do not. What this example shows is that the main effect of a term in the model, here the quadratic term for `meanFamiliarity`, should be specified explicitly in the model when the question of interest is whether an interaction term is justified.

The conventions governing the specification of main effects and interactions in the formula of a model are both straightforward and flexible. It is often convenient not to have to spell out all interactions for models with many predictors. The following overview shows how combinations of predictors and their interactions can be specified using parentheses, the plus and minus symbols, and the ^ operator. With ^2, for instance, we denote that all interactions involving pairwise combinations of the predictors enclosed within parentheses should be included in the model:

```
a + b + c
a + b + c + a:b                        or   a * b + c
a + b + c + a:b + a:c + b:c            or   (a + b + c)^2
a + b + c + a:b + a:c + b:c + a:b:c    or   (a + b + c)^3
a + b + c + a:b + a:c                  or   (a + b + c)^2 - b:c
```

Thus, the formula for `ratings.lm5`, for instance, can be simplified to:

```
meanSizeRating ~ (meanFamiliarity + I(meanFamiliarity^2)) * Class
```

6.2   Ordinary least squares regression

This section introduces the `Design` package for multiple regression. This package is described in detail by its author in Harrell (2001), a highly recommended monograph on regression and modeling strategies. In what follows, we work through an example that illustrates the full range of complexities that we may encounter in multiple regression using the data on 2284 monomorphemic and monosyllabic English nouns and verbs that we have already encountered in the preceding chapters. A detailed analysis of a subset of these data can be found in Baayen *et al.* (2006). Short descriptions of each of the predictors are available in the on-line documentation (`help(english)`). We begin by considering whether a word's reaction time in visual lexical decision can be predicted from its frequency of use in written English and from its length in letters. We have data for 2197 words, divided over two word categories, nouns and verbs:

```
> xtabs(~english$WordCategory)
english$WordCategory
    N     V
 2904  1664
```

The reaction times (`RTlexdec`) are log-transformed averages calculated for two subject groups differentiated by age:

```
> xtabs(~english$AgeSubject)
english$AgeSubject
  old young
 2284  2284
```

The structure of this data set is made more clear by cross-tabulation:

```
> xtabs(~english$AgeSubject + english$WordCategory)
                   english$WordCategory
english$AgeSubject    N     V
             old   1452   832
           young   1452   832
```

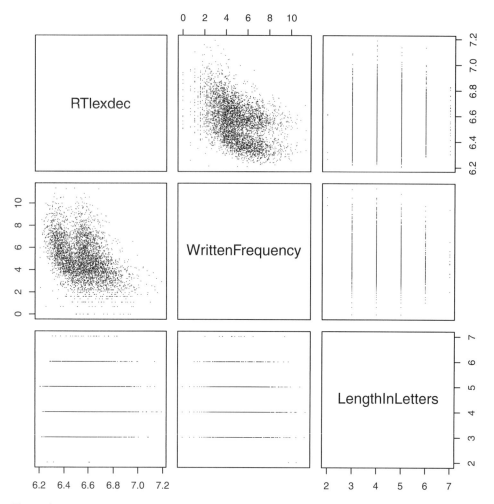

Figure 6.1. *Pairs plot for written frequency, length in letters, and reaction time in visual lexical decision, for English nouns and verbs. For each word, an average reaction time is plotted for two groups of subjects, differentiated by age.*

Each word occurs on two lines in the data frame, once for the young subject group and once for the old subject group. We begin with a visual inspection of our variables using the pairs plot shown in Figure 6.1:

```
> pairs(english[,c("RTlexdec", "WrittenFrequency", "LengthInLetters")],
+ pch = ".")
```

A negative correlation is visible for frequency and reaction time, which seems to be non-linear. There also appear to be two parallel bands of points. These are due, as will become apparent below, to the slower responses of the older subjects. Finally, we note that there is not much to be seen for length in letters, an integer-valued variable with a highly restricted range of values.

When working with data using the `Design` package, it is recommended that you first make an object that summarizes the distribution of your data with the `datadist()` function. Such a summary includes, for instance, the ranges of the predictors, which in turn guide the plot methods of `Design` objects:

```
> library(Design)
> english.dd = datadist(english)
```

It often happens that we have more than one data distribution object in the current workspace, so we need to tell the functions of the `Design` package which of these objects it should use. This is accomplished with the `options()` function, which sets a variable with the name `datadist` to point to the appropriate data distribution object:

```
> options(datadist = "english.dd")
```

In what follows, we switch from `lm()` to `ols()` as our tool for regression modeling. The name of this function is an acronym for ORDINARY LEAST SQUARES, the method by means of which the coefficients of the linear model are estimated and that is used by both `lm()` and `ols()`. This estimation method seeks to minimize the squared vertical distances of data points to the regression line, hence the terminology of "least squares." We use `ols()` in the same way as `lm()`:

```
> english.ols = ols(RTlexdec~WrittenFrequency+LengthInLetters, english)
```

A summary of the model is obtained simply by typing the name of the model object at the prompt:

```
> english.ols
Linear Regression Model
ols(formula = RTlexdec ~ WrittenFrequency + LengthInLetters, english)

   n Model L.R.       d.f.          R2       Sigma
4568      959.7          2      0.1895      0.1413

Residuals:
      Min         1Q     Median          3Q         Max
-0.455240  -0.115826  -0.001086   0.103922    0.562429

Coefficients:
                      Value Std. Error        t Pr(>|t|)
Intercept           6.71845   0.012728 527.832   0.0000
WrittenFrequency   -0.03689   0.001137 -32.456   0.0000
LengthInLetters     0.00389   0.002489   1.563   0.1182

Residual standard error: 0.1413 on 4565 degrees of freedom
Adjusted R-Squared: 0.1891
```

The summary begins with describing `english.ols` as a linear regression model object, and specifies the function call with which it was obtained. It then lists the number of observations (4568), followed by the likelihood ratio statistic (`L.R.`), a measure of goodness of fit. Together with its associated degrees of freedom (2), this statistic can be used to test whether the model as a whole is explanatory as follows:

```
> 1 - pchisq(959.7, 2)
[1] 0
```

The extremely small p-value is reassuring.

The proportion of the variance explained by the model, R^2, is 0.1895, and the standard deviation of the RESIDUAL STANDARD ERROR (Sigma) is estimated at 0.14. To understand these measures, it is helpful to make a table listing the observed (log) RTs, the EXPECTED or FITTED values of these RTs predicted by the model, and the difference between the observed and expected values, the RESIDUALS. We use the functions fitted() and resid() and bring the result together in a data frame:

```
> x = data.frame(obs = english$RTlexdec,
+ exp = fitted(english.ols), resid = resid(english.ols))
> x[1:5,]
       obs      exp       resid
1  6.543754 6.585794 -0.04203996
2  6.397596 6.571078 -0.17348145
3  6.304942 6.501774 -0.19683156
4  6.424221 6.548908 -0.12468768
5  6.450597 6.553591 -0.10299411
```

The values of R^2 and Sigma are now straightforward to calculate:

```
> cor(x$obs, x$exp)^2
[1] 0.1894976           # R-squared
> sd(x$resid)
[1] 0.1412707           # Sigma
```

R^2 tells us how tight the fit is between what we observe and what we predict. Sigma, on the other hand, summarizes the variability in the residuals. The better the model, the smaller Sigma will be.

The summary proceeds with a description of the distribution of the residuals. The mathematics underlying ordinary least squares regression depends on the assumption that the residuals are normally distributed. The summary therefore lists the quartiles:

```
> quantile(x$resid)
          0%          25%           50%          75%         100%
-0.455239802 -0.115826341 -0.001086030  0.103922388  0.562429031
```

which suggest a reasonably symmetrical distribution. We can also inspect the normality of the residuals by means of density and quantile-quantile plots:

```
> par(mfrow = c(1, 2))
> plot(density(x$resid), main = "")
> qqnorm(x$resid, pch = ".", main = "")
> qqline(x$resid)
> par(mfrow = c(1, 1))
```

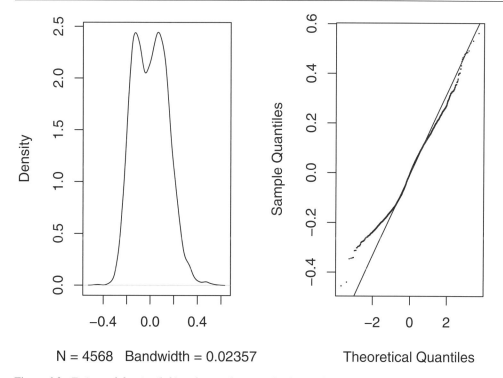

Figure 6.2. *Estimated density (left) and quantile-quantile plot (right) for the residuals of* english.ols.

Figure 6.2 shows that there is something wrong with the residuals. Both panels suggest departure from normality. The density plot, furthermore, indicates that we are missing an important predictor, and that we have here two normal or near-normal distributions with different means, instead of a single normal distribution.

Next in the summary is the table of coefficients. WrittenFrequency is a significant predictor, LengthInLetters apparently not. The summary concludes with listing the residual standard error, so Sigma again, and its associated degrees of freedom, 4565. This number is equal to the total number of observations, 4568, minus the number of coefficients in the model, 3. The last line of the summary mentions the adjusted R^2, a conservative version of R^2 optimized for comparing different models with respect to the amount of variance that they explain.

The density in Figure 6.2 suggests we have failed to bring an important predictor into the model. This predictor turns out to be the age group (young versus old) of the subjects in the experiment. We therefore include AgeSubject as a predictor, and rerun ols():

```
> english.olsA = ols(RTlexdec ~ WrittenFrequency + AgeSubject +
+ LengthInLetters, data = english)
> english.olsA
Linear Regression Model
ols(formula = RTlexdec ~ WrittenFrequency + AgeSubject +
  LengthInLetters, data = english)
```

```
        n Model L.R.       d.f.          R2      Sigma
     4568      5331           3      0.6887    0.08758


     Residuals:
        Min      1Q   Median       3Q      Max
     -0.34438 -0.06041 -0.00695  0.05241  0.45157


     Coefficients:
                        Value Std. Error       t Pr(>|t|)
     Intercept            6.82931  0.0079946 854.245  0.00000
     WrittenFrequency    -0.03689  0.0007045 -52.366  0.00000
     AgeSubject=young    -0.22172  0.0025915 -85.556  0.00000
     LengthInLetters      0.00389  0.0015428   2.521  0.01173


     Residual standard error: 0.08758 on 4564 degrees of freedom
     Adjusted R-Squared: 0.6885
```

Note, first of all, that R^2 is very much higher, and that Sigma is substantially reduced. We now have a much better model. With the most important source of variation under control, LengthInLetters emerges as significant as well.

Thus far, we have assumed that our predictors are linear. Given the curvature visible in Figure 6.1, we need to address the possibility that this convenient assumption is too simplistic.

6.2.1   Nonlinearities

We have already studied a regression model with a nonlinear relation between the predictor and the dependent variable. We could add a quadratic term to the model, using lm(),

```
> english.lm = lm(RTlexdec ~ WrittenFrequency + I(WrittenFrequency^2) +
+ AgeSubject + LengthInLetters,  data = english)
> summary(english.lm)
Coefficients:
                     Estimate Std. Error t value Pr(>|t|)
(Intercept)          6.9181819  0.0100832 686.112   < 2e-16
WrittenFrequency    -0.0773456  0.0029733 -26.013   < 2e-16
I(WrittenFrequency^2) 0.0038209  0.0002732  13.987   < 2e-16
AgeSubjectyoung     -0.2217215  0.0025380 -87.362   < 2e-16
LengthInLetters      0.0050257  0.0015131   3.321 0.000903
```

and it is clear from the summary that the quadratic term for WrittenFrequency is justified. The technical term for this way of handling nonlinearities is that we made use of a QUADRATIC POLYNOMIAL.

It is not possible (nor necessary, as we shall see) to add a quadratic term in the same way to the model formula when using ols(). This is because ols() tries to look up the quadratic term in the data distribution object that we constructed for our data frame. As there is no separate quadratic term available in our data frame, ols() reports an error and quits. Fortunately, ols() provides alternative ways of modeling nonlinearities that are in fact simpler to specify in the model formula. In order to include a quadratic term for WrittenFrequency, we use the function `pol()`, an abbreviation for POLYNOMIAL. It takes two arguments, the name of the predictor, and a number specifying the complexity of the polynomial function. A 2 specifies a linear and a quadratic component, a 3 defines the combination of a linear, a quadratic, and a cubic component, etc. Here, we opt for minimal nonlinearity with a quadratic fit:

```
> english.olsB = ols(RTlexdec ~ pol(WrittenFrequency, 2) + AgeSubject +
+ LengthInLetters,  data = english)
> english.olsB
Coefficients:
                        Value Std. Error        t  Pr(>|t|)
Intercept            6.918182  0.0100832 686.112 0.0000000
WrittenFrequency    -0.077346  0.0029733 -26.013 0.0000000
WrittenFrequency^2   0.003821  0.0002732  13.987 0.0000000
AgeSubject=young    -0.221721  0.0025380 -87.362 0.0000000
LengthInLetters      0.005026  0.0015131   3.321 0.0009026
```

The estimates of the coefficients are identical to those estimated by `lm()`, but we did not have to spell out the quadratic term ourselves.

The use of `ols()` has some further, more important advantages, however. First, the anova table lists the overall significance of `WrittenFrequency`, and separately the significance of its nonlinear component(s):

```
> anova(english.olsB)
Analysis of Variance            Response: RTlexdec

        Factor       d.f. Partial SS MS                F        P
WrittenFrequency     2 21.3312650 10.665632502 1508.39 <.0001
Nonlinear            1  1.4462474  1.446247447  204.54 <.0001
AgeSubject           1 54.4400676 54.440067616 7699.22 <.0001
LengthInLetters      1  0.0821155  0.082115506   11.61 7e-04
REGRESSION           4 76.0907743 19.022693573 2690.30 <.0001
ERROR             4461 31.5430668  0.007070851
```

Unlike when `anova()` is applied to model objects produced by `lm()`, the `anova()` method for `ols` objects provides a NON-SEQUENTIAL analysis of variance table. This table lists, for each predictor, the F-statistics and associated p-values, given that all the other predictors are already in the model.

A second advantage of `ols()` is that it is straightforward to visualize the effects of the predictors. For this example, we begin with creating space for three panels with `mfrow()`, and then we apply `plot()` to the model object. When setting up the plot regions, we also specify that we need a smaller font size (0.6 of the standard) with the `cex` parameter, so that the text accompanying each panel is fully readable:

```
> par(mfrow = c(2, 2), cex = 0.6)
> plot(english.olsB)
> par(mfrow = c(1, 1), cex = 1.0)
```

Figure 6.3 shows the PARTIAL EFFECTS of each of the predictors, i.e. the effect of a given predictor when the other predictors in the model are held constant. The position of each curve with respect to the vertical axis depends on the actual values

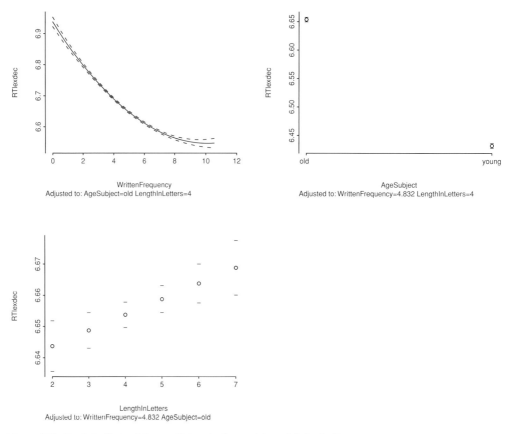

Figure 6.3. *Partial effects of the predictors in the model* english.olsB.

for which the other parameters in the model are held constant. These values are spelled out beneath each panel. For instance, the curve for frequency represents the old subjects, and words with four letters (the median word length). The line for the effect of length is adjusted so that it describes the effect for the old subjects and for a written frequency of 4.8 (the median frequency). The dashed lines show the 95% confidence bands for the regression lines. Confidence intervals are indicated by hyphens above and below the points representing factor levels. For AgeSubject, the intervals are so small that the hyphens coincide with the point symbols.

There are disadvantages to the use of polynomials, however. A quadratic polynomial presupposes the data follow part of a parabola. For more complex curvature, higher-order polynomials can be used (i.e. models including additional cubic or higher terms), but they are costly in the number of parameters they require, they tend to overfit the data, and a priori impose a very specific functional form on the curve. A more flexible alternative is to use RESTRICTED CUBIC SPLINES. In construction, a spline is a flexible strip of metal or a piece of rubber that is used for drawing the curved parts of objects. In statistics, a spline is a function for modeling nonlinear relations. The spline function combines a series of simpler functions (in fact, cubic polynomials) defined over a corresponding series of intervals. These simpler functions are constrained to have smooth transitions where they meet, at the KNOTS of the spline. The number of knots determines the number of intervals. When you use more intervals, the simpler functions are defined over smaller intervals, so this allows you to model more subtle nonlinearities. In other words, the number of knots controls how smooth your curve will be. The minimum number of knots is three (so two intervals), in which case the curve is maximally smooth. As more knots are added, more wriggly curves can be fitted. Restricted cubic splines are cubic splines that are adjusted to avoid overfitting for the more extreme values of the predictor. For details, see Harrell, 2001:16–24, and references cited there.

Let's consider two models, one with a restricted cubic spline with three knots, and one with seven knots. In the model formula, we replace `pol()` by `rcs()`. The number of knots is the second parameter for `rcs()`, the first parameter specifies what predictor a spline is requested for:

```
> english.olsC = ols(RTlexdec ~ rcs(WrittenFrequency, 3) + AgeSubject +
+ LengthInLetters, data = english)
> english.olsC
                        Value Std. Error      t Pr(>|t|)
Intercept            6.903062   0.009248 746.411 0.000000
WrittenFrequency    -0.059213   0.001650 -35.882 0.000000
WrittenFrequency'    0.030576   0.002055  14.881 0.000000
AgeSubject=young    -0.221721   0.002531 -87.598 0.000000
LengthInLetters      0.004875   0.001508   3.232 0.001238
```

The mathematics of restricted cubic splines work out so that the number of parameters required is one less than the number of knots. This explains why the summary lists two coefficients for `WrittenFrequency`. For seven knots, we get six coefficients:

```
> english.olsD = ols(RTlexdec ~ rcs(WrittenFrequency,7) + AgeSubject +
+ LengthInLetters, data = english)
> english.olsD
                          Value Std. Error       t  Pr(>|t|)
Intercept              6.794645   0.013904 488.697 0.000e+00
WrittenFrequency      -0.010971   0.005299  -2.070 3.847e-02
WrittenFrequency'     -0.348645   0.052381  -6.656 3.147e-11
WrittenFrequency''     2.101416   0.474765   4.426 9.814e-06
WrittenFrequency'''   -2.987002   1.081374  -2.762 5.764e-03
WrittenFrequency''''   1.880416   1.121685   1.676 9.372e-02
WrittenFrequency'''''  -0.951205   0.649998  -1.463 1.434e-01
AgeSubject=young      -0.221721   0.002497 -88.784 0.000e+00
LengthInLetters        0.005238   0.001491   3.513 4.468e-04
```

Note that the last two coefficients for `WrittenFrequency` have large *p*-values. This suggests that five knots should be sufficient to capture the nonlinearity without undersmoothing or oversmoothing. Figure 6.4 compares the different spline curves with the curve obtained with a quadratic polynomial. With only three knots (so two intervals), we basically get two straight lines with a smooth bend, that together are very similar to the polynomial curve. With seven knots, the curve becomes somewhat wriggly in the center, with several points of inflection. These are removed when the number of intervals is reduced to four.

Figure 6.4 is built panel by panel. Presuming the plot region is defined properly with `mfrow()`, we obtain the upper left panel by setting `WrittenFrequency` to `NA`:

```
> plot(english.olsC, WrittenFrequency=NA, ylim=c(6.5, 7.0), conf.int=F)
```

This tells the plot method for `ols` objects that it should suppress panels for the other predictors in the model. As we want to avoid cluttering our plot with very similar confidence intervals, we set `conf.int = F`. In order to add the polynomial curve to the same plot we specify `add = T`:

```
> plot(english.olsB, WrittenFrequency = NA, add = T,
+ lty = 2, conf.int = F)
> mtext("3 knots, undersmoothing", 3, 1, cex = 0.8)
```

The other two panels are obtained in a similar way. Note that we force the same interval on the vertical axis across all panels:

```
> plot(english.olsD, WrittenFrequency=NA, ylim=c(6.5, 7.0), conf.int=F)
> plot(english.olsB, WrittenFrequency=NA, add=T, lty=2, conf.int=F)
> mtext("7 knots, oversmoothing", 3, 1, cex = 0.8)
> english.olsE = ols(RTlexdec ~ rcs(WrittenFrequency,5) + AgeSubject +
+ LengthInLetters, english)
> plot(english.olsE, WrittenFrequency=NA, ylim=c(6.5, 7.0), conf.int=F)
> plot(english.olsB, WrittenFrequency=NA, add=T, lty=2, conf.int=F)
> mtext("5 knots", 3, 1, cex = 0.8)
```

It turns out that there is an interaction of `WrittenFrequency` by age:

```
> english.olsE = ols(RTlexdec ~ rcs(WrittenFrequency, 5) + AgeSubject +
+ LengthInLetters + rcs(WrittenFrequency,5) : AgeSubject,
+ data = english)
```

The summary shows that there are four coefficients for the interaction of age by frequency, matching the four coefficients for frequency by itself:

```
> english.olsE
Coefficients:
                                           Value  ...
Intercept                                6.856846
WrittenFrequency                        -0.039530
WrittenFrequency'                       -0.136373
WrittenFrequency''                       0.749955
WrittenFrequency'''                     -0.884461
AgeSubject=young                        -0.275166
LengthInLetters                          0.005218
WrittenFrequency * AgeSubject=young      0.017493
WrittenFrequency' * AgeSubject=young    -0.043592
WrittenFrequency'' * AgeSubject=young    0.010664
WrittenFrequency''' * AgeSubject=young   0.171251 ...

Residual standard error: 0.08448 on 4557 degrees of freedom
Adjusted R-Squared: 0.7102
```

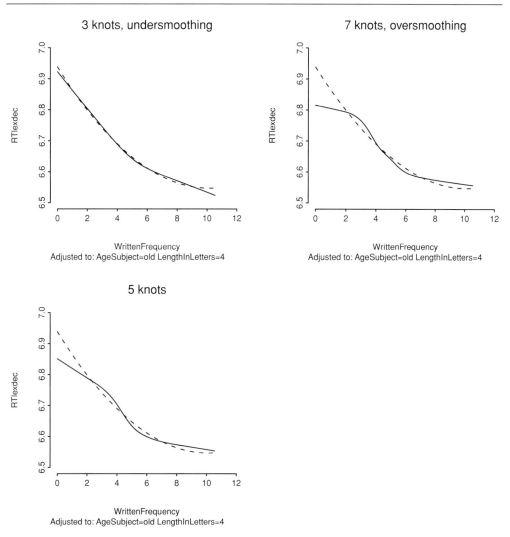

Figure 6.4. *The partial effect of written frequency using a restricted cubic spline with three knots (upper left), seven knots (upper right), and five knots (lower left). The dashed line represents a quadratic polynomial.*

The anova table confirms that all these coefficients are really necessary:

```
> anova(english.olsE)
Analysis of Variance          Response: RTlexdec

Factor                          df    SS        MS       F       P
WrittenFrequency
 (Factor+Higher Order Factors)   8 23.5123     2.9390   411.80 <.0001
 All Interactions                4  0.1093     0.0273     3.83 0.0041
 Nonlinear
 (Factor+Higher Order Factors)   6  2.4804     0.4134    57.92 <.0001
AgeSubject
 (Factor+Higher Order Factors)   5 56.2505    11.2501  1576.29 <.0001
 All Interactions                4  0.1093     0.0273     3.83 0.0041
```

LengthInLetters	1	0.0874	0.0874	12.24	0.0005
WrittenFrequency * AgeSubject					
(Factor+Higher Order Factors)	4	0.1093	0.0273	3.83	0.0041
Nonlinear	3	0.1092	0.0364	5.10	0.0016
TOTAL NONLINEAR	6	2.4804	0.4134	57.92	<.0001
TOTAL NONLINEAR + INTERACTION	7	2.4806	0.3544	49.65	<.0001
REGRESSION	10	79.9318	7.9932	1119.95	<.0001
ERROR	4557	32.5237	0.0071		

It is worth taking a closer look at this anova table. It first lists the statistics for Written Frequency as a whole, including its nonlinear terms and its interactions. The column labeled df lists the number of coefficients in the model for the different predictors and their interactions. For WrittenFrequency, for instance, we have 8 coefficients, 4 for the main effect and another 4 for the interaction with AgeSubject. The nonlinearity of WrittenFrequency is accounted for with 6 coefficients (the ones listed with one or more apostrophes in the summary table for the coefficients and their p-values). For AgeSubject, we spend 5 parameters: one coefficient for AgeSubject itself, and 4 for the interaction with Written-Frequency. The last lines of the summary evaluate the combined nonlinearities as well as the nonlinearities and interactions considered jointly, and conclude with the F-test for the regression model as a whole.

Each coefficient costs us a degree of freedom. In the present model, we have 4557 degrees of freedom left. If we were to add another predictor requiring one coefficient, the residual degrees of freedom would become 4556. Since p-values for the t- and F-tests become smaller for larger degrees of freedom, it becomes more and more difficult to observe significant effects as we add more parameters to the model. This is exactly what is needed, as we want our model to be parsimonious and to avoid overfitting the data.

Figure 6.5 shows the partial effects of the predictors in this model. As before, we add the curve representing WrittenFrequency for the young subjects to the plot for the old subjects with the option add=T:

```
> par(mfrow = c(2, 2), cex = 0.7)
> plot(english.olsE, WrittenFrequency = NA, ylim = c(6.2, 7.0))
> plot(english.olsE, WrittenFrequency = NA, AgeSubject = "young",
+ add = T, col = "darkgrey")
> plot(english.olsE, LengthInLetters = NA, ylim = c(6.2, 7.0))
> plot(english.olsE, AgeSubject = NA, ylim = c(6.2, 7.0))
> par(mfrow = c(1, 1), cex = 1)
```

With the same range of values on the vertical axis, the huge differences in the sizes of the partial effects of frequency, length, and age group become apparent.

You now know how to run a multiple regression with ols(), how to handle potential nonlinearities, and how to plot the partial effects of the predictors. For the present data set, the analysis is far from complete, however, as there are many more variables in the model that we have not yet considered. As many of these additional predictors are pairwise correlated, we run into the problem of collinearity.

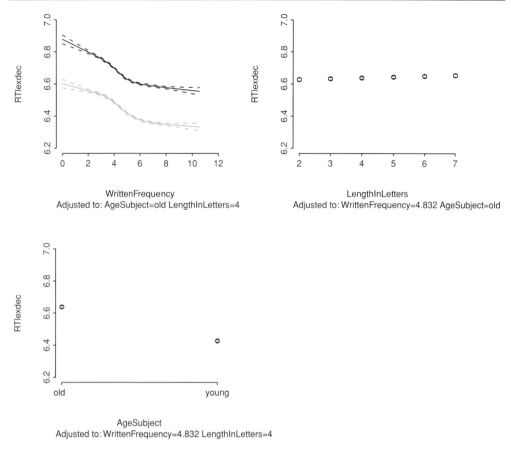

Figure 6.5. *The partial effects according to model* `english.olsE`. *As the vertical axes are all on the same scale, the huge differences in the sizes of the effects are clearly visible.*

6.2.2   Collinearity

The ideal data set for multiple regression is one in which all the predictors are uncorrelated. Severe problems may arise if the predictors enter into strong correlations, a phenomenon known as COLLINEARITY (Belsley *et al.*, 1980). A metaphor for understanding the problem posed by collinearity builds on Figure 6.6. The ideal situation is shown to the left. The variance to be explained is represented by the square. The small circles represent the part of the variance captured by four predictors. In the situation shown on the left, each predictor captures its own unique portion of the variance. In this case, the predictors are said to be ORTHOGONAL; they are uncorrelated. The situation depicted to the right illustrates collinear predictors. There is little variance that is captured by just one predictor. Instead, almost the same part of the variance is captured by all four predictors. Hence, it becomes difficult to tease the explanatory values of these predictors apart.

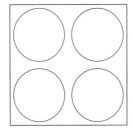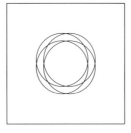

Figure 6.6. *Orthogonal (left) and collinear (right) predictors.*

Collinearity is generally assessed by means of the condition number κ. The greater the collinearity, the closer the matrix of predictors is to becoming SINGU-LAR. When a matrix is singular, the problem that arises is similar to attempting to divide a number by zero: the operation is not defined. The condition number estimates the extent to which a matrix is singular, i.e. how close the task of estimating the parameters is to being unsolvable. R provides a function, kappa(), for estimating the condition number, but we calculate κ with collin.fnc() following Belsley *et al.* (1980). These authors argue that not only the predictors, but also the intercept should be taken into account when evaluating the condition number. When the condition number is between 0 and 6, there is no collinearity to speak of. Medium collinearity is indicated by condition numbers around 15, and condition numbers of 30 or more indicate potentially harmful collinearity.

In order to assess the collinearity of our lexical predictors, we first remove word duplicates from the english data frame by selecting those rows that concern the young age group. We then apply collin.fnc() to the resulting data matrix of items, restricted to the columns of the 23 numerical variables in which we are interested (in columns 7 through 29 of our data frame). From the list of objects returned by collin.fnc() we select the condition number with the $ operator:

```
> collin.fnc(english[english$AgeSubject == "young",], 7:29)$cnumber
[1] 132.0727
```

Note that the second argument to collin.fnc() specifies the columns to be selected from the data frame specified as its first argument. A condition number as high as 132 indicates that it makes no sense to consider these 23 predictors jointly in a multiple regression model. Too many variables tell the same story. The numerical algorithms used to estimate the coefficients may even run into problems with machine precision.

As a first step towards addressing this problem, we visualize the correlational structure of our predictors. In section 5.1.4 we studied this correlational structure with the help of hierarchical clustering. The Design package provides a convenient function for visualizing clusters of variables, varclus(), that obviates intermediate steps:

```
> plot(varclus(as.matrix(english[english$AgeSubject == "young", 7:29])))
```

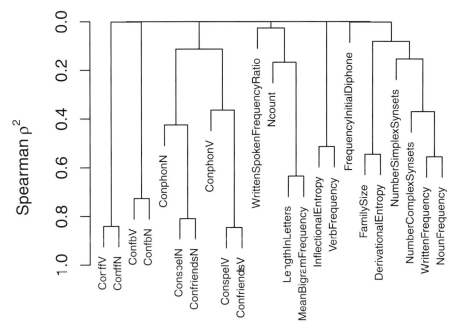

Figure 6.7. *Hierarchical clustering of* 23 *predictors in the* english *data set, using the square of Spearman's rank correlation as similarity measure.*

The varclus() function carries out a hierarchical cluster analysis, using the square of Spearman's rank correlation as a similarity metric to obtain a more robust insight into the correlational structure of (possibly nonlinear) predictors. Figure 6.7 shows that there are several groups of tightly correlated predictors. For instance, the second cluster from the left brings together six correlated measures for orthographic consistency, which subdivide by whether they are based on token counts (the left subcluster with variable names ending in N) or whether they are based on type counts (the right subcluster with names ending in V).

There are several strategies that one can pursue to reduce collinearity. The simplest strategy is to select one variable from each cluster. The problem with this strategy is that we may be throwing out information that is actually useful. Belsley *et al.* (1980) give as example an entrance test gauging skills in mathematics and physics. Normally, grades for these subjects will be correlated, and one could opt for looking only at the grades for physics. But some students might like only math, and basing a selection criterion on the grades for physics would exclude students with excellent grades for math but low grades for physics. In spite of this consideration, one may have theoretical reasons for selecting one variable from a cluster. For instance, FamilySize and DerivationalEntropy are measures that are mathematically related, and that gauge the same phenomenon. As we are not interested in which of the two is superior in this study, we select one.

In the case of our 10 measures for orthographic consistency, we can do more. We can orthogonalize these predictors using principal components analysis, a technique that was introduced in Chapter 5. Columns 19 through 28 contain the orthographic consistency measures for our words, and just for these 10 variables by themselves, the condition number is already quite large:

```
> collin.fnc(english[english$AgeSubject == "young",], 18:27)$cnumber
[1] 49.05881
```

We reduce these 10 correlated predictors to 4 uncorrelated, orthogonal, predictors as follows. With `prcomp()` we create a principal components object. Next, we inspect the proportions of variance explained by the successive principal components:

```
> items = english[english$AgeSubject == "young",]
> items.pca = prcomp(items[ , c(18:27)], center = T, scale = T)
> summary(items.pca)
Importance of components:
                          PC1    PC2    PC3    PC4    PC5 ...
Standard deviation      2.087  1.489  1.379 0.9030 0.5027 ...
Proportion of Variance  0.435  0.222  0.190 0.0815 0.0253 ...
Cumulative Proportion   0.435  0.657  0.847 0.9288 0.9541 ...
```

The first four PCs each capture more than 5% of the variance, and jointly account for 93% of the variance,

```
> sum((items.pca$sdev^2/sum(items.pca$sdev^2))[1:4])
[1] 0.9288
```

so they are excellent candidates for replacing the 10 original consistency measures. Inspection of the rotation matrix allows insight into the relation between the original and new variables. For instance, sorting the rotation matrix by PC4 shows that this component distinguishes between the token-based and type-based measures:

```
> x = as.data.frame(items.pca$rotation[,1:4])
> x[order(x$PC4), ]
                   PC1         PC2         PC3         PC4
ConfriendsN 0.37204438 -0.28143109  0.07238358 -0.44609099
ConspelN    0.38823175 -0.22604151 -0.15599471 -0.40374288
ConphonN    0.40717952  0.17060014  0.07058176 -0.35127339
ConfbN      0.24870639  0.52615043  0.06499437 -0.06059884
ConffN      0.10793431  0.05825320 -0.66785576  0.05538818
ConfbV      0.25482902  0.52696962  0.06377711  0.10447280
ConffV      0.09828443  0.03862766 -0.67055578  0.13298443
ConfriendsV 0.33843465 -0.35438183  0.20236240  0.38326779
ConphonV    0.38450345  0.22507258  0.13966044  0.38454580
ConspelV    0.36685237 -0.32393895 -0.03194922  0.42952573
```

The principal components themselves are available in `items.pca$x`. That there is indeed no collinearity among these four principal components can be verified by application of `collin.fnc()`:

```
> collin.fnc(items.pca$x, 1:4)$cnumber
[1] 1
```

Finally, we add these four principal components to our data, first for the young age group, and then for the old age group. We then combine the two data frames into an expanded version of the original data frame `english` with the help of `rbind()`, which binds vectors or data frames row-wise:

```
> items$PC1 =  items.pca$x[,1]
> items$PC2 =  items.pca$x[,2]
> items$PC3 =  items.pca$x[,3]
> items$PC4 =  items.pca$x[,4]
> items2 = english[english$AgeSubject != "young", ]
> items2$PC1 =  items.pca$x[,1]
> items2$PC2 =  items.pca$x[,2]
> items2$PC3 =  items.pca$x[,3]
> items2$PC4 =  items.pca$x[,4]
> english2 = rbind(items, items2)
```

Sometimes, simpler solutions are possible. For the present data, one question of interest concerned the potential consequences of the frequency of use of a word as a noun or as a verb (e.g. *the work, to work*). Including two correlated frequency vectors is not advisable. As a solution, we include as a predictor the difference of the log frequency of the noun and that of the verb. (This is mathematically equivalent to considering the log of the ratio of the unlogged nominal and verbal frequencies.) With this new predictor, we can investigate whether it matters whether a word is used more often as a noun, or more often as a verb:

```
> english2$NVratio =
+ log(english2$NounFrequency+1) - log(english2$VerbFrequency+1)
```

Similarly, the frequencies of use in written and spoken language can be brought together in a ratio, `WrittenSpokenFrequencyRatio`, that is already available in the data frame. With just three frequency measures, `WrittenFrequency`, `WrittenSpokenFrequency Ratio`, and `NVratio`, instead of four frequency measures, we reduce the condition number for the frequency measures from 9.45 to 3.44. In what follows, we restrict ourselves to the following predictors,

```
> english3 = english2[,c("RTlexdec", "Word", "AgeSubject",
+ "WordCategory", "WrittenFrequency",
+ "WrittenSpokenFrequencyRatio", "FamilySize",
+ "InflectionalEntropy", "NumberSimplexSynsets",
+ "NumberComplexSynsets", "LengthInLetters", "MeanBigramFrequency",
+ "Ncount",  "NVratio", "PC1", "PC2", "PC3", "PC4", "Voice")]
```

and create the corresponding data distribution object:

```
> english3.dd = datadist(english3)
> options(datadist = "english3.dd")
```

We also include the interaction of `WrittenFrequency` by `AgeSubject` observed above in the new model:

```
> english3.ols = ols(RTlexdec ~ Voice + PC1 + PC2 + PC3 + PC4 +
+ LengthInLetters + MeanBigramFrequency + Ncount +
+ rcs(WrittenFrequency, 5) + WrittenSpokenFrequencyRatio +
```

```
+ NVratio + WordCategory + AgeSubject +
+ FamilySize + InflectionalEntropy +
+ NumberSimplexSynsets + NumberComplexSynsets +
+ rcs(WrittenFrequency, 5) * AgeSubject, data = english3)
```

An `anova` summary shows remarkably few non-significant predictors: the principal components PC2–4, length, neighborhood density, and the number of simplex synsets. A procedure in the `Design` package for removing superfluous predictors from the full model is `fastbw()`, which implements a fast backwards elimination routine:

```
> fastbw(english3.ols)

Deleted              Chi-Sq df P    Residual df     P    AIC   R2
NumberSimplexSynsets 0.00   1  0.9742  0.00   1 0.9742 -2.00 0.734
Ncount               0.05   1  0.8192  0.05   2 0.9737 -3.95 0.734
PC3                  0.74   1  0.3889  0.80   3 0.8505 -5.20 0.734
PC2                  0.90   1  0.3441  1.69   4 0.7924 -6.31 0.734
LengthInLetters      1.15   1  0.2845  2.84   5 0.7252 -7.16 0.734
PC4                  1.40   1  0.2364  4.24   6 0.6445 -7.76 0.734
NVratio              4.83   1  0.0279  9.07   7 0.2476 -4.93 0.734
WordCategory         2.01   1  0.1562 11.08   8 0.1971 -4.92 0.733


Approximate Estimates after Deleting Factors

Coef        S.E.      Wald Z         P
Intercept                    6.865088 0.0203124 337.97550 0.000e+00
Voice=voiceless             -0.009144 0.0025174  -3.63235 2.808e-04
PC1                          0.002687 0.0005961   4.50736 6.564e-06
MeanBigramFrequency          0.007509 0.0018326   4.09740 4.178e-05
WrittenFrequency            -0.041683 0.0047646  -8.74852 0.000e+00
WrittenFrequency'           -0.114355 0.0313057  -3.65285 2.593e-04
WrittenFrequency''           0.704428 0.1510582   4.66329 3.112e-06
WrittenFrequency'''         -0.886685 0.1988077  -4.46002 8.195e-06
WrittenSpokenFrequencyRatio  0.009739 0.0011305   8.61432 0.000e+00
AgeSubject=young            -0.275166 0.0187071 -14.70915 0.000e+00
FamilySize                  -0.010316 0.0022198  -4.64732 3.363e-06
InflectionalEntropy         -0.021827 0.0022098  -9.87731 0.000e+00
NumberComplexSynsets        -0.006295 0.0012804  -4.91666 8.803e-07
Frequency * AgeSubject=young     0.017493 0.0066201   2.64244 8.231e-03
Frequency' * AgeSubject=young   -0.043592 0.0441450  -0.98747 3.234e-01
Frequency'' * AgeSubject=young   0.010664 0.2133925   0.04998 9.601e-01
Frequency''' * AgeSubject=young  0.171251 0.2807812   0.60991 5.419e-01


Factors in Final Model

[1] Voice            PC1                       MeanBigramFrequency
[4] WrittenFrequency WrittenSpokenFrequencyRatio AgeSubject
[7] FamilySize       InflectionalEntropy       NumberComplexSynsets
[10] WrittenFrequency * AgeSubject
```

The output of `fastbw()` has two parts. The first part lists statistics summarizing why factors are deleted. As can be seen in the two columns of *p*-values, none

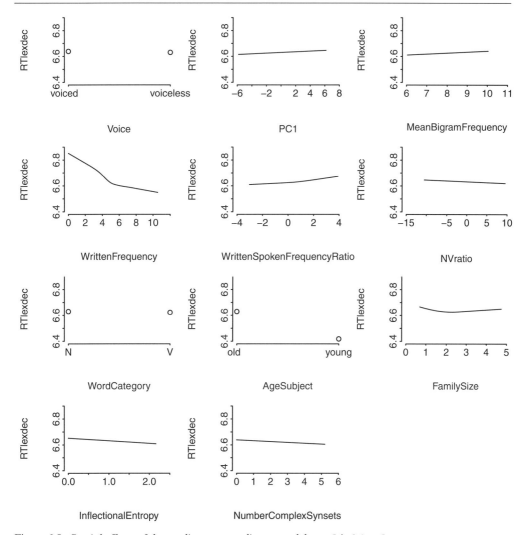

Figure 6.8. *Partial effects of the predictors according to model* english3.olsA.

of the deleted variables comes anywhere near explaining a significant part of the variance. Unsurprisingly, all predictors that did not reach significance in the anova table are deleted. In addition, WordCategory and NVratio, which just reached significance at the 5% level, are removed as well. The second part of the output of fastbw() lists the estimated coefficients for the remaining predictors, together with their associated statistics.

We should not automatically accept the verdict of fastbw(). First, it is only one of many available methods for searching for the most parsimonious model. Second, it often makes sense to remove predictors by hand, guided by our theoretical knowledge of the predictors. In the present example, PC1 remains in the model as the single representative of ten control variables for orthographic consistency. We gladly accept the removal of the other three principal components.

LengthInLetters is also deleted. Given the very small effect size we observed above for this variable, and given that a highly correlated control variable for orthographic form, MeanBigramFrequency, remains in the model, we have no regrets either for word length. With respect to WordCategory and NVratio, we need to exercise some caution. Not only did these predictors reach significance at the 5% level, we also have theoretical reasons for predicting that nouns should have a processing advantage compared to verbs in visual lexical decision. Third, we need to check at this point whether there are nonlinearities for other predictors besides written frequency. In fact, nonlinearities turn out to be required for Fam-ilySize and WrittenSpokenFrequencyRatio, and once these nonlinearities are brought into the model, WordCategory and NVratio emerge as predictive after all (both $p < 0.05$):

```
> english3.olsA = ols(RTlexdec ~ Voice + PC1 + MeanBigramFrequency +
+ rcs(WrittenFrequency, 5) + rcs(WrittenSpokenFrequencyRatio, 3) +
+ NVratio + WordCategory + AgeSubject + rcs(FamilySize, 3) +
+ InflectionalEntropy + NumberComplexSynsets +
+ rcs(WrittenFrequency, 5):AgeSubject, data=english3, x=T, y=T)
```

We summarize this model by means of Figure 6.8, removing confidence bands (which are extremely narrow) and the subtitles specifying how the partial effects are adjusted for the other predictors in the model (as this is a very long list with so many predictors):

```
> par(mfrow = c(4, 3), mar = c(4, 4, 1, 1), oma = rep(1, 4))
> plot(english3.olsA, adj.subtitle=F, ylim=c(6.4, 6.9), conf.int=F)
> par(mfrow = c(1, 1))
```

6.2.3   Model criticism

Before we can accept the model we have now arrived at, we need to ascertain whether this model provides a satisfactory fit to the data. There are a number of things to be checked. First of all, we check whether the residuals properly follow a normal distribution. The estimated probability density in the upper left panel of Figure 6.9 has a right tail that is somewhat thicker and longer than expected for a normal distribution. This asymmetry is also reflected in the quantile-quantile plot in the upper right panel. This shows that the model is stressed when it tries to fit the longest response latencies:

```
> english3$rstand = as.vector(scale(resid(english3.olsA)))
> plot(density(english3$rstand), main=" ")
> qqnorm(english3$rstand, cex = 0.5, main = " ")
> qqline(english3$rstand)
```

The lower left panel plots standardized residuals against the fitted values. There is a small increase in the residuals for larger fitted values, suggesting HETEROSKEDAS-TICITY, but the number of potentially offending data points is small and the of-fending points are outside the range of -2.5 to 2.5 and hence probably OUTLIERS:

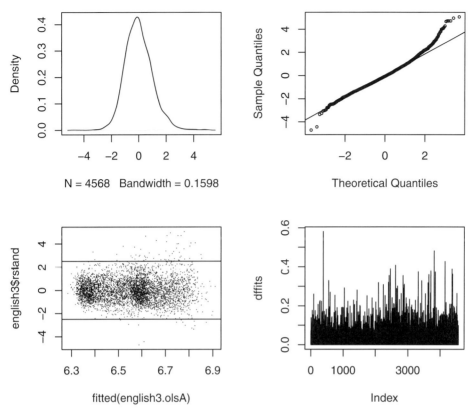

Figure 6.9. *Model criticism for* `english3.olsA`: *a density plot of the standardized residuals (upper left), the corresponding quantile-quantile plot (upper right), standardized residuals by predicted reaction time (lower left), and dffits (lower right).*

```
> plot(english3$rstand ~ fitted(english3.olsA), pch=".")
> abline(h = c(-2.5, 2.5))
```

There are many diagnostics for identifying outliers. One such diagnostic calculates, for each data point, a scaled difference between the fitted value given the full data set and the fitted value when that data point is not included when building the model. The resulting numbers are known as DFFITS (differences in the fits). If the two values are very different, a data point has atypical LEVERAGE, and may have undue influence on the values of the model's coefficients. The lower right panel of Figure 6.9 plots the absolute values of the DFFITS for each successive data point in `english3`, where we use the function `abs()` to obtain absolute values:

```
> dffits = abs(resid(english3.olsA, "dffits"))
> plot(dffits, type="h")
```

Observations for which the absolute DFFITS stand out from the others are suspect as exerting undue leverage. A metaphor may help explain this. Consider a flock of sheep, moving north, and one sheep moving west. One would like to say that the sheep are actually moving north, but the one exceptional sheep may

cause the model to report the sheep are moving to the northwest. To obtain a
good estimate of the direction in which the flock is moving, we need to identify
atypical individuals, and check whether they are distorting the general pattern.

The DFFITS provide a global measure for detecting leverage. There are also
measures for detecting leverage with respect to specific predictors. The function
dfbetas() (differences with respect to the betas, i.e. the values of the coefficients) gives the change in the estimated coefficients if an observation is excluded,
relative to its standard error. For a linear model obtained with ols(), the function
which.influence() returns a list with, for each predictor, the row numbers of
high-leverage observations in the data frame english3 that we used to obtain the
model english3.olsA. A data point is marked as influential when the absolute
relative change exceeds 0.2 (the default cutoff):

```
> w = which.influence(english3.olsA)
> w
$Intercept
[1] 2844 3714 3815

$PC1
[1] 4365

$WrittenFrequency
[1] 2419 2458 2844 2883 3628 3714 3815 3850 4381

$WrittenSpokenFrequencyRatio
[1] 1036 2400 2612 3320 3328 4148 4365

$AgeSubject
[1]  385 2097 2419 2458 2844 3628 3714 3815 3850 4381

$"WrittenFrequency * AgeSubject"
[1]  385 2419 2458 2844 3628 3714 3815 3850 4381
```

It can be useful to inspect the individual data points that are a potential source
of trouble. We do so with a FOR LOOP over the elements of the list returned by
which.influence, after isolating the names of the elements in a separate vector.
Within the loop, we use cat(), which echoes its arguments to the console, to
report on the subsets of outliers:

```
> nam = names(w)
> for (i in 1:length(nam)) {
+   cat("Influential observations for effect of", nam[i], "\n")
+   print(english3[w[[i]], 1:3])
+ }
```

Note that w[[i]] is a vector of row numbers, the row numbers of a subset of
outliers in english3. For each of the selected rows, we print the first three
columns to the console:

```
Influential observations for effect of Intercept
     RTlexdec Word AgeSubject
2012 6.578709 skit        old
2882 6.722401 slat        old
```

```
3815 6.648596 wilt        old
Influential observations for effect of  PC1
     RTlexdec Word AgeSubject
4365 7.006052 piss        old
Influential observations for effect of WrittenFrequency
     RTlexdec  Word AgeSubject
1587 7.097689 nonce       old
1626 6.549551 champ       old
2012 6.578709  skit       old
2051 6.631857   cox       old
2796 6.751335  mitt       old
2882 6.722401  slat       old
3815 6.648596  wilt       old
3850 6.549551 champ       old
4381 6.606934 broil       old
Influential observations for effect of WrittenSpokenFrequencyRatio
     RTlexdec Word AgeSubject
1036 6.571149  mum      young
1568 6.956155 boon        old
1780 7.078021  gel        old
2488 6.760079  mum        old
2496 6.867641  god        old
4148 7.086813  dun        old
4365 7.006052 piss        old
Influential observations for effect of AgeSubject
     RTlexdec  Word AgeSubject
385  6.253194  jape      young
3549 6.369661 broil      young
1587 7.097689 nonce       old
1626 6.549551 champ       old
2012 6.578709  skit       old
2796 6.751335  mitt       old
2882 6.722401  slat       old
3815 6.648596  wilt       old
3850 6.549551 champ       old
4381 6.606934 broil       old
Influential observations for effect of WrittenFrequency * AgeSubject
     RTlexdec  Word AgeSubject
385  6.253194  jape      young
1587 7.097689 nonce       old
1626 6.549551 champ       old
2012 6.578709  skit       old
2796 6.751335  mitt       old
2882 6.722401  slat       old
3815 6.648596  wilt       old
3850 6.549551 champ       old
4381 6.606934 broil       old
```

Many of the words identified as outliers are unknown words or words that are relatively uncommon, or uncommon in written form (e.g. *mum*). It is not at all surprising that these words elicited atypical reaction times. Their removal will allow us to obtain improved insight into the processing complexity of more normal words. We therefore create a vector with the row numbers of the offending data points:

```
> outliers=as.numeric(rownames(english3[abs(english3$rstand) > 2.5,]))
> dfBetas=as.numeric(unique(unlist(as.vector(w))))
> outliers2=unique(c(dfBetas, outliers))
```

The resulting vector of unique row names accounts for less than 2% of the data points:

```
> length(outliers2)/nrow(english3)
[1] 0.01904553
```

We use negative subscripting to take the outliers out of the data, create an updated data distribution object,

```
> english4 = english3[-outliers2, ]
> english4.dd = datadist(english4)
> options(datadist = "english4.dd")
```

and refit the model:

```
> english4.ols = ols(RTlexdec ~ Voice + PC1 + MeanBigramFrequency +
+ rcs(WrittenFrequency, 5) + rcs(WrittenSpokenFrequencyRatio, 3) +
+ NVratio + WordCategory + AgeSubject + rcs(FamilySize, 3) +
+ rcs(WrittenFrequency, 5):AgeSubject + InflectionalEntropy +
+ NumberComplexSynsets, data = english4, x = T, y = T)
```

The specification of `x = T, y = T` instructs `ols()` to create a model object that stores detailed information about the input (such as the internal coding for restricted cubic splines) and the output. This is essential for later plotting and model validation:

```
> anova(english4.ols)
              Analysis of Variance          Response: RTlexdec
```

Factor	d.f.	Part SS	MS	F	P
Voice	1	0.0629	0.0629	10.50	0.0012
PC1	1	0.1355	0.1355	22.63	<.0001
MeanBigramFrequency	1	0.1247	0.1247	20.82	<.0001
WrittenFrequency					
(Factor+Higher Order Factors)	8	8.7284	1.0910	182.09	<.0001
All Interactions	4	0.1464	0.0366	6.11	0.0001
Nonlinear					
(Factor+Higher Order Factors)	6	1.5158	0.2526	42.16	<.0001
WrittenSpokenFrequencyRatio	2	0.5377	0.2688	44.88	<.0001
Nonlinear	1	0.0269	0.0269	4.50	0.0340
NVratio	1	0.0446	0.0446	7.46	0.0063
WordCategory	1	0.0427	0.0427	7.14	0.0076
AgeSubject					
(Factor+Higher Order Factors)	5	54.9897	10.9979	1835.51	<.0001
All Interactions	4	0.1464	0.0366	6.11	0.0001
FamilySize	2	0.4368	0.2184	36.46	<.0001
Nonlinear	1	0.3250	0.3250	54.25	<.0001
InflectionalEntropy	1	0.2668	0.2668	44.53	<.0001
NumberComplexSynsets	1	0.1354	0.1354	22.60	<.0001
WrittenFrequency * AgeSubject					
(Factor+Higher Order Factors)	4	0.1464	0.0366	6.11	0.0001
Nonlinear	3	0.1461	0.0487	8.13	<.0001

```
Nonlinear Interaction :
    f(A,B) vs. AB                    3  0.1461  0.0487   8.13 <.0001
TOTAL NONLINEAR                      8  2.6352  0.3294  54.98 <.0001
TOTAL NONLINEAR + INTERACTION        9  2.6356  0.2928  48.87 <.0001
REGRESSION                          20 81.1652  4.0582 677.31 <.0001
ERROR                             4460 26.7232  0.0059
```

Compared to `english3.olsA`, most predictors have become more significant. In addition, the proportion of variance explained increased as well, as witnessed by the change in the adjusted R^2 from 0.736 to 0.751 (the adjusted R^2 is provided by the summary, not shown here, obtained when you type the name of the model object at the prompt). In short, we have identified those data points for which we do not have a good theory, and we have developed a model with improved goodness of fit for the remaining data points.

6.2.4   Validation

We are still not there. We need to ascertain to what extent we have been overfitting the model to this specific set of data points. To do so, we make use of the BOOTSTRAP. The bootstrap proceeds as follows. From our data set with 4492 words, we randomly draw 4492 observations WITH REPLACEMENT. This is called a bootstrap sample. For our data set, something like 2820 of the original observations will be present in such a bootstrap sample, many of which will be represented more than once, compare:

```
> length(unique(sample(1:4492, replace=T)))
[1] 2838
> length(unique(sample(1:4492, replace=T)))
[1] 2820
> length(unique(sample(1:4492, replace=T)))
[1] 2824
```

(The total number of data points in each bootstrap sample is always 4492.) We now fit our model to the data in the sample, and use this model to predict the reaction times for the original full data set, which contains many data points on which the bootstrap model has not been trained. Next, we compare the resulting goodness of fit of the bootstrap model with the goodness of fit of the original model, in our case, `english4.ols`. Averaged over a large number of bootstrap samples, these comparisons reveal to what extent the original model overfits the data. To see how this works, we make use of the `validate()` function in the `Design` package. It takes as arguments the model that is to be validated, and the number of bootstrap runs, as specified by the argument `B`. In the following example, we also specify that fast backwards elimination of superfluous predictors should be allowed, both for the input model and for the bootstrap models. (For `validate()` to work, the model object should have been created with the options `x = T` and `y = T`, as in the function call to `ols()` above that created `english4.ols`. These are instructions to store more information about the model in the model object.)

```
> validate(english4.ols, bw = T, B = 200)
Backwards Step-down - Original Model
```

```
No Factors Deleted
Frequencies of Numbers of Factors Retained
   9   10   11   12
   3   16   28  153
              index.orig    training         test       optimism
R-square   0.748543387   0.74942258   0.747215839    2.206745e-03
MSE        0.006095415   0.00609558   0.006127595   -3.201435e-05
Intercept  0.000000000   0.00000000   0.015134152   -1.513415e-02
Slope      1.000000000   1.00000000   0.997676416    2.323584e-03
              index.corrected    n
R-square      0.746336642      200
MSE           0.006127429      200
Intercept     0.015134152      200
Slope         0.997676416      200
```

For the present model, no predictors are removed by the backwards step-down algorithm for the input model. The summary then specifies the numbers of predictors retained by the step-down algorithm across 200 bootstrap runs. All twelve predictors are retained for 153 runs, one predictor is removed for 28 runs, two predictors for 16 runs, and three for 9 runs. (When you rerun this validation, the numbers will change slightly.) The final part of the summary compares goodness of fit statistics for the input model with the average of the corresponding statistics for the model fitted to the bootstrap samples. The first row lists the R^2, the second the MEAN SQUARED ERROR, which is the mean of the squared residuals:

```
> sum(resid(english4.ols)^2)/length(resid(english4.ols))
[1] 0.006095415
```

The third and fourth line list the intercept and slope of the regression line obtained when the observed reaction times are regressed against the fitted values:

```
> coef(lm(english4$RTlexdec~fitted(english4.ols)))
 (Intercept) fitted(english4.ols)
3.998611e-15          1.000000e-00
```

Slope and intercept are by necessity 0 and 1 for the original data. However, when we regress the observed reaction times in the full data set against the fitted values obtained in a simulation run, the slope may be less than one, in which case the intercept will shift away from zero to compensate. Therefore, these bootstrap slopes and intercepts may also shed light on the degree of overfitting.

The next column in the output of `validate()` reports the average of these four statistics for the 200 models fitted to the bootstrap samples. The third column lists these statistics when the bootstrap models are used to predict the reaction times in the full data set. Prediction for the test set is less accurate than for the training set: the R^2 decreases by $0.748543387 - 0.746336642 = 0.002206745$, and the mean squared error increases from 0.006095415 to 0.006127429 by $-3.2014e - 05$. These (in this example minute) differences between the training and the test statistics are listed in the column labeled OPTIMISM. Comparing training and test statistics, we find that we are too optimistic about the R^2, our undue optimism is 0.002. Similarly, the mean squared error is somewhat larger that we thought; here we were too optimistic as well. Similarly, intercept and slope move away from 0 and 1. The last column in the summary corrects the original estimates in the first column for optimism. Thus, the corrected value for R^2 is $0.748543387 - 2.206745e - 03 = 0.7463366$. For the present data, the bootstrap corrections are minimal, which allows us to conclude that we are not overfitting the data. Likewise, there are relatively few bootstrap runs in which the fast backwards elimination routine decides that predictors can be dispensed with. The tiny amount of overfitting in the present example does not come as a surprise in the light of the large number of data points compared to the number of coefficients in the model. As a rule of thumb, there should be at least fifteen times more observations than coefficients (for more precise estimates depending on the kind of regression analysis used, see Harrell (2001:61)). For small data sets and large numbers of predictors, it is not unusual to find that the amount of variance explained is halved or even decimated when adjusted for optimism.

6.3   Generalized linear models

GENERALIZED LINEAR MODELS are an important extension to ordinary least squares regression models. Parameter estimation, however, is not based on minimizing the sum of squared errors. Instead, parameters are chosen such that, given the data and our choice of model, they make the model's predicted values most similar to the observed values. This general technique is known as MAXIMUM LIKELIHOOD ESTIMATION. Maximum likelihood estimation for generalized linear models makes use of iterative fitting techniques.

6.3.1   Logistic regression

Thus far, we have been concerned with observations involving measurements. In many experiments, however, outcomes are not real numbers, but take one of two possible values: head or tail, success or failure, correct versus incorrect, regular or irregular, direct object construction versus prepositional object construction, etc. For data sets with such BINARY dependent variables, we would like to be able to estimate the probability of a given outcome (e.g. head, or success, or regular, or direct object construction) given the predictors. This is accomplished with logistic regression, a technique that is widely used in sociolinguistics where it is known as VARBRUL analysis.

To see how logistic regression works, we return to the visual lexical decision data (`english`), but now consider the accuracy of the responses. In lexical decision, subjects have to decide whether the letter string presented on the screen is a word. If they press the NO button when a real word is presented, this is counted as an error. Is the probability of an error determined by the same predictors that we observed to be significant for the reaction times? The column `CorrectLexdec` lists for each word the number of subjects, out of a total of 30, that provided the correct (yes) response. Let's look at the counts of correct responses for the first ten words in the data frame:

```
> nCorrect = english2$CorrectLexdec[1:10]
> nCorrect
 [1] 27 30 30 30 26 28 30 28 25 29
```

At first, you might think that it would be useful to transform these counts into proportions (or percentages, when multiplied by 100),

```
> proportions = nCorrect/30
> proportions
 [1] 0.9000000 1.0000000 1.0000000 1.0000000 0.8666667
 [5] 0.9333333 1.0000000 0.9333333 0.8333333 0.9666667
```

and to use these proportions as the dependent variable in a standard linear regression model. There are several considerations that argue against this approach. First, proportions are bounded between 0 and 1, but `lm()` and `ols()` don't know about this and might come up with predicted proportions greater than one or smaller than zero. Second, proportions have the property that the variance increases with the mean. But `lm()` (and `ols()`) presuppose that the variance is constant and does not vary with the values of any of the predictors. Third, proportions don't provide information about how many observations went into the calculation of the proportion. In a lexical decision experiment, for instance, observations are sometimes lost due to failure of the button box. Suppose that only 4 responses are available, 2 correct and 2 errors, and compare this with the case that 30 responses are available, 15 correct and 15 incorrect. With 30 responses, we can be more confident that the probability of an error is 0.5 than for just four responses. What needs to be done is to weight the proportions for the number of contributing observations.

The solution is to model the probabilities indirectly through a LINK FUNCTION. For binary data, this link function is the LOGIT transformation of the probability. For the above proportions, we obtain the corresponding logits (log odds ratios) as follows:

```
> logits = log(nCorrect/(30 - nCorrect))
> logits
 [1] 2.197225      Inf      Inf      Inf 1.871802
 [6] 2.639057      Inf 2.639057 1.609438 3.367296
```

Note that there are four cases where the logit is infinite. This happens when there are no errors, in which case we are dividing 30 by 0, to which R responds with the error code `Inf`. Fortunately, the R functions for logistic modeling have principled methods for backing away from zero, so we will not calculate logits ourselves. Instead, we will leave these calculations to the proper functions, `glm()` and, in the `Design` package, `lrm()`. The choice between these functions depends on the form of your data frame. When there is a single elementary observation in a row of the data frame, with a column specifying the value of the binary predictor, we use `lrm()`. If our data is in a format in which the numbers of successes and failures are listed for each line in the data frame, we use `glm()`. We begin with an example requiring `glm()`, an acronym for Generalized Linear Model.

As always, `glm()` requires us to specify the model that we want to fit to the data by means of a formula. The dependent variable requires special care: `glm()` needs to know both the number of successes and the number of failures. This information is supplied in the form of a two-column matrix, which we create with the `cbind()` (column bind) function as follows:

```
> cbind(english$CorrectLexdec, 30 - english$CorrectLexdec)
       [,1] [,2]
[1,]    27   3
[2,]    30   0
[3,]    30   0
[4,]    30   0
[5,]    26   4
[6,]    28   2
 . . .
```

We specify the same model for the error data as for the decision latencies, using `english2` (which includes `CorrectLexdec` as predictor) as the input data frame:

```
> english2.glm =
+ glm(cbind(english2$CorrectLexdec, 30 - english2$CorrectLexdec) ~
+ Voice + PC1 + MeanBigramFrequency + LengthInLetters + Ncount +
+ WordCategory + NVratio + poly(WrittenFrequency, 2) +
+ poly(WrittenSpokenFrequencyRatio, 2) + poly(FamilySize, 2) +
+ InflectionalEntropy + NumberComplexSynsets + AgeSubject, english2,
+ family = "binomial")
```

The last line of this command is new: `family = "binomial"`. It tells `glm()` to expect two-column input, to use the logit link function, and to assume that the variance increases with the mean according to the binomial distribution:

```
> summary(english2.glm)
Deviance Residuals:
     Min       1Q    Median       3Q      Max
 -8.5238  -0.6256   0.4419   1.3549   6.5136


Coefficients:
                              Estimate Std. Error z value Pr(>|z|)
(Intercept)                   2.282741   0.144491  15.798  < 2e-16
Voicevoiceless                0.010561   0.019964   0.529    0.597
PC1                          -0.020694   0.004857  -4.261 2.03e-05
MeanBigramFrequency          -0.131139   0.023195  -5.654 1.57e-08
LengthInLetters               0.269007   0.023088  11.651  < 2e-16
Ncount                        0.002157   0.002694   0.800    0.423
WordCategoryV                 0.138718   0.031253   4.439 9.06e-06
NVratio                       0.021836   0.005156   4.235 2.28e-05
poly(WrittenFrequency, 2)1   40.896851   1.099373  37.200  < 2e-16
poly(WrittenFrequency, 2)2  -14.810919   0.757810 -19.544  < 2e-16
poly(WrSpFrequencyRatio, 2)1 -10.882376  0.717038 -15.177  < 2e-16
poly(WrSpFrequencyRatio, 2)2  0.181922   0.549843   0.331    0.741
poly(FamilySize, 2)1          6.962633   1.060134   6.568 5.11e-11
poly(FamilySize, 2)2        -10.258182   0.703623 -14.579  < 2e-16
```

```
InflectionalEntropy                        0.361696   0.023581  15.338  < 2e-16
NumberComplexSynsets                       0.120928   0.011454  10.558  < 2e-16
AgeSubjectyoung                           -0.873541   0.020179 -43.290  < 2e-16

(Dispersion parameter for binomial family taken to be 1)

    Null deviance: 24432  on 4567  degrees of freedom
Residual deviance: 12730  on 4551  degrees of freedom
AIC: 21886

Number of Fisher Scoring iterations: 5
```

After repeating the call to `glm()` (not shown), the summary provides a brief overview by means of quartiles of the distribution of the deviance residuals, the differences between the observed and expected values. These deviances are comparable to the residuals of an ordinary least squares regression. However, the deviance residuals are expressed in logits, and unlike the residuals of `lm()` or `ols()`, they need not follow a normal distribution.

The next part of the summary lists the estimates of the coefficients. These coefficients also pertain to the logits. The coefficient for `AgeSubject`, for instance, which expresses the contrast between the old subjects (the reference level mapped onto the intercept) and the young subjects is negative. Negative coefficients indicate that the probability of a correct response (the first column of the two-column matrix for the dependent variable) goes down. A positive coefficient indicates that this probability increases. What we see here, then, is that the older subjects were more accurate responders. This ties in nicely with the observation that they were also slower responders.

Each estimated coefficient is accompanied by its estimated standard error, a Z-score, and the associated p-value. The p-value for the Noun-to-Verb frequency ratio, for instance, can be calculated simply with:

```
> 2 * (1 - pnorm(4.235))
[1] 2.285517e-05
```

The next line in the summary mentions that the dispersion parameter for the binomial family is taken to be 1. This note is to remind us that the variance of a binomial random variable depends entirely on the mean, and that the model assumed that this property characterizes our data. The next two lines in the summary provide the information necessary to check whether this assumption is met.

The null deviance is the deviance that you get with a model with only an intercept. In the present example, this is a model that thinks that the probability of an error is the same for all words. By itself, the null deviance is uninteresting. It is useful, though, for ascertaining whether the predictors in the full model jointly earn their keep. The difference between the null deviance and the residual deviance approximately follows a chi-squared distribution with, as degrees of freedom, the difference between the degrees of freedom of the two deviances:

```
> 1 - pchisq(24432 - 12730, 4567 - 4551)
[1] 0
```

The very small *p*-value shows that we have a model with explanatory value. The reason that glm() does not list this *p*-value is that the approximation to the chi-squared distribution is valid only for large expected counts. So be warned: these *p*-values may provide a rough indication only.

The residual deviance is used to examine whether the assumption of non-constant, binomial variance, holds. We again use a test based on the chi-squared approximation, that again is approximate only (perhaps even useless, according to Harrell (2001:231)):

```
> 1 - pchisq(12730, 4551)
[1] 0
```

The very small *p*-value indicates that the assumption of binomial variance is probably not met. The variance is much larger than expected — if it had been in accordance with our modeling assumption, the residual deviance should be approximately the same as the number of degrees of freedom. Here it is more than four times too large. This is called OVERDISPERSION. Overdispersion indicates a lack of goodness of fit. We may be missing crucial predictors, or we may have missed nonlinearities in the predictors.

The final line of the summary mentions the number of scoring iterations, 5 in the present example. The algorithm for estimating the coefficients of a general linear model is iterative. It starts with an initial guess at the coefficients, and refines this guess in subsequent iterations until the guesses become sufficiently stable.

Recall that there is a second function summarizing the model, anova(). For lm() and glm() it has two functions. Its first function is to allow us to carry out a sequential analysis in which terms are added successively to the model. In the summary table shown above, we see that Voice is not predictive. But the analysis of deviance table produced by the anova() function seems to provide a different verdict:

```
> anova(english2.glm, test = "Chisq")
Analysis of Deviance Table

Model: binomial, link: logit

Terms added sequentially (first to last)
```

	Df	Deviance	Resid. Df	Resid. Dev	P(>|Chi|)
NULL			4567	24432.1	
Voice	1	52.6	4566	24379.5	4.010e-13
PC1	1	169.2	4565	24210.3	1.123e-38
MeanBigramFrequency	1	109.4	4564	24100.9	1.317e-25
LengthInLetters	1	11.7	4563	24089.2	6.370e-04
Ncount	1	27.0	4562	24062.2	2.003e-07

```
...
```

This is because Voice is explanatory only when there are no other predictors in the model. If we enter Voice and Ncount last to the model formula, then the results are in harmony with the table of coefficients:

```
> english2.glm =
+ glm(cbind(english2$CorrectLexdec, 30 - english2$CorrectLexdec) ~
+ MeanBigramFrequency + LengthInLetters + WordCategory + NVratio +
+ poly(WrittenFrequency, 2) + WrittenSpokenFrequencyRatio +
+ poly(FamilySize, 2) + InflectionalEntropy + NumberComplexSynsets +
+ AgeSubject + PC1 + Voice + Ncount, data=english2, family="binomial")
> anova(english2.glm, test = "Chisq")
...
Voice            1      0.3      4553     12730.9         0.6
Ncount           1      0.6      4552     12730.2         0.4
```

The second function of `anova()` is to allow us to evaluate the overall significance of factors. When a factor has only two levels, the test for the (single) coefficient based on its Z-score is very similar to the test in the `anova()` function when the relevant factor is entered last into the model equation. But when a factor has more than two levels, the table of coefficients lists a t-value or a Z-score for each coefficient. In order to assess whether the factor as a whole is explanatory, the `anova()` table is essential.

You may have noted that we called the `anova()` function with an argument that we did not need before, `test = "Chisq"`. This is because there are two kinds of tests that we can run for a logistic model, a test that makes use of the chi-squared distribution, and a test that makes use of the F-distribution. The latter test is more conservative, but is sometimes recommended (see, e.g. Crawley, 2002) when there is evidence for overdispersion. The most recent implementation of the `anova()` function, however, adds a warning that the F-test is inappropriate for binomial models.

Let's look at the predictions of the model by plotting the predicted counts against the observed counts. The left panel of Figure 6.10 shows that the model is far too optimistic about the probability of a correct response, especially for words for which many incorrect responses were recorded. Our model is clearly unsatisfactory, even though it supports the relevance of most of our predictors. What is needed is model criticism.

First, however, we consider how to obtain the left panel of Figure 6.10. We extract the predicted probabilities of a correct response with `predict()`, which we instruct to produce probabilities rather than logits by means of the option `type = "response"`. In order to proceed from probabilities (proportions) to counts, we multiply by the total number of subjects (30):

```
> english2$predictCorrect = predict(english2.glm, type = "response")*30
```

The plot is now straightforward:

```
> plot(english2$CorrectLexdec, english2$predictCorrect, cex = 0.5)
> abline(0,1)
```

Let's now remove observations from the data set for which the standardized residual falls outside the interval $(-5, 5)$, in the hope that this will reduce overdispersion:

```
> english2A = english2[abs(rstandard(english2.glm)) < 5, ]
```

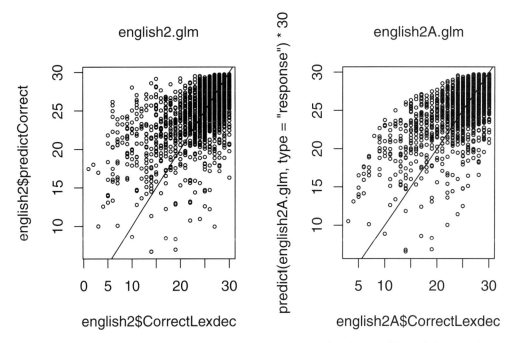

Figure 6.10. *Predicted and observed counts of correct responses for the visual lexical decision data in* english2 *(left panel). This model seriously overestimates the number of correct responses for words where many mistakes are observed. The right panel shows the improvement obtained after removal of data points with extreme residuals.*

It is easy to see that this amounts to removing slightly more than 1% of the data points:

```
> (nrow(english2) - nrow(english2A)) / nrow(english2)
[1] 0.01357268
```

We now refit our model,

```
> english2A.glm =
+ glm(cbind(english2A$CorrectLexdec, 30 - english2A$CorrectLexdec) ~
+ MeanBigramFrequency + LengthInLetters + WordCategory + NVratio +
+ poly(WrittenFrequency, 2) + WrittenSpokenFrequencyRatio +
+ poly(FamilySize, 2) + InflectionalEntropy + NumberComplexSynsets +
+ AgeSubject + Voice + PC1 + Ncount, english2A, family = "binomial")
```

and inspect the table of coefficients:

```
> summary(english2A.glm)
Deviance Residuals:
    Min       1Q   Median       3Q      Max
-5.3952  -0.6600   0.3552   1.2885   4.7383

Coefficients:
                         Estimate Std. Error z value Pr(>|z|)
(Intercept)              2.905725   0.151493  19.181  < 2e-16
MeanBigramFrequency     -0.195028   0.024326  -8.017 1.08e-15
```

```
LengthInLetters                    0.303197   0.024159  12.550  < 2e-16
WordCategoryV                      0.123030   0.032056   3.838 0.000124
NVratio                            0.023568   0.005226   4.510 6.48e-06
poly(WrittenFrequency, 2)1        40.133735   1.092606  36.732  < 2e-16
poly(WrittenFrequency, 2)2       -17.077597   0.753239 -22.672  < 2e-16
WrSpFrequencyRatio                -0.153989   0.009509 -16.194  < 2e-16
poly(FamilySize, 2)1               5.327479   1.082136   4.923 8.52e-07
poly(FamilySize, 2)2              -8.887187   0.715517 -12.421  < 2e-16
InflectionalEntropy                0.334942   0.024447  13.701  < 2e-16
NumberComplexSynsets               0.107175   0.011763   9.111  < 2e-16
AgeSubjectyoung                   -0.882157   0.020997 -42.013  < 2e-16
Voicevoiceless                     0.060491   0.020699   2.922 0.003473
PC1                               -0.020570   0.005076  -4.052 5.07e-05
Ncount                            -0.001153   0.002792  -0.413 0.679692

(Dispersion parameter for binomial family taken to be 1)

    Null deviance: 20894  on 4505  degrees of freedom
Residual deviance: 10334  on 4490  degrees of freedom
```

Voice now emerges as significant. This illustrates the importance of model criticism: the distorting presence of just a few atypical outliers may obscure effects that characterize the majority of the data points. Also note that the residual deviance is substantially reduced, from 12730 to 10334, but, with 4490 degrees of freedom, we still have overdispersion. This leads to the conclusion that there may be important predictors for subjects' accuracy scores that we have failed to take into account. As can be seen in the right panel of Figure 6.10, the removal of a few atypical outliers has led to a visible improvement in the fit:

```
> plot(english2A$CorrectLexdec,
+ predict(english2A.glm, type = "response")*30, cex = 0.5)
> abline(0,1)
```

This completes this example of a logistic regression for a data set in which the successes and failures are available in tabular format. The next example illustrates the lrm() function from the Design package for logistic regression modeling of data in LONG FORMAT, i.e. data in which each row of the data frame specifies a single outcome, either a success or a failure. We consider a data set reported by Tabak *et al.* (2005) that specifies, for 700 Dutch verbs that belong to the Germanic stratum of the Dutch vocabulary, whether that verb is regular or irregular, together with a series of other predictors, such as the auxiliary selected by the verb in the present and past perfect, its frequency, and its morphological family size. Further information is available through help(regularity). We begin by creating a data distribution object, and specify that this is the current data distribution object with options():

```
> regularity.dd = datadist(regularity)
> options(datadist = "regularity.dd")
> xtabs( ~ regularity$Regularity)
 regularity$Regularity
 irregular    regular
       159        541
```

Fitting a logistic regression model with `lrm()` is straightforward:

```
> regularity.lrm = lrm(Regularity ~ WrittenFrequency+rcs(FamilySize,3)+
+ NcountStem + InflectionalEntropy + Auxiliary + Valency + NVratio +
+ WrittenSpokenRatio, data = regularity, x = T, y = T)
```

The `anova()` function applied to an `lrm` object does *not* produce a sequential analysis of deviance table, but a table listing the partial effects of the predictors, which, in the present example, are all significant. Significance is evaluated by means of the chi-squared test statistic:

```
> anova(regularity.lrm)
Wald Statistics          Response: Regularity

Factor               Chi-Square d.f.  P
WrittenFrequency        8.76      1   0.0031
FamilySize             15.92      2   0.0003
 Nonlinear             11.72      1   0.0006
NcountStem             14.21      1   0.0002
InflectionalEntropy     9.73      1   0.0018
Auxiliary              16.12      2   0.0003
Valency                10.29      1   0.0013
NVratio                 7.79      1   0.0053
WrittenSpokenRatio      4.61      1   0.0318
TOTAL                 126.86     10   <.0001
```

A table with the coefficients of the model and further summary statistics is obtained by typing the name of the fitted model at the prompt:

```
> regularity.lrm
Logistic Regression Model

lrm(formula = Regularity ~ WrittenFrequency + rcs(FamilySize, 3) +
  NcountStem + InflectionalEntropy + Auxiliary + Valency +
  NVratio + WrittenSpokenRatio, data = regularity, x = T, y = T)

Frequencies of Responses
irregular    regular
    159        541

  Obs  Max Deriv  Model L.R.      d.f.        P        C
  700    1e-05      215.62         10         0      0.843
   Dxy      Gamma       Tau-a        R2      Brier
  0.687     0.688       0.241      0.403     0.121

                      Coef     S.E.   Wald Z  P
Intercept            4.4559  0.97885   4.55   0.0000
WrittenFrequency    -0.2749  0.09290  -2.96   0.0031
FamilySize          -1.2608  0.31684  -3.98   0.0001
FamilySize'          1.1752  0.34333   3.42   0.0006
NcountStem           0.0730  0.01937   3.77   0.0002
InflectionalEntropy  0.9999  0.32049   3.12   0.0018
Auxiliary=zijn      -1.9484  0.57629  -3.38   0.0007
Auxiliary=zijnheb   -0.6974  0.28433  -2.45   0.0142
Valency             -0.1448  0.04514  -3.21   0.0013
NVratio              0.1323  0.04739   2.79   0.0053
WrittenSpokenRatio  -0.2146  0.09993  -2.15   0.0318
```

The summary first lists how the model object was created, as well as the frequencies of the two levels of our dependent variable: 159 irregulars, and 541 regulars. The regulars (listed last) are interpreted as successes, and the irregulars as failures. The next section of the summary lists a series of statistics that assess the goodness of fit. It starts off with the number of observations, 700. The most important statistics are `Model L.R.`, `C`, `Dxy` and `R2`. `Model L.R.` stands for model likelihood chi-square, the difference between the Null Deviance and the Residual Deviance that we encountered above with `glm()`. In the summary, it is followed by its associated degrees of freedom and p-value. The very small p-value indicates that jointly the predictors are explanatory.

The remaining statistics address the predictive ability of the model. Recall that for normal regression models, the R^2 measure provides insight into how accurate the predictions of the model are. The problem with dichotomous response variables such as `Regularity` is that the model produces estimates of the *probability* that a verb is regular, whereas our observations simply state *whether* a verb is regular or irregular. We could dichotomize our probabilities by mapping probabilities greater than 0.5 onto success and probabilities less than 0.5 onto failure, but this implies a substantial loss of information. (Consider the consequences for a data set in which success probabilities all range between 0 and 0.4.) Fortunately, `lrm()` provides a series of measures that deal with this problem in a more principled way.

The measure named `C` is an index of concordance between the predicted probability and the observed response. `C` is obtained by inspecting all pairs of verbs with both a regular and an irregular verb for which the regular verb does indeed have the higher expected probability of being regular. When `C` takes the value 0.5, the predictions are random, when it is 1, prediction is perfect. A value above 0.8 indicates that the model may have some real predictive capacity. Since `C` is listed with the value 0.843, our confidence in the model is strengthened. A related measure is Somers' D_{xy}, a rank correlation between predicted probabilities and observed responses. This measure, 0.687 for our data, which can be obtained from `C` (0.843) as follows,

```
> 2 * (0.843 - 0.5)
[1] 0.686
```

ranges between 0 (randomness) and 1 (perfect prediction). Finally, the R^2 mentioned in the table is a generalized index that is calculated from log-likelihood ratio statistics, and also provides some indication of the predictive strength of the model.

Bootstrap validation provides further evidence that we have a reasonable model:

```
> validate(regularity.lrm, bw = T, B = 200)
Backwards Step-down - Original Model
No Factors Deleted
Factors in Final Model

[1] WrittenFrequency    FamilySize         NcountStem
```

```
[4] InflectionalEntropy Auxiliary              Valency
[7] NVratio              WrittenSpokenRatio
Iteration:
1 2 3 4 5 6 7 8 9 10 11 12 13 14 15 16 17 18 19 20
...
Frequencies of Numbers of Factors Retained

   4    5    6    7    8
   1   11   24   46  118
          index.orig training    test optimism index.corrected
Dxy           0.6869   0.7026  0.6713   0.0313          0.6556
R2            0.4032   0.4216  0.3839   0.0377          0.3655
Intercept     0.0000   0.0000  0.0758  -0.0758          0.0758
Slope         1.0000   1.0000  0.9128   0.0872          0.9128
Emax          0.0000   0.0000  0.0336   0.0336          0.0336
D             0.3066   0.3234  0.2896   0.0339          0.2727
U            -0.0029  -0.0029  0.0019  -0.0047         -0.0019
Q             0.3095   0.3263  0.2877   0.0386          0.2709
B             0.1210   0.1175  0.1243  -0.0068          0.1278
```

The fast backwards elimination algorithm reports that all predictors are retained. During the bootstrap runs, it does eliminate predictors, most likely those with weak p-values in the summary() and anova() tables. Except for 12 out of 200 bootstrap validation runs, at most two predictors are deleted. The optimism with respect to D_{xy}, and R_N^2 is somewhat larger than in the previous example of bootstrap validation. The changes in slope and intercept are also more substantial. In all, there is evidence that we are somewhat overfitting the data.

Overfitting is an adverse effect of fitting a model to the data. In the process of selecting coefficients that approximate the data to the best of our abilities, it is unavoidable that noise is also fitted. Data points with extreme values due to noise are taken just as seriously as normal data points. Across experiments, it is unlikely that the extreme values will be replicated. As a consequence, coefficients in the fitted model run the risk of having values that are also too extreme: In replication studies, the values of these coefficients will generally be somewhat closer to zero. This phenomenon is known as SHRINKAGE. For models fitted by means of maximum likelihood estimation, the Design package offers a tool, pentrace(), that helps us find estimates of the coefficients that anticipate this shrinkage. Because the coefficients in a penalized model have been shrunk towards zero, their values are less vulnerable to overfitting and more accurate for prediction for unseen data. The pentrace() function makes use of a technique known as PENALIZED MAXIMUM LIKELIHOOD ESTIMATION. This technique introduces a penalty factor into the estimation process that discourages large values for the coefficients. We do not know beforehand what the best penalty is, so a series of penalty values has to be considered. For each penalty, a model is fitted to the data. The penalized model with the best fit is then selected.

Applied to the current data, pentrace() expects as first argument the fitted model, and as second argument the penalties that should be considered. Its output informs us about what the best penalty is:

```
> pentrace(regularity.lrm, seq(0, 0.8, by = 0.05))
Best penalty:
penalty       df
   0.6 9.656274
     simple        df      aic      bic     aic.c
1     0.00 10.000000 195.6179 150.1071 195.2986
2     0.05  9.967678 195.6792 150.3155 195.3619
3     0.10  9.936161 195.7327 150.5124 195.4173
4     0.15  9.905399 195.7789 150.6986 195.4654
5     0.20  9.875348 195.8184 150.8749 195.5067
6     0.25  9.845965 195.8519 151.0421 195.5419
7     0.30  9.817215 195.8796 151.2007 195.5714
8     0.35  9.789063 195.9021 151.3513 195.5957
9     0.40  9.761478 195.9198 151.4945 195.6150
10    0.45  9.734432 195.9330 151.6308 195.6298
11    0.50  9.707899 195.9420 151.7606 195.6404
12    0.55  9.681853 195.9472 151.8843 195.6471
13    0.60  9.656274 195.9487 152.0023 195.6502
14    0.65  9.631140 195.9470 152.1149 195.6499
15    0.70  9.606432 195.9421 152.2225 195.6465
16    0.75  9.582133 195.9343 152.3253 195.6402
17    0.80  9.558225 195.9239 152.4236 195.6311
```

The best penalty is 0.60, for which we have the largest values of `aic` (the Akaike Information Criterion) and `aic.c` (a corrected version of `aic`). Larger values of these measures imply improved goodness of fit.

Now that we know the optimal value for the penalty, we take our original unpenalized model and update it with this penalty to obtain the corresponding penalized model:

```
> regularity.lrm.pen = update(regularity.lrm, penalty = 0.6)
> regularity.lrm.pen
Frequencies of Responses
irregular    regular
      159        541
Penalty factors:
 simple nonlinear interaction nonlinear.interaction
    0.6      0.6         0.6                   0.6
Final penalty on -2 log L: 3.24

        Obs  Max Deriv Model L.R.       d.f.          P        C
        700     1e-06      215.26       9.66          0    0.843
        Dxy      Gamma      Tau-a         R2      Brier
      0.686      0.688      0.241      0.397      0.121

                     Coef    S.E.   Wald Z  P      Penalty Scale
Intercept         4.18590 0.93607   4.47  0.0000 0.0000
WrittenFrequency -0.27410 0.09125  -3.00  0.0027 1.5030
FamilySize       -1.10885 0.28526  -3.89  0.0001 0.9161
FamilySize'       1.01248 0.31279   3.24  0.0012 0.7468
NcountStem        0.07153 0.01911   3.74  0.0002 5.0767
InflectionalEntropy 0.96949 0.31762 3.05  0.0023 0.3114
Auxiliary=zijn   -1.74304 0.53771  -3.24  0.0012 0.6325
Auxiliary=zijnheb -0.70646 0.27883 -2.53  0.0113 0.6325
Valency          -0.14079 0.04429  -3.18  0.0015 2.7047
```

```
        NVratio                0.12880 0.04660   2.76   0.0057 2.6535
        WrittenSpokenRatio    -0.21421 0.09850  -2.17   0.0297 1.1694
```

The summary has a structure that is very similar to that of the unpenalized model. It adds the information that (in this example) the same penalty was applied to all types of terms in the model. (This is the default, other options are available. For instance, only nonlinear terms and interactions can be penalized. Consult the documentation for `lrm()` for further details.)

To see what penalization has accomplished, we arrange the coefficients of the two models side by side, and also list the difference between the two:

```
> cbind(coef(regularity.lrm), coef(regularity.lrm.pen),
+ abs(coef(regularity.lrm)  - coef(regularity.lrm.pen)))
                               [,1]          [,2]          [,3]
Intercept                4.45591812    4.18590117  0.2700169476
WrittenFrequency        -0.27489322   -0.27410296  0.0007902561
FamilySize              -1.26081754   -1.10884722  0.1519703217
FamilySize'              1.17521466    1.01248128  0.1627333834
NcountStem               0.07300013    0.07153112  0.0014690074
InflectionalEntropy      0.99994212    0.96948811  0.0304540066
Auxiliary=zijn          -1.94843887   -1.74304390  0.2053949677
Auxiliary=zijnheb       -0.69740672   -0.70645984  0.0090531198
Valency                 -0.14480320   -0.14078808  0.0040151257
NVratio                  0.13228590    0.12880451  0.0034813886
WrittenSpokenRatio      -0.21457506   -0.21421097  0.0003640932
```

Note that with the exception of `Auxiliary=zijnheb` all coefficients are SHRUNK towards zero. The largest adjustments are those for Family Size and for `Auxiliary=zijn`. For the latter predictor, this does not come as a surprise, as there are only a few verbs in the data set that select *zijn*:

```
> table(regularity$Auxiliary)

 hebben     zijn zijnheb
    577       20     103
```

It is precisely the magnitude of the contrast coefficient for *zijn* that is reduced substantially. Here, our data are most sparse, and hence we should be restrained most for prediction.

Let's finally inspect the partial effects of the model by plotting all effects with the same range on the vertical axis:

```
> par(mfrow = c(3, 3))
> plot(regularity.lrm.pen, fun = plogis, ylab = "Pr(regular)",
+ adj.subtitle = F, ylim = c(0, 1))
> par(mfrow = c(1, 1))
```

Figure 6.11 shows that the probability of a verb being regular decreases with increasing frequency, as expected. But it is clear that in addition to frequency, there are many other predictors that have similar effect sizes, such as inflectional entropy, valency (a variable that is strongly correlated with number of meanings), and the noun-to-verb frequency ratio. Tabak *et al.* (2005) and Baayen and

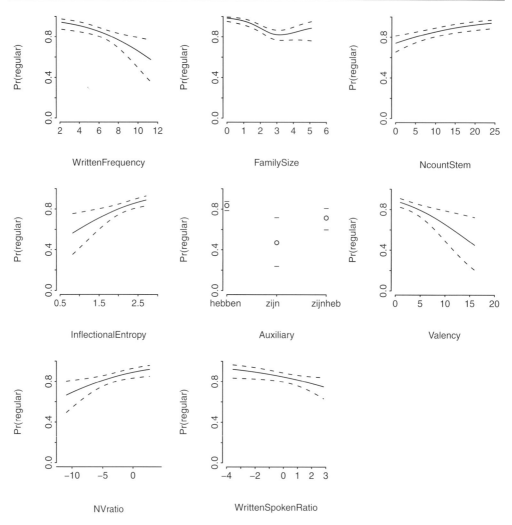

Figure 6.11. *Partial effects of the predictors for the log odds ratio of a Dutch simplex verb from the native (Germanic) stratum being regular.*

Moscosodel Prado Martín (2005) discuss these results in the context of the hypothesis that irregular verbs live in denser semantic similarity neighborhoods than do regular verbs.

6.3.2   Ordinal logistic regression

Logistic regression is appropriate for dichotomous response variables. ORDINAL REGRESSION is appropriate for dependent variables that are factors with ordered levels. For a factor such as gender in German, the factor levels "masculine," "feminine," and "neuter" are not intrinsically ordered. In contrast, vowel length in Estonian has the ordered levels "short," "long," and "extra long."

Regression models for such ORDERED FACTORS are available. The technique that we introduce here, ORDINAL LOGISTIC REGRESSION, is a generalization of the logistic regression technique.

As an example, we consider the data set studied by Tabak *et al.* (2005). The model predicting regularity for Dutch verbs developed in the preceding section showed that the likelihood of regularity decreased with increasing valency. An increase in valency (here, the number of different subcategorization frames in which a verb can be used) is closely related to an increase in the verb's number of meanings.

Irregular verbs are generally described as the older verbs of the language. Hence, it could be that they have more meanings and a greater valency because they have had a longer period of time in which they could spawn new meanings and uses. Irregular verbs also tend to be more frequent than regular verbs, and it is reasonable to assume that this high frequency protects irregular verbs through time against regularization.

In order to test these lines of reasoning, we need some measure of the age of a verb. A rough indication of this age is the kind of cognates a Dutch verb has in other Indo-European languages. On the basis of an etymological dictionary, Tabak *et al.* (2005) established whether a verb appears only in Dutch, in Dutch and German, in Dutch, German and other West-Germanic languages, in any Germanic language, or in Indo-European. This classification according to etymological age is available in the column labeled `EtymAge` in the data set `etymology`:

```
> colnames(etymology)
 [1] "Verb"                "WrittenFrequency"      "NcountStem"
 [4] "MeanBigramFrequency" "InflectionalEntropy"   "Auxiliary"
 [7] "Regularity"          "LengthInLetters"       "Denominative"
[10] "FamilySize"          "EtymAge"               "Valency"
[13] "NVratio"             "WrittenSpokenRatio"
```

When a data frame is read into R, the levels of any factor are assumed to be unordered by default. In order to make `EtymAge` into an ORDERED FACTOR with the levels in the appropriate order, we use the function `ordered()`:

```
> etymology$EtymAge = ordered(etymology$EtymAge, levels = c("Dutch",
+ "DutchGerman", "WestGermanic", "Germanic", "IndoEuropean"))
```

When we inspect the factor,

```
> etymology$EtymAge
...
[276] WestGermanic Germanic      IndoEuropean Germanic     Germanic
[281] Germanic      WestGermanic Germanic      Germanic     DutchGerman
Levels: Dutch < DutchGerman < WestGermanic < Germanic < IndoEuropean
```

we see that the ordering relation between its levels is now made explicit. We leave it as an exercise for you to verify that etymological age is a predictor for whether a verb is regular or irregular over and above the predictors studied in the preceding section. Here, we study whether etymological age itself can be predicted from frequency, regularity, family size, etc. We create a data distribution object, set the appropriate variable to point to this object,

```
> etymology.dd = datadist(etymology)
> options(datadist = "etymology.dd")
```

and fit a logistic regression model to the data with `lrm()`:

```
> etymology.lrm = lrm(EtymAge ~ WrittenFrequency + NcountStem +
+ MeanBigramFrequency + InflectionalEntropy + Auxiliary +
+ Regularity + LengthInLetters + Denominative + FamilySize + Valency +
+ NVratio + WrittenSpokenRatio, data = etymology, x = T, y = T)
> anova(etymology.lrm)
Wald Statistics          Response: EtymAge


Factor                  Chi-Square d.f.  P
WrittenFrequency         0.45        1   0.5038
NcountStem               3.89        1   0.0487
MeanBigramFrequency      1.89        1   0.1687
InflectionalEntropy      0.94        1   0.3313
Auxiliary                0.38        2   0.8281
Regularity              14.86        1   0.0001
LengthInLetters          0.30        1   0.5827
Denominative             8.84        1   0.0029
FamilySize               0.42        1   0.5191
Valency                  0.26        1   0.6080
NVratio                  0.07        1   0.7894
WrittenSpokenRatio       0.18        1   0.6674
TOTAL                   35.83       13   0.0006
```

The anova table suggests three significant predictors, `Regularity`, as expected, the neighborhood density of the stem (`NcountStem`), and whether the verb is denominative (`Denominative`). We simplify the model, and inspect the summary:

```
> etymology.lrmA = lrm(EtymAge ~ NcountStem + Regularity + Denominative,
+ data = etymology, x = T, y = T)
> etymology.lrmA
Frequencies of Responses
Dutch  DutchGerman WestGermanic   Germanic IndoEuropean
    8           28           43        173           33

Obs  Max Deriv Model L.R.       d.f.         P          C
285      2e-08     30.92          3         0      0.661
  Dxy      Gamma       Tau-a        R2      Brier
0.322      0.329       0.189     0.114      0.026

                      Coef     S.E.    Wald Z P
y>=DutchGerman     4.96248  0.59257    8.37   0.0000
y>=WestGermanic    3.30193  0.50042    6.60   0.0000
y>=Germanic        2.26171  0.47939    4.72   0.0000
y>=IndoEuropean   -0.99827  0.45704   -2.18   0.0289
NcountStem         0.07038  0.02014    3.49   0.0005
Regularity=regular -1.03409 0.25123   -4.12   0.0000
Denominative=N    -1.48182  0.43657   -3.39   0.0007
```

The summary lists the frequencies with which the different levels of our ordered factor for etymological age are attested, followed by the usual measures for gauging the predictivity of the model. The values of C, D_{xy}, and R_N^2 are all low, so we have to be careful when drawing conclusions.

The first four lines of the table of coefficients are new, and specific to ordinal logistic regression. These four lines represent four intercepts. The first intercept is for a normal binary logistic model that contrasts data points with Dutch as etymological age with all other data points, for which the etymological age (represented by y in the summary) is greater or equal than DutchGerman. For this standard binary model, the probability of greater age increases with neighborhood density, it is smaller for regular verbs, and also smaller for denominative verbs. The second intercept represents a second binary split, now between Dutch and DutchGerman on the one hand, and WestGermanic, Germanic, and IndoEuropean on the other. Again, the coefficients for the three predictors show how the probability of having a greater etymological age has to be adjusted for neighborhood density, regularity, and whether the verb is denominative. The remaining two intercepts work in the same way, each shift the criterion for "young" versus "old" further towards the greatest age level.

There are two things to note here. First, the four intercepts are steadily decreasing. This simply reflects the distribution of successes (old etymological age) and failures (young etymological age) as we shift our cutoff point for old versus young further towards IndoEuropean. To see this, we first count the data points classified as "old" versus "young":

```
> tab = xtabs(~etymology$EtymAge)
> tab
etymology$EtymAge
  Dutch  DutchGerman WestGermanic      Germanic IndoEuropean
      8           28           43           173           33
> sum(tab)
[1] 285
```

For the cutoff point between Dutch and DutchGerman, we have $285 - 8 = 277$ old observations (successes) and 8 young observations (failures), and hence a log odds ratio of 3.54. The following code loops through the different cutoff points and lists the counts of old and young observations, and the corresponding log odds ratio:

```
> for (i in 0:3) {
+   cat(sum(tab[(2 + i) : 5]), sum(tab[1 : (1 + i)]),
+   log(sum(tab[(2 + i) : 5]) / sum(tab[1 : (i + 1)])), "\n")
+ }
277 8 3.544576
249 36 1.933934
206 79 0.9584283
33 252 -2.032922
```

We see the same downwards progression in the logits as in the table of intercepts. The numbers are not the same, as our logits do not take into account any of the other predictors in the model. In other words, the progression of intercepts is by

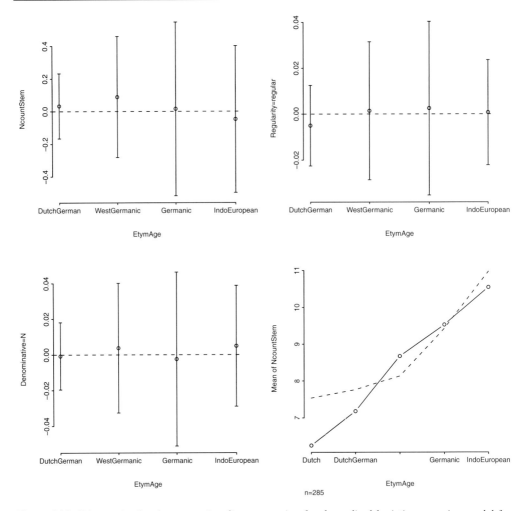

Figure 6.12. *Diagnostics for the proportionality assumption for the ordinal logistic regression model for etymological age. The lower right panel compares observed (observed) and expected (given proportionality, dashed) mean neighborhood density for each level of etymological age, the remaining panels plot for each predictor the distribution of residuals for each cutoff point.*

itself not of interest, just as the intercept in least squares regression or standard logistic regression is generally not of interest by itself.

The second thing to note is that lrm() assumes that the effects of our predictors, NcountStem, Regularity, and Denominative, are the same, irrespective of the cutoff point for etymological age. In other words, these predictors are taken to have the same proportional effect across all levels of our ordered factor. Hence, this kind of model is referred to as a PROPORTIONAL ODDS MODEL. The assumption of proportionality should be checked. One way of doing so is to plot, for each cutoff point, the mean of the partial binary residuals together with their 95% confidence intervals. If the proportionality assumption holds, these means should be close to zero. As can be seen in the first three panels of Figure 6.12, the proportionality assumption is not violated for our data. The means are very close to zero in all cases. The last panel takes a closer look at our continuous predictor, NcountStem. For each successive factor level, two points are plotted. The circles connected by the solid line show the means as actually observed; the dashed line shows what these means should be if the proportionality assumption would be satisfied perfectly. There is a slight discrepancy for the first level, Dutch, for which we also have the lowest number of observations. But since the two lines are otherwise quite similar, we conclude that a proportional odds model is justified. The diagnostic plots shown in Figure 6.12 were produced with two functions from the Design package, resid() and plot.xmean.ordinaly() as follows:

```
> par(mfrow = c(2, 2))
> resid(etymology.lrmA, 'score.binary', pl = T)
> plot.xmean.ordinaly(EtymAge ~ NcountStem, data = etymology)
> par(mfrow = c(1, 1))
```

Bootstrap validation calls attention to changes in slope and intercept,

```
> validate(etymology.lrmA, bw=T, B=200)
  1   2   3
  2   7 191
          index.orig  training       test    optimism index.corrected
Dxy       0.3222059 0.3314785 0.31487666  0.01660182      0.30560403
R2        0.1138586 0.1227111 0.10597692  0.01673422      0.09712436
Intercept 0.0000000 0.0000000 0.04821578 -0.04821578      0.04821578
Slope     1.0000000 1.0000000 0.95519326  0.04480674      0.95519326
Emax      0.0000000 0.0000000 0.01871305  0.01871305      0.01871305
D         0.1049774 0.1147009 0.09714786  0.01755301      0.08742437
```

but the optimism is fairly small, and a pentrace recommends a penalty of zero,

```
> pentrace(etym.lrmA, seq(0, 0.8, by=0.05))
Best penalty:
penalty df
      0  3
```

so we accept etymology.lrmA as our final model, and plot the partial effects (Figure 6.13):

```
> plot(etymology.lrmA, fun = plogis, ylim = c(0.8, 1))
```

We conclude that the neighborhood density of the stem is a predictor for the age of a verb. Words with a higher neighborhood density are phonologically more regular, and easier to articulate. Apparently, phonological regularity and ease of articulation contribute to a verb's continued existence through time, in addition to morphological regularity. It is remarkable that frequency is not predictive at all.

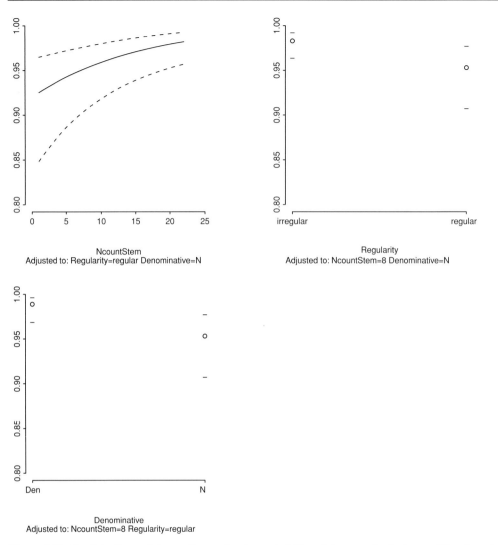

Figure 6.13. *Partial effects of the predictors for the probability of the etymological age of Dutch verbs. Den: denominative; N: not denominative.*

6.4   Regression with breakpoints

Thus far, all examples of nonlinear relations involved smooth, continuous functions that we modeled with polynomials or with splines. However, one may also encounter situations in which there is a discontinuity in an otherwise linear relation. An example is a study of the frequency with which years were referenced in the *Frankfurter Allgemeine Zeitung* (Pollman and Baayen, 2001). The relevant data are available as the data set `faz`:

```
> head(faz, 3)
    Year Frequency
1   1993     12068
2   1992      6338
3   1991      3791
> tail(faz, 3)
    Year Frequency
798 1196         0
799 1195         1
800 1194         2
```

For each year in the time period 1993–1194, `faz` lists the frequency of that year as referenced in this newspaper in 1994. Most of the year references in the issues of 1994 were to the previous year, 1993, followed by 1992, then by 1991, etc. We add a column to `faz` specifying the distance from 1994,

```
> faz$Distance = 1:nrow(faz)
```

and plot log frequency of use as a function of log distance from 1994, as shown in the upper left panel of Figure 6.14:

```
> plot(log(faz$Distance), log(faz$Frequency + 1),
+ xlab = "log Distance", ylab = "log Frequency")
```

What is of interest in this plot is that there seems to be a linear relation up till approximately a log distance of four. Around the location of the vertical solid line, the slope of the regression line changes fairly abruptly. This suggests that the collective consciousness of events in the past is substantially reduced for events occurring more than a lifetime (some 60 years) ago. The dashed vertical line marks 1945, the end of the Second World War. Therefore, an alternative explanation of the observed change is that the Second World War is the dividing line between recent and more distant history. In order to evaluate these hypotheses, we need to establish whether there is indeed a sudden change—a significant change in the slope—and if so, where this discontinuity is located.

The simplest regression model for this data that takes the discontinuity into account is one with a single linear regression line that changes slope at a so-called BREAKPOINT. Let's assume that the breakpoint is at distance 59. For convenience, we log frequency and distance,

```
> faz$LogFrequency = log(faz$Frequency + 1)
> faz$LogDistance = log(faz$Distance)
> breakpoint = log(59)
```

and then shift all the data points leftwards along the horizontal axis, so that the breakpoint coincides with the vertical axis. This is shown in the upper right panel of Figure 6.14:

```
> faz$ShiftedLogDistance = faz$LogDistance - breakpoint
> plot(faz$ShiftedLogDistance, faz$LogFrequency,
+ xlab = "log Shifted Distance", ylab = "log Frequency")
```

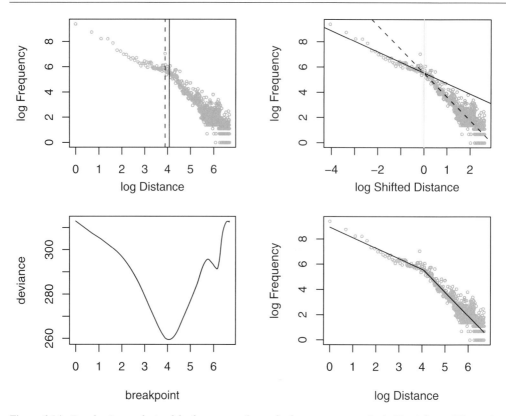

Figure 6.14. *Breakpoint analysis of the frequency of use of references to years in the* Frankfurter Allgemeine Zeitung *in* 1994 *as a function of the distance of the year name from* 1994.

We can now fit two regression models to the data, one for the data points to the left of the vertical axis, and one for the data points to its right. As can be seen in the upper right panel of Figure 6.14, the two lines cross the vertical axis at nearly the same place:

```
> faz.left = lm(LogFrequency ~ ShiftedLogDistance,
+ data = faz[faz$ShiftedLogDistance <= 0,])
> faz.right = lm(LogFrequency ~ ShiftedLogDistance,
+ data = faz[faz$ShiftedLogDistance >= 0,])
> abline(faz.left, lty = 1)
> abline(faz.right, lty = 2)
```

What we need to do is to integrate these two models into a single regression model. We do this by introducing an INDICATOR VARIABLE that specifies whether the shifted log distance is greater than zero,

```
> faz$PastBreakPoint = as.factor(faz$ShiftedLogDistance > 0)
```

and by constructing a model in which the only term in the formula is the interaction of `ShiftedLogDistance` with this indicator variable `PastBreakPoint`:

```
> faz.both = lm(LogFrequency ~ ShiftedLogDistance : PastBreakPoint,
+ data=faz)
```

Normally, one would not include an interaction without including the main effects, but in this special case we do not want these main effects to be present. To see why, consider the table of coefficients in the summary:

```
> summary(faz.both)
...

Residuals:
     Min       1Q    Median       3Q      Max
-1.76242 -0.31593 -0.02271  0.34838  1.87073
Coefficients:
                                 Estimate Std. Error t value Pr(>|t|)
(Intercept)                       5.52596    0.05434  101.70   <2e-16
ShiftedLogDist:PastBreakPointFALSE -0.84124    0.06460  -13.02   <2e-16
ShiftedLogDist:PastBreakPointTRUE  -1.88383    0.02872  -65.60   <2e-16

Residual standard error: 0.5705 on 797 degrees of freedom
Multiple R-Squared: 0.8898,      Adjusted R-squared: 0.8895
F-statistic:   3218 on 2 and 797 DF,  p-value: < 2.2e-16
```

We have three coefficients, one for the intercept, one for the slope when we are to the left of the breakpoint, and one for when we are to the right of the breakpoint. Since the intercept represents the frequency when the shifted distance is zero, we have succeeded in building a model that combines the first half of the solid line in the upper right panel with the second half of the dashed line. An anova test comparing this model with a model with just a simple regression line shows that the extra parameter for modeling the breakpoint is justified:

```
> anova(faz.both, lm(LogFrequency ~ ShiftedLogDistance, data = faz))
Analysis of Variance Table

Model 1: LogFrequency ~ ShiftedLogDistance:PastBreakPoint
Model 2: LogFrequency ~ ShiftedLogDistance
  Res.Df     RSS Df Sum of Sq      F    Pr(>F)
1    797 259.430
2    798 312.945 -1   -53.515 164.41 < 2.2e-16
```

Up till now, we have worked with one sensible breakpoint, but we still need to ascertain what the most likely breakpoint is. To do so, we fit a series of models, one for each possible breakpoint. For each model, we calculate the deviance; the sum of the squared differences between the observed and the fitted values:

```
> sum((fitted(faz.both) - faz$LogFrequency)^2)
[1] 259.4298
> deviance(faz.both)
[1] 259.4298
```

The following lines of code implement this idea. We begin by creating a vector in which we store the deviances for the models. We then loop over all sensible breakpoints, and carry out the same sequence of steps as above:

```
> deviances = rep(0, nrow(faz)-1)
> for (pos in 1 : (nrow(faz)-1)) {
+   breakpoint = log(pos)
+   faz$ShiftedLogDistance = faz$LogDistance - breakpoint
+   faz$PastBreakPoint = as.factor(faz$ShiftedLogDistance > 0)
+   faz.both = lm(LogFrequency ~ ShiftedLogDistance:PastBreakPoint,
+       data = faz)
+   deviances[pos] = deviance(faz.both)
+ }
```

We select the breakpoint for which the deviance is smallest,

```
> best = which(deviances == min(deviances))
> best
[1] 58
> breakpoint = log(best)
```

and refit the model one last time for this breakpoint:

```
> faz$ShiftedLogDistance = faz$LogDistance - breakpoint
> faz$PastBreakPoint = as.factor(faz$ShiftedLogDistance > 0)
> faz.both = lm(LogFrequency ~ ShiftedLogDistance:PastBreakPoint,
+ data = faz)
```

We now add the lower panels to Figure 6.14:

```
> plot(log(1:length(deviances)), deviances, type = "l",
+ xlab = "breakpoint", ylab = "deviance")
> plot(faz$LogDistance, faz$LogFrequency,
+ xlab = "log Distance", ylab = "log Frequency", col = "darkgrey")
> lines(faz$LogDistance, fitted(faz.both))
```

Note that the final plot has the unshifted distances on the horizontal axis, and the fitted values (obtained for the shifted values) on the vertical axis. (A moment's thought should reveal why this is legitimate.) The breakpoint is at distance 58 from 1994, in 1936, so this suggests that the change in historical consciousness is located well before the beginning of the Second World War.

A second example illustrating the use of indicator variables addresses changes in the frequency with which constructions with periphrastic *do* were used in English from the end of the fourteenth to the end of the sixteenth century. Ellegård (1953) studied the use of periphrastic *do* in 107 texts. Counts of periphrastic *do* for four sentence types are available as the data set periphrasticDo:

```
> head(periphrasticDo)
  begin  end     type    do other
1  1390 1425  affdecl    17 49583
2  1425 1475  affdecl   121 45379
3  1475 1500  affdecl  1059 58541
4  1500 1525  affdecl   396 28204
5  1525 1535  affdecl   494 18306
6  1535 1550  affdecl  1564 17636
> table(periphrasticDo$type)
affdecl affquest  negdecl negquest
     11       11       11       11
```

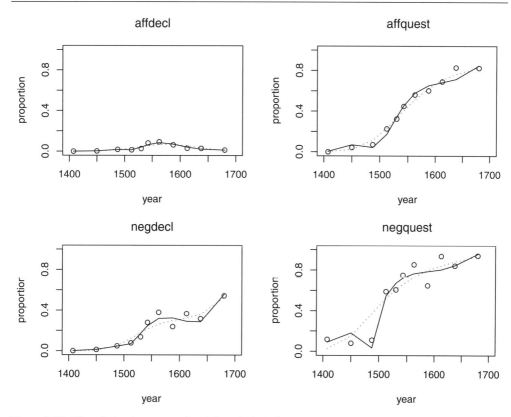

Figure 6.15. *The relative frequency of periphrastic* do *in four sentence types across three centuries. Circles represent observed relative frequencies, dashed and solid lines a regression model without and with an indicator variable adjusting for the fifteenth century.*

The columns `begin` and `end` list the beginning and end of the period for which Ellegård counted the occurrences of `do` and `other` constructions for affirmative declarative sentences (`affdecl`), affirmative questions (`affquest`), negative declarative sentences (`negdecl`), and negative questions (`negquest`). Figure 6.15 shows, for each sentence type, the observed proportion of sentences with periphrastic *do* for the midpoints of each time period. Except for affirmative declarative sentences, the use of periphrastic *do* increased over the years.

The curve for affirmative questions has been analyzed with a logistic regression model by Kroch (1989); see Vulanović and Baayen (2006) for further references to studies that propose models for subsets of the sentence types. The question considered by the latter study is whether a single model can be fitted to the data of all four sentence types. After all, each sentence type shows a pattern of linguistic change, including the affirmative declarative sentences, for which the change did not carry through.

Since we are dealing with binary data (counts of sentences with and without periphrastic *do*) in tabular format, we use `glm()` and allow points of inflection into the curves by using both quadratic and cubic polynomial terms, which we allow to interact with sentence type:

```
> periphrasticDo$year = periphrasticDo$begin +
+     (periphrasticDo$end-periphrasticDo$begin)/2          # midpoints
> periphrasticDo.glm = glm(cbind(do, other) ~
+ (year + I(year^2) + I(year^3)) * type,
+ data = periphrasticDo, family = "binomial")
> summary(periphrasticDo.glm)
Deviance Residuals:
     Min         1Q     Median         3Q        Max
-18.4741    -1.7182    -0.1357     1.7668    14.8644


Coefficients:
                             Estimate Std. Error z value Pr(>|z|)
(Intercept)                -4.901e+02  2.163e+02  -2.266   0.0235
year                        6.024e-01  4.167e-01   1.445   0.1483
I(year^2)                  -1.759e-04  2.675e-04  -0.658   0.5107
I(year^3)                  -6.345e-09  5.720e-08  -0.111   0.9117
typeaffquest               -6.073e+02  9.088e+02  -0.668   0.5040
typenegdecl                -4.009e+03  7.325e+02  -5.473 4.42e-08
typenegquest               -8.083e+02  1.229e+03  -0.658   0.5106
year:typeaffquest           1.328e+00  1.726e+00   0.769   0.4418
year:typenegdecl            7.816e+00  1.392e+00   5.613 1.99e-08
year:typenegquest           1.790e+00  2.365e+00   0.757   0.4492
I(year^2):typeaffquest     -9.591e-04  1.092e-03  -0.878   0.3800
I(year^2):typenegdecl      -5.078e-03  8.816e-04  -5.760 8.43e-09
I(year^2):typenegquest     -1.299e-03  1.517e-03  -0.856   0.3918
I(year^3):typeaffquest      2.298e-07  2.303e-07   0.998   0.3183
I(year^3):typenegdecl       1.100e-06  1.860e-07   5.915 3.32e-09
I(year^3):typenegquest      3.111e-07  3.241e-07   0.960   0.3370


(Dispersion parameter for binomial family taken to be 1)

Null deviance: 20431.1  on 43  degrees of freedom
Residual deviance:  1236.0  on 28  degrees of freedom
AIC: 1504.6
```

Since the residual deviance is much larger than the corresponding degrees of freedom, we have overdispersion, so we use the F-test to evaluate the significance of the interactions, following Crawley (2002):

```
> anova(periphrasticDo.glm, test = "F")
Analysis of Deviance Table
Model: binomial, link: logit
Terms added sequentially (first to last)
                Df Deviance Resid. Df Resid. Dev       F     Pr(>F)
NULL                              43    20431.1
year             1   6302.2       42    14128.9 6302.225 < 2.2e-16
I(year^2)        1   4085.6       41    10043.3 4085.613 < 2.2e-16
I(year^3)        1     31.3       40    10012.0   31.321 2.187e-08
type             3   7810.5       37     2201.4 2603.510 < 2.2e-16
year:type        3    750.9       34     1450.5  250.296 < 2.2e-16
I(year^2):type   3    173.3       31     1277.2   57.767 < 2.2e-16
I(year^3):type   3     41.3       28     1236.0   13.754 5.752e-09
```

The dotted lines in Figure 6.15 show that this model captures the main trends for all sentence types, but the fit is rather poor for especially the negative questions.

In order to improve the fit, we note that there is very little development during the fifteenth century. We therefore create an indicator variable that is zero for the first three time periods, and one for the remaining periods:

```
> periphrasticDo$Indicator = rep(c(rep(0, 3), rep(1, 8)), 4)
> periphrasticDo.glmA = glm(cbind(do, other) ~
+ (year + I(year^2) + I(year^3)) * type +
+ Indicator * type + Indicator * year,
+ data = periphrasticDo, family = "binomial")
```

The anova summary shows that the indicator variable is significant,

```
> anova(periphrasticDo.glmA, test = "F")
```

	Df	Deviance	Resid. Df	Resid. Dev	F	Pr(>F)
NULL			43	20431.1		
year	1	6302.2	42	14128.9	6302.225	< 2.2e-16
I(year^2)	1	4085.6	41	10043.3	4085.613	< 2.2e-16
I(year^3)	1	31.3	40	10012.0	31.321	2.187e-08
type	3	7810.5	37	2201.4	2603.510	< 2.2e-16
Indicator	1	174.7	36	2026.8	174.663	< 2.2e-16
year:type	3	717.0	33	1309.8	238.990	< 2.2e-16
I(year^2):type	3	199.9	30	1109.9	66.636	< 2.2e-16
I(year^3):type	3	46.1	27	1063.8	15.359	5.459e-10
type:Indicator	3	48.2	24	1015.6	16.081	1.891e-10
year:Indicator	1	485.8	23	529.8	485.820	< 2.2e-16

so it does indeed make sense to allow coefficients to change when going from the fifteenth century to the next two centuries. The solid lines in Figure 6.15 show that the new model is superior to the old model for all sentence types, with the exception of the affirmative declaratives, for which there is no improvement that is visible to the eye.

Compared to previous models proposed in the literature, the present model has the advantage of fitting all sentence types simultaneously. This brings out a similarity between the two types of declarative clauses. For both, an initial increase is followed by a decrease that perseveres in the case of affirmative sentences, but that is followed by a slight increase in the case of negative declaratives. For further discussion of the mathematics of the functional considerations motivating these patterns of language change, see Vulanović and Baayen (2006).

At this point, you might be asking yourself whether we are overfitting the data, with 21 coefficients for 4 sentence types with 11 time points each. The rule of thumb given by Harrell (2001:61) is that for logistic models, the number of coefficients should be smaller than the total number of observations with the minority outcome, divided by 20. For the present data,

```
> min(apply(periphrasticDo[, c("do", "other")], 2, sum))
[1] 9483
```

the 9483 observations for the less frequent outcome (do) is much larger than the number of parameters (21) multiplied by 20, so we are doing fine.

Figure 6.15 was made by looping over the level of sentence type in order to create the successive panels:

```
> periphrasticDo$predict = predict(periphrasticDo.glm, type="response")
```

```
> periphrasticDo$predictA=predict(periphrasticDo.glmA, type="response")
> par(mfrow=c(2, 2))
> for (i in 1:nlevels(periphrasticDo$type)) {
+    subset = periphrasticDo[periphrasticDo$type ==
+      levels(periphrasticDo$type)[i], ]
+    plot(subset$year,
+        subset$do/(subset$do + subset$other),
+        type = "p", ylab = "proportion", xlab = "year",
+        ylim = c(0, 1), xlim = c(1400, 1700))
+    mtext(levels(periphrasticDo$type)[i], line = 2)
+    lines(subset$year, subset$predict, lty = 3)
+    lines(subset$year, subset$predictA, lty = 1)
+ }
```

6.5   Models for lexical richness

The frequencies of linguistic units such as words, word bigrams
and trigrams, syllables, constructions, etc. pose a special challenge for statistical analysis. This section illustrates this challenge by means of an in-
vestigation of lexical richness in *Alice's Adventures in Wonderland*. The
data set alice is based on a version obtained from the project Guten-
berg (http://www.gutenberg.org/wiki/MainPage) from which header
and trailer were removed. The resulting text was loaded into R with
scan("alice.txt", what="character") and converted to lower case with
tolower(). This ensures that variants such as Went and went are considered
as tokens of the same word type. To clarify the distinction between TYPES and
TOKENS, consider the first sentence of *Alice's Adventures in Wonderland*:

*Alice was beginning to get very tired of sitting by her sister on the bank and
of having nothing to do.*

There are 21 words in this sentence, of which two are used twice. We will refer to
the number of unique words as the number of types, and to the number of words
regardless of their identity as the number of tokens.

The question that we consider here is how to characterize the vocabulary richness of *Alice's Adventures in Wonderland*. Intuitively, vocabulary richness (or
lexical richness) should be quantifiable in terms of the number of different word
types. However, the number of different word types depends on the number of
tokens.

If we read through a text or corpus, and at regular intervals keep note of
how many different types we have encountered, we find that, unsurprisingly, the
number of types increases, first rapidly, and then more and more slowly. This
phenomenon is illustrated in the upper left panel of Figure 6.16. For 40 equally
spaced measurement points in "token time," the corresponding count of different
types is graphed. I refer to this curve as the GROWTH CURVE OF THE VOCABULARY.
The panel to its right shows the rate at which the vocabulary is increasing, quickly

at first, more and more slowly as we proceed through the text. The VOCABULARY GROWTH RATE is estimated by the ratio of the number of HAPAX LEGOMENA (types with a frequency of 1) to the number of tokens sampled. The growth rate is a probability, the probability that, after having read N tokens, the next token sampled represents an unseen type, a word type that did not occur among the preceding N tokens (Good, 1953; Baayen, 2001).

The problem that arises is that, although we could select the total number of types counted for the full text as a measure of lexical richness, this measure would not lend itself well for comparison with longer or with shorter texts. Therefore, considerable effort has been invested in developing measures of lexical richness that would supposedly be independent of the number of tokens sampled. The remaining six panels of Figure 6.16 illustrate that these measures have not been particularly successful. The third panel on the upper row shows the worst measure of all, the type-token ratio, obtained by dividing the number of types by the number of tokens. It is highly correlated ($r = 0.99$) with the growth rate of the vocabulary shown in the panel to its left. The panel in the upper right explores the idea that word frequencies might follow a lognormal distribution. If so, the mean log frequency might be expected to remain roughly constant and in fact to narrow down to its true value as the sample size increases. We return to this issue below; here we note that there is no sign that the curve is anywhere near reaching a stable value. The bottom panels illustrate the systematic variability in four more complex measures that have been put forward in the literature. None of these putative constants is a true constant. The only measure of these last four that is, at least under the simplifying assumption that words are used randomly and independently, truly constant is Yule's K, but due to the non-random way in which Lewis Carroll used the words in *Alice's Adventures in Wonderland*, even K fails to be constant.

Before considering the implications of this conclusion, we first introduce the function that was used to obtain Figure 6.16, `growth.fnc()`. We instruct it to calculate lexical measures at 40 intervals with 648 tokens in each interval:

```
> alice[1:5]
[1] "alice"        "s"           "adventures" "in"          "wonderland"
> alice.growth = growth.fnc(text = alice, size = 681, nchunks = 40)
```

The output of `growth.fnc()` is a growth object, and its contents can be inspected with `head.growth()` or `tail.growth()`:

```
> head.growth(alice.growth, 3)
  Chunk Tokens Types HapaxLegomena DisLegomena TrisLegomena
1     1    681   280           179          42           21
2     2   1362   450           269          71           27
3     3   2043   590           344          92           41
      Yule       Zipf TypeTokenRatio    Herdan  Guiraud
1 107.38290 -0.6634960      0.4111601 0.7410401 10.72962
2 102.02453 -0.7365004      0.3303965 0.7150101 12.19338
3  98.60922 -0.7691661      0.2887910 0.7041325 13.05323
```

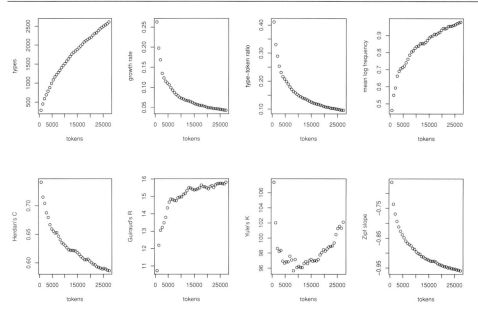

Figure 6.16. *The vocabulary growth curve and selected measures of lexical richness, all of which depend on the text size.*

```
        Sichel Lognormal
1 0.1500000 0.4604566
2 0.1577778 0.5503570
3 0.1559322 0.5926050
```

The first three columns list the indices of the chunks, the corresponding (cumulative) number of tokens, and the counts of different types in the text up to and including the current chunk. The next three columns list the numbers of HAPAX, DIS, AND TRIS LEGOMENA, the words that are counted exactly once, exactly twice, or exactly three times at a given text size. The remaining columns list various measures of lexical richness: Yule's K (Yule, 1944), the Zipf slope (Zipf, 1935), the type-token ratio, Herdan's C (Herdan, 1960), Guiraud's R (Guiraud, 1954), Sichel's S (Sichel, 1986), and the mean of log frequency (Carroll, 1967). Once a growth object has been created, Figure 6.16 is obtained straightforwardly by applying the standard `plot()` function to the growth object:

```
> plot(alice.growth)
```

Let's return to the issue of the variability of the lexical constants. This variability would not be much of a problem if a constant's range of variability within a given text would be very small compared to its range of variability across texts. Unfortunately, this is not the case, as shown by Tweedie and Baayen (1998) and Hoover (2003). The within-text variability can be of the same order of magnitude as the between-text variability.

There are two approaches to overcome this problem. A practical solution is to compare the vocabulary size (number of types) across texts for the same text sizes. For larger texts, a random sample of the same size as the smallest text in the comparison set has to be selected. The concomitant data loss (all the other words in the larger text that are discarded) is taken for granted. The function `compare.richness.fnc()` carries out such comparisons. By way of example, we split the text of *Alice's Adventures in Wonderland* into unequal parts:

```
> aiw1 = alice[1:17000]
> aiw2 = alice[17001:27269]
```

If we straightforwardly compare these texts by examining the number of types, we find that there is a highly significant difference in vocabulary richness:

```
> compare.richness.fnc(aiw1, aiw2)
comparison of lexical richness for aiw1 and aiw2
with approximations of variances based on the LNRE models
gigp (X2 = 12.17) and gigp (X2 = 22.29)

      Tokens Types HapaxLegomena GrowthRate
aiw1  17000  2020           941    0.05535
aiw2  10269  1522           736    0.07167

two-tailed tests:
                            Z p
Vocabulary Size       14.0246 0
Vocabulary Growth Rate -5.8962 0
```

In order to evaluate differences in the observed numbers of types, the variances of these type counts have to be estimated. `compare.richness.fnc()` does this by fitting word frequency models (see below) to each text, and selecting for each text the model with the best goodness of fit. (Models with a better goodness of fit have a lower chi-squared value). Given the estimates of the required variances, Z-scores are obtained that evaluate the difference between the number of types in the first and the second text. Because `aiw1` has more tokens than `aiw2`, this difference is positive. Hence the Z-score is also positive. Its very large value, 14.02, is associated with a very small p-value, effectively zero.

When we reduce the size of the larger text to that of the smaller one, the differences in lexical richness are no longer significant, as expected:

```
> aiw1a = aiw1[1:length(aiw2)]
> compare.richness.fnc(aiw1a, aiw2)
comparison of lexical richness for aiw1a and aiw2
with approximations of variances based on the LNRE models
gigp (X2 = 23.19) and gigp (X2 = 22.29)

       Tokens Types HapaxLegomena GrowthRate
aiw1a  10269  1516           740    0.07206
aiw2   10269  1522           736    0.07167

two-tailed tests:
                             Z       p
Vocabulary Size       -0.1795 0.8575
Vocabulary Growth Rate 0.1201 0.9044
```

Note that `compare.richness.fnc()` compares texts not only with respect to their vocabulary sizes, but also with respect to their growth rates. A test of growth rates is carried out because two texts may have made use of the same number of types, but may nevertheless differ substantially with respect to the rate at which unseen types are expected to appear.

The other approach to the problem of lexical richness is to develop better statistical models. The challenge that this poses is best approached by first considering in some more detail the problems with the models proposed by Herdan (1960) and Zipf (1935). In fact, there are two kinds of problems. The first is illustrated in Figure 6.17. The upper left panel plots log types against log tokens. The double log transformation changes a curve into what looks like a straight line. Herdan proposed that the slope of this line is a text characteristic that is invariant with respect to text length. This slope is known as Herdan's C and was plotted in the lower left panel of Figure 6.16 for a range of text sizes. A plot of the residuals, shown in the upper right panel of Figure 6.17, shows that the residuals are far from random. Instead, they point to the presence of some curvature that the straight line fails to capture. In other words, the regression model proposed by Herdan is too simple. This is the first problem. The second problem is that when we estimate the slope of the regression line at forty equally spaced intervals for varying text sizes, the estimated slope changes systematically. This is clearly visible in the lower left panel of Figure 6.16.

Zipf's law is beset by exactly the same problems. The lower left panel of Figure 6.17 plots log frequency against log rank. The overall pattern is that of a straight line, as shown by the ordinary least squares regression line shown in grey. The slope of this line, the Zipf slope, is supposed to be a textual characteristic independent of the sample size. But the residuals (see the lower right panel of Figure 6.17) again point to systematic problems with the goodness of fit. And the lower right panel of Figure 6.16 shows that the slope of this regression line also changes systematically as we vary the size of the text, a phenomenon first noted by Orlov (1983). We could try to fit more complicated regression models to the data using quadratic terms or cubic splines. Unfortunately, although this might help to obtain a better fit for a fixed text size, it would leave the second problem unsolved. Any non-trivial change in the text size leads to a non-trivial change in the values of the regression coefficients. Before explaining why these changes occur, we pause to discuss the code for Figure 6.17.

The object `alice.growth` is a growth object. Internal to that object is a data frame, which we extract as follows:

```
> alice.g = alice.growth@data$data
> head(alice.g, 3)
  Chunk Tokens Types HapaxLegomena DisLegomena TrisLegomena      Yule
1     1    681   280           179          42           21 107.38290
2     2   1362   450           269          71           27 102.02453
3     3   2043   590           344          92           41  98.60922
        Zipf TypeTokenRatio   Herdan   Guiraud    Sichel Lognormal
1 -0.6634960      0.4111601 0.7410401  10.72962 0.1500000 0.4604566
```

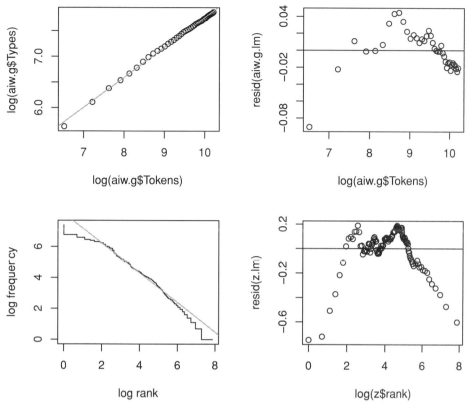

Figure 6.17. *Herdan's law (upper left) and Zipf's law (lower left) and the corresponding residuals (right panels) for* Alice's Adventures in Wonderland.

```
2 -0.7365004      0.3303965 0.7150101 12.19338 0.1577778 0.5503570
3 -0.7691661      0.2887910 0.7041325 13.05323 0.1559322 0.5926050
```

The upper left panel of Figure 6.17 is obtained by regressing log `Types` on log `Tokens`:

```
> plot(log(alice.g$Tokens), log(alice.g$Types))
> alice.g.lm = lm(log(alice.g$Types)~log(alice.g$Tokens))
> abline(alice.g.lm, col="darkgrey")
```

The summary of the model,

```
> summary(alice.g.lm)
Coefficients:
                       Estimate Std. Error t value Pr(>|t|)
(Intercept)            1.900790   0.041020   46.34   <2e-16
log(alice.g$Tokens) 0.586259   0.004401  133.22   <2e-16

Residual standard error: 0.024 on 38 degrees of freedom
Multiple R-Squared: 0.9979,     Adjusted R-squared: 0.9978
F-statistic: 1.775e+04 on 1 and 38 DF,  p-value: < 2.2e-16
```

shows we have been extremely successful with an R-squared of 0.998. But the residual plot shows the model is nevertheless inadequate:

```
> plot(log(alice.g$Tokens), resid(alice.g.lm))
> abline(h=0)
```

The lower left panel of Figure 6.17 is obtained with `zipf.fnc()`. Its output is a data frame with the word frequencies, the frequencies of these frequencies, and the associated ranks:

```
> z = zipf.fnc(alice, plot = T)
> head(z, n = 3)
    frequency freqOfFreq rank
117      1639          1    1
116       866          1    2
115       725          1    3
> tail(z, n = 3)
  frequency freqOfFreq rank
3         3        228 1052
2         2        397 1449
1         1       1166 2615
```

When plot is set to true, it shows the RANK-FREQUENCY STEP FUNCTION in the graphics window, as illustrated in the lower left panel of Figure 6.17. The code it executes is simply:

```
> plot(log(z$rank), log(z$frequency), type = "S")
```

The step function (obtained with `type = "S"`) highlights that, especially for the lowest frequencies, large numbers of words share exactly the same frequency but have different (arbitrary) ranks. We fit a linear model predicting frequency from the highest rank with that frequency, and add the regression line:

```
> z.lm = lm(log(z$frequency) ~ log(z$rank))
> abline(z.lm, col = "darkgrey")
```

Finally, we add the plot with the residuals at each rank:

```
> plot(log(z$rank), resid(z.lm))
> abline(h=0)
```

So why is it that the slopes of the regression models proposed by Herdan and Zipf change systematically as the text size is increased? A greater text size implies a greater sample size, and under normal circumstances, a greater sample size would lead us to expect not only more precise estimates but also more stable estimates. Consider, for instance, what happens if we regress reaction time on frequency for increasing samples of words from the data set of English monomorphemic and monosyllabic words in the data set `english`. We simplify by restricting ourselves to the data pertaining to the young age group, and by ignoring all other predictors in the model:

```
> young = english[english$AgeSubject == "young",]
> young = young[sample(1:nrow(young)), ]
```

The last line randomly reorders the rows in the data frame. We next define a vector with sample sizes,

```
> samplesizes = seq(57, 2284, by = 57)
```

and create vectors for storing the coefficients, their standard errors, and the lower bound of the 95% confidence interval:

```
> coefs  = rep(0, 40)
> stderr = rep(0, 40)
> lower  = rep(0, 40)
```

We loop over the sample sizes, select the relevant subset of the data, fit the model, and extract the statistics of interest:

```
> for (i in 1:length(samplesizes)) {
+    young.s      = young[1:samplesizes[i], ]
+    young.s.lm = lm(RTlexdec ~ WrittenFrequency, data = young.s)
+    coefs[i]     = coef(young.s.lm)[2]
+    stderr[i]    = summary(young.s.lm)$coef[2, 2]
+    lower[i]     = qt(0.025, young.s.lm$df.residual) * stderr[i]
+ }
```

Finally, we plot the coefficients as a function of sample size, and add the 95% confidence intervals:

```
> plot(samplesizes, coefs, ylim = c(-0.028, -0.044), type = "l",
+ xlab = "sample size", ylab = "coefficient for frequency")
> points(samplesizes, coefs)
> lines(samplesizes, coefs - lower, col = "darkgrey")
> lines(samplesizes, coefs + lower, col = "darkgrey")
```

What we see, as shown in Figure 6.18, is that after some initial fluctuations the estimates of the coefficient become stable, and that the confidence interval becomes narrower as the sample size is increased. This is the normal pattern: we expect that as the sample size grows larger, the difference between the sample mean and the population mean will approach zero. (This is known as the LAW OF LARGE NUMBERS.) However, this pattern is unlike anything that we see for our lexical measures.

The reason that our lexical measures misbehave is that word frequency distributions, and even more so the distributions of bigrams and trigrams, are characterized by large numbers of very low probability elements. Such distributions are referred to as LNRE distributions, where the acronym LNRE stands for Large Number of Rare Events (Chitashvili and Khmaladze, 1989; Baayen, 2001). Many of the rare events in the population do not occur in a given sample, even when that sample is large. The joint probability of the unseen words is usually so substantial that the relative frequencies in the sample become inaccurate estimates of the real probabilities. Since the relative frequencies in the sample sum up to 1, they leave no space for probabilities of the unseen types in the population. Hence, the sample relative frequencies have to be adjusted so that they become slightly smaller, in order to free probability space for the unseen types (Good, 1953; Gale

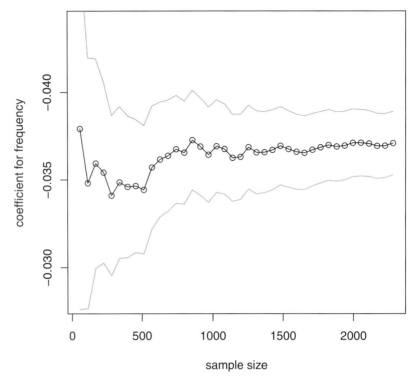

Figure 6.18. *Estimated coefficient for written frequency for English lexical decision times for increasing sample size, with 95% confidence interval.*

and Sampson, 1995; Baayen 2001). An estimate for the joint probability of the unseen types is the growth rate of the vocabulary. For *Alice's Adventures in Wonderland*, this probability equals 0.05. In other words, the likelihood of observing a new word at the end of the text is 1 out of 20. It is not surprising, therefore, that lexical measures have to be updated continuously as the text sample is increased.

The package `zipfR`, developed by Evert and Baroni (2006), provides tools for fitting the two most important and useful LNRE models, the Generalized Inverse Gauss-Poisson model of Sichel (1986), and the finite Zipf-Mandelbrot model of Evert (2004). An object type that is fundamental to the `zipfR` package is the FREQUENCY SPECTRUM. A frequency spectrum is a table with frequencies of frequencies. When working with raw text we can make a frequency spectrum within R. (This, however, is feasible only with texts or small corpora with less than a million words.) By way of illustration, we return to *Alice's Adventures in Wonderland*, and apply `table()` twice:

```
> alice.table = table(table(alice))
> head(alice.table)
   1    2    3    4    5    6
1166  397  228  147   94   58
```

```
> tail(alice.table)
553  595  631  725  866 1639
  1    1    1    1    1    1
```

There are 1166 hapax legomena, 397 dis legomena, 228 tris legomena, and steadily decreasing counts of words with higher frequencies. At the tail of the frequency spectrum we see that the highest frequency, 1639, is realized by only a single word. To see which words have the highest frequencies, we apply `table()` to the text, but now only once. After sorting, we see that the highest frequency is realized by the definite article:

```
> tail(sort(table(alice)))
alice
she   it    a   to  and  the
553  595  631  725  866 1639
```

In order to convert `alice.table` into a spectrum object, we apply `spc()`. Its first argument, m, should specify the word frequencies, its second argument, Vm, should specify the frequencies of these word frequencies:

```
> alice.spc = spc(m = as.numeric(names(alice.table)),
+ Vm = as.numeric(alice.table))
> alice.spc
    m    Vm
1   1  1166
2   2   397
3   3   228
4   4   147
5   5    94
6   6    58
7   7    61
8   8    51
9   9    33
10 10    37
        ...

      N    V
  27269 2615
```

Spectrum objects have a summary method, which lists the first ten elements of the spectrum, together with the number of tokens N and the number of types V in the text. A spectrum behaves like a data frame, so we can verify that the counts of types and tokens are correct with:

```
> sum(alice.spc$Vm)              # types
[1] 2615
> sum(alice.spc$m * alice.spc$Vm)    # tokens
[1] 27269
```

For large texts and corpora, frequency spectra should be created by independent software. For a corpus of Dutch newspapers of some 80 million words (part of the Twente News Corpus), a frequency spectrum is available as the data set `twente`. We convert this data frame into a `zipfR` spectrum object with `spc()`:

```
> twente.spc = spc(m=twente$m, Vm = twente$Vm)
> N(twente.spc)    # ask for number of tokens
[1] 78934379
> V(twente.spc)    # ask for number of types
[1] 912289
```

Note that a frequency spectrum provides a very concise summary of a frequency distribution. We have nearly a million different words (defined as sequences of characters separated by spaces), but `twente.spc` has a mere 4639 rows.

We return to *Alice's Adventures in Wonderland* and fit an LNRE model to this text with `lnre()`. This function takes two arguments, the type of model and a frequency spectrum. We first choose as a model the Generalized Inverse Gauss-Poisson model, `gigp`:

```
> alice.lnre.gigp = lnre("gigp", alice.spc)
```

A summary of the model is obtained by typing the name of the model object at the prompt:

```
> alice.lnre.gigp
Generalized Inverse Gauss-Poisson (GIGP) LNRE model.
Parameters:
Shape:          gamma = -0.7054636
Lower decay:      B = 0.02646131
Upper decay:      C = 0.0358188
[ Zipf size:      Z = 27.9183 ]
Population size: S = 5901.3
Sampling method: Poisson, with exact calculations.

Parameters estimated from sample of size N = 27269:
            V      V1     V2     V3     V4     V5
Observed: 2615.00 1166.00 397.00 228.00 147.00 94.00 ...
Expected: 2600.98 1149.66 450.99 227.14 136.58 91.84 ...

Goodness-of-fit (multivariate chi-squared test):
     X2 df          p
61.72194 13 2.580101e-08
```

The summary first lists the model and its parameters. It then mentions the population size S, an estimate of the number of types in the population sampled by the text. Because LNRE models take the probability mass of unseen word types into account, they are able to provide estimates of the number of unseen types. By combining the count of observed types with the estimated count of unseen types, an estimate of the population number of types is obtained. For the present example, this estimate concerns the number of words Lewis Carroll might have found appropriate to use when writing stories about Alice.

Of course, the accuracy of this estimate depends on how well the model fits the data. Skipping a technical comment about the sampling method, we therefore inspect the final part of the summary, which provides information about the goodness of fit. It first lists the observed and expected counts for the total vocabulary as well as for the numbers of types with frequencies 1 through 5. A visual comparison of the first 15 observed and expected spectrum elements, shown in the upper left panel of Figure 6.19, is obtained with the help of the `lnre.spc()` function, which takes as argument an LNRE model and the sample size (in tokens) for which a spectrum is required, here 25942, the number of tokens in *Alice's Adventures in Wonderland*:

```
> plot(alice.spc, lnre.spc(alice.lnre.gigp, 27269))
```

Note that the observed number of dis legomena is somewhat smaller than the expected number. This lack of goodness of fit is also highlighted by a special version of the chi-squared test, listed at the end of the summary. For a good fit, the X^2-value should be low, and the corresponding p-value large and preferably well above 0.05. In the present example, the model is clearly unsatisfactory. It should be kept in mind that the statistical theory underlying these LNRE models proceeds on the assumption that words are used at random and independently of each other in text. This is obviously a simplification and may underlie the present lack of goodness of fit.

A more successful fit is obtained for the spectrum of the Dutch newspaper corpus with the finite Zipf-Mandelbrot model:

```
> twente.lnre.fzm = lnre("fzm", twente.spc)
> twente.lnre.fzm
finite Zipf-Mandelbrot LNRE model.
Parameters:
Shape:          alpha = 0.5446703
Lower cutoff:       A = 3.942826e-11
Upper cutoff:       B = 0.0005977105
[ Normalization:    C = 13.37577 ]
Population size: S = 11402151
Sampling method: Poisson, with exact calculations.

Parameters estimated from sample of size N = 78934379:
               V        V1       V2       V3       V4       V5
Observed: 912289 478416.0 119055.0 56944.00 35373.00 24330.0 ...
Expected: 912289 478358.3 118540.7 57515.25 35304.73 24397.9 ...

Goodness-of-fit (multivariate chi-squared test):
      X2 df          p
17.05788 13 0.1966717
```

The excellent fit is also apparent from the plot of the observed and expected spectrum shown in the upper right panel of Figure 6.19:

```
> plot(twente.spc, lnre.spc(twente.lnre.fzm, N(twente.spc)))
```

Note that the function `N()` extracts the number of tokens from the spectrum object to which it is applied. Also note that the expected number of string types in the population is an order of magnitude larger than the observed number of types.

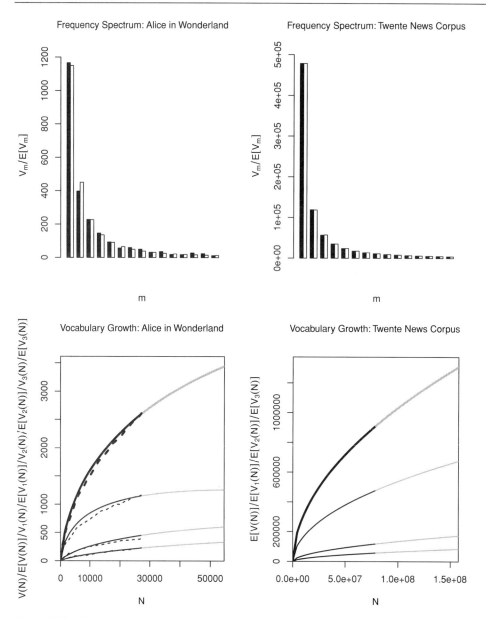

Figure 6.19. *Observed (black) and expected (white) frequency spectrum for* Alice's Adventures in Wonderland *and the* Twente News Corpus *(upper panels) and the corresponding vocabulary growth curves (lower panels). For the growth curves, black lines represent interpolation, grey lines extrapolation to twice the observed sample size, and dashed lines the observed growth curves (only available for* Alice's Adventures in Wonderland*).*

This is probably due to the productivity of typos, morphology, brand names, and names for people and places, both nationally and internationally.

Once an LNRE model has been fitted to a frequency spectrum, the model can be used to obtain expected values for the vocabulary size and the spectrum elements both at smaller sample sizes (interpolation) and at larger sample sizes (extrapolation). The lower panels of Figure 6.19 illustrate these possibilities for *Alice's Adventures in Wonderland* (left) and the Twente News Corpus (right). The black lines represent interpolated values, the grey lines extrapolated values.

The lower left panel was obtained with the following lines of code. First, the extrapolated curves were determined with the help of `lnre.vgc()`, which takes as arguments a fitted model, a sequence of sample sizes, and the number of required spectrum elements:

```
> alice.ext.gigp = lnre.vgc(alice.lnre.gigp,
+ seq(N(alice.lnre.gigp), N(alice.lnre.gigp)*2, length = 20), m.max = 3)
```

The interpolated curves are obtained similarly:

```
> alice.int.gigp = lnre.vgc(alice.lnre.gigp,
+ seq(0, N(alice.lnre.gigp), length=20), m.max=3)
```

In order to plot the observed growth curves, we use `growth2vgc.fnc()` to convert a growth object into a `vgc` object (vocabulary growth object) as required for the `zipfR` functions:

```
> alice.vgc = growth2vgc.fnc(alice.growth)
```

The plot itself is straightforward:

```
> plot(alice.int.gigp,alice.ext.gigp,alice.vgc,add.m = 1:3,main = " ")
> mtext("Vocabulary Growth: Alice in Wonderland", cex = 0.8, side = 3,
+ line=2)
```

In the case of *Alice's Adventures in Wonderland* we are dealing with continuous text rather than with a compilation of text fragments, so here we can compare the actual observed growth curves (dashed lines) with the expected interpolated growth curves. Note that the interpolated values for the vocabulary size and the hapax legomena tend to be slightly too high. This overestimation bias is probably due to discourse structure. In cohesive discourse, topical words tend to be used intensively. As a consequence, new types are sampled at a slower rate than one would expect if words were used randomly and independently of each other (see Baayen 2001, Chapter 5). Another consequence of this overestimation bias for interpolation is an underestimation bias for extrapolation. Hence, the number of types estimated for the population, S, the asymptote that the vocabulary growth curve approaches when the sample size becomes infinitely large, probably is a lower bound.

For corpora consisting of collections of randomly sampled short text fragments, this overestimation bias tends to be attenuated. In this case, the interpolated vocabulary and spectrum can be viewed as the counts one would obtain on average when randomly permuting the texts in the corpus. (For the problems that may arise due to sampling asymmetries when dealing with diachronic corpora, see, e.g., Lüdeling and Evert (2005).)

In summary, comparing texts with respect to their lexical richness is a tricky business. Standard linear modeling of the growth curve of the vocabulary may at first sight provide excellent fits, but due to the LNRE property of many linguistic frequency distributions, these fits are misleading. LNRE models provide a principled solution, that, however, will remain approximate for many actual data sets. As mentioned above, a practical solution is to compare texts for a fixed text size, or to plot interpolated growth curves for different texts side by side (see, e.g., the tutorial referenced in the documentation of the `zipfR` package).

6.6   General considerations

There are two very different ways in which statistical models are used. Ideally, a model is used to test a pre-specified hypothesis, or a set of hypotheses. We fit a model to the data, remove overly influential outliers, use bootstrap validation, and if required shrink the estimated coefficients. Only after this process is completed do we inspect the anova and summary tables, to see whether the p-values and the direction of the effects are as predicted by our hypotheses. The p-values in the summary tables are correct under these circumstances, and only under these circumstances.

In practice, this ideal procedure is hardly ever realistic, for a variety of reasons. First, it is often the case that our initial hypotheses are very underspecified. Under these circumstances, we engage in statistical modeling in order to explore the potential relevance of predictors, to learn about their functional form, and to come to a better understanding of the structure of our data. In this exploratory process, we screen predictors for significant p-values, remove variables accordingly, and gradually develop a model that we feel is both parsimonious and adequate. The p-values of such a final model are still informative, but far from exact. According to some, they are even totally worthless and completely uninterpretable. This highlights the crucial importance of model validation, for instance by means of the bootstrap, as this will inform us about the extent to which we might be overfitting the data. It is equally crucial to replicate our experiment with new materials. The same factors should be predictive, the magnitudes of the coefficients should be similar, and we would hope to find that the model for the original experiment provides reasonable predictions for the new data.

What you should avoid at all times is what statisticians refer to as cherry-picking. You should not tweak the data by removing data points so that a non-significant effect becomes significant. It is not bad to remove data points, but you should have reasons for removing them that are completely independent of whether as a result predictors will be significant. Overly influential outliers have to be removed, and any other data points that are suspect. For instance, in experiments using lexical decision, response latencies of less than 200 milliseconds are probably artefactual, simply because the time for reading the stimulus combined with the time required for planning and carrying out the movements involved in pushing the response button already require at least 200 milliseconds.

Similarly, you should not hunt around for a method that will make an effect significant. It is true that there are often several different methods available for modeling a given data set. And yes, there is no single best model. However, when different modeling techniques have been considered, and when each technique is appropriate, then the combined evidence should be taken into account. A predictor that happens to be significant in only one analysis but not in the others should not be reported as significant.

The examples in this chapter illustrate the steps in data analysis: the construction of an initial model, the exploration of nonlinear relations, model criticism, and validation. All these steps are important, and crucial for understanding your data. As you build up experience with regression modeling, you will find that notably model criticism almost always allows theoretically well-supported predictors to emerge more strongly.

A final methodological issue that should be mentioned is the unfortunate practice in psycholinguistics of dichotomizing continuous variables. For instance, Baayen *et al.* (1997) studied frequency effects in visual word recognition by contrasting high-frequency words with low-frequency words. The two sets of words were matched in the mean for a number of other lexical variables. However, this dichotomization of frequency reduces an information-rich continuous variable into an information-poor two-level factor. If frequency were a treatment that we could administer to words, like raising the temperature or the humidity in an agricultural experiment, then it would make sense to maximize our chances of finding an effect by contrasting observations subjected to a fixed very low level of the treatment with observations subjected to a fixed very high level of the treatment. Unfortunately, frequency is a property of our experimental units; it cannot be administered independently, and it is correlated with many other lexical variables. Due to this correlational structure, dichotomization of linguistic variables almost always leads to factor levels with overlapping or nearly overlapping distributions of the original variable—it is nearly impossible to build contrasts for extreme values on one linguistic variable while matching for a host of other correlated linguistic variables. As a consequence, the enhanced statistical power obtained by comparing two very different treatment levels is not available. In these circumstances, dichotomization comes with a severe loss of statistical power, precise information is lost and nonlinearities become impossible to detect. Furthermore, samples obtained through dichotomization tend to be small and to get ever smaller the more variables are being matched for. Such samples are also non-random in the extreme, and hence do not allow proper statistical inference. To make matters even worse, dichotomization may also have various other adverse side effects, including spurious significance (see, e.g., Cohen, 1983; Maxwell and Delaney, 1993; MacCallum *et al.*, 2002). Avoid it. Use regression.

Workbook section

Exercises

1. Analyze the effect of PC1 on the naming latencies in the english2 data set that we created in section 6.2.2. Attach the Design package, make a data distribution object, and set the datadist variable to point to this object with the options() function. First fit a model with AgeSubject and WrittenFrequency, and PC1 as predictors. Use a restricted cubic spline with three knots for WrittenFrequency, and include an interaction of WrittenFrequency by AgeSubject. Is the linear effect of PC1 significant? Now allow the effect of PC1 to be nonlinear with a restricted cubic spline with three knots. Plot the partial effect of PC1 in this new model, and explain the difference with respect to the first model.

2. Exercise 5.3 addressed the prediction of the underlying voice specification of the stem-final obstruent in Dutch words with the help of a classification tree. Ernestus and Baayen (2003) compared several statistical models for the finalDevoicing data set, including a logistic regression model. Load the data, and use the lrm() function from the Design package to model the dependent variable Voice as a function of the other variables in the data frame. Use fastbw() to remove irrelevant predictors from the model.

3. Check that the danger of overfitting has been reduced for the penalized model dutch.lrm.pen by means of bootstrap validation.

4. We fit a logistic regression model to the data set etymology with, as dependent variable, the Regularity of the verb, and the ordered factor EtymAge (etymological age) as etymological age as main predictor of interest:

```
> etymology$EtymAge = ordered(etymology$EtymAge, levels=c("Dutch",
+ "DutchGerman", "WestGermanic", "Germanic", "IndoEuropean"))
> library(Design)
> etym.dd = datadist(etym)
> options(datadist='etym.dd')
> etymology.lrm = lrm(Regularity ~ rcs(WrittenFrequency,3) +
+ rcs(FamilySize,3) + NcountStem + InflectionalEntropy +
+ Auxiliary + Valency + NVratio + WrittenSpokenRatio + EtymAge,
+ data=etymology, x=T, y=T)
 Warning message: Variable EtymAge is an ordered factor.
 You should set
 options(contrasts=c("contr.treatment","contr.treatment"))
 or Design will not work properly. in: Design(eval(m, sys.parent()))
```

The warning message tells us that the defaults for the dummy coding of factors have to be reset. We do as instructed:

```
> options(contrasts = c("contr.treatment", "contr.treatment"))
```

Rerun the model, inspect the result by means of an ANOVA table, and validate it. You will observe considerable overfitting, so use the `pentrace()` function to find an optimal penalty for shrinking the coefficients. Make a plot of the partial effects of the predictors in the penalized model.

5. Consider again the breakpoint analysis of the frequencies of references to years in the *Frankfurter Allgemeine Zeitung* (`faz`). Explain why the model,

```
> faz.bothA = lm(LogFrequency ~ ShiftedLogDistance +
+ ShiftedLogDistance : PastBreakPoint, data = faz)
```

is a correct alternative formulation of the model presented in the main text, and also explain why the model,

```
> faz.bothA = lm(LogFrequency~ShiftedLogDistance * PastBreakPoint,
+ data = faz)
```

is incorrect for our purposes.

6. Compare the lexical richness of Lewis Carroll's *Alice's Adventures in Wonderland* with that of his *Through the Looking-Glass*, available as the data set `through`, using `compare.richness.fnc()` for equal text sizes, i.e. for the number of tokens in the smallest of the two texts. Use the same method to compare *Alice's Adventures in Wonderland* with Baum's *The Wonderful Wizard of Oz* (`oz`) and with Melville's *Moby Dick* (`moby`).

7. Plag *et al.* (1999) studied morphological productivity for selected affixes in the British National Corpus (BNC). The BNC consists of three subcorpora: written English, spontaneous conversations (the demographic subcorpus), and spoken English in more formal settings (the context-governed subcorpus). Frequency spectra for the English suffix *-ness* calculated for these subcorpora are available as the data sets `nessw`, `nessdemog`, and `nesscg`. Convert them into `scp` objects with `spc()`. Then fit the finite Zipf-Mandelbrot LNRE model to each of the spectra. Inspect the goodness of fit, and refit with the Generalized Inverse Gauss-Poisson model where necessary. Plot the growth curve of the vocabulary at 40 equally spaced intervals in the range from zero to the size of the sample of written words with *-ness*. Comment on the relation between the shape of the growth curves and the estimated numbers of types in the population. Finally, calculate the growth rates of the vocabulary both at the sample size of the largest subcorpus, and for that of the smallest subcorpus. Use the function `Vm()` from the `zipfR` package, which takes as first argument a frequency spectrum and as second argument the spectrum element (1 for the hapax legomena).

8. Tyler *et al.* (2005) combined fMRI and priming data in a study addressing the extent to which phonological and semantic processes recruit the same brain areas. Figure 6.20, reconstructed from the graphics coordinates of their Figure 2b, summarizes the main structure of one of their subanalyses. The authors argue that the priming scores (horizontal axis) for the semantic condition are significantly correlated with the intensity of the most significant voxel (vertical axis), which is located in an area of the brain typically associated with semantic processing.

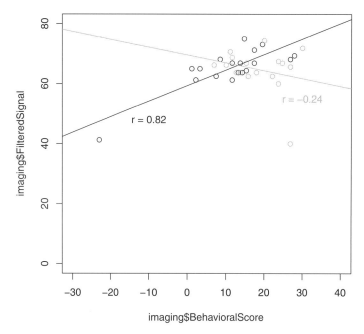

Figure 6.20. *Signal intensity in fMRI at the peak voxel in the left medial fusiform gyrus and priming scores for semantically related (*card/paper*) and morphologically related (*begin/began*) conditions. Each data point represents a brain-damaged patient. (After Tyler* et al. (2005)).

They also argue that there is no such correlation for the morphological condition. Figure 6.20 is based on the data set `imaging`. Carry out an analysis of covariance with `FilteredSignal` as dependent variable in the model, and test whether there is a significant interaction of `BehavioralScore` by `Condition`. Then apply model criticism, and use this to evaluate the conclusions reached by Tyler and colleagues.

7 Mixed models

Consider a study addressing the consequences of adding white noise to the comprehension of words presented auditorily over headphones to a group of subjects, using auditory lexical decision latencies as a measure of speed of lexical access. In such a study, the presence or absence of white noise would be the treatment factor, with two levels (noise versus no noise). In addition, we would need identifiers for the individual words (items), and identifiers for the individual participants (or subjects) in the experiment. The item and subject factors, however, differ from the treatment factor in that we would normally only regard the treatment factor as REPEATABLE.

A factor is repeatable, if the set of possible levels for that factor is fixed, and if, moreover, each of these levels can be repeated. In our example, the treatment factor is repeatable, because we can take any new acoustic signal and either add or not add a fixed amount of white noise. We would not normally regard the identifiers of items or subjects as repeatable. Items and subjects are sampled randomly from populations of words and participants, and replicating the experiment would involve selecting other words and other participants. For these new units, we would need new identifiers. In other words, we would be introducing new levels of these subject and item factors in the experiment that had not been seen previously.

To see the far-reaching consequences of this, imagine that we have eight subjects and eight items, and that we create two factors, each with eight levels, using contrast coding. One of the subjects and one of the items will be mapped onto the intercept, the other subjects and items will receive coefficients specifying how they differ from the intercept. How useful is this model for predicting response latencies for new subjects and items? A moment's thought will reveal that it is completely useless. New subjects and new items have new identifiers that do not match the identifiers that were used in building the contrasts and the model using these contrasts. We can still assign new data points to the levels of the treatment factor, noise versus no noise, because these levels are repeatable. But subjects and items are not repeatable, hence we cannot use our model to make predictions for new subjects and new items. In short, the model does not generalize to the populations of subjects and items. It is tailored to the specific subjects and items in the experiment only.

The statistical literature therefore makes a crucial distinction between factors with repeatable levels, for which we use FIXED-EFFECTS terms, and factors with levels randomly sampled from a much larger population, for which we use

RANDOM-EFFECTS terms. MIXED-EFFECTS MODELS, or more simply, MIXED MOD-
ELS, are models which incorporate both fixed and random effects.

While fixed-effect factors are modeled by means of contrasts, random effects
are modeled as random variables with a mean of zero and unknown variance. For
instance, the participants in a reaction time experiment will differ with respect to
how quickly they respond. Some tend to be slow, others tend to be fast. Across
the population of participants, the average adjustment required to account for
differences in speed will be zero. The adjustments required for individual subjects
will in general not be zero, instead, they will vary around zero with some unknown
standard deviation. In mixed models, the standard deviations associated with
random effects are parameters that are estimated, just as the coefficients for the
fixed effects are parameters that are estimated.

7.1   Modeling data with fixed and random effects

The package for building mixed-effects models is named LME4. This
package automatically loads two other libraries, `lattice` and `Matrix`. The key
function in this package is `lmer()`. Bates (2005) provides a brief introduction with
examples of its use, and Faraway (2006) provides more extensive examples for
a variety of experimental designs. The `lme4` package is still under development.
Results with newer versions may differ slightly from the examples in this chapter,
which are based on `lme4` version 0.99875-6 running under R version 2.5.1.

We illustrate how to use the `lmer()` function by returning to the `lexdec`
data set that we have already considered in Chapter 2. Recall that this data set
provides visual lexical decision latencies elicited from 21 subjects for a set of 79
words: 44 nouns for animals, and 35 nouns for plants (fruits and vegetables). An
experimental design in which we have multiple subjects responding to multiple
items is referred to as a repeated measures design. For each word (item), we have
21 repeated measures (one measure from each subject). At the same time, we have
79 repeated measures for each subject (one for each item). Subject and item are
random-effects factors; fixed-effects factors that are of interest include whether
the subject was a native speaker of English, and whether the word referred to an
animal or a plant, as well as lexical covariates such as frequency and length.

The reaction times in `lexdec` are already logarithmically transformed. Nevertheless, it makes sense to inspect the distribution of the reaction times before
beginning with fitting a model to the data. We do so with quantile-quantile plots
for each subject separately, using the `qqmath()` function from the `lattice`
package. Similar plots should be made for the items:

```
> qqmath(~RT|Subject, data = lexdec)
```

The result is shown in Figure 7.1. For data sets with more subjects than can be
plotted on a single page, we use the `layout` parameter. Its first argument specifies

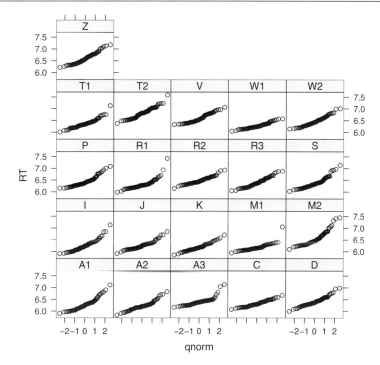

Figure 7.1. *Quantile-quantile plots for the log-transformed reaction times in visual lexical decision grouped by subject.*

the number of columns, the second argument the number of rows, and the third argument the number of pages. To inspect the graphs page by page, we instruct R to ask us to hit the `<return>` key to see the next plot, at the same time saving the old prompting value. We then run the plot function itself, and finally reset the prompting option to its old value once we have paged through the lattice graphs:

```
> old.prompt = grid::grid.prompt(TRUE)
> qqmath(~RT|Word, data = lexdec, layout = c(5,5,4))
> grid::grid.prompt(old.prompt)
```

As can be seen in Figure 7.1, subjects such as C and W1 have reaction times that follow a normal distribution, whereas subjects such as S and M2 have thick right tails. We also see that there are subjects such as R1 or M1 with clear outliers, but also subjects such as C or Z with no outliers at all.

The question that arises at this point is whether to clean the data before fitting the model. In answer to this question, we note first of all that data points that are suspect for experimental reasons should be removed. For instance, reaction times of less than 200 milliseconds in visual lexical decision are probably erroneous button presses, as visual uptake and response execution normally require 200 milliseconds if not more. Similarly, very long reaction times and error responses can be removed from the data set. It is less straightforward what to do with outlier responses. In the present data set, many individual outliers will be removed by setting a threshold at log RT = 7, which amounts to roughly 1100 milliseconds. You may verify this with,

```
> qqmath(~RT|Subject, data = lexdec[lexdec$RT<7,])
```

all potentially troublesome outliers (0.025% of the data) have now been eliminated. Since these outliers might obscure the initial model fitting stages, I tend to take them out, especially as they almost always will be eliminated anyway at the stage of model criticism:

```
> lexdec2 = lexdec[lexdec$RT < 7, ]
> nrow(lexdec) - nrow(lexdec2)
[1] 45
> (nrow(lexdec) - nrow(lexdec2)) / nrow(lexdec)
[1] 0.02471368
> lexdec3 = lexdec2[lexdec2$Correct == "correct", ]
```

Alternatively, individual outliers can be identified for each subject and item separately in the quantile-quantile plots and then removed manually from the data frame (which would then need to be sorted first by subject (or item), and then by RT). A procedure that is certain to lead to unnecessary data loss is to blindly remove data points with extreme values (more than two or three standard deviations away from an item's or subject's group mean) a priori, as subjects and items with perfectly regular distributions will undergo completely unnecessary data trimming.

We begin our analysis by examining a control variable for possible longitudinal effects of familiarization or fatigue during the experiment, using the position (or rank) of a trial in the experimental list:

```
> xylowess.fnc(RT ~ Trial | Subject, data = lexdec3, ylab = "log RT")
```

Figure 7.2 shows a clear effect of familiarization for, for instance, subject T2, and a clear effect of fatigue for subject D. Is there a main effect of Trial? Let's fit a mixed-effects model with Trial as covariate and Subject and Word as random effects as a first step towards answering this question:

```
> lexdec3.lmer = lmer(RT ~ Trial + (1|Subject) + (1|Word), lexdec3)
```

The lmer() function call has the familiar components of a formula followed by the data frame to be used. The first part of the formula is also familiar: reaction times are modeled as depending on Trial. The remainder of the formula specifies the random-effects terms for Subject and Word. The vertical line in an expression such as (1|Subject) separates the grouping factor (to its right) from the fixed-effects terms for which random effects have to be included. In the present example, there is only a 1, which represents the intercept. Recall that in linear models the intercept provides a kind of baseline mean. Changing from one factor level to another, or changing the value of a covariate, provides fine-tuning with respect to this baseline. Lowering the intercept for a subject implies that all reaction times for that subject become somewhat shorter. This is what we want to do for a subject who happens to be a quick responder. For

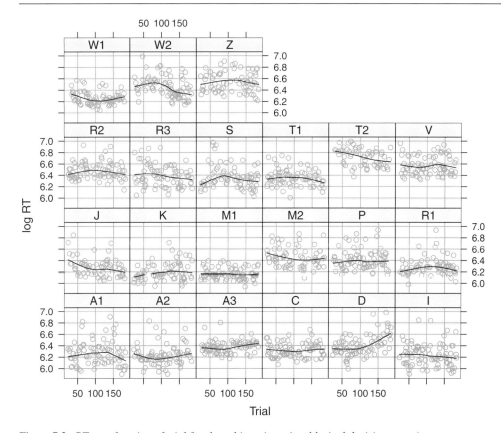

Figure 7.2. *RT as a function of trial for the subjects in a visual lexical decision experiment.*

slower subjects, we may need to increase the intercept, so that all their responses become longer. The random-effects term (1|Subject) specifies that the model will make such by-subject adjustments for the average speed by means of small changes to the intercept. Similarly, some words may be more difficult than other words, and elicit longer response latencies. Just as for the subjects, we may have to adjust the intercept for the individual words by means of a random-effects term (1|Word). Importantly, such by-subject or by-word adjustments are *not* parameters (coefficients) of the model. Only two parameters are involved, one parameter specifying the variance of the random variable for the subjects, and one parameter for the variance of the random variable for the words. Given these two parameters, the individual by-word and by-subject adjustments simply follow.

To make this more concrete, consider the summary of the model that we just obtained by typing the name of the model object at the prompt:

```
> lexdec3.lmer
Linear mixed-effects model fit by REML
Formula: RT ~ Trial + (1 | Subject) + (1 | Word)
   Data: lexdec3
   AIC   BIC logLik MLdeviance REMLdeviance
 -1243 -1222  625.7      -1274         -1251
```

```
Random effects:
 Groups    Name         Variance   Std.Dev.
 Word      (Intercept) 0.0046579 0.068249
 Subject   (Intercept) 0.0186282 0.136485
 Residual              0.0225642 0.150214
number of obs: 1557, groups: Word, 79; Subject, 21

Fixed effects:
              Estimate Std. Error t value
(Intercept)  6.394e+00  3.217e-02  198.74
Trial       -1.835e-04  8.194e-05   -2.24

Correlation of Fixed Effects:
      (Intr)
Trial -0.268
```

The summary begins with telling you what kind of object you are looking at:
a linear mixed-effects model fit by a technique called RELATIVIZED MAXIMUM
LIKELIHOOD, also known as RESTRICTED or RESIDUAL maximum likelihood. The
next line reminds you of how the object was created. After a list of summary
statistics that describe the quality of the fit of the model to the data, we come to
the more interesting sections of the summary: a table with the random effects in
the model, followed by a table with the fixed effects. The summary concludes
with a table listing the correlations of the fixed effects. The numbers listed here
can be used to construct confidence ellipses for pairs of fixed-effects parameters,
and should not be confused with the normal correlations obtained by applying
cor() to pairs of predictor vectors in the input data. For models with many predictors this table may become very large. Since constructing confidence ellipses
is beyond the scope of this book, we will often suppress this table in our output as
follows:

```
> print(lexdec3.lmer, corr=FALSE)
```

First consider the table with random effects. It provides information on three
random effects, listed under the heading Groups: Word, Subject, and Residual. Residual stands for the residual error, the unexplained variance. This
is a random variable with mean zero and unknown variance, and is therefore a random effect just as are the random effects of Subject and Word.
The next column shows that the random effects of Subject and Word are
defined with respect to the intercept, in accordance with the specifications
(1|Subject) and (1|Word). The third and fourth columns show the estimated
variances and the corresponding standard deviations for these random effects.
The means of these three random variables are not listed, as they are always
zero.

The summary of the random effects lists the *parameters* for the random effects: the three variances, or, equivalently, the three corresponding standard deviations (their square roots). The actual *adjustments* for specific subjects and
specific words to the intercept can be extracted from the model with the ranef()

function, an abbreviation for RANdom EFfects. The adjustments for words are,

```
> ranef(lexdec3.lmer)$Word
                (Intercept)
almond        0.0076094201
ant          -0.0409265042
apple        -0.1040504847
apricot      -0.0086191706
asparagus     0.1002836459
avocado       0.0218818091
. . .
```

and their variance is similar in magnitude to the variance listed for `Word` in the summary table, 0.0046579:

```
> var(ranef(lexdec3.lmer)$Word)
                (Intercept)
(Intercept)  0.003732362
```

It should be kept in mind that the variance in the summary is a parameter of the model, and that the BEST LINEAR UNBIASED PREDICTORS (or BLUPs in short) for the by-word adjustments produced by `ranef()` are derived given this parameter. Hence the sample variance of the BLUPs is not identical to the estimate in the summary table. The BLUPs for the intercept are often referred to as RANDOM INTERCEPTS. In the present example, we have both by-subject random intercepts and by-word random intercepts.

The part of the summary dealing with the fixed effects is already familiar from the summaries for objects created by the `lm()` and `ols()` functions for models with fixed effects only. The table lists the coefficients of the fixed effects, in this case the coefficient for the intercept and for the slope of `Trial`, and their associated standard errors and t-values. The slope of `Trial` is small in part because `Trial` ranges from 23 to 185 and reaction time is on a log scale.

The fitted values can be extracted from the model object by means of `fitted()`:

```
> fitted(lexdec3.lmer)[1:4]
6.272059 6.318508 6.245524 6.254167
```

Let's reconstruct how the model arrived at the fitted reaction time of 6.272 for subject `A1` to item `owl` at trial 23 (the first word trial after an initial practice session familiarizing the participants with the experiment). We begin with the coefficient for the intercept, 6.394, and adjust this intercept for the specified subject and item, and then add the effect of `Trial`:

```
> 6.394 + ranef(lexdec3.lmer)$Word["owl",] +
+ ranef(lexdec3.lmer)$Subject["A1",] -1.835e-04*23
[1] 6.272  # 6.394 - 0.01449 - 0.1031  - 1.8350e-04*23
```

The current version of the `lme4` package does not provide p-values for t- and F-tests. The reason is that it is at present unclear how to calculate the appropriate degrees of freedom. An upper bound for the degrees of freedom for the *t*-tests can be obtained by taking the number of observations (1557) and subtracting the number of fixed-effects parameters (2). This allows us to estimate the *p*-value for `Trial` as usual:

```
> 2 * (1 - pt(abs(-2.24), 1557 - 2))
[1] 0.02523172
```

As we shall see below, this upper bound works reasonably well for large data sets with thousands of observations, but it is ANTICONSERVATIVE for small data sets: for small data sets, the *p*-values may be too small. Since for large numbers of degrees of freedom (>100) the *t*-distribution approximates the normal distribution, a simple way of assessing significance at the 5% significance level is to check whether the absolute value of the *t*-statistic exceeds 2.

An alternative that works very well for both small and large samples is to make use of Markov chain Monte Carlo (MCMC) sampling. Each MCMC sample contains one number for each of the parameters in our model. For `lexdec3.lmer`, we obtain five such numbers, three variances for the random effects and two coefficients for the fixed effects. With many such samples, we obtain insight into what is called the POSTERIOR DISTRIBUTIONS of the parameters. On the basis of these distributions we can estimate *p*-values and confidence intervals known as HIGHEST POSTERIOR DENSITY (HPD) intervals. The functions for Markov chain Monte Carlo sampling are `mcmcsamp()` and `HPDinterval()` in the `coda` package. The function `pvals.fnc()` carries out MCMC sampling (with by default 10000 samples) and also reports the *p*-values based on the *t*-statistic:

```
> pvals.fnc(lexdec3.lmer)$fixed
                Estimate    MCMCmean HPD95lower   HPD95upper  pMCMC Pr(>|t|)
(Intercept)  6.3939620   6.3938802  6.3246413   6.45951910 0.0001   0.0000
Trial       -0.0001835  -0.0001845 -0.0003468  -0.00002344 0.0224   0.0253
```

In the light of Figure 7.2, it remains somewhat surprising that the effect of `Trial` does seem to reach significance, even if only at the 5% level. What we see in Figure 7.2 is that some subjects show an effect, sometimes in opposite directions, but also that many subjects have no clear effect at all. In terms of model building, what we would like to do is to allow the slope of the effect of `Trial` to vary across subjects. In other words, what we need here are by-subject RANDOM SLOPES for `Trial`. We build these into the model by expanding the expression for the subject random-effects structure:

```
> lexdec3.lmerA = lmer(RT ~ Trial + (1+Trial|Subject) + (1|Word),
+ data = lexdec3)
> print(lexdec3.lmerA, corr = FALSE)
Random effects:
 Groups    Name          Variance    Std.Dev.   Corr
 Word      (Intercept)   4.7620e-03  0.0690074
 Subject   (Intercept)   2.9870e-02  0.1728293
           Trial         4.4850e-07  0.0006697  -0.658
 Residual                2.1600e-02  0.1469704
number of obs: 1557, groups: Word, 79; Subject, 21
```

```
Fixed effects:
              Estimate Std. Error t value
(Intercept)  6.3963562  0.0396077  161.49
Trial       -0.0002033  0.0001669   -1.22
```

In this new model, the estimate of `Trial` is very similar to the previous model, but it is now no longer significant. In what follows, we leave `Trial` as a main fixed effect in the model because we also have random slopes for `Trial` in the model. (The by-subject random effect of `Trial` is the functional equivalent of an interaction of `Subject` by `Trial` in a model treating `Subject` as a fixed effect.) We compare the predictions of the new model with the predictions of the simpler model graphically, using a customized panel function for `xyplot()`:

```
> xyplot(RT ~ Trial | Subject, data = lexdec3,
+   panel = function(x, y, subscripts) {
+     panel.xyplot(x, y)                          # the scatterplot
+     subject = as.character(lexdec3[subscripts[1], "Subject"])
+     coefs = as.numeric(unlist(coef(lexdec3.lmer)$Subject[subject,]))
+     panel.abline(coefs, col = "black", lty = 2)    # add first line
+     coefs = as.numeric(unlist(coef(lexdec3.lmerA)$Subject[subject,]))
+     panel.abline(coefs, col = "black", lty = 1)    # add second line
+ })
```

We first add the data points to a given panel with `panel.xyplot()`. When a panel is prepared for a given subject, the vector `subscripts` contains the row indices in `lexdec3` of this subject's data points in `lexdec3`. This allows us to identify the name of the subject under consideration by taking the first row in the data frame with data for this subject, and extracting the value in its `Subject` column. With the subject name in hand, we proceed to extract that subject's coefficients from the two models. Finally, we feed these coefficients to `panel.abline()`, which adds lines to panels.

The dashed lines in Figure 7.3 illustrate that the first model assigns the same slope to each subject, the solid lines show that the second model adjusts the slopes to fit the data of each individual subject. It is clear that the second model provides an improved fit to the data. It seems that subjects went through the experiment in somewhat different ways, with some adapting to the task, and others becoming tired.

Does the experiment also reveal differences between native and non-native speakers of English? The data frame `lexdec3` contains a column labeled `NativeLanguage` for this fixed-effects factor, with levels `English` and `Other`:

```
> lexdec3.lmerB = lmer(RT ~ Trial + NativeLanguage +
+ (1+Trial|Subject) + (1|Word), lexdec3)
> lexdec3.lmerB
Fixed effects:
                      Estimate Std. Error t value
(Intercept)          6.3348827  0.0435378  145.50
Trial               -0.0002026  0.0001669   -1.21
NativeLanguageOther  0.1433655  0.0506176    2.83
```

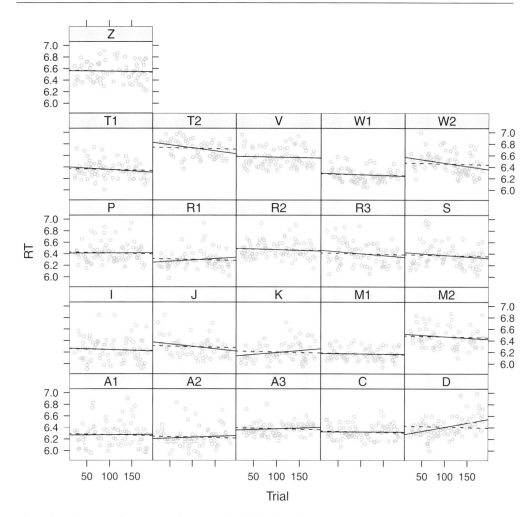

Figure 7.3. *Response latency as a function of trial. The black lines represent the slopes estimated by model* lexdec3.lmerA, *which allows slopes to vary among subjects. The dashed lines are those obtained with* lexdec3.lmer, *which assigns the same slope to all subjects.*

There indeed appears to be support for the possibility that the non-native speakers are the slower responders. Since native speakers have more experience with their language, the frequency effect might be stronger for native speakers, leading to greater facilitation. We test this hypothesis by including Frequency as a predictor, together with an interaction of NativeLanguage by Frequency:

```
> lexdec3.lmerC = lmer(RT ~ Trial + Frequency*NativeLanguage +
+ (1+Trial|Subject) + (1|Word), lexdec3)
> lexdec3.lmerC
Fixed effects:
                                Estimate Std. Error t value
(Intercept)                    6.4797681  0.0512770  126.37
```

```
Trial                                -0.0002036   0.0001658   -1.23
Frequency                            -0.0305036   0.0058148   -5.25
NativeLanguageOther                   0.2353085   0.0584242    4.03
Frequency:NativeLanguageOther        -0.0190195   0.0060335   -3.15
```

Since the reference level for `NativeLanguage` is `English`, we note that non-native speakers of English had significantly longer response latencies. Furthermore, we find that the coefficient for the frequency effect for native speakers of English is -0.03, while for non-native speakers, this coefficient is -0.030 $-0.019 = -0.049$. Apparently, the frequency effect is stronger and more facilitative for non-native speakers, contrary to what we expected. Why would this be so? Possibly, we are led astray by a confound with word length — more frequent words tend to be shorter, and non-native readers might find shorter words easier to read compared to native readers. When we add a `Length` by `NativeLanguage` interaction to the model, inspection of the summary shows that the `Frequency` by `NativeLanguage` interaction is no longer significant, in contrast to the interaction of `NativeLanguage` by `Length`:

```
> lexdec3.lmerD = lmer(RT ~ Trial + Length*NativeLanguage  +
+ NativeLanguage*Frequency + (1+Trial|Subject) + (1|Word), lexdec3)
> lexdec3.lmerD
Fixed effects:
                                Estimate Std. Error t value
(Intercept)                    6.4548536  0.0637955  101.18
Trial                         -0.0002128  0.0001677   -1.27
Length                         0.0029408  0.0042965    0.68
NativeLanguageOther            0.0973266  0.0706921    1.38
Frequency                     -0.0286264  0.0062827   -4.56
Length:NativeLanguageOther     0.0154950  0.0045037    3.44
NativeLanguageOther:Frequency -0.0093742  0.0066275   -1.41
```

We therefore take the spurious `NativeLanguage:Frequency` interaction out of the model. Note that the `Length` by `NativeLanguage` interaction makes sense. For native readers, there is no effect of `Length`, while non-native readers require more time to respond to longer words.

Thus far, we have examined only the table of coefficients. Let's redress our neglect of the table of random effects:

```
> lexdec3.lmerD
Random effects:
 Groups   Name        Variance   Std.Dev.   Corr
 Word     (Intercept) 2.2525e-03 0.04746081
 Subject  (Intercept) 2.7148e-02 0.16476753
          Trial       4.5673e-07 0.00067582 -0.740
 Residual             2.1286e-02 0.14589823
number of obs: 1557, groups: Word, 79; Subject, 21
```

In addition to the usual standard deviations listed in the fourth column, the final column of the random effects table lists a correlation. This correlation concerns the by-subject random intercepts and the by-subject random slopes for `Trial`. Since we have random slopes and random intercepts that are paired by subject, it is possible that the vectors of random slopes and random intercepts are correlated.

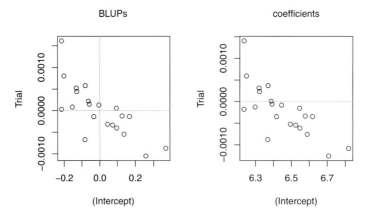

Figure 7.4. *Best linear unbiased predictors (*BLUPs*) for the by-subject random effects for model* lexdec3.lmerD *(left panel), and the corresponding by-subject coefficients (right panel).*

The way in which we specified the random-effects structure for Subject, (1 + Trial | Subject), explicitly instructed lmer() to allow for this possibility by including a special parameter for this correlation of the BLUPs for the intercept and the BLUPs for Trial. The left panel of Figure 7.4 is a scatterplot that visualizes this correlation for these BLUPs:

```
> ranefs = ranef(lexdec3.lmerD)$Subject
> head(ranefs)
     (Intercept)        Trial
A1 -0.057992023 1.368812e-04
A2 -0.127666091 4.443818e-04
A3 -0.131176609 5.246854e-04
C  -0.004438559 1.274880e-04
D  -0.215372691 1.617985e-03
I  -0.216234737 3.445517e-05
> plot(ranefs)
> abline(h = 0, col = "grey")
> abline(v = 0, col = "grey")
```

In this scatterplot, each data point represents a subject. Subjects with a large negative adjustment for the intercept are fast responders, subjects with a large positive adjustment are slow responders. Fast responders have positive adjustments for Trial, while slow responders have negative adjustments for Trial. Since the estimated fixed-effects coefficient for Trial equals a mere -0.0002, the fastest responders appear to slow down in the course of the experiment, whereas the slowest responders speed up. This is also visible, perhaps more clearly so, when we plot the by-subject coefficients, as shown in the right panel of Figure 7.4. These by-subject coefficients differ for the intercept and for Trial (where they are adjusted by the BLUPs), and are identical for all other predictors:

```
> coefs = coef(lexdec3.lmerD)$Subject
> round(head(coefs),4)
     (Intercept)    Trial Length NativeLanguageOther Frequency
A1       6.3969 -0.0001 0.0029              0.0973   -0.0286
A2       6.3272  0.0002 0.0029              0.0973   -0.0286
A3       6.3237  0.0003 0.0029              0.0973   -0.0286
C        6.4504 -0.0001 0.0029              0.0973   -0.0286
D        6.2395  0.0014 0.0029              0.0973   -0.0286
I        6.2386 -0.0002 0.0029              0.0973   -0.0286
     Length:NativeLanguageOther NativeLanguageOther:Frequency
A1                       0.0155                       -0.0094
A2                       0.0155                       -0.0094
A3                       0.0155                       -0.0094
C                        0.0155                       -0.0094
D                        0.0155                       -0.0094
I                        0.0155                       -0.0094
> plot(coefs[,1:2])
```

The right panel of Figure 7.4 shows straightforwardly that subjects with a large intercept have a large negative coefficient for `Trial`, while subjects with a small intercept have a large positive coefficient for `Trial`.

The total number of parameters in `lexdec3.lmerD` is 12: we have 7 fixed-effects coefficients (including the intercept), and 5 random-effects parameters. The question that arises at this point is whether all these random-effects parameters are justified. The significance of parameters for random effects is assessed by means of likelihood ratio tests, which are carried out by the `anova()` function when supplied with two mixed-effects models that have the same fixed-effects structure but different numbers of random-effects parameters. For instance, we can evaluate the significance of the two by-subject random effects for `Subject` by fitting a simpler model with only a by-subject random intercept that we then compare with the full model:

```
> lexdec3.lmerD1 = lmer(RT ~ Trial + Length * NativeLanguage +
+ NativeLanguage * Frequency + (1|Subject) + (1|Word),  data = lexdec3)
> anova(lexdec3.lmerD, lexdec3.lmerD1)
                Df      AIC      BIC   logLik  Chisq Chi Df Pr(>Chisq)
lexdec3.lmerD1   9 -1327.88 -1279.73   672.94
lexdec3.lmerD   11 -1361.28 -1302.42   691.64 37.398      2   7.572e-09
```

The likelihood ratio test takes the log likelihood (`logLik`, an important measure of goodness of fit) for the smaller model with 9 parameters (`Df`) and compares it with the log likelihood for the larger model with 11 parameters. The difference between the two log likelihoods (692.76 − 673.85), multiplied by 2, follows a chi-squared distribution with as degrees of freedom the difference in the number of parameters, $11 - 9 = 2$. As the associated probability is small, the additional parameters in the more complex model are justified. Similarly, we can peel off the random effect for `Word` to see whether the inclusion of by-word random intercepts is justified:

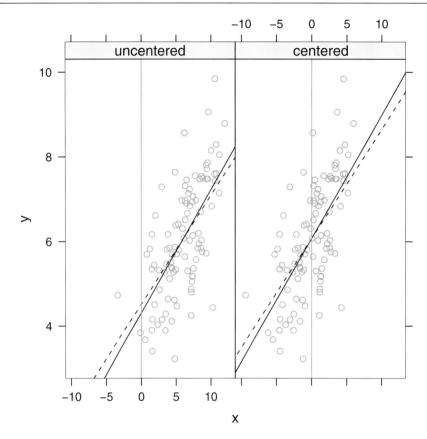

Figure 7.5. *A small change in the data may change the slope of the regression line, with a concomitant change in the intercept when the X-values are not centered. (The vertical grey lines represent the Y-axes.) As a consequence, random intercepts and slopes may be correlated in uncentered data (left panel) but uncorrelated in centered data (right panel).*

```
> lexdec3.lmerD2 = lmer(RT ~ Trial + Length * NativeLanguage +
+ NativeLanguage * Frequency + (1|Subject),  data = lexdec3)
> anova(lexdec3.lmerD1, lexdec3.lmerD2)
                Df      AIC      BIC   logLik  Chisq Chi Df Pr(>Chisq)
lexdec3.lmerD2   8 -1280.36 -1237.55   648.18
lexdec3.lmerD1   9 -1327.88 -1279.73   672.94 49.522      1  1.962e-12
```

The large chi-squared value indicates that the random effect for `Word` is fully justified.

There is one potential problem with the correlation parameter for the by-subject random slopes and intercepts, however. The values of `Trial` are all greater than zero; they are bounded by zero to the left. As a consequence, a change in the slope may correlate with a change in the intercept. This is illustrated in the left panel of Figure 7.5. The solid line fits the bivariate normal simulated data points shown in the scatterplot. When we take the *y*-value for the minimum of *x* and increase it by 2, and likewise take the *y*-value for the maximum of *x* and decrease it by 2, and then refit the model, we obtain the dashed regression line. The resulting small shift in the slope of the regression line is accompanied by a small change in the intercept. Suppose that we have many parallel plots like the one shown in the left panel of Figure 7.5, one for each subject. Then we may expect that across subjects, slopes and intercepts will covary. The way to eliminate such a spurious correlation is to center the data by subtracting the mean of x from each x-value, as shown in the right panel of Figure 7.5. Both regression lines cross the vertical axis at the same point: intercept and slope can now be varied independently. We therefore center `Trial` and refit the model:

```
> lexdec3$cTrial = lexdec3$Trial - mean(lexdec3$Trial)
> lexdec3.lmerD3 = lmer(RT ~ cTrial + Length*NativeLanguage +
+ NativeLanguage*Frequency + (1+cTrial|Subject) + (1|Word), lexdec3)
> lexdec3.lmerD3
Random effects:
 Groups    Name        Variance    Std.Dev.    Corr
 Word      (Intercept) 2.2520e-03  0.04745557
 Subject   (Intercept) 1.4874e-02  0.12195041
           cTrial      4.5662e-07  0.00067573  -0.417
 Residual              2.1286e-02  0.14589851
```

The likelihood ratio test shows that after centering, the correlation parameter has nearly halved. We can test formally whether its presence in the model is still justified by fitting a new model without the correlation parameter, which we then compare with our present model using the likelihood ratio test. In the model formula we first specify the random intercepts for `Subject`. We then add a second term with `Subject` as grouping factor, `(0+cTrial|Subject)`, which specifies the random by-subject slopes for `Trial`, with the zero indicating not to add the correlation parameter. An alternative equivalent notation is `(cTrial-1|Subject)`, where the -1 indicates that the correlation parameter should be taken out:

```
> lexdec3.lmerD3a = lmer(RT ~ cTrial + Length*NativeLanguage +
+ NativeLanguage*Frequency + (1|Subject)+(0+cTrial|Subject)+(1|Word),
+ lexdec3)
> anova(lexdec3.lmerD3a,lexdec3.lmerD3)
                 Df      AIC       BIC    logLik  Chisq Chi Df Pr(>Chisq)
lexdec3.lmerD3a 10 -1360.25 -1306.74   690.12
lexdec3.lmerD3  11 -1361.28 -1302.42   691.64 3.0282      1      0.08183
```

The p-value of the likelihood ratio test suggests that the correlation parameter may be superfluous. This impression receives support from an inspection of the MCMC distribution of the correlation parameter, obtained by running `pvals.fnc()` but now extracting the `random` component of the list that it returns:

```
x = pvals.fnc(lexdec3.lmerD3, nsim = 10000)
x$random
            MCMCmean HPD95lower HPD95upper
sigma       0.1459890  0.1408218   0.151687
Word.(In)   0.0470265  0.0359103   0.059393
Sbjc.(In)   0.1330270  0.0950869   0.188165
Sbjc.cTrl   0.0007254  0.0004736   0.001123
Sbj.(I).cTr -0.4361482 -0.7714082  0.114836
```

For each random effect in the model, the MCMC mean of the corresponding standard deviation is listed, together with its 95% HPD interval. When the model contains correlation parameters, these are also listed, in this example at the bottom of the table. When reading tables like this, it is important to carefully distinguish between the standard deviations on the one hand, and the correlations on the other. Correlations are bounded between minus one and plus one by definition. Hence it makes sense to ask ourselves whether zero is contained in a correlation's 95% confidence interval. For the present correlation this is indeed the case, so we conclude that a model without the correlation parameter is adequate.

Standard deviations, by contrast, are always positive, so their HPD interval will *never ever* contain zero. As a consequence, we cannot use these confidence intervals to ascertain whether the random effect is significant. In this case significance testing has to be done by means of the likelihood ratio test. However, the HPD intervals do provide important information about the standard deviations. They allow us to check whether the spread in the distribution of the parameter makes sense. For all standard deviations in the above table the intervals are narrow, which is good. But if the upper and lower limits of the HPD interval differ substantially, this indicates there is something wrong with the model. For instance, a by-item standard deviation with MCMC mean 0.02 and a 95% confidence interval ranging from 0.00000001 to 0.6 would indicate that it is actually completely impossible to estimate this parameter. With so much uncertainty about its actual value, it should be taken out of the model.

Our model for the reaction times in this lexical decision experiment is still incomplete. Another predictor that we should consider is the by-subject mean of the estimated weight of the referents of the words presented to the subjects, available in the data frame by the column name `meanWeight`. (As the `Native-Language` by `Frequency` interaction was not significant, we remove it from the model specification.)

```
> lexdec3.lmerE = lmer(RT ~ cTrial + Frequency +
+ NativeLanguage * Length + meanWeight +
+ (1|Subject) + (0+cTrial|Subject) + (1|Word), lexdec3)
> lexdec3.lmerE
Fixed effects:
                                Estimate Std. Error t value
(Intercept)                    6.4319956  0.0545209  117.97
cTrial                        -0.0002089  0.0001668   -1.25
Frequency                     -0.0404232  0.0057107   -7.08
NativeLanguageOther            0.0303136  0.0594427    0.51
Length                         0.0028283  0.0039709    0.71
meanWeight                     0.0235385  0.0064834    3.63
NativeLanguageOther:Length     0.0181745  0.0040862    4.45
```

We see that objects that are judged to be heavier elicited longer response latencies.

As always, we have to check the residuals for potential problems with the model specification. The upper panels of Figure 7.6 show that the model is not coping properly with especially the longer response latencies. A simple solution for checking that the pattern of results obtained is not due to the presence of outliers is to remove the extreme outliers from the data, to refit the model, and to

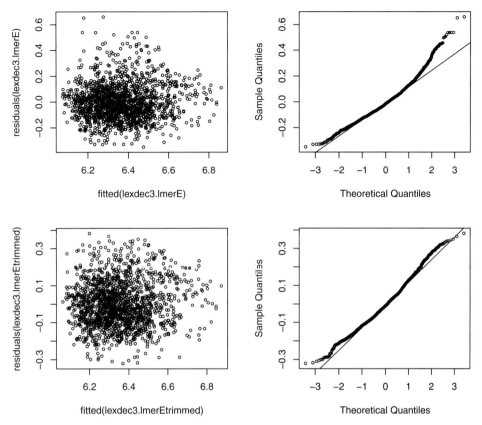

Figure 7.6. *Residual diagnostics for the models before (upper panels) and after (lower panels) removal of 37 data points with extreme residuals.*

inspect whether the non-normality of the residuals has been removed or at least attenuated. Refitting the model after excluding the 37 outliers with a standardized residual at a distance greater than 2.5 standard deviations from zero,

```
> lexdec3.lmerEtrimmed =
+ lmer(RT ~ cTrial + Frequency + meanWeight + NativeLanguage * Length +
+ (1|Subject) + (0+cTrial|Subject) + (1|Word),
+ data = lexdec3, subset = abs(scale(resid(lexdec3.lmerE))) < 2.5)
> nrow(lexdec3)-nrow(lexdec3[abs(scale(resid(lexdec3.lmerE))) < 2.5,])
[1] 37
```

we find that that the quantile-quantile plot has improved somewhat, as shown in the lower panels of Figure 7.6:

```
> par(mfrow=c(2,2))
> plot(fitted(lexdec3.lmerE), residuals(lexdec3.lmerE))
> qqnorm(residuals(lexdec3.lmerE), main=" ")
> qqline(residuals(lexdec3.lmerE))
> plot(fitted(lexdec3.lmerEtrimmed), residuals(lexdec3.lmerEtrimmed))
> qqnorm(residuals(lexdec3.lmerEtrimmed), main=" ")
> qqline(residuals(lexdec3.lmerEtrimmed))
> par(mfrow=c(1,1))
```

In the trimmed model, the same predictors have remained significant. The estimates of the coefficients have changed slightly, however, and may now be somewhat more precise. Since very long reaction times in lexical decision are likely to be codetermined by later processes that are usually not of primary interest to the researcher, trimming the model is justified not only technically but also conceptually:

```
> x = pvals.fnc(lexdec3.lmerEtrimmed)
> x$fixed
                Estimate   MCMCmean HPD95lower HPD95upper  pMCMC  Pr(>|t|)
(Intercept)     6.411494   6.4117333  6.3084566  6.5264888 0.0001  0.0000
cTrial         -0.000192  -0.0001945 -0.0004923  0.0001250 0.2082  0.2058
Frequency      -0.037813  -0.0377575 -0.0490303 -0.0264884 0.0001  0.0000
meanWeight      0.020679   0.0206687  0.0079811  0.0337784 0.0030  0.0015
NatLanOther     0.039060   0.0389072 -0.0828886  0.1585393 0.5166  0.5091
Length          0.003183   0.0031761 -0.0044192  0.0110505 0.4142  0.4157
NatLanOth:Len   0.017492   0.0174837  0.0103630  0.0243377 0.0001  0.0000
> x$random
                MCMCmean    HPD95lower    HPD95upper
sigma           0.1269356    0.1223552     0.1317316
Word.(In)       0.0448592    0.0354490     0.0568323
Sbjc.cTrl       0.0006203    0.0004132     0.0009482
Sbjc.(In)       0.1274543    0.0930270     0.1781425
deviance     -1741.5971505 -1750.1482009 -1731.9742494
> lexdec3.lmerEtrimmed
Random effects:
 Groups   Name         Variance    Std.Dev.
 Word     (Intercept)  2.0464e-03  0.04523680
 Subject  cTrial       3.8438e-07  0.00061998
 Subject  (Intercept)  1.5506e-02  0.12452139
 Residual              1.6083e-02  0.12682059
```

Unlike summaries for `lm` or `ols` model objects, summary tables for mixed-effects models obtained with `lmer()` do not list the proportion of variance (R^2) accounted for. This is not without reason, as there are a number of different sources of variance that are modeled jointly. In addition to the variance explained by fixed effects, we have the variance explained by one or more random effects. As a consequence, an R^2 calculated by correlating observed and fitted values,

```
> cor(fitted(lexdec3.lmerE), lexdec3$RT)^2
[1] 0.5296985
```

does not inform us at all about the variance explained by just the fixed effects, the variance that would be comparable to the explained variance by models obtained with `lm()` or `ols()` (which contain fixed effects only). For mixed-effects models fitted to experimental data, a large part of the explained variance is often due to by-item and by-subject variability. We can gain some insight into the amount of variance accounted for by only non-linguistic variables by fitting a model without lexical fixed-effects predictors and without `Word` as random effect:

```
> lexdec3.lmer00 = lmer(RT ~ Trial +
+ (1|Subject) + (0+Trial|Subject), data = lexdec3)
```

```
> cor(fitted(lexdec3.lmer00), lexdec3$RT)^2
[1] 0.4005094
```

This linguistically uninteresting model captures $0.4005/0.5297 = 76\%$ of the variance explained by our full model. As is often the case in these kinds of experiments, a large proportion of the variance is accounted for just by variability among subjects. In this example, only $100 - 76 = 24\%$ of the variance that we can account for can be traced to linguistic variables, and almost all of this linguistic variance can already be captured just by including the random effect for word:

```
> lexdec3.lmer0 = lmer(RT ~ 1+(1|Subject)+(0+Trial|Subject)+(1|Word),
+ data = lexdec3)
> cor(fitted(lexdec3.lmer0), lexdec3$RT)^2
[1] 0.5263226
```

Only 0.3% of the overall variance can therefore be traced to the lexical predictors in the fixed-effects structure of the model. Fortunately, inspection of the random-effects structure of these models shows that including the lexical predictors does lead to a reduction in the standard deviation for Word by $1 - (0.0419/0.0687) = 39\%$:

```
> lexdec3.lmer0
Random effects:
 Groups    Name        Variance    Std.Dev.
 Word      (Intercept) 4.7232e-03  0.06872577
 Subject   Trial       3.7151e-07  0.00060951
 Subject   (Intercept) 2.5022e-02  0.15818286
 Residual              2.1663e-02  0.14718479
> lexdec3.lmerE
Random effects:
 Groups    Name        Variance    Std.Dev.
 Word      (Intercept) 1.7537e-03  0.04187756
 Subject   Trial       3.5455e-07  0.00059544
 Subject   (Intercept) 2.2573e-02  0.15024339
 Residual              2.1375e-02  0.14620023
```

This example is typical of what we find across many psycholinguistic tasks, where the method of data acquisition is inherently very noisy. The low signal-to-noise ratio is of course exactly the reason why these experiments are generally run with many different subjects and a wide range of items.

7.2   A comparison with traditional analyses

Mixed-effects models with crossed random effects are a recent development in statistics. Because these models are new, the present section discusses three common designs in psycholinguistic studies, and compares the advantages of the mixed-effects approach to the gold standards imposed over the last decades by many psycholinguistics journals. Pinheiro and Bates (2000) is the authoritative reference on mixed-effects modeling in R, but the software they discuss is suited primarily for analyzing hierarchical, nested designs (e.g. children nested under schools nested under cities). A short introduction to the more recent package (lme4) used in this chapter is Bates (2005); Everitt and Hothorn (2006) provide some introductory discussion as well. More comprehensive discussion is available in Faraway (2006) and Wood (2006). A technical overview of the mathematics underlying the implementation of mixed-effects models in the lme4 package is Bates (2006).

7.2.1   Mixed-effects models and quasi-*F*

Mixed-effects models are the response of the statistical community to a problem that was first encountered in the 1940s. The quasif data set illustrates this problem. This (constructed) data set is taken from Raaijmakers *et al.* (1999:see their Table 2). Their data concern reaction times (RT) with Subject and Item as random effects and SOA (stimulus onset asynchrony, the time between the presentation of a prime or distractor and the presentation of the target in chronometric experiments) as a fixed-effects factor:

```
> quasif[1:4,]
  Subject  RT Item    SOA
1      S1 546   W1  short
2      S2 566   W1  short
3      S3 567   W1  short
4      S4 556   W1  short
```

We inspect the experimental design by means of summary tables:

```
> table(quasif$SOA)
long short
  32    32
```

The treatment factor SOA has two levels, long and short. Each subject responds to each word once:

```
> table(quasif$Subject, quasif$Item)
   W1 W2 W3 W4 W5 W6 W7 W8
S1  1  1  1  1  1  1  1  1
S2  1  1  1  1  1  1  1  1
S3  1  1  1  1  1  1  1  1
S4  1  1  1  1  1  1  1  1
S5  1  1  1  1  1  1  1  1
S6  1  1  1  1  1  1  1  1
S7  1  1  1  1  1  1  1  1
S8  1  1  1  1  1  1  1  1
```

Subject and item are CROSSED in this design. Subject and the SOA treatment are also crossed, and each subject responds an equal number of times to the items presented in the two SOA conditions:

```
> table(quasif$Subject, quasif$SOA)
   long short
S1    4     4
S2    4     4
S3    4     4
```

```
S4   4   4
S5   4   4
S6   4   4
S7   4   4
S8   4   4
```

The items, however, are NESTED under SOA: items 1 through 4 are always used in
the short condition, and items 5 through 8 in the long condition:

```
> table(quasif$Item, quasif$SOA)

     long short
 W1   0    8
 W2   0    8
 W3   0    8
 W4   0    8
 W5   8    0
 W6   8    0
 W7   8    0
 W8   8    0
```

It is straightforward to fit a linear mixed-effects model to this data set. We
begin with a model in which subjects and items receive random intercepts and in
which subjects also receive random slopes for the SOA treatment:

```
> quasif.lmer = lmer(RT ~ SOA + (1+SOA|Subject) + (1|Item),
+ data = quasif)
> quasif.lmer
Random effects:
 Groups    Name         Variance Std.Dev. Corr
 Subject   (Intercept)  861.99   29.360
           SOAshort     502.65   22.420   -0.813
 Item      (Intercept)  448.29   21.173
 Residual               100.31   10.016
number of obs: 64, groups: Subject, 8; Item, 8

Fixed effects:
             Estimate Std. Error t value
(Intercept)   540.91      14.93   36.23
SOAshort       22.41      17.12    1.31
```

We check that we really need this complex random-effects structure for Subject
by comparing it with a simpler model using the likelihood ratio test:

```
> quasif.lmerA = lmer(RT ~ SOA + (1|Subject) + (1|Item),
+ data = quasif)
> anova(quasif.lmer, quasif.lmerA)
               Df    AIC     BIC  logLik  Chisq Chi Df Pr(>Chisq)
quasif.lmerA   4  580.29  588.92 -286.14
quasif.lmer    6  555.72  568.67 -271.86 28.570      2  6.255e-07
```

The small p-value shows that we need to stay with the original, full model. Note
that we do not have to take special measures to indicate that the items are nested
under SOA, the determination of nested or non-nested is done for us by lmer().

The *t*-value for SOA is well below 2, so it is clear that it is not significant. For this small data set with only 64 observations, it is crucial to use the *p*-values obtained through MCMC sampling — the *p*-value based on the *t*-statistic is too small:

```
> pvals.fnc(quasif.lmer, nsim = 50000)$fixed
            Estimate MCMCmean HPD95lower HPD95upper   pMCMC Pr(>|t|)
(Intercept)   540.91   540.95     500.03     580.97 0.00002   0.0000
SOAshort       22.41    22.33     -22.83      65.17 0.27224   0.1956
```

Doing the analysis the traditional way recommended by Raaijmakers *et al.* (1999) is a pain. We begin by fitting a simple linear model with lm(), without distinguishing between fixed and random-effects terms.

```
> quasif.lm = lm(RT ~ SOA + Item + Subject + SOA:Subject +
+ Item:Subject, data = quasif)
> anova(quasif.lm)
              Df  Sum Sq Mean Sq F value Pr(>F)
SOA            1  8032.6  8032.6
Item           6 22174.5  3695.7
Subject        7 26251.6  3750.2
SOA:Subject    7  7586.7  1083.8
Item:Subject  42  4208.8   100.2
Residuals      0     0.0
```

The anova() summary does not produce any *p*-values. The model is SATURATED, the residual error is zero, and the number of parameters in the model,

```
> length(coef(quasif.lm))
[1] 72
```

exceeds the number of data points:

```
> nrow(quasif)
[1] 64
```

In fact, 8 of the coefficients in the model are inestimable:

```
> sum(is.na(coef(quasif.lm)))
[1] 8
```

This model is completely useless for prediction for new subjects or new items; it overfits the data, but we can squeeze out a *p*-value. Recall that in analysis of variance, the idea is to compare variances in the form of mean squares. The problem that the present experimental design causes for classical analysis of variance is that there is no proper mean squares to test the mean squares of SOA against. The way out of this dilemma was developed by Satterthwaite (1946) and Cochran (1951). They devised an approximative *F*-value known as quasi-*F*. For the present design, we can calculate this quasi-*F* ratio with the function quasiF.fnc, which takes as input four mean squares and their associated degrees of freedom as listed in the above anova() table:

```
> x = anova(quasif.lm)
> quasiF.fnc(x["SOA","Mean Sq"], x["Item:Subject", "Mean Sq"],
+            x["SOA:Subject", "Mean Sq"], x["Item", "Mean Sq"],
```

```
+               x["SOA","Df"], x["Item:Subject", "Df"],
+               x["SOA:Subject", "Df"], x["Item", "Df"])
$F
[1] 1.701588

$df1
[1] 1.025102

$df2
[1] 9.346185

$p
[1] 0.2239887
```

Instead of specifying the cells in the ANOVA table, we could also have plugged in the values listed in the tables directly. The *p*-value returned for the quasi-*F* ratio, 0.224, is slightly smaller than the *p*-value suggested by MCMC sampling.

In psycholinguistics, a specific methodology evolved over the years to work around having to calculate quasi-*F* ratios, which were computationally very demanding thirty years ago. Clark (1973) suggested an easy-to-calculate conservative estimate for quasi-*F* ratios which involved two simpler *F*-values. These *F*-values were obtained by averaging over the items to obtain subject means for each level of the treatment effect, and similarly by averaging over subjects to obtain item means. Forster and Dickinson (1976) proposed an alternative procedure, which has become the gold standard of psycholinguistics. In this procedure, separate analyses of variance are carried out on the by-item and the by-subject means. The by-item analysis is supposed to be informative over the reliability of an effect across items, and the by-subject analysis is likewise supposed to ascertain reliability across subjects. A predictor is accepted as significant only when it is significant both by subjects and by items.

For the present example, the by-subject analysis proceeds as follows. We calculate the mean RTs averaged over the items for each combination of `Subject` and `SOA` with the help of `aggregate()`, which has a syntax similar to that of `tapply()`:

```
> subjects = aggregate(quasif$RT, list(quasif$Subject,
+   quasif$SOA),mean)
> subjects
    Group.1 Group.2      x
1        S1    long 553.75
2        S2    long 532.00
3        S3    long 546.25
4        S4    long 521.00
5        S5    long 569.75
6        S6    long 529.50
7        S7    long 490.00
8        S8    long 585.00
9        S1   short 556.50
10       S2   short 556.50
11       S3   short 579.25
12       S4   short 551.75
```

```
13      S5    short 594.25
14      S6    short 572.50
15      S7    short 535.75
16      S8    short 560.00
```

The column labels are unhelpful, however, so we rename them:

```
> colnames(subjects) = c("Subject", "SOA", "MeanRT")
```

We now test for an effect of SOA by means of an analysis of variance. Since subjects are crossed with SOA, we have to use the aov() function with Subject specified explicitly as ERROR STRATUM (random effect):

```
> summary(aov(MeanRT ~ SOA + Error(Subject), data = subjects))

Error: Subject
Df Sum Sq Mean Sq F value Pr(>F)
Residuals  7 6562.9   937.6

Error: Within
Df  Sum Sq Mean Sq F value  Pr(>F)
SOA         1 2008.16 2008.16   7.4114 0.02966
Residuals  7 1896.68  270.95
```

The summary reports two error strata, one concerning the variance between subjects, and one concerning the variance within subjects. It is in the second part of the table that we find the F-value for SOA, which for 1 and 7 degrees of freedom happens to be significant.

For the by-item analysis, we proceed along similar lines. We first construct a data frame with the by-item means,

```
> items = aggregate(quasif$RT, list(quasif$Item, quasif$SOA),
+   mean)
> items
  Group.1 Group.2       x
1     W5    long 533.125
2     W6    long 529.250
3     W7    long 583.250
4     W8    long 518.000
5     W1   short 559.625
6     W2   short 575.250
7     W3   short 553.375
8     W4   short 565.000
> colnames(items) = c("Item", "SOA", "MeanRT")
```

and then run the by-item analysis of variance. Because items are nested under SOA instead of crossed, we can simply run a one-way analysis of variance:

```
> summary(aov(MeanRT ~ SOA, items))
Df  Sum Sq Mean Sq F value Pr(>F)
SOA         1 1004.08 1004.08  2.1735 0.1908
Residuals  6 2771.81  461.97
```

In contrast to the by-subject analysis, there is no trace of significance in the by-item analysis. As it is not the case that both the by-subject (or F_1) analysis and the by-item (or F_2) analysis are both significant, the effect of SOA is evaluated as not significant. Thus, we reach the same conclusion as offered by the quasi-*F* test and the mixed-effects model.

Inspection of a single data set is not that informative about how the different techniques perform across experiments. The `simulateQuasif.fnc()` function allows us to examine multiple simulated data sets with the same underlying structure. It takes three arguments: a data set with the same design and variable names as our current example data frame `quasif`, the number of simulation runs required, and whether an effect of SOA should be present (`with = TRUE`) or absent (`with = FALSE`). The function estimates fixed and random effects by fitting a mixed-effects model to the input data frame, and then constructs simulated data sets that follow the corresponding theoretical distribution. Its output is a list that specifies for both the 95% and 99% significance levels what the proportion of simulation runs is for which a significant effect for SOA is observed.

We apply this simulation function, once with and once without an effect of SOA. The first simulation will tell us how successful our models are in detecting an effect that is really there. It informs us about the POWER of the models. The second simulation will tell us how often the models incorrectly lead us to believe that there is a significant effect. It provides an estimate of the TYPE I ERROR RATE of the models. (These simulations may take a long time to run.)

```
> y3 = simulateQuasif.fnc(quasif, nruns=1000, with=FALSE)
> y3$alpha05
   quasi-F by-subject    by-item     F1+F2  lmer:pt lmer:pMCMC
     0.055      0.310      0.081     0.079    0.088      0.032
> y3$alpha01
   quasi-F by-subject    by-item     F1+F2  lmer:pt lmer:pMCMC
     0.005      0.158      0.014     0.009    0.031      0.000
```

The error rates for the quasi-*F* test are close to the nominal levels. The by-subject analysis by itself is far off, and the by-item analysis by itself has a high error rate for $\alpha = 0.05$. This high error rate carries over to the `F1+F2` procedure. As expected for small samples, the *p*-values for `lmer()` based on the *t*-statistic are clearly anticonservative. By contrast, the *p*-values based on MCMC sampling are somewhat conservative. When we consider the power for those techniques with nominal Type I error rates (editing the output of `simulateQuasif.fnc()`),

```
> x3 = simulateQuasif.fnc(quasif, nruns=1000, with=TRUE)
> x3$alpha05
   quasi-F              lmer:pMCMC
     0.233                   0.163
> x3$alpha01
   quasi-F     F1+F2  lmer:pMCMC
     0.087     0.089       0.043
```

we find that the quasi-*F* test has the greatest power. This suggests that for small data sets as typically found in textbooks, the quasi-*F* test is to be preferred. We should keep in mind, however, that in real life experiments are characterized by missing data and that, unlike mixed-effects models, the quasi-*F* test is highly vulnerable to missing data and inapplicable to unbalanced designs.

This example illustrates that the *p*-values based on the *t*-statistic in mixed-effects models are anticonservative for small data sets with the present design. For larger numbers of subjects and items, this anticonservatism is largely eliminated. This is easy to see in a series of simulations in which we use 20 instead of 8 subjects and 40 instead of 8 items:

```
> y4 = simulateQuasif.fnc(quasif, nruns=1000, nsub=20, nitem=40,
+ with = F)
> y4$alpha05
   quasi-F by-subject    by-item      F1+F2    lmer:pt lmer:pMCMC
     0.052     0.238       0.102       0.099      0.055      0.027
> y4$alpha01
   quasi-F by-subject    by-item      F1+F2    lmer:pt lmer:pMCMC
     0.009     0.120       0.036       0.036      0.013      0.001
```

The F1+F2 procedure emerges as slightly anticonservative at both alpha levels. If we now consider the power for the subset of techniques with nominal error rates,

```
> x4 = simulateQuasif.fnc(quasif, nruns=1000, nsub=20, nitem=40)
> x4$alpha05
   quasi-F    lmer:pt lmer:pMCMC
     0.809      0.823      0.681
> x4$alpha01
   quasi-F    lmer:pt lmer:pMCMC
     0.587      0.618      0.392
```

we find that lmer()'s *p*-values based on the *t*-distribution are now an excellent choice. The MCMC *p*-values remain conservative.

In summary, for realistic data sets mixed-effects models have at least the same power as the quasi-*F* test of detecting an effect if it is there, while the risk of incorrectly concluding a predictor is significant is comparable. Mixed-effects models offer the advantages of being robust with respect to missing data, of allowing covariates to be taken into account, and of providing insight into the full structure of your data, including the random effects. They can also be applied straightforwardly to other designs for which quasi-*F* ratios would be difficult and cumbersome to derive.

7.2.2   Mixed-effects models and Latin Square designs

For a second design that is commonly encountered in psycholinguistic studies, Raaijmakers *et al.* (1999) recommend an F_1 analysis. Let's consider this recommendation in some more detail as well. We load the data set that they discuss (their Table 4), available as latinsquare:

```
> latinsquare[1:4, ]
   Group Subject Word  RT    SOA List
1    G1      S1    W1 532  short   L1
2    G1      S2    W1 542  short   L1
3    G1      S3    W1 615  short   L1
4    G1      S4    W1 547  short   L1
```

In this (constructed) data set, the factor SOA has three levels (short, medium, long). The design underlying this data set is that of the LATIN SQUARE. The twelve words in this experiment were divided into three lists with four words each. These three lists were rotated over subjects, such that each subject was exposed to a given list for a single condition of SOA. There were three groups of four subjects, which differed only with respect to which combination of List and SOA was presented to them:

```
> table(latinsquare$Group,
+   as.factor(paste(latinsquare$List, latinsquare$SOA)))
    L1 long L1 medium L1 short
G1       0         0        16
G2       0        16         0
G3      16         0         0

    L2 long L2 medium L2 short
G1       0        16         0
C2      16         0         0
G3       0         0        16

    L3 long L3 medium L3 short
G1      16         0         0
G2       0         0        16
G3       0        16         0
```

Analyzing these data with lmer() is again straightforward:

```
> latinsquare.lmer = lmer(RT ~ SOA + (1|Word) + (1|Subject),
+ data = latinsquare)
```

We use pvals.fnc() to generate *p*-values, and specify that it should also save the matrix with the simulated MCMC data:

```
> x = pvals.fnc(latinsquare.lmer, nsim=10000, withMCMC=TRUE)
> names(x)
[1] "fixed"  "random" "mcmc"
> x$fixed
            Estimate MCMCmean HPD95lower HPD95upper  pMCMC Pr(>|t|)
(Intercept) 533.9583 533.7189    504.252    562.985 0.0001   0.0000
SOAmedium     2.1250   2.1363     -1.767      6.197 0.2886   0.2912
SOAshort     -0.4583  -0.4463     -4.297      3.648 0.8184   0.8196
```

Since SOA is now a factor with three levels, we have two contrast coefficients, neither of which is significantly different from zero. In order to evaluate the significance of the factor SOA as a whole, we use aovlmer.fnc(). Its arguments are a fitted mixed-effects model, a matrix of MCMC samples as provided by pvals.fnc(), and the row names of the factor levels that are to be evaluated:

```
> latinsquare.aov = aovlmer.fnc(latinsquare.lmer, x$mcmc,
+ c("SOAmedium", "SOAshort"))
```

The output is a list with two elements. The first element is a list with the MCMC
p-value and the factor levels that are jointly evaluated. The second element is an
anova table with a potentially anticonservative *p*-value:

```
> latinsquare.aov
$MCMC
$MCMC$p
[1] 0.3855
$MCMC$which
[1] "SOAmedium" "SOAshort"

$Ftests
Analysis of Variance Table
    Df  Sum Sq Mean Sq      F     Df2      p
SOA  2 182.389  91.194 0.9444 141.000  0.391
```

For the present design, the *p*-values based on the MCMC samples and those based on
the *t*-statistic are very similar. Both suggest that SOA is not a significant predictor.

The by-subject analysis recommended by Raaijmakers *et al.* requires more
work. We first average RTs for each combination of List, SOA, and Subject:

```
> subjects = aggregate(latinsquare$RT, list(latinsquare$Subject,
+ latinsquare$Group, latinsquare$SOA, latinsquare$List), mean)
> colnames(subjects) = c("Subject", "Group", "SOA", "List", "MeanRT")
> subjects[1:12,]
   Subject Group    SOA List MeanRT
1      S10    G3   long   L1 592.25
2      S11    G3   long   L1 508.75
3      S12    G3   long   L1 483.00
4       S9    G3   long   L1 534.25
5       S5    G2 medium   L1 590.50
6       S6    G2 medium   L1 483.25
7       S7    G2 medium   L1 513.50
8       S8    G2 medium   L1 560.50
9       S1    G1  short   L1 511.00
10      S2    G1  short   L1 521.50
11      S3    G1  short   L1 588.50
12      S4    G1  short   L1 554.75
```

As a next step, we fit a model with Subject nested under Group and with SOA
in interaction with List:

```
> subjects.lm = lm(MeanRT ~ Group/Subject + SOA*List, data = subjects)
```

We then obtain an analysis of variance table, but we ignore the last two columns
because the *F*-values and *p*-values are based on the assumption that all factors
are fixed, contrary to fact:

```
> anova(subjects.lm)[,1:3]
               Df Sum Sq Mean Sq  F value     Pr(>F)
Group           2   1696     848  28.9395 2.379e-06
SOA             2     46      23   0.7781    0.4741
List            2   3116    1558  53.1724 2.791e-08
Group:Subject   9  47305    5256 179.3974 9.422e-16
SOA:List        2     40      20   0.6830    0.5177
Residuals      18    527      29
```

In order to obtain the desired *p*-value, we compare the `Mean Sq` for `SOA` with that for `SOA:List`, and obtain an *F*-value of $23/20 = 1.15$ and a *p*-value of:

```
> 1 - pf(23/20, 2, 2)
[1] 0.4651163
```

This by-subject analysis also points to a non-significant effect of `SOA`.

The averaging procedure of Raaijmakers and colleagues yields a larger *p*-value than the mixed-effects model, suggesting that it is more conservative and may have less power to detect the significance of predictors. We investigate whether this is indeed the case with `simulateLatinsquare.fnc()`. This function takes a data set as input, fits a mixed-effects model to this data set, extracts the coefficients of the fixed effects (using `fixef()`) and the random-effects parameters (estimating standard deviations from the output of `ranef()`), and uses the values obtained to generate random samples according to the theoretical distribution of the fitted model. When the option `with` is set to `FALSE`, the contrasts for `SOA` are set to zero. The Type I error rates are in conformity with the nominal levels,

```
> latinsqY = simulateLatinsquare.fnc(latinsquare, nruns=1000, with=F)
> latinsqY$alpha05
Ftest   MCMC     F1
0.055 0.053 0.052
> latinsqY$alpha01
Ftest   MCMC     F1
0.011 0.011 0.010
```

irrespective of whether we use the by-subject analysis (`F1`), the *F*-test of the mixed model (`Ftest`), or the MCMC-based test (`MCMC`). However, the mixed-effects model has greater power:

```
> latinsqX = simulateLatinsquare.fnc(latinsquare, nruns=1000, with=T)
> latinsqX$alpha05
Ftest   MCMC     F1
0.262 0.257 0.092
> latinsqX$alpha01
Ftest   MCMC     F1
0.082 0.080 0.020
```

Raaijmakers, Schrijnemakers, and Gremmen (1999) suggest a somewhat more powerful test that can be applied when the interaction of `SOA` by `List` is not significant. When this interaction is not significant it can be removed from the model. The treatment effect can now be tested against a larger error term, leading to smaller *p*-values. The power of this test is closer to that of the mixed-effects analysis, but even this test tends to be slightly more conservative (Baayen, Davidson, and Bates, forthcoming).

7.2.3   Regression with subjects and items

In the psycholinguistics literature, a range of regression techniques are in use for data sets with subjects and items. We illustrate this by means of simulated data sets in which reaction time is defined as linearly dependent on three fixed-effects predictors, X, Y, and Z. The fixed effects are tied to the items and quantify properties of these items. For items that are words, these properties could be word length, word frequency, and inflectional entropy. Each subject provides one RT to each item. The function `make.reg.fnc()` creates simulated data sets with this layout.

A simulated data set obtained with `make.reg.fnc()` allows us to reconstruct exactly how the RTs depend on the fixed and random effects:

```
> simdat = make.reg.fnc()
> simdat[1:4, ]
  Intr X  Y  Z  Item RanefItem RanefSubj Subject    Error      RT
1    1 1  8  7 Item1 -81.56308  137.1683   Subj1  16.22481 549.8300
2    1 2 13  8 Item2  14.27047  137.1683   Subj1 -16.89636 648.5424
3    1 3  5  1 Item3  19.51690  137.1683   Subj1  34.03299 630.7182
4    1 4 19 18 Item4 -63.28945  137.1683   Subj1  68.03613 735.9150
```

The RT on the first line, for instance, can be reconstructed given the vector of fixed-effects coefficients $(400, 2, 6, 4)$ for the intercept and X, Y, and Z that `make.reg.fnc()` works with by default, together with the random-effects adjustments for subject and item and the error term:

```
> 400*1 + 2*1 + 6*8 + 4*7 - 81.56308 + 137.1683 + 16.22481
[1] 549.83
```

The task of a regression analysis is to infer from the data the parameters of the model: the coefficients for the fixed effects, and the standard deviations for the random effects. Here is what `lmer()` reports for this particular simulation run:

```
> simdat.lmer = lmer(RT ~ X+Y+Z+(1|Item)+(1|Subject), data=simdat)
> simdat.lmer
Random effects:
 Groups    Name         Variance Std.Dev.
 Item      (Intercept) 2051.4    45.293
 Subject   (Intercept) 3881.5    62.301
 Residual               2645.7    51.436
number of obs: 200, groups: Item, 20; Subject, 10

Fixed effects:
             Estimate Std. Error t value
(Intercept)   436.490     39.320  11.101
X               2.410      2.008   1.200
Y               5.178      1.926   2.689
Z               2.643      1.988   1.329
```

The estimates for the fixed effects in the summary table of this MIXED-EFFECTS REGRESSION model are close to the values that we used to generate this data set, $(400, 2, 6, 4)$. Averaged over a large series of simulated data sets, these estimates become more and more similar to the values that we actually used to construct the data sets. Turning to the random effects, we observe that the estimated standard deviations are also well-estimated: the standard deviations that `make.reg.fnc()` assumes by default are 40 for item, 80 for subject, and 50 for the residual error.

Traditionally, regression for data with subjects and items is carried out with the help of two separate regression analyses. One regression begins with calculating by-item means, averaging over subjects, and then proceeds with ordinary least squares regression. We will refer to this as BY-ITEM REGRESSION:

```
> items = aggregate(simdat$RT, list(simdat$Item), mean)
> colnames(items) = c("Item", "Means")
> items = merge(items, unique(simdat[,c("Item", "X", "Y", "Z")]),
+   by.x = "Item", by.y = "Item")
> items.lm = lm(Means ~ X + Y + Z, data = items)
> summary(items.lm)
Residuals:
     Min       1Q   Median       3Q      Max
-100.570   -6.932    4.895   20.553   85.639

Coefficients:
            Estimate Std. Error t value Pr(>|t|)
(Intercept)  436.490     34.029  12.827 7.79e-10
X              2.410      2.008   1.200   0.2476
Y              5.178      1.926   2.689   0.0161
Z              2.643      1.988   1.329   0.2024

Residual standard error: 48.12 on 16 degrees of freedom
Multiple R-Squared: 0.4299,     Adjusted R-squared: 0.323
F-statistic: 4.022 on 3 and 16 DF,  p-value: 0.02611
```

These estimates for the fixed-effects coefficients are identical to those returned by lmer(). Across regression techniques, this is almost always the case. When we compare *p*-values for the by-item regression with those for mixed-effects regression, we also obtain comparable values:

```
> pvals.fnc(simdat.lmer)$fixed
            Estimate MCMCmean HPD95lower HPD95upper  pMCMC Pr(>|t|)
(Intercept)  436.490  436.247    356.687    520.706 0.0001   0.0000
X              2.410    2.425     -2.021      6.498 0.2326   0.2316
Y              5.178    5.188      1.037      8.923 0.0106   0.0078
Z              2.643    2.653     -1.429      6.913 0.1996   0.1853
```

Rather different *p*-values are obtained with a second regression technique known as RANDOM REGRESSION. This kind of regression has been advocated in psychology by Lorch and Myers (1990), and has become the gold standard in psycholinguistics. In random regression, we fit a separate model to the data for each individual subject. The function from the lme4 package that calculates these by-subject coefficients is lmList():

```
> simdat.lmList = lmList(RT ~ X + Y + Z | Subject, simdat)
> coef(simdat.lmList)
        (Intercept)          X        Y          Z
Subj1     628.1484 -1.9141021 1.649215  3.4021119
Subj2     458.7045  3.1036178 3.374996  1.5192233
Subj3     469.3044  2.9379676 3.484233  2.8355168
Subj4     418.5968  5.6396018 4.241479 -0.4764763
Subj5     467.6317  4.1477264 7.123812 -0.6388146
Subj6     328.9318  3.8245708 7.373426  2.5304837
Subj7     308.7975  3.0110525 6.709779  1.7966127
Subj8     360.2321  2.6404247 7.098332  6.0430440
Subj9     473.5752  0.1909166 3.849270  5.4122264
Subj10    450.9785  0.5152209 6.873633  4.0021081
```

We note that for Y, the coefficient is greater than zero for all subjects, while for X, one coefficient is negative and nine are positive. For Z, two coefficients are negative and eight are positive. We formally test whether the coefficients are significantly different from zero (at the risk of combining precise and imprecise information) by means of one-sample t-tests. We do so for all four columns simultaneously with `apply()`:

```
> apply(coef(simdat.lmList), 2, t.test)
```

Abbreviating the output, we obtain means that are again identical to the estimates obtained with `lmer()` and by-item regression:

```
$'(Intercept)'
t = 15.1338, df = 9, p-value = 1.044e-07; mean of x 436.4901
$X
t = 3.4527, df = 9, p-value = 0.007244; mean of x 2.409700
$Y
t = 7.8931, df = 9, p-value = 2.464e-05; mean of x 5.177817
$Z
t = 3.7716, df = 9, p-value = 0.004406; mean of x 2.642604
```

However, the p-values are much smaller, and would suggest that all predictors are significant. Interestingly, when we run a mixed-effects model with only `Subject` as random effect, omitting `Item`, we also obtain similarly small p-values:

```
> simdat.lmerS = lmer(RT ~ X+Y+Z + (1|Subject), data=simdat)
> pvals.fnc(simdat.lmerS)$fixed
       Estimate MCMCmean HPD95lower HPD95upper  pMCMC Pr(>|t|)
Intr   436.490  436.746   386.3913   490.913  0.0001   0.0000
X        2.410    2.420     0.7133     4.111  0.0070   0.0065
Y        5.178    5.168     3.4939     6.838  0.0001   0.0000
Z        2.643    2.639     0.8610     4.301  0.0036   0.0026
```

Inspection of the random-effects structure of the model,

```
> simdat.lmerS
Random effects:
 Groups    Name         Variance  Std.Dev.
 Subject   (Intercept)  3793.7    61.593
 Residual               4401.0    66.340
```

and a comparison with the random-effects structure for the model including `Item` as a random effect shows that the standard deviation for the residual error is over-estimated: the value used when constructing the data set was 50, the model with subject and item as random effects estimated it at 51, but the present model at 66. This model is confounding item-bound systematic error with the residual error.

Because mixed-effects models were developed historically for NESTED designs, there are proposals in the literature that items should be analyzed as nested under subjects (see, e.g., Quené and Van den Bergh, 2004). It is important to realize the consequences of this proposal. Nesting items under subjects implies that we allow ourselves to assume that each subject is exposed to in principle a completely different set of items. The idea that a given item has basically the same effect on any subject (modulo the residual error) is completely given up. The design of the lmer() function forces the distinction between crossed and nested effects out into the open. Because lmer() figures out from the input data frame whether subject and item are crossed or nested, crossing versus nesting has to be made fully explicit in the input. In simdat, every level of Subject occurs in conjunction with the same 20 levels of item, as shown by cross-tabulation of subject and item:

```
> table(simdat$Subject, simdat$Item)[1:4, 1:4]

      Item1 Item10 Item11 Item12
Subj1     1      1      1      1
Subj2     1      1      1      1
Subj3     1      1      1      1
Subj4     1      1      1      1
```

In order to specify that the items are nested under subject instead of crossed, we have to create new names for the items, such that the labels for the 20 items will be different for each subject. We can achieve this by pasting the name of the item onto the name of the subject, by converting the resulting character vector into a factor, and adding the result as a new column to simdat:

```
> simdat$Item2 = factor(paste(simdat$Subject, simdat$Item, sep = "."))
```

A cross-tabulation now results in a table of 10 rows (subjects) by 200 columns (the new items). Most of the cells of this table are zero:

```
> table(simdat$Subject, simdat$Item2)[1:10, 1:4]

       Subj10.Item1 Subj10.Item10 Subj10.Item11 Subj10.Item12
Subj1             0             0             0             0
Subj2             0             0             0             0
Subj3             0             0             0             0
Subj4             0             0             0             0
Subj5             0             0             0             0
Subj6             0             0             0             0
Subj7             0             0             0             0
Subj8             0             0             0             0
Subj9             0             0             0             0
Subj10            1             1             1             1
```

Note that effectively we now have 200 different items, instead of just 20 items. In other words, nesting implies that one subject may respond to, say, *scythe*, in the way another subject might respond to, say, *antidisestablishmentarianism*, once the fixed-effects predictors have been accounted for. This is not what we want, not for the present data, and more generally not for linguistic data sets in which the items are sensibly distinct. Proponents of nesting argue that nesting does justice to the idea that each subject has her own experience with a given item. With respect to the mental lexicon, for instance, expertise in the nautical domain and expertise in the medical domain will lead to differential familiarity with nautical terms and medical terms across subpopulations. However, nesting gives up on the commonality of words altogether. Also note that with full nesting structure the random effect for Item is CONFOUNDED with the residual error. We have 200 data points, so 200 residual error values, but also 200 by-item adjustments. As

Table 7.1. *Type I error rate and power comparison for four regression models (*lmer*: mixed-effects regression with crossed random effects for subject and item,* lmerS*: mixed-effects regression with random effect for subject only,* lmList*: random regression,* item*: by-item regression) across 1000 simulation runs. The* mcmc *extension denotes p-values based on 10000 Markov chain Monte Carlo samples.*

| | $\beta_Z = 0$ | | | | | |
| | $\alpha = 0.05$ | | | $\alpha = 0.01$ | | |
	X	Y	Z	X	Y	Z
lmer	0.248	0.898	0.077	0.106	0.752	0.018
lmer-mcmc	0.219	0.879	0.067	0.069	0.674	0.013
lmerS	0.609	0.990	**0.380**	0.503	0.982	**0.238**
lmerS-mcmc	0.606	0.991	**0.376**	0.503	0.982	**0.239**
lmList	0.677	0.995	**0.435**	0.519	0.979	**0.269**
item	0.210	0.873	0.063	0.066	0.670	0.012
	$\beta_Z = 4$					
	$\alpha = 0.05$			$\alpha = 0.01$		
	X	Y	Z	X	Y	Z
lmer	0.219	0.897	0.626	0.089	0.780	0.415
lmer-mcmc	0.190	0.881	0.587	0.061	0.651	0.304
lmerS	0.597	0.989	0.925	0.488	0.978	0.867
lmerS-mcmc	0.594	0.989	0.924	0.485	0.978	0.869
lmList	0.650	0.992	0.931	0.487	0.979	0.868
item	0.183	0.875	0.574	0.055	0.642	0.295

a consequence, nesting of items under subjects leads to an ill-defined model. If items are truly nested, then the simpler model with only Subject as random effect is appropriate.

Thus far, we have considered only one simulated data set. But it is useful to know how these regression techniques perform across many simulated data sets. The function simulateRegression.fnc() applies the different regression techniques to a series of simulated data sets. We apply it once with and once without an effect for the predictor Z. Table 7.1 summarizes the results. The upper half of the table shows that the by-subject methods (lmerS and lmList) so badly inflate the Type I error compared to the nominal 0.05 and 0.01 values that it does not make sense to consider them in the power comparison. The rows for these models are therefore shown in grey in the lower half of Table 7.1. It is clear that the only acceptable models are the by-item regression and the mixed-effects regression with crossed random effects for subject and item. Of these two, the mixed-effects model has slightly greater power.

It is also worth noting that the mixed-effects model with only subject as random effect (`lmerS`) does not provide proper estimates of the standard deviations of the random effects (defined in the model as 40 for `Item`, 80 for `Subject`, and 50 for the residual error). Averaged across 1000 simulation runs for the simulation without an effect for Z,

```
> s = simulateRegression.fnc(beta = c(400, 2, 6, 0), nruns = 1000)
> s$ranef
          Item  Subject Residual
lmer   39.35468 77.22093 49.84096
lmerS       NA 76.74287 62.04566
```

we find that the estimate provided by `lmerS` for the residual error is too high, and that for subject is too low. The same pattern emerges for the simulation with an effect of Z included.

Mixed-effects regression with crossed random effects for subject and item therefore offers several advantages. First, it provides insight into the full random-effects structure. Second, it has slightly superior power. Third, it allows us to bring into the model longitudinal effects and also to study more complex random-effects structure with random slopes. Finally, mixed-effects regression makes it possible to include in the model by-subject predictors such as age or education level along with by-item predictors such as frequency and length.

Under what conditions, then, is random regression or mixed-effects regression with subject as only random effect, appropriate? The answer is simple: when the predictors are true TREATMENT factors that have no relation to the properties of the basic unit in the experiment. Consider, for instance, an experiment measuring the velocity of a tennis ball with as predictors the humidity of the air and wind force. When the same tennis ball is tested under different treatments of humidity and wind force, there is no by-item random effect. When the same experiment is repeated across laboratory, laboratory can be included as random effect. But no random effect is necessary at the item level. However, in linguistics and psycholinguistics, we hardly ever study just a single linguistic object. A word's frequency, for instance, is not a treatment that can be applied to it. Frequency is an intrinsic property of individual words, and it is highly correlated to many other lexical properties, as we have seen in preceding chapters. We have no guarantee that all relevant item-specific properties are actually captured adequately by our item-specific predictors. It is much more likely that there is still unexplained by-item variance. In these circumstances, one must bring item as random effect into the model.

7.3   Shrinkage in mixed-effects models

Linear mixed-effects models are also attractive compared to classical analysis of variance and multiple regression because they provide SHRINKAGE estimates for the by-subject and by-item adjustments — the best linear unbiased predictors or BLUPS. To illustrate shrinkage in mixed-effects models, it is useful to

consider a simple simulated experiment with 10 subjects and 20 words in which we
have a dependent variable (RT) that is modeled as a straightforward linear function
(with an intercept of 400 and a slope of 5) of a numerical predictor (frequency).
The frequencies of the 20 items were simulated by sampling 20 random numbers
from a normal distribution with a mean of 20 and a standard deviation of 4. This
data set, available as shrinkage, was created with two random effects: random
intercepts for subject, and the residual error. For simplicity, there are no random
intercepts for item. The standard deviation for the subject random effect for the
intercept was 20, and the standard deviation of the residual error was 50. We load
these data, and run lmer() to see how it reconstructs the parameters that we used
to construct the data set:

```
> shrinkage.lmer = lmer(RT ~ frequency + (1|subject), data = shrinkage)
> shrinkage.lmer
Random effects:
 Groups    Name          Variance Std.Dev.
 subject   (Intercept)   185.99   13.638
 Residual                2444.57  49.443
number of obs: 200, groups: subject, 10

Fixed effects:
             Estimate Std. Error t value
(Intercept) 393.0311    21.4566  18.318
frequency     1.0866     0.1936   5.613
```

The summary reports the estimates for our four parameters. The estimate for
the intercept is close, as is the estimate of the standard deviation of the residual
error. The standard deviation for subjects is somewhat too low, and the slope for
frequency is likewise underestimated. This is the best we can do, given the level
of noise in this data set:

   Now consider a random regression on this data set:

```
> shrinkage.lmList = lmList(RT ~ frequency | subject, data = shrinkage)
> coef(shrinkage.lmList)
     (Intercept)   frequency
S1     365.2841   1.2281146
S10    377.3522   1.1365690
S2     319.4524   1.7300404
S3     445.8967   0.6943159
S4     542.5428  -0.2364537
S5     325.6736   1.6250778
S6     478.6631   0.2033189
S7     471.4654   0.6686009
S8     367.1283   1.5067342
S9     236.8524   2.3100814
```

A *t*-test on the slope for frequency yields a significant *p*-value, as expected
given that only subject S4 had a negative slope:

```
> t.test(coef(shrinkage.lmList)$frequency)
t = 4.4952, df = 9, p-value = 0.001499
mean of x
 1.08664
```

As before, the mean slope, 1.08664, is indistinguishable from the slope estimated by `lmer()`.

However, mixed-effects models provide improved estimates of the by-subject differences compared to random regression. To see this, we first tabulate the estimated coefficients for the two models side by side:

```
> coef(shrinkage.lmList)              > coef(shrinkage.lmer)$subject
     (Intercept)   frequency              (Intercept)   frequency
S1    365.2841    1.2281146         S1    385.4278     1.08664
S10   377.3522    1.1365690         S10   386.7957     1.08664
S2    319.4524    1.7300404         S2    390.1994     1.08664
S3    445.8967    0.6943159         S3    399.5851     1.08664
S4    542.5428   -0.2364537         S4    397.7705     1.08664
S5    325.6736    1.6250778         S5    387.1721     1.08664
S6    478.6631    0.2033189         S6    387.6356     1.08664
S7    471.4654    0.6686009         S7    413.3528     1.08664
S8    367.1283    1.5067342         S8    404.5415     1.08664
S9    236.8524    2.3100814         S9    377.8304     1.08664
```

There are two striking differences. First, the mixed-effects model does not vary the coefficient for `frequency` across subjects, as there is no random slope in the model. Second, the random regression offers estimates for the intercept that have a much wider range than those for the mixed-effects model. This is illustrated graphically in Figure 7.7. In both panels, the circles represent the intercepts that were actually used to construct the RTs in the simulated data set. The intercepts labeled S1, S2, ..., S10 represent the estimated intercepts. The left panel shows the estimates for random regression, the right panel shows the estimates for mixed-effects regression. It is immediately apparent that the mixed-effects model does a much better job at getting accurate estimates that approach the true by-subject differences in the intercept.

The reason that `lmer()` is so much more successful is that `lmer()` considers a given subject in the light of what it knows about the other subjects. Consider again the left panel of Figure 7.7. The horizontal axis ranks the subjects from short to long RTs (intercepts). Subject S9 is extremely fast, and subject S4 extremely slow. Such extremes are unlikely to be observed for the same subjects in a second experiment with these same subjects. In such a second experiment, they are much more likely to have less extreme intercepts. In other words, the estimates for the intercepts are subject to a general phenomenon known as RE-GRESSION TOWARDS THE MEAN: in replication studies with the same subjects, the extremely slow subjects will be faster, and the extremely fast subjects will be slower responders. SHRINKAGE towards the mean across replication studies is an adverse result of traditional modeling. The model provides too tight a fit to the data. In mixed-effects regression, this shrinkage is anticipated and brought into the model. Informally, you can think of this in terms of the model considering the behavior of any given subject in the light of what it knows about the behavior of all the other subjects. In the present example, for instance, the assumption of a common slope in the `lmer` model damps the variation in the intercept. As a

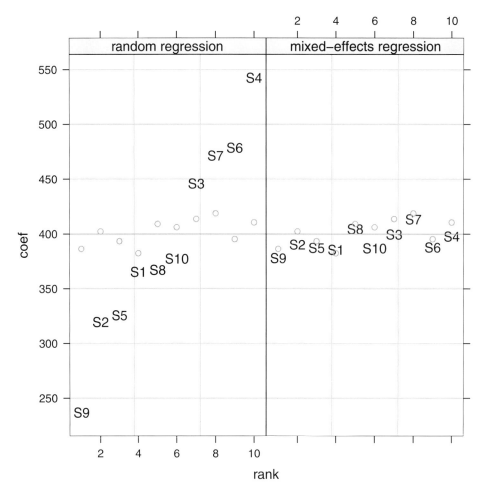

Figure 7.7. *The estimated intercepts for subjects (S1, S2, ..., S10) in random regression (left panel) and mixed-effects regression (right panel). The grey circles represent the actual intercepts that were present in the simulation. The dark grey horizontal line denotes the true mean of the intercept (400). The horizontal axes represent the rank of the intercept as estimated in the random regression model.*

consequence, the BLUPs produced by lmer() are much closer to the actual values. Because they have already been shrunk towards the mean in the model, they no longer shrink towards the mean when you repeat the experiment. Hence, they make more precise prediction possible.

7.4   Generalized linear mixed models

Thus far, we have considered mixed-effects models that extend ordinary least squares models fitted with lm() or ols(). In this section we consider the mixed-effects parallel to glm() and lrm(), the GENERALIZED LINEAR MIXED

MODEL. We return for a final time to the data of Bresnan *et al.* (2007), addressing the choice between the PP and NP realization of the dative in English, available as the data set `dative`. In Chapter 5 we analyzed this data set by means of a CART tree. Here, we use logistic regression. We begin with an analysis using the `lrm()` function from the `Design` package discussed in Chapter 6, and consider a model with main effects only:

```
> library(Design)
> dative.dd = datadist(dative)
> options(datadist = 'dative.dd')
> dative.lrm = lrm(RealizationOfRecipient ~
+ AccessOfTheme + AccessOfRec + LengthOfRecipient + AnimacyOfRec +
+ AnimacyOfTheme + PronomOfTheme + DefinOfTheme + LengthOfTheme+
+ SemanticClass + Modality,
+ data = dative)
> anova(dative.lrm)
Wald Statistics
```

Factor	Chi-Square	d.f.	P
AccessOfTheme	30.79	2	<.0001
AccessOfRec	258.06	2	<.0001
LengthOfRecipient	69.87	1	<.0001
AnimacyOfRec	93.35	1	<.0001
AnimacyOfTheme	3.71	1	0.0542
PronomOfTheme	54.42	1	<.0001
DefinOfTheme	28.72	1	<.0001
LengthOfTheme	79.03	1	<.0001
SemanticClass	166.55	4	<.0001
Modality	49.91	1	<.0001
TOTAL	747.64	15	<.0001

The animacy of the theme is the only potentially irrelevant predictor. However, the problem with this analysis is that we have repeated measures for many of the verbs:

```
> rev(sort(table(dative$Verb)))
    give      pay     sell     send     cost     tell
    1666      207      206      172      169      128
   offer    teach     take     show    bring   charge
      79       64       58       58       55       43
     owe       do     loan     lend    award    write
      31       31       21       20       19       17
    feed     hand     mail    grant    allow     deny
      17       15       14       13       13       12
 ...
     get   funnel    float     flip    carry bequeath
       1        1        1        1        1        1
  assess   afford    accord
       1        1        1
```

The structure of this data set differs from the data set of Dutch verbs that we analyzed in Chapter 4. The Dutch data set contained nearly 1100 verbs, but each verb occurred only once. In the data of Bresnan and colleagues, some verbs occur only once, but others are highly frequent, with *give* the most frequent verb of all.

It is not unlikely that the data of just the single verb *give* dominate the effects observed with `lrm()`. To alleviate this problem, we rerun the analysis with a mixed-effects logistic regression with a random effect for `Verb`. It remains unfortunate that the numbers of observations for the different verbs are so different. This is a problem that one often encounters in corpus studies. We will therefore have to depend on the robustness of the mixed-effects algorithms with respect to unequal numbers of observations.

For a generalized linear mixed-effects model, we again use `lmer()`, but now select the binomial distribution and the logistic link function with `family = "binomial"`:

```
> library(lme4, keep.source=F)
> dative.glmm = lmer(RealizationOfRecipient ~ AccessOfTheme +
+ AccessOfRec + LengthOfRecipient + AnimacyOfRec + AnimacyOfTheme +
+ PronomOfTheme + DefinOfTheme + LengthOfTheme + SemanticClass +
+ Modality + (1|Verb), data = dative, family = "binomial")
```

I have used the extension `glmm` to mark the object as a Generalized Linear Mixed Model, in order to distinguish it from "normal" mixed models, to which I give the extension `lmer`:

```
> print(dative.glmm, corr = FALSE)
Random effects:
 Groups Name        Variance Std.Dev.
 Verb   (Intercept) 4.3982   2.0972
number of obs: 3263, groups: Verb, 75

Estimated scale (compare to  1 )  0.870155

Fixed effects:
                         Estimate Std. Error  z value Pr(>|z|)
(Intercept)               1.29308    0.65005    1.989   0.0467
AccessOfThemegiven        1.50541    0.25504    5.903 3.58e-09
AccessOfThemenew         -0.41979    0.19067   -2.202   0.0277
AccessOfRecgiven         -2.46129    0.17761  -13.858  < 2e-16
AccessOfRecnew            0.12461    0.24423    0.510   0.6099
LengthOfRecipient         0.41485    0.04754    8.727  < 2e-16
AnimacyOfRecinanimate     2.24228    0.25864    8.669  < 2e-16
AnimacyOfThemeinanimate  -0.86354    0.48283   -1.788   0.0737
PronomOfThemepronominal   2.20501    0.24624    8.955  < 2e-16
DefinOfThemeindefinite   -0.93295    0.19024   -4.904 9.39e-07
LengthOfTheme            -0.23354    0.02766   -8.443  < 2e-16
SemanticClassc            0.38583    0.34929    1.105   0.2693
SemanticClassf            0.02204    0.57971    0.038   0.9697
SemanticClassp           -3.77588    1.47575   -2.559   0.0105
SemanticClasst            0.31043    0.20895    1.486   0.1374
Modalitywritten           0.85021    0.18536    4.587 4.50e-06
```

The estimated scale parameter at the beginning of the summary is a measure of how the actual variance in the data compares to the variance assumed by the binomial model. Ideally, it is close to 1. In the present example, it is somewhat smaller than 1 (underdispersion), probably because of the very unequal numbers of verbs in the data. It is not so low as to be a cause of serious concern.

The estimates of the coefficients are very similar to those estimated by `lrm()`:

```
> cor.test(coef(dative.lrm), fixef(dative.glmm))
t = 8.5114, df = 14, p-value = 6.609e-07
      cor
0.9154485
```

The main difference concerns the *p*-values for the contrasts for semantic class. According to `lrm()`, most contrasts are highly significant, but once we have taken by-verb variability into account, there is little left for semantic class to explain. Apparently, there is much more variation among individual verbs than among semantic classes. In other words, semantic class was an indirect and imperfect means for accounting for by-verb variability.

Unlike `lrm()`, `lmer()` does not specify Somers' D_{xy} or the *C* index of concordance,. A function from the `Hmisc` package that calculates these measures for a vector of predicted probabilities and a vector of observed binary outcomes is `somers2()`. We transform the fitted log odds ratios into probabilities either by hand,

```
> probs = 1/(1+exp(-fitted(dative.glmm)))
```

or with,

```
> probs = binomial()$linkinv(fitted(dative.glmm))
```

and then apply `somers2()`:

```
> somers2(probs, as.numeric(dative$RealizationOfRec)-1)
        C           Dxy           n       Missing
0.9613449   0.9226899 3263.0000000   0.0000000
```

Both measures indicate the fit is excellent.

Another way of inspecting the goodness of fit is to divide the range of possible expected probabilities into ten equally sized bins $(0 - 0.1, 0.1 - 0.2, \ldots, 0.9 - 1.0)$, and to compare for each bin the mean expected proportion of successes with the observed proportion of successes for the data points falling into that bin. `plot.logistic.fit.fnc` carries out this comparison. It takes as arguments a model fit by either `lrm()` or `lmer()`, and the corresponding data frame:

```
> par(mfrow=c(1,2))
> plot.logistic.fit.fnc(dative.lrm, dative)
> mtext("lrm", 3, 0.5)
> plot.logistic.fit.fnc(dative.glmm, dative)
> mtext("lmer", 3, 0.5)
> par(mfrow=c(1,1))
```

As can be seen in Figure 7.8, the observed proportions and the corresponding mean expected probabilities are very similar for both models.

In our analyses thus far, we have ignored a potentially important source of variation, the speakers whose utterances were sampled. For the subset of spoken

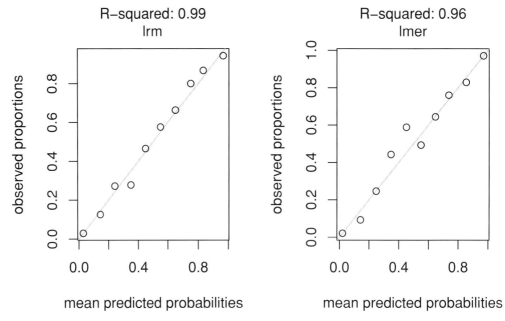

Figure 7.8. *Observed proportions of* PP *realizations and the corresponding mean predicted probabilities for* `dative.lrm` *(left) and* `dative.glmm` *(right).*

English, identifiers for the individual speakers are available. It turns out that the numbers of observations contributed by a given speaker vary substantially:

```
> spoken = dative[dative$Modality != "written",]
> spoken$Speaker = spoken$Speaker[drop=TRUE]
> range(table(spoken$Speaker))
[1]  1 40
```

In principle, we can include a random effect for `Speaker` in our model, accepting that subjects with few observations contribute almost no information:

```
> spoken.glmm = lmer(RealizationOfRecipient ~
+ AccessOfTheme + AccessOfRec + LengthOfRecipient + AnimacyOfRec +
+ AnimacyOfTheme + PronomOfTheme + DefinOfTheme + LengthOfTheme +
+ SemanticClass + (1|Verb) + (1|Speaker),
+ data = spoken, family = "binomial")
```

However, the estimated variance for factor `Speaker` is effectively zero, as is evident from the table of random effects:

```
> print(spoken.glmm, corr=FALSE)
Random effects:
 Groups  Name         Variance     Std.Dev.
 Speaker (Intercept) 5.0000e-10   2.2361e-05
 Verb    (Intercept) 4.3753e+00   2.0917e+00
```

The random effect for `Speaker` is superfluous. From this we conclude that speaker variation is unlikely to distort our conclusions. Another way in which we may ascertain that our results are valid across speakers is to run a bootstrap validation in which we sample speakers (and all their data points) with replacement:

```
> speakers = levels(spoken$Speaker)
+ nruns = 100 # number of bootstrap runs
+ for (run in 1:nruns) {
+   # sample with replacement from the speakers
+   mysampleofspeakers = sample(speakers, replace = TRUE)
+   # select rows from data frame for the sampled speakers
+   mysample = spoken[is.element(spoken$Speaker, mysampleofspeakers),]
+   # fit a mixed effects model
+   mysample.lmer = lmer(RealizationOfRecipient ~ SemanticClass +
+     AccessOfRec + AccessOfTheme + PronomOfRec + PronomOfTheme +
+     DefinOfRec + DefinOfTheme + AnimacyOfRec + LengthOfTheme +
+     LengthOfRecipient + (1|Verb), family="binomial", data=mysample)
+   # extract fixed effects from the model
+   fixedEffects = fixef(mysample.lmer)
+   # and save them for later inspection
+   if (run == 1) res = fixedEffects
|   else res = rbind(res, fixedEffects)
+   # this takes time, so output dots to indicate progress
+   cat(".")
+ }
+ cat("\n")  # add newline to console
+ # assign sensible rownames
+ rownames(res) = 1:nruns
+ # and convert into data frame
+ res = data.frame(res)
```

The `res` data frame contains, for each of the predictors, 100 bootstrap estimates of the coefficients:

```
> res[1:4, c("AccessOfThemegiven", "AccessOfThemenew")]
    AccessOfThemegiven AccessOfThemenew
1             1.928998       -0.2662725
2             1.894876       -0.4450632
3             1.891211       -0.6237502
4             1.347860       -0.3443248
```

With the help of the `quantile()` function we obtain for a given column the corresponding 95% confidence interval as well as the median:

```
> quantile(res$AccessOfThemegiven, c(0.025, 0.5, 0.975))
    2.5%      50%     97.5%
1.248588 1.682959 2.346539
```

We apply the quantile function to all columns simultaneously, and transpose the resulting table for expository convenience:

```
> t(apply(res, 2, quantile, c(0.025, 0.5, 0.975)))
                         2.5%         50%        97.5%
X.Intercept.       -0.75399640  0.07348911   1.07283054
SemanticClassc     -0.68274579  0.16244792   0.80071553
SemanticClassf     -1.51546566  0.12709561   1.62158050
SemanticClassp   -216.54050927 -4.40976146  -3.65166274
SemanticClasst     -0.03004542  0.32834900   0.89482430
AccessOfRecgiven   -1.98532032 -1.41952502  -0.83553953
```

```
AccessOfRecnew              -1.40423078  -0.64366428  -0.04868748
AccessOfThemegiven           1.14068980   1.73408922   2.07713229
AccessOfThemenew            -0.65928103  -0.28711212   0.14225554
PronomOfRecpronominal       -2.35856122  -1.76332487  -1.17819294
PronomOfThemepronominal      2.14508430   2.45161684   2.80406841
DefinOfRecindefinite         0.24902836   0.58052840   1.14548685
DefinOfThemeindefinite      -1.65686315  -1.14979881  -0.72662940
AnimacyOfRecinanimate        1.86492658   2.53141426   3.13096327
LengthOfTheme               -0.31025375  -0.19152255  -0.12557149
LengthOfRecipient            0.29265114   0.43854148   0.65946138
```

Confidence intervals that do not include zero, i.e. rows with only positive or only negative values, characterize coefficients that are significantly different from zero at the 5% significance level. For instance, since the 95% confidence interval for `AccessOfThemegiven` does not include zero, in contrast to the 95% confidence interval for `AccessOfThemenew`, only the former coefficient is significant.

7.5   Case studies

This section discusses four case studies that illustrate some of the new possibilities offered by mixed-effects models for coming to grips with the structure of your data.

7.5.1   Primed lexical decision latencies for Dutch neologisms

De Vaan *et al.* (2007) report a priming study using visual lexical decision that addressed the question of whether new complex words that subjects have not seen before are processed differently when encountered for the first time or for the second time. The data set `primingHeid` concerns 40 newly created neologisms with the Dutch suffix *-heid*, e.g. *lobbigheid* "fluffiness," which we presented to 26 subjects in two conditions. In the first condition, subjects first responded to the base (*lobbig*) and 40 trials later encountered its derivative (*lobbigheid*). In the alternative condition, they were exposed to the complex word (*lobbigheid*), and 40 trials later this same word was repeated. A given subject was exposed to a word in either the base-priming condition or in the derivative-priming condition. Our expectation was that subjects who had seen the complex word before would respond more quickly at the second exposure compared to subjects who had only seen the stem before, due to a nascent frequency effect:

```
> primingHeid.lmer0 = lmer(RT ~ Condition +
+ (1|Subject) + (1|Word), data = primingHeid)
> print(primingHeid.lmer0, corr = FALSE)
Random effects:
 Groups    Name        Variance   Std.Dev.
 Word      (Intercept) 0.0034119  0.058412
 Subject   (Intercept) 0.0408438  0.202098
 Residual              0.0440838  0.209962
```

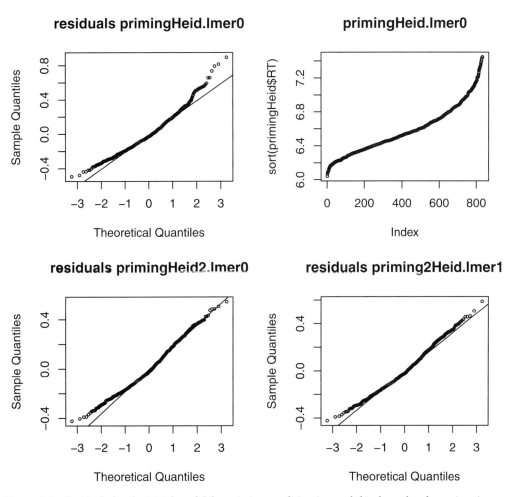

Figure 7.9. *Residuals for the initial model for priming condition (upper left), the ordered reaction times, and the residuals for the model with* 45 *extremely long and atypical reaction times removed.*

```
number of obs: 832, groups: Word, 40; Subject, 26

Fixed effects:
                Estimate Std. Error t value
(Intercept)      6.60297    0.04215  156.66
Conditionheid    0.03127    0.01467    2.13
```

The *p*-value suggests there is indeed an effect of condition, surprisingly an effect that is inhibitory instead of facilitatory. Inspection of the residuals reveals that the model fails to fit the longer reaction times, as shown in the upper panels of Figure 7.9:

```
> qqnorm(residuals(primingHeid.lmer0),
+ main = "residuals primingHeid.lmer0")
> qqline(residuals(primingHeid.lmer0))
> plot(sort(primingHeid$RT), main = "primingHeid.lmer0")
```

We remove the outliers with the greatest reaction times,

```
> primingHeid2 = primingHeid[primingHeid$RT < 7.1,]
> nrow(primingHeid)-nrow(primingHeid2)
[1] 45
> 45/nrow(primingHeid)
[1] 0.05408654
```

and refit the model:

```
> primingHeid2.lmer0 = lmer(RT~Condition+
+ (1|Subject)+(1|Word), data = primingHeid2)
> primingHeid2.lmer0
Fixed effects:
               Estimate Std. Error t value
(Intercept)    6.580379   0.035929  183.15
Conditionheid 0.009115   0.012695    0.72
```

The effect of `Condition` is no longer significant. Thus it would seem that the effect of priming condition is carried only by 45 atypical data points, a mere 5% of the full data set.

It is at this point that we can profit from the full power of mixed-effects modeling. The central concept of priming is that prior processing affects later processing of related words. By only looking at the effect of condition by itself, we are in fact ignoring two important sources of variation. First, a subject may have decided that the base or the neologism was a non-word 40 trials back. If so, that prior rejection must have been revised, as the data that we are analyzing only contains the yes-responses. Such a revision may introduce variance, variance that we have left unaccounted for thus far. Furthermore, the latency elicited for the prime may help predict the latency for the target word. Again, this is a source of variation that we can bring into the model. Finally, it is conceivable that the latency for the prime is not a good predictor for the latency to the target in case the prime was rejected as a word, as a process of revision of opinion is then superimposed—only targets eliciting a yes response are considered here. We therefore include as new predictors the reaction time for the prime (`RTtoPrime`), whether the prime was accepted or rejected as a word (`ResponseToPrime`), and the interaction of these two predictors. This leads to the following model:

```
> primingHeid2.lmer1 = lmer(RT ~ RTtoPrime*ResponseToPrime+Condition+
+ (1|Subject) + (1|Word), data = primingHeid2)
> pvals.fnc(primingHeid2.lmer1, nsim=10000)$fixed
                Estimate MCMCmean HPD95lower HPD95upper  pMCMC Pr(>|t|)
(Intercept)      5.27072  5.33992    4.93105    5.78696 0.0001   0.0000
RTtoPrime        0.19871  0.18840    0.12483    0.25336 0.0001   0.0000
Respincrrct      1.63316  1.50885    0.75650    2.23385 0.0001   0.0000
Conditionheid   -0.03876 -0.03845   -0.06644   -0.01127 0.0060   0.0055
RTtoPrime:
  Respincorrct  -0.22877 -0.21081   -0.32099   -0.10025 0.0001   0.0000
```

We see that the two new predictors are relevant. The RT for the prime is a predictor for the RT to the target. However, the interaction indicates that this positive correlation holds only when the prime was accepted as a word. When it was rejected, we have to adjust the coefficient for the RT to the prime down to roughly zero. As expected, revision of opinion masks the correlation with earlier processing. Crucially, we now see a solidly significant effect of Condition, indicating that indeed a neologism is responded to more quickly upon the second exposure. This may indicate that memory traces for complex words already begin to develop after the very first time they have been encountered. A check of the residuals of this model (as depicted in the lower right panel of Figure 7.9) shows that there is still room for improvement, but there is no serious worry about atypical outliers driving the effects.

```
> qqnorm(residuals(primingHeid2.lmer1),
+ main="residuals primingHeid2.lmer1")
> qqline(residuals(primingHeid2.lmer1))
```

It is left to you as an exercise to verify that none of the other predictors in the data frame (family size, length in letters, number of synsets, or trial) are sufficient by themselves to pull the effect of condition out of the noise. To do so, it is crucial to have access to the specific response latencies of subjects to the specific primes they encountered earlier in the experiment. There is no way in which this can be accomplished with the traditional by-subject and by-item analyses.

7.5.2 Self-paced reading latencies for Dutch neologisms

De Vaan *et al.* (2007) also used the experimental design described in the previous section with another task, self-paced reading. Instead of embedding primes and targets in a list of isolated words, they embedded them in short texts. The question is whether neologisms will similarly benefit from prior exposure when there is meaningful context to guide interpretation. We remove a few extremely low-valued outliers and a few high-valued outliers, 13 data points in all:

```
> selfPacedReadingHeid=selfPacedReadingHeid[selfPacedReadingHeid$RT>5 &
+ selfPacedReadingHeid$RT < 7.2,]
```

A simple model with Condition as the only predictor does not support an effect for this predictor:

```
> selfPacedReadingHeid.lmer = lmer(RT ~ Condition +
+ (1|Subject) + (1|Word), data = selfPacedReadingHeid)
> selfPacedReadingHeid.lmer
Fixed effects:
                  Estimate Std. Error t value
(Intercept)        5.95569    0.05023  118.57
Conditionheidheid  0.01157    0.02139    0.54
```

Adding the reading latency for the prime as covariate does help:

```
> selfPacedReadingHeid.lmer = lmer(RT ~ RTtoPrime + Condition +
+ (1|Subject) + (1|Word),  data = selfPacedReadingHeid)
```

```
> selfPacedReadingHeid.lmer
Fixed effects:
                    Estimate Std. Error t value
(Intercept)          4.91831    0.15260   32.23
RTtoPrime            0.17574    0.02485    7.07
Conditionheidheid   -0.01648    0.02148   -0.77
```

What we need to do at this point is examine whether we can control for differences in how the words immediately preceding the target word were read. The preceding discourse context may lead up to the target to a greater or lesser extent. It may be necessary to bring this source of variance under control in order for the effect of `Condition` to become fully visible. We therefore inspect the correlations of the reading latency for the target word with the latencies to the four words preceding the target word:

```
> round(cor(selfPacedReadingHeid[,c(3, 12:15)]),3)
               RT RT4WordsBack RT3WordsBack RT2WordsBack RT1WordBack
RT          1.000        0.453        0.490        0.408       0.453
RT4WordsBack 0.453        1.000        0.484        0.387       0.391
RT3WordsBack 0.490        0.484        1.000        0.405       0.397
RT2WordsBack 0.408        0.387        0.405        1.000       0.453
RT1WordBack  0.453        0.391        0.397        0.453       1.000
```

There is considerable correlational structure here. Including four correlated variables as separate predictors makes no sense, as it would give rise to very high collinearity. A solution is to orthogonalize the latencies for the preceding words using principal components analysis, and to add the first three (orthogonal) principal components as predictors to the model:

```
> x = selfPacedReadingHeid[,12:15]
> x.pr = prcomp(x, center = T, scale = T)
> selfPacedReadingHeid$PC1 = x.pr$x[,1]
> selfPacedReadingHeid$PC2 = x.pr$x[,2]
> selfPacedReadingHeid$PC3 = x.pr$x[,3]
> selfPacedReadingHeid.lmer = lmer(RT ~ RTtoPrime + PC1 + PC2 + PC3 +
+ Condition + (1|Subject) + (1|Word), data = selfPacedReadingHeid)
> selfPacedReadingHeid.lmer
Fixed effects:
                    Estimate Std. Error t value
(Intercept)         5.250310   0.139242   37.71
RTtoPrime           0.119199   0.023283    5.12
PC1                 0.150975   0.008757   17.24
PC2                -0.010937   0.012907   -0.85
PC3                 0.020720   0.013742    1.51
Conditionheidheid  -0.003850   0.020160   -0.19
```

Only the first principal component (which captures 55.4% of the variance of the four preceding reading latencies) is required in the model. We remove the other principal components, and test for interactions with `PC1`:

```
> selfPacedReadingHeid.lmer = lmer(RT ~ (RTtoPrime + Condition)*PC1 +
+ (1|Subject) + (1|Word), data = selfPacedReadingHeid)
> pvals.fnc(selfPacedReadingHeid.lmer, nsim=10000)$fixed
                    Estimate HPD95lower HPD95upper  pMCMC Pr(>|t|)
```

```
(Intercept)                 5.244705    4.95947   5.523279 0.0001   0.0000
RTtoPrime                   0.119359    0.07438   0.169190 0.0001   0.0000
Conditionheidheid          -0.005128   -0.04612   0.034474 0.7878   0.7991
PC1                         0.080316   -0.05934   0.225098 0.2654   0.2729
RTtoPrime:PC1               0.013893   -0.01027   0.037403 0.2504   0.2549
Conditionheidheid:PC1      -0.028234   -0.05575  -0.001841 0.0390   0.0367
```

Since PC1 is positively correlated with the latencies to the preceding words,

```
> cor(selfPacedReadingHeid[,c(19,12:15)])[,"PC1"]
      PC1 RT4WordsBack RT3WordsBack RT2WordsBack  RT1WordBack
1.0000000    0.7536694    0.7636564    0.7446181    0.7432292
```

we may interpret PC1 as a measure of the difficulty of the immediately preceding discourse. The more difficult the preceding discourse is, the longer the reading latencies for the target, as witnessed by the positive sign of the coefficient of PC1. The interaction with Condition shows that if the neologism had been read 40 words earlier in the discourse, the inhibitory effect of PC1 is attenuated compared to when the base had been read previously. Inspection of the residuals shows that there still is some lack of goodness of fit for the longest latencies. The effect of Condition remains stable after removal of outliers with high standardized residuals, however, so it is not driven by a few atypical data points:

```
> selfPacedReadingHeid.lmer = lmer(RT ~ RTtoPrime +
+ PC1 * Condition + (1|Subject) + (1|Word),
+ data = selfPacedReadingHeid)
> selfPacedReadingHeid.lmerA = lmer(RT ~ RTtoPrime +
+ PC1 * Condition + (1|Subject) + (1|Word), data =
+ selfPacedReadingHeid[abs(scale(residuals(selfPacedReadingHeid.lmer)))
+ < 2.5, ])
> pvals.fnc(selfPacedReadingHeid.lmerA,nsim=10000)$fixed
                        Estimate HPD95lower HPD95upper  pMCMC Pr(>|t|)
(Intercept)              5.32173    5.07890   5.559462 0.0001   0.0000
RTtoPrime                0.10532    0.06571   0.145635 0.0001   0.0000
PC1                      0.15057    0.13161   0.169758 0.0001   0.0000
Conditionheidheid       -0.01810   -0.05148   0.015194 0.2848   0.2836
PC1:Conditionheidheid   -0.02673   -0.04882  -0.005017 0.0184   0.0175
```

To conclude, this example shows how an effect that is masked initially by a strong effect of context can nevertheless be detected, but only by taking into account the correlational structure with the reading times of the words in the immediately preceding discourse. There is no way of doing so with traditional analyses requiring prior averaging over subjects and items.

7.5.3   Visual lexical decision latencies of Dutch eight-year-olds

Perdijk *et al.* (2007) studied the reading skills of eight-year-old Dutch children using visual lexical decision. Key questions addressed by this experiment are whether the morphological family size measure is predictive for beginning readers, and whether systematic differences between beginning readers can be traced to lexical predictors such as a word's frequency and orthographic length. Perdijk's data, with the latencies of 59 children to 184 words, are available as the data set `beginningReaders`. The list of column names,

```
> colnames(beginningReaders)
 [1] "Word"           "Subject"       "LogRT"
 [4] "Trial"          "OrthLength"    "LogFrequency"
 [7] "LogFamilySize"  "ReadingScore"  "ProportionOfErrors"
[10] "PC1"            "PC2"           "PC3"
[13] "PC4"
```

includes two random-effects variables, `Subject` and `Word`, and as the dependent variable the log-transformed reaction time (`LogRT`). Predictors are `Trial` (the rank of a trial in the experimental list), length in letters (`OrthLength`), log frequency in a word frequency list based on reading materials for children (`LogFrequency`), log morphological family size with counts of words not known to young children removed (`LogFamilySize`), by-word error proportions (`ProportionOfErrors`), a score for reading proficiency (`Reading Score`), and four principal components orthogonalizing the reaction times to the preceding four trials. We centralize `OrthLength` and `LogFrequency` because, as we shall see shortly, by-subject random slopes are required for these predictors and we want to avoid running into spurious correlation parameters for our random effects:

```
> beginningReaders$OrthLength = scale(beginningReaders$OrthLength,
+ scale=FALSE)
> beginningReaders$LogFrequency = scale(beginningReaders$LogFrequency,
+ scale=FALSE)
```

A first mixed-effects model for this data set is:

```
> beginningReaders.lmer = lmer(LogRT ~ PC1+PC2+PC3 + ReadingScore +
+ OrthLength + I(OrthLength^2) + LogFrequency + LogFamilySize +
+ (1|Word) + (1 |Subject), data = beginningReaders)
> pvals.fnc(beginningReaders.lmer, nsim = 1000)$fixed
                Estimate  MCMCmean HPD95lower HPD95upper pMCMC Pr(>|t|)
(Intercept)     7.545557  7.547105   7.476803   7.617784 0.001   0.0000
PC1             0.135777  0.135792   0.129275   0.142626 0.001   0.0000
PC2             0.056464  0.056584   0.047318   0.068183 0.001   0.0000
PC3            -0.027804 -0.027779  -0.039130  -0.017392 0.001   0.0000
ReadingScore   -0.004119 -0.004141  -0.005425  -0.002939 0.001   0.0000
OrthLength      0.045510  0.045346   0.036436   0.053244 0.001   0.0000
I(OrthLen^2)   -0.004114 -0.004107  -0.007593  -0.001189 0.020   0.0165
LogFrequency   -0.043652 -0.043798  -0.057531  -0.031607 0.001   0.0000
LogFamilySize  -0.014483 -0.014721  -0.031604   0.002729 0.090   0.0908
```

We note that there is an effect of family size, facilitatory as expected given previous work, and significant at the 5% level when evaluated with one-tailed tests.

Of special interest in this data set is the random-effects structure. In our initial model, we included only random intercepts, one for `Word` and one for `Subject`. However, in general, predictors tied to subjects (age, sex, handedness, education level, etc.) may require by-item random slopes, and predictors related to items (frequency, length, number of neighbors, etc.) may require by-subject random slopes. For the present example, it turns out we need by-subject random slopes for word length. These random slopes allow us to bring into the model that children cope in rather different ways with reading long words:

```
> beginningReaders.lmer1 = lmer(LogRT ~ PC1+PC2+PC3 + ReadingScore +
+ OrthLength + I(OrthLength^2) + LogFrequency + LogFamilySize +
+ (1|Word) + (1|Subject)+(0+OrthLength|Subject), beginningReaders)
> anova(beginningReaders.lmer1, beginningReaders.lmer)
                Df     AIC     BIC  logLik  Chisq Chi Df Pr(>Chisq)
begReaders.lmer 11  6019.1  6095.9 -2998.6
begReaders.lmer1 12 5976.8  6060.5 -2976.4 44.383      1   2.701e-11
> beginningReaders.lmer2 = lmer(LogRT ~ PC1+PC2+PC3 + ReadingScore +
+ OrthLength + I(OrthLength^2) + LogFrequency + LogFamilySize +
+ (1|Word) + (1|Subject)+(1+OrthLength|Subject), beginningReaders)
> anova(beginningReaders.lmer1, beginningReaders.lmer2)
                 Df     AIC     BIC  logLik  Chisq Chi Df Pr(>Chisq)
begReaders.lmer1 12  5976.8  6060.5 -2976.4
begReaders.lmer2 14  5980.1  6077.8 -2976.0 0.6781      2     0.7125
```

A similar series of steps shows we also need random slopes for `LogFrequency` and that again the correlation parameter can be dispensed with:

```
> beginningReaders.lmer3 = lmer(LogRT ~ PC1+PC2+PC3 + ReadingScore +
+ OrthLength + I(OrthLength^2) + LogFrequency + LogFamilySize +
+ (1|Word) + (1|Subject)+(0+OrthLength|Subject) +
+ (1+LogFrequency|Subject), data = beginningReaders)
> anova(beginningReaders.lmer1, beginningReaders.lmer3)
                 Df     AIC     BIC  logLik  Chisq Chi Df Pr(>Chisq)
begReaders.lmer1 12  5976.8  6060.5 -2976.4
begReaders.lmer3 15  5962.1  6066.8 -2966.1 20.647      3   0.0001246
> beginningReaders.lmer4 = lmer(LogRT ~ PC1+PC2+PC3 + ReadingScore +
+ OrthLength + I(OrthLength^2) + LogFrequency + LogFamilySize +
+ (1|Word) + (1|Subject)+(0+OrthLength|Subject) +
+ (0+LogFrequency|Subject), data = beginningReaders)
> anova(beginningReaders.lmer4, beginningReaders.lmer3)
                 Df     AIC     BIC  logLik  Chisq Chi Df Pr(>Chisq)
begReaders.lmer4 13  5961.1  6051.8 -2967.6
begReaders.lmer3 15  5962.1  6066.8 -2966.1 2.9944      2     0.2238
> anova(beginningReaders.lmer4, beginningReaders.lmer1)
                 Df     AIC     BIC  logLik  Chisq Chi Df Pr(>Chisq)
begReaders.lmer1 12  5976.8  6060.5 -2976.4
begReaders.lmer4 13  5961.1  6051.8 -2967.6 17.652      1   2.652e-05
```

After removal of outliers and refitting, we make sure that the random-effects parameters have sensible values and have properly constrained confidence intervals:

```
> beginningReaders.lmer4a = lmer(LogRT ~ PC1+PC2+PC3 + ReadingScore +
+ OrthLength + I(OrthLength^2) + LogFrequency + LogFamilySize +
+ (1|Word) + (1|Subject)+(0+OrthLength|Subject) +
+ (0+LogFrequency|Subject), data = beginningReaders,
+ subset=abs(scale(resid(beginningReaders.lmer4)))<2.5)
> x = pvals.fnc(beginningReaders.lmer4a, nsim=10000)
> x$random
           MCMCmean HPD95lower HPD95upper
sigma       0.30937    0.30436    0.31441
Word.(In)   0.06650    0.05690    0.07781
Sbjc.(In)   0.11441    0.09364    0.13845
Sbjc.OrtL   0.03182    0.02443    0.04168
```

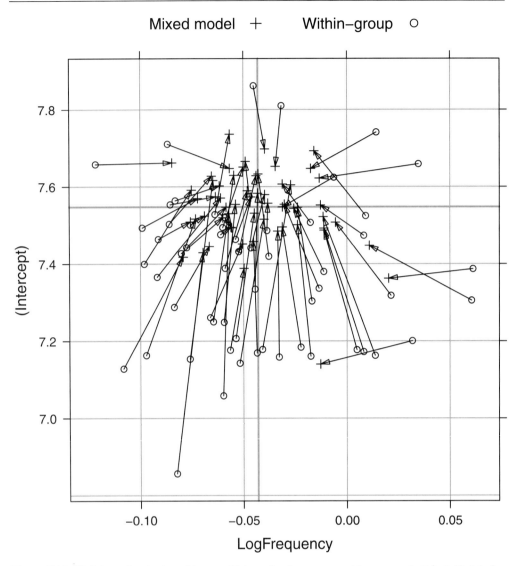

Figure 7.10. *Shrinkage for the by-subject coefficients for frequency and intercept:* `lmList()` *(circles, within-group estimates) versus* `lmer()` *(+ symbols). Solid grey lines denote the population means.*

```
Sbjc.LgFr    0.03191    0.02258    0.04416
deviance  4327.23205 4315.36462 4340.66993
```

Without linear mixed-effects models, it would be a formidable task to trace differential effects for frequency and word length such as observed for the children in this reading experiment in a principled way. Estimates of by-subject differences, which in actual tests evaluating reading skills in schools may be quite important, would be suboptimal without shrinkage (see Figure 7.10).

Finally, we examine the table of coefficients. The morphological family size effect (`LogFamilySize`) is now significant at the 5% level (one-tailed tests) according to both the MCMC p-value and the p-value based on the t-statistic:

```
> x = pvals.fnc(beginningReaders.lmer4a, nsim = 10000, withMCMC=TRUE)
> x$fixed
                Estimate   MCMCmean HPD95lower HPD95upper   pMCMC Pr(>|t|)
(Intercept)     7.584160   7.584132   7.505149   7.659856  0.0001   0.0000
PC1             0.127112   0.127097   0.120748   0.133404  0.0001   0.0000
PC2             0.050347   0.050476   0.040787   0.059970  0.0001   0.0000
PC3            -0.024551  -0.024680  -0.034846  -0.014469  0.0001   0.0000
ReadingScore   -0.004687  -0.004687  -0.006160  -0.003246  0.0001   0.0000
OrthLength      0.048587   0.048587   0.036764   0.060110  0.0001   0.0000
I(OrthLen^2)   -0.004540  -0.004530  -0.007847  -0.001198  0.0084   0.0076
LogFrequency   -0.046391  -0.046363  -0.061484  -0.030940  0.0001   0.0000
LogFamSize     -0.015548  -0.015412  -0.031732   0.001559  0.0756   0.0669
```

It is often useful to plot the fixed effects, but as yet there is no general plot method for `lmer` objects. As a consequence, we have to make the plots ourselves. As a first step, we extract the coefficients with `fixef()`:

```
> coefs = fixef(beginningReaders.lmer4a)
> coefs
  (Intercept)            PC1            PC2            PC3    ReadingScore
 7.584160135    0.127111560    0.050346964   -0.024551161    -0.004687245
   OrthLength I(OrthLength^2)   LogFrequency   LogFamilySize
 0.048587098    -0.004540186   -0.046390578    -0.015547652
```

We also attach the data frame: attaching a data frame makes the columns of the data frame immediately available.

```
> attach(beginningReaders)
```

Next, we select the ranges for each of the predictors for which we want to graph the partial effect on the reaction times, using the `max()` and `min()` functions, and feed these extreme values to `seq()` with the specification that it should create a vector with 40 equally spaced points in the range specified, except for the discrete length variable:

```
> pc1     = seq(min(PC1), max(PC1), length = 40)
> pc2     = seq(min(PC2), max(PC2), length = 40)
> pc3     = seq(min(PC3), max(PC3), length = 40)
> score   = seq(min(ReadingScore), max(ReadingScore), length = 40)
> freq    = seq(min(LogFrequency), max(LogFrequency), length = 40)
> olength = sort(unique(OrthLength))
> famsize = seq(min(LogFamilySize), max(LogFamilySize), length = 40)
```

Now consider plotting the partial effect for `LogFrequency`. We start with the intercept, and add the product of the coefficient for frequency and the vector of frequencies `freq`:

```
> plot(freq, coefs["(Intercept)"] + coefs["LogFrequency"] * freq)
```

This is sufficient to visualize the shape of the frequency effect, but if we would stop here the intercept of the regression line would be positioned for words with zero as the value for all other predictors. This is undesirable, as there are no words with zero length, for instance. To obtain an intercept that is appropriate for the most typical values of the other predictors, we adjust the intercept for the effects of the other predictors at their medians. We therefore define a vector with these adjustments:

```
> adjustments = c(coefs["PC1"] * median(PC1),
+    coefs["PC2"] * median(PC2),
+    coefs["PC3"] * median(PC3),
+    coefs["ReadingScore"] * median(ReadingScore),
+    coefs["OrthLength"] * median(OrthLength) +
+    coefs["I(OrthLength^2)"] * median(OrthLength)^2,
+    coefs["LogFrequency"] * median(LogFrequency),
+    coefs["LogFamilySize"] * median(LogFamilySize))
> adjustments
           PC1            PC2           PC3   ReadingScore
 2.653726e-02  -4.719135e-04  3.194531e-05  -2.192327e-01
   OrthLength   LogFrequency LogFamilySize
 1.101314e-02   3.487795e-03 -2.105395e-02
```

The required adjustment to the intercept for the partial effect of frequency is the sum of all these individual adjustments, with the exception of the adjustment for frequency itself, the sixth element of the vector of adjustments:

```
> sum(adjustments[-6])
[1] -0.2031762
```

We combine all bits and pieces into a data frame,

```
> dfr = data.frame(
+ x =
+  c(pc1, pc2, pc3, score, olength, freq, famsize),
+ y =
+  c(coefs["(Intercept)"] + coefs["PC1"] * pc1 + sum(adjustments[-1]),
+  coefs["(Intercept)"] + coefs["PC2"] * pc2 + sum(adjustments[-2]),
+  coefs["(Intercept)"] + coefs["PC3"] * pc3 + sum(adjustments[-3]),
+  coefs["(Intercept)"] + coefs["ReadingScore"] * score +
+    sum(adjustments[-4]),
+  coefs["(Intercept)"] + coefs["OrthLength"] * olength +
+  coefs["I(OrthLength^2)"] * olength^2 + sum(adjustments[-5]),
+  coefs["(Intercept)"] + coefs["LogFrequency"] * freq +
+    sum(adjustments[-6]),
+  coefs["(Intercept)"] + coefs["LogFamilySize"]*famsize +
+    sum(adjustments[-7])),
+ which =   # the grouping factor for xyplot()
+  c(rep("PC1", length(pc1)), rep("PC2", length(pc2)),
+  rep("PC3", length(pc3)), rep("Reading Score", length(score)),
+  rep("Length in Letters", length(olength)),
+  rep("Log Frequency", length(freq)), rep("Log Family Size",
+      length(famsize))))
```

and produce Figure 7.11 with xyplot():

```
> xyplot(y~x|which, data=dfr, ylim=c(6.5,8.0), scales="free",
+ as.table = TRUE, xlab=" ", ylab="Log RT",
+ panel = function(x, y) panel.lines(x,y))
```

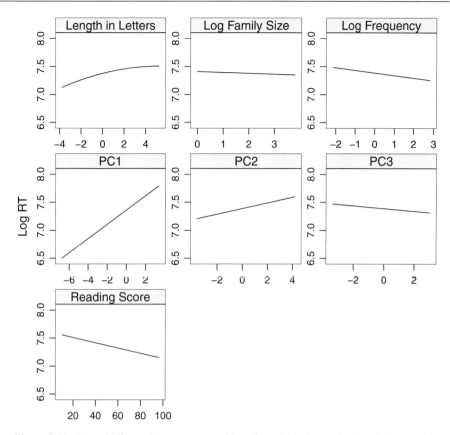

Figure 7.11. *Partial effects of frequency, word length, and family size for Dutch 8-year-olds in visual lexical decision. Length in letters and Log Frequency have been centralized.*

The effects for frequency, word length, and reading score are large compared to the effect of family size, but small compared to that of PC I. Note that the nonlinear effect for length suggests a ceiling effect — beginning readers have difficulties with longer word lengths, but by a length of 9, reaction times are just about as slow as they can be. We should keep in mind that we imposed a functional form on the effect of length by using a quadratic polynomial, and a restricted cubic spline could be considered instead. To visualize mixed-effects models with splines obtained with `rcs()`, you can use the plot function for mixed-effects models in the `languageR` package, `plotLMER.fnc()` (see the on-line help for details).

7.5.4   Mixed-effects models in corpus linguistics

The final example of a mixed-effects model comes from corpus linguistics. Keune *et al.* (2005) studied the frequency of use of words ending in the Dutch suffix *-lijk* (compare *-ly* in English) in written Dutch in the Netherlands and in Flanders. The data, available as `writtenVariationLijk`, bring together counts in seven newspapers, four from Flanders and three from the

Netherlands, representing three global registers (Regional, National, and Quality newspapers). From each of these newspapers, the first 1.5 million words available in the condiv corpus (Grondelaers *et al.*, 2000) were selected. The frequencies for the 80 most frequent words in *-lijk* are available in the column labeled Count:

```
> writtenVariationLijk[1:4,]
    Corpus        Word Count     Country Register
1   belang aantrekkelijk   26    Flanders Regional
2    gazet aantrekkelijk   17    Flanders Regional
3 laatnieu aantrekkelijk   19    Flanders National
4  limburg aantrekkelijk   33 Netherlands Regional
```

There are two sets of questions that we want to address. First of all, are words in *-lijk* used more often in the Netherlands, or more often in Flanders? Are there similar differences in their use across written registers? These are questions that concern the presence or absence of main effects of Country and Register, as well as their interaction. Second, to what extent might main effects be modulated by differences that are specific to the individual words in *-lijk*? Questions of this kind concern the random effects of Word.

We analyze the data with a generalized mixed-effects model, but we do not use the BINOMIAL DISTRIBUTION, which is appropriate for counts of successes and failures. Instead, we use the POISSON DISTRIBUTION (with a log link function), which is appropriate for counts of events in a fixed time window. Here, the fixed time window is 1.5 million words. Note that a count of, e.g. 26 occurrences for *aantrekkelijk* in a subcorpus of 1.5 million words, defines the rate at which this word appears in that subcorpus.

We begin with a simple model with only random intercepts,

```
> writtenVariationLijk.lmer = lmer(Count ~ Country*Register + (1|Word),
+ data = writtenVariationLijk, family = "poisson")
```

and then fit a more complex model with random slopes for Country:

```
> writtenVariationLijk.lmer1 = lmer(Count ~ Country * Register +
+ (1+Country|Word), data = writtenVariationLijk,
+ family = "poisson")
```

A likelihood ratio test shows that adding random slopes is fully justified, and the summary of the model provides reasonable estimates:

```
> anova(writtenVariationLijk.lmer, writtenVariationLijk.lmer1)
                   Df     AIC     BIC  logLik  Chisq Chi Df Pr(>Chisq)
writVarLijk.lmer    7  4505.6  4535.9 -2245.8
writVarLijk.lmer1   9  2856.5  2895.5 -1419.3 1653.1      2  < 2.2e-16
> print(writtenVariationLijk.lmer1, corr=FALSE)
Random effects:
 Groups Name                 Variance Std.Dev. Corr
 Word   (Intercept)          0.87432  0.93505
        CountryNetherlands   0.40269  0.63458  -0.356
number of obs: 560, groups: Word, 80

Estimated scale (compare to  1 )  1.948123
```

```
Fixed effects:
                                Estimate Std. Error z value Pr(>|z|)
(Intercept)                      3.62081    0.10576   34.24  < 2e-16
CountryNetherlands               0.28381    0.07421    3.82 0.000131
RegisterQuality                 -0.04582    0.01992   -2.30 0.021447
RegisterRegional                 0.14419    0.01667    8.65  < 2e-16
CountryNeth:RegisterQuality      0.02022    0.02649    0.76 0.445275
CountryNeth:RegisterRegional    -0.22597    0.02432   -9.29  < 2e-16
```

However, the choice of the Poisson distribution entails the assumption that the variance of the errors increases with the mean. The ratio of the two should be 1. The estimated actual ratio for our data, listed as `Estimated scale` is 1.9, so we are running the risk of overdispersion. There are several ways in which this lack of goodness of fit can be addressed. One option is to allow the variance of the errors to increase with the square of the mean, instead of with the mean, retaining the log link function to constrain the predicted counts to be non-negative:

```
> writtenVariationLijk.lmer1A = lmer(Count ~ Country * Register +
+ (1|Word) + (1+Country|Word), data = writtenVariationLijk,
+ family = quasi(link = "log", variance = mu^2))
```

We inspect the coefficients with `pvals.fnc()`. As Markov chain Monte Carlo sampling is not yet implemented for generalized linear mixed models, p-values are based on the t-statistic:

```
> pvals.fnc(writtenVariationLijk.lmer1A)
                                          Estimate Pr(>|t|)
(Intercept)                              3.5683284   0.0000
CountryNetherlands                       0.3867314   0.0000
RegisterQuality                          0.1518658   0.0825
RegisterRegional                         0.2493743   0.0010
CountryNetherlands:RegisterQuality      -0.1162445   0.3469
CountryNetherlands:RegisterRegional     -0.3455769   0.0029
```

An alternative for count data is to apply either a square root transformation or a log transformation. We select the square root transformation here, leaving the log transformation as an exercise, and now fit a straightforward linear mixed-effects model:

```
> writtenVariationLijk.lmer1B = lmer(sqrt(Count) ~ Country * Register +
+ (1+Country|Word), data = writtenVariationLijk)
> pvals.fnc(writtenVariationLijk.lmer1B)$fixed
                      Estimate HPD95lower HPD95upper  pMCMC Pr(>|t|)
(Intercept)            6.5878    5.60904     7.5638 0.0001   0.0000
CountryNetherlands     1.2284    0.69321     1.7596 0.0001   0.0000
RegisterQuality        0.3026   -0.04734     0.6415 0.0872   0.0885
RegisterRegional       0.7884    0.49056     1.0944 0.0001   0.0000
CountryNeth:RegQuality -0.2273   -0.74825     0.2355 0.3506   0.3652
CountryNeth:RegRegional -1.1157  -1.58444    -0.6503 0.0001   0.0000
```

Since the two alternative models support the presence of the same main effects and their interaction, we return to the original Poisson model. We add the fitted counts to the data, and compare them with the observed counts:

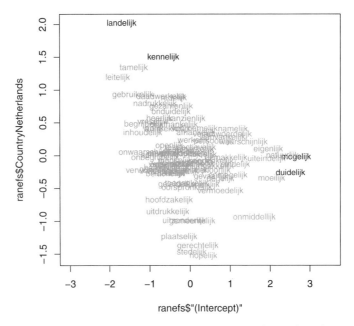

Figure 7.12. *The* BLUPs *for intercept and CountryNetherlands in the Poisson model fit to counts of words with the Dutch suffix* -lijk *in seven Dutch and Flemish newspapers.*

```
> writtenVariationLijk$fitted = exp(fitted(writtenVariationLijk.lmer1))
> cor(writtenVariationLijk$fitted, writtenVariationLijk$Count)^2
[1] 0.9709
```

It is clear that the fit is good. (An alternative option that we might consider here is to use `family="quasipoisson"` instead of `family="poisson"`. This option relaxes the requirement that the dispersion parameter should be close to 1.)

We can visualize how the coefficients of individual words compare to the population means by plotting pairs of random effects. For instance, suppose we want to compare differences in the frequencies of the words as they are used in the Dutch and Flemish national newspapers. Since the national newspapers represent the reference level, this comparison can be carried out graphically by plotting the BLUPs for the intercept against the BLUPs for `CountryNetherlands`, as shown in Figure 7.12. One can read off the scatterplot that *mogelijk* ("possible") and *duidelijk* ("clear") are words that appear more often in the Flemish newspaper (they are at the far right of the plot), whereas *landelijk* ("country-specific") and *kennelijk* ("apparently") are more fashionable in the corresponding Dutch newspaper (they are at the top of the graph):

```
> ranefs = ranef(writtenVariationLijk.lmer1)$Word
> plot(ranefs$"(Intercept)", ranefs$CountryNetherlands, type="n")
> text(ranefs$"(Intercept)", ranefs$CountryNetherlands,
+ rownames(ranefs), cex = 0.8)
```

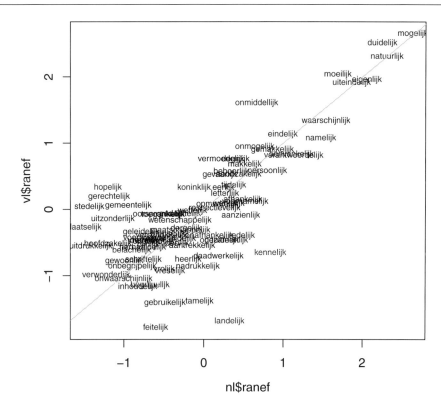

Figure 7.13. *By-word adjustments for Flanders and the Netherlands according to a mixed-effects Poisson model with equal variances for the random effects for Country. Words with positive scores are used more often than the population average; words above the diagonal are used preferentially in Flanders.*

When we are dealing with random slopes for a factor, a different parameterization is available that assumes: (i) that the adjustments for different levels are uncorrelated; and (ii) that the variances for the different factor levels are identical. This is often useful for factors with more than two levels. We illustrate it here for the two-level factor `Country`:

```
> writtenVariationLijk.lmer2 = lmer(Count ~ Country * Register +
+ (1|Word)+(1|Country:Word), writtenVariationLijk, family="poisson")
> writtenVariationLijk.lmer2
Random effects:
 Groups        Name         Variance Std.Dev.
 Country:Word (Intercept) 0.20135  0.44872
 Word         (Intercept) 0.66323  0.81439
number of obs: 560, groups: Country:Word, 160; Word, 80
```

The BLUPs for word now specify adjustments for the words with respect to their population average,

```
> words = ranef(writtenVariationLijk.lmer2)[[2]]
> head(words, 3)
```

```
                     (Intercept)
aantrekkelijk   -0.3008298
aanvankelijk     0.8413145
aanzienlijk      0.1609281
```

and the BLUPs for Country now specify independent country-specific adjustments:

```
> countries = ranef(writtenVariationLijk.lmer2)[[1]]
> head(countries,3)
                            (Intercept)
Flanders:aantrekkelijk -0.24646081
Flanders:aanvankelijk  -0.01005619
Flanders:aanzienlijk    -0.25390726
> tail(countries, 3)
                                (Intercept)
Netherlands:werkelijk            0.13987759
Netherlands:wetenschappelijk -0.09695836
Netherlands:wettelijk           -0.07178403
```

We can combine these BLUPs to obtain by-word adjustments for Flanders and for the Netherlands. When plotted (see Figure 7.13) they provide an intuitive overview of the country-specific preferences:

```
> countries$which = factor(substr(rownames(countries),1,4))
> countries$words = rep(rownames(words),2)
> countries$intWords = rep(words[,1], 2)
> countries$ranef = countries$"(Intercept)" + countries$intWords
> vl = countries[countries$which=="Flan",]
> nl = countries[countries$which!="Flan",]
> plot(nl$ranef, vl$ranef, type="n")
> text(nl$ranef, vl$ranef, nl$words, cex=0.7)
> abline(0, 1, col="grey")
```

Mixed-effects models thus provide a useful tool side by side with principal components analysis and correspondence analysis for the joint study of the textual frequencies of a large number of words. They offer the advantage that the significance of main effects and interactions can be ascertained directly, while offering insight into the specific properties of the individual words through their BLUPs.

Workbook section

Exercises

1. Consider our final model for the visual lexical decision data lexdec3.lmerE, and test whether subjects differ in their sensitivity to word length. Answering this exercise involves three steps. First, recreate lexdec3 and make sure that Trial and also Length are centered. Then recreate lexdec3.lmerE with the centered version of word length as predictor. Second, add Length as a random slope for subject, once without and once with a correlation parameter for the random intercepts and random slopes for length. Third, use the anova() function to select the appropriate model.

2. Above, we modeled the reaction times of young children to Dutch words with a mixed-effects model with both `Subject` and `Word` as random effect:

```
> beginningReaders.lmer4 = lmer(LogRT ~  PC1 + PC2 + PC3  +
+ ReadingScore + OrthLength + I(OrthLength^2) + LogFrequency +
+ LogFamilySize + (1|Word) + (1|Subject)+(0+LogFrequency|Subject) +
+ (0+OrthLength|Subject), data = beginningReaders)
```

Show that the presence of the random effect for `Word` is justified by first fitting a model with the same fixed effects but without `Word` as random effect, followed by a likelihood ratio test comparing `beginningReaders.lmer4` with this new, more parsimonious model. Next, consider whether random slopes are required for `PC1`. Do not include parameters for correlations with other random slopes.

3. Investigate whether the following predictors should be added to the model for the self-paced reading latencies (`reading.lmerA`): subjective frequency rating (`Rating`), word length (`LengthInLetters`), and the number of synsets (`NumberOfSynsets`). The starting model of this exercise is obtained with the following lines of code:

```
> selfPacedReadingHeid =
+  selfPacedReadingHeid[selfPacedReadingHeid$RT > 5 &
+  selfPacedReadingHeid$RT < 7.2,]
> x = selfPacedReadingHeid[,12:15]
> x.pr = prcomp(x, center = T, scale = T)
> selfPacedReadingHeid$PC1 = x.pr$x[,1]
> selfPacedReadingHeid$PC2 = x.pr$x[,2]
> selfPacedReadingHeid$PC3 = x.pr$x[,3]
> selfPacedReadingHeid.lmer = lmer(RT ~ RTtoPrime +
+ LengthInLetters + PC1 * Condition + (1|Subject) + (1|Word),
+ data = selfPacedReadingHeid)
```

4. Use the `writtenVariationLijk` data set to fit a mixed-effects model with the logarithm of `Count` as the dependent variable, with `Country` and `Register` and their interaction as fixed-effects predictors, and with random intercepts for `Word` and by-word random slopes for `Country`. Consider the residuals, remove outliers, refit the model, and inspect the residuals of the trimmed model.

5. We return to the data on the use of word order and ergative case marking in Lajamanu Warlpiri for which the first exercise of Chapter 2 considered a mosaic plot. Use a mixed-effects logistic regression model with `Speaker` and `Text` as random effects, `CaseMarking` (ergative versus other) as dependent variable, and as predictors `AnimacyOfSubject`, `AnimacyOfObject`, `OvertnessOfObject`, `WordOrder` (whether the subject is initial), and `AgeGroup` (child versus adult) to study how children and adults use the ergative case. Begin with a simple main effects model with all predictors included. Then remove the two object-related predictors, and refit. Finally include an interaction of `AgeGroup` by `WordOrder`. The data set is available as `warlpiri`.

6. In Chapter 4 (section 4.4.1) we fitted a model of covariance to size ratings obtained by averaging over subjects. The question addressed here is whether the results of this by-item

analysis are supported by a mixed-effects model. The data are available as the data set `sizeRatings`. Fit a model with `Subject` and `Word` as crossed random effects, with `Rating` as dependent variable, and with the `MeanFamiliarity` ratings for the words and `Class` as predictors. Also include two variables that provide information on the subjects: `Language`, which specifies whether their native language is English, and `Naive`, which specifies whether the subjects were informed about the purpose of the experiment. Include interactions of `Class` by `Naive` and of `Language` by the linear and quadratic terms of `MeanFamiliarity`.

7. Verify that the simpler model for the corpus data, `writtenVariationLijk.lmer2`, is justified compared to the more complex model `writtenVariationLijk.lmer1`, using a likelihood ratio test.

Appendix A   Solutions to the exercises

1.1

```
> spanishMeta
    Author YearOfBirth  TextName PubDate Nwords    FullName
1        C        1916 X14458gll    1983   2972        Cela
2        C        1916 X14459gll    1951   3040        Cela
...
> colnames(spanishMeta)
[1] "Author"      "YearOfBirth" "TextName"    "PubDate"     "Nwords"
[6] "FullName"
> nrow(spanishMeta)
[1] 15
```

1.2

```
> xtabs(~ Author, data=spanishMeta)
Author
C M V
5 5 5
```

The means can be obtained in two ways:

```
> aggregate(spanishMeta$PubDate, list(spanishMeta$Author), mean)
  Group.1      x
1       C 1956.0
2       M 1990.2
3       V 1974.6
> tapply(spanishMeta$PubDate, list(spanishMeta$Author), mean)
     C      M      V
1956.0 1990.2 1974.6
```

1.3

```
> spanishMeta[order(spanishMeta$YearOfBirth, spanishMeta$Nwords),]
```

1.4

```
> v = spanishMeta$PubDate
> sort(v)
 [1] 1942 1948 1951 1956 1963 1965 1977 1981 1982 1983
[11] 1986 1987 1989 1992 2002
> ?sort
> sort(v, decreasing=T)
 [1] 2002 1992 1989 1987 1986 1983 1982 1981 1977 1965
[11] 1963 1956 1951 1948 1942
> sort(rownames(spanishMeta))
```

```
[1] "1"   "10" "11" "12" "13" "14" "15" "2"   "3"   "4"
[11] "5"   "6"   "7"   "8"   "9"
```

1.5

```
> spanishMeta[spanishMeta$PubDate < 1980, ]
```

1.6

```
> mean(spanishMeta$PubDate)
[1] 1973.6
> sum(spanishMeta$PubDate)/length(spanishMeta$PubDate)
[1] 1973.6
```

1.7

```
> spanishMeta = merge(spanishMeta, composer, by.x="FullName",
+ by.y="Author")
```

2.1

```
> warlpiri.xtabs= xtabs( ~ CaseMarking + AnimacyOfSubject + AgeGroup +
+ WordOrder, data = warlpiri)
> mosaicplot(warlpiri.xtabs,xlab="",ylab="",main="")
```

Figure A.1 reveals an asymmetry in how frequently adults and children use ergative case marking across word orders. For instance, in subject-initial sentences,
adults are more likely to use ergative case marking for animate subjects than
children.

2.2 (Figure A.2)

```
> par(mfrow = c(1, 2))
> plot(exp(heid2$BaseFrequency), exp(heid2$MeanRT))
> plot(heid2$BaseFrequency, heid2$MeanRT)
> par(mfrow=c(1, 1))
```

2.3 (Figure A.3)

```
> plot(log(ranks), log(moby.table),
+ xlab = "log rank", ylab = "log frequency")
```

2.4

```
> xylowess.fnc(RT   Trial | Subject, data = lexdec, ylab="log RT")
```

Figure A.4 suggests that subject T2 speeds up as the experiment proceeds, possibly
due to within-experiment learning of how to do lexical decision efficiently. Subject
D started out with fast response latencies, but slowed down later in the experiment,
possibly because of fatigue.

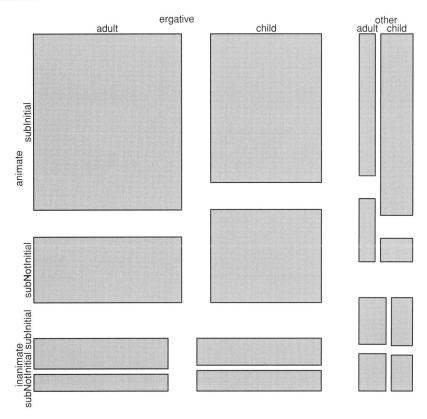

Figure A.1. *Mosaic plot for the use of ergative case marking in Lajamanu Warlpiri, cross-classified by the animacy of the subject (left: inanimate versus animate), word order (left: initial versus non-initial subject), case-marking (top: ergative versus other) and age group (top: adult versus child).*

2.5

```
> library(MASS)
> par(mfrow = c(1, 2))
> truehist(english$RTnaming)
> plot(density(english$RTnaming))
> par(mfrow = c(1, 1))
```

The histogram and the density of Figure A.5 show two separate peaks or MODES. This BIMODAL distribution consists of two almost separate distributions, one for the younger subjects, and one for the older subjects.

```
> library(lattice)
> bwplot(RTnaming ~ Voice | AgeSubject, data = english)
```

The trellis boxplot (not shown) illustrates that the distribution of longer latencies belongs to the older subjects. The boxplot also visualizes the effect of the differential sensitivity of the voicekey for how naming latencies are registered: Voiced phonemes are registered earlier.

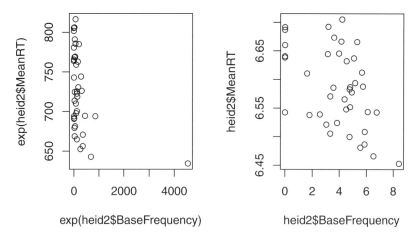

Figure A.2. *Scatterplots of reaction time in visual lexical decision by base frequency for neologisms in -heid without (left) and with (right) logarithmically transformed variables. Note that without the log transformation, the pattern in the data is dominated by just one word with a very high base frequency.*

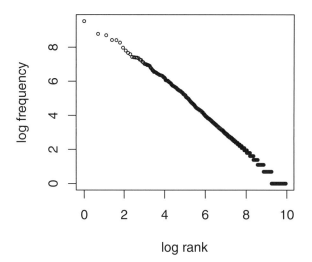

Figure A.3. *Scatterplot for frequency and rank in the double logarithmic plane for Melville's* Moby Dick. *Except for the six highest-frequency words, the pattern is reasonably linear, as expected on the basis of Zipf's law.*

3.1

```
> wonderland$hare = wonderland$word=="hare"    #March Hare
> countOfHare = tapply(wonderland$hare, wonderland$chunk, sum)
> countOfHare.tab = xtabs(~countOfHare)
> wonderland$very = wonderland$word=="very"
> countOfVery = tapply(wonderland$very, wonderland$chunk, sum)
> countOfVery.tab = xtabs(~countOfVery)
```

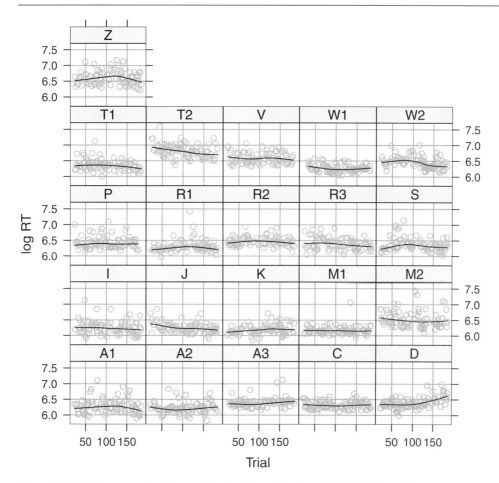

Figure A.4. *Trellis scatterplot with smoother for RT as a function of Trial. Each panel represents one subject.*

3.2

```
> plot(1:40, countOfAlice, type = "h")
> plot(1:40, countOfVery,  type = "h")
> plot(1:40, countOfHare,  type = "h")
```

The three leftmost panels in Figure A.6 illustrate that *Alice* and *very* occur relatively uniformly through the text, but that *hare* occurs only in the second half of the text (in the collocate *March Hare*), and even there it is bursty instead of being relatively evenly distributed across the chunks.

3.3

```
> plot(as.numeric(names(countOfAlice.tab)), countOfAlice.tab/
+ sum(countOfAlice.tab), type = "h", xlim = c(0,18), ylim = c(0,0.9))
> plot(as.numeric(names(countOfVery.tab)), countOfVery.tab/
```

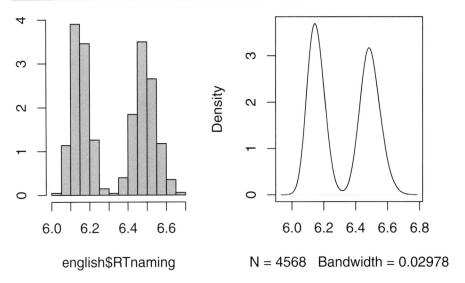

Figure A.5. *Histogram and density of the naming latencies to* 2197 *English monomorphemic monosyllabic words, collected for two subject populations (old and young speakers).*

```
+ sum(countOfVery.tab), type = "h", xlim = c(0,18), ylim = c(0,0.4))
> plot(as.numeric(names(countOfHare.tab)), countOfHare.tab/
+ sum(countOfHare.tab), type = "h", xlim = c(0,18), ylim = c(0,0.9))
```

See the three panels in the second column of Figure A.6.

3.4

```
> plot(0:18, dpois(0:18, mean(countOfAlice)), type = "h",
+ xlim = c(0, 18), ylim = c(0, 0.9))
> plot(0:18, dpois(0:18, mean(countOfVery)), type = "h",
+ xlim = c(0, 18), ylim = c(0, 0.4))
> plot(0:18, dpois(0:18, mean(countOfHare)), type = "h",
+ xlim = c(0, 18), ylim = c(0, 0.9))
```

See the third column of panels in Figure A.6. Note that for *Alice* and *very*, the Poisson densities might be smoothed versions of the sample densities. However, for *hare* the sample densities are very unevenly distributed compared to the Poisson density.

3.5

```
> plot(qpois(1:20 / 20, mean(countOfAlice)), quantile(countOfAlice,
+ 1:20 / 20), xlab="theoretical quantiles", ylab = "sample quantiles")
> plot(qpois(1:20 / 20, mean(countOfVery)), quantile(countOfVery,
+ 1:20 / 20), xlab="theoretical quantiles", ylab = "sample quantiles")
> plot(qpois(1:20 / 20, mean(countOfHare)), quantile(countOfHare,
+ 1:20 / 20), xlab="theoretical quantiles", ylab = "sample quantiles")
```

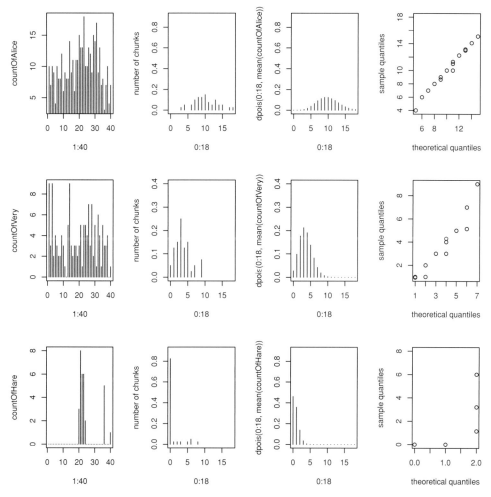

Figure A.6. *Counts of the occurrences of* Alice, hare *and* very *across text chunks (left), sample densities (second column), the corresponding Poisson densities (third column), and quantile-quantile plots (right).*

See the fourth column of panels in Figure A.6. The quantile-quantile plots are roughly linear for *Alice* and *very*, and therefore support the possibility that *Alice* and *very* are Poisson-distributed. By contrast, *hare* clearly does not follow a Poisson distribution.

3.6

```
> 1 - ppois(10, 4)
[1] 0.002839766
```

A much better estimate of λ is the mean across chunks, 9.95:

```
> 1 - ppois(10, 9.95)
[1] 0.410705
```

That this is a good estimate of the actual proportion of chunks with 10 or more occurrences is verified with the `quantile()` function, supplied with the complementary proportion:

```
> quantile(countOfAlice, 0.589295)
58.9295%
      10
```

4.1

```
> chisq.test(verbs.xtabs)

        Pearson's Chi-squared test with Yates' continuity correction

data:  verbs.xtabs
X-squared = 13.9948, df = 1, p-value = 0.0001833
```

4.2 We first estimate the rate at which *het* appears in chunks of 1000 words:

```
> lambda = mean(havelaar$Frequency)
```

Given `lambda`, we apply a Kolmogorov-Smirnov test, with the vector of frequencies as its first argument, the distribution function `ppois()` as its second argument, and the Poisson parameter `lambda` as its third argument:

```
> ks.test(havelaar$Frequency, "ppois", lambda)

        One-sample Kolmogorov-Smirnov test

D = 0.1198, p-value = 0.1164

Warning message: cannot compute correct p-values with ties
```

The large *p*-value suggests that there is no reason to suppose that the frequency of *het* does not follow a Poisson distribution. However, if we resolve the ties using `jitter()`, we do find evidence against *het* following a Poisson distribution:

```
> ks.test(jitter(havelaar$Frequency), "ppois", lambda)
D = 0.1738, p-value = 0.004389
```

4.3 Density plots (Figure A.7) show that `DurationOfPrefix` is roughly symmetrically distributed, but that `Frequency` is roughly symmetrical only after a log transform:

```
> par(mfrow = c(1, 3), pty = "s")
> plot(density(durationsGe$DurationOfPrefix), main="duration")
> plot(density(durationsGe$Frequency), main = "frequency")
> plot(density(log(durationsGe$Frequency)), main = "log frequency")
> par(mfrow = c(1, 1), pty = "m")
```

Both distributions have slightly thicker right tails, so it does not come as a surprise that the Shapiro-Wilk test of normality is significant:

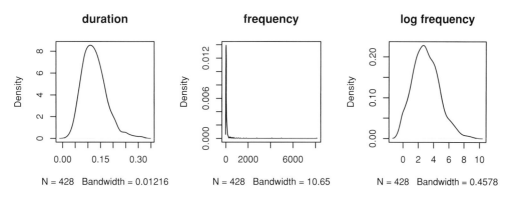

Figure A.7. *Densities for the duration of the Dutch prefix* ge- *and the frequencies of its carrier words.*

```
> shapiro.test(durationsGe$DurationOfPrefix)
...
W = 0.9633, p value = 7.37e 09

> shapiro.test(log(durationsGe$Frequency))
...
W = 0.9796, p-value = 9.981e-06
```

There is sufficient symmetry to run a linear model, although we should keep an eye open for the harmful effect of outliers (see Chapter 6 for further discussion):

```
> ge.lm = lm(DurationOfPrefix ~ log(Frequency + 1), data = durationsGe)
> summary(ge.lm)

Call:
lm(formula = DurationOfPrefix ~ log(Frequency + 1), data = ge)

Residuals:
      Min        1Q    Median        3Q       Max
-0.101404 -0.031994 -0.006107  0.027866  0.185379

Coefficients:
                    Estimate Std. Error t value Pr(>|t|)
(Intercept)         0.139883   0.005028   27.82  < 2e-16
log(Frequency + 1) -0.004658   0.001429   -3.26  0.00121
---

Residual standard error: 0.04689 on 426 degrees of freedom
Multiple R-Squared: 0.02433,    Adjusted R-squared: 0.02204
F-statistic: 10.62 on 1 and 426 DF,  p-value: 0.001205
```

We observe significant predictivity for frequency: more frequent words tend to have past participles with a shorter prefix. The *R*-squared, however, is only a mere 2%. On the one hand, this is not surprising, as the model neglects many other potential predictors such as speech rate. On the other hand, these data do not suggest that the quality of a speech synthesis system would benefit greatly by making the duration of the prefix depend on word frequency.

4.4 A model with an interaction with the quadratic term is specified as follows:

```
> ratings.lm = lm(meanSizeRating ~ meanFamiliarity * Class +
+ I(meanFamiliarity^2)*Class, data = ratings)
```

Inspection of the summary,

```
> summary(ratings.lm)
...
Coefficients:
                                Estimate Std. Error t value Pr(>|t|)
(Intercept)                      4.16838    0.59476   7.008 8.95e-10
meanFamiliarity                 -0.48424    0.32304  -1.499   0.1381
Classplant                       1.02187    1.86988   0.546   0.5864
I(meanFamiliarity^2)             0.09049    0.04168   2.171   0.0331
meanFamiliarity:Classplant      -1.18747    0.87990  -1.350   0.1812
Classplant:I(meanFamiliarity^2)  0.11254    0.10087   1.116   0.2681
...
```

shows that this interaction is not significant. Note that by including one superfluous interaction the significance of the majority of other predictors in the model is masked.

4.5 Given the objects `alice`, `very`, and `hare` as created in the exercise for Chapter 3, we carry out the Kolmogorov-Smirnov tests as follows:

```
> ks.test(countOfAlice, ppois, mean(countOfAlice))
D = 0.1181, p-valuc = 0.6325
> ks.test(countOfVery, ppois, mean(countOfVery))
D = 0.1902, p-value = 0.1106
> ks.test(countOfHare, ppois, mean(countOfHare))
D = 0.4607, p-value = 8.449e-08
```

There is no evidence that *Alice* and *very* do not follow a Poisson distribution. *Hare*, however, is clearly not Poisson-distributed.

4.6 We have the choice between using `lm()` for a one-way analysis of variance,

```
> english.lm = lm(RTlexdec ~ AgeSubject, data = english)
> summary(english.lm)$coef
Coefficients:
                  Estimate Std. Error t value Pr(>|t|)
(Intercept)       6.493500   0.001069  6073.7   <2e-16
AgeSubjectyoung  -0.341989   0.001512  -226.2   <2e-16
```

or between using the `aov()` function:

```
> summary(aov(RTnaming ~ AgeSubject, data = english))
             Df  Sum Sq Mean Sq F value    Pr(>F)
AgeSubject    1 133.564 133.564   51161 < 2.2e-16
Residuals  4566  11.920   0.003
```

The `lm()` function is more useful, because it informs us that the difference between the two group means is −0.34, and that the group mean for the old subjects is 6.49. To obtain the group mean for the young subjects, we subtract 0.34:

```
> 6.493500 - 0.341989
[1] 6.151511
```

4.7 We use `lm()` for the analysis of covariance:

```
> summary(lm(DurationPrefixNasal ~ PlosivePresent + Frequency,
+ data = durationsOnt, subset = DurationPrefixNasal > 0))
Coefficients:
                    Estimate Std. Error t value Pr(>|t|)
(Intercept)        0.0723609  0.0037796  19.145  < 2e-16
PlosivePresentyes -0.0218871  0.0034788  -6.292 9.88e-09
log(Frequency)    -0.0016590  0.0009575  -1.733   0.0864
---
Residual standard error: 0.0155 on 94 degrees of freedom
Multiple R-Squared: 0.3194,      Adjusted R-squared: 0.305
F-statistic: 22.06 on 2 and 94 DF,  p-value: 1.395e-08
```

The effect of frequency is in the expected direction: a greater frequency of use implies greater reduction. Hence, we are allowed to use a one-tailed test, and accept it as a significant predictor. If the plosive is present, the nasal is realized shorter than when it is absent, which is suggestive of a compensatory lengthening effect.

5.1

```
> dat = affixProductivity[affixProductivity$Registers == "L", ]
> dat.pr = prcomp(dat[ , 1:27], center = T, scale = T)
> summary(dat.pr)
Importance of components:
                         PC1   PC2   PC3    PC4    PC5
Standard deviation      2.030 1.768 1.635 1.5789 1.5271
Proportion of Variance 0.153 0.116 0.099 0.0923 0.0864
Cumulative Proportion  0.153 0.268 0.367 0.4597 0.5461
```

We visually inspect the first four PCs with `pairscor.fnc()`:

```
> pairscor.fnc(data.frame(dat.pr$x[,1:4], birth = dat$Birth))
```

The result is shown in Figure A.8. Date of birth is significantly correlated with PC2, also when Milton and Startrek are removed from the data set:

```
> dat2 = dat[-c(21, 18),]
> dat2.pr = prcomp(dat2[ , 1:27], center = T, scale = T)
> cor.test(dat2.pr$x[,2], dat2$Birth)
t = -4.3786, df = 24, p-value = 0.0002017
        cor
-0.6663968
```

A biplot (Figure A.9) suggests that the early authors used *-able, est*, and *be-* more productively, and that the late authors used *-ize* and *-less* more productively:

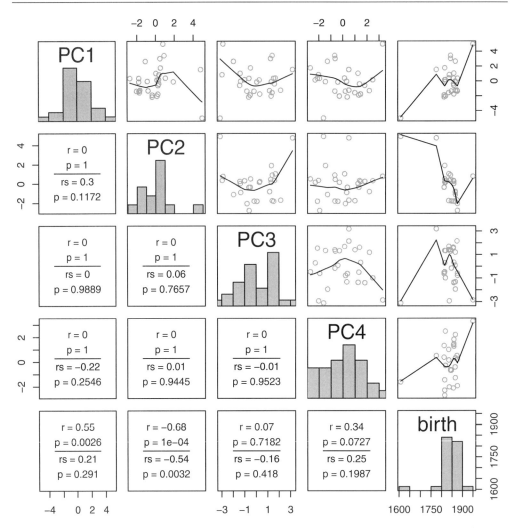

Figure A.8. *Scatterplot matrix for the correlations of the principal components for 27 texts in productivity space. Note that all PCs are pairwise uncorrelated, as expected, and that PC2 is significantly correlated with year of birth.*

```
> biplot(dat2.pr, var.axes = F)
```

5.2

```
> lexicalMeasures.cor = cor(lexicalMeasures[, -1], method = "spearman")^2
> lexicalMeasures.scale = cmdscale(dist(lexicalMeasures.cor), k = 2)
```

To plot the two kinds of measures in black and grey, we define a vector with the semantic measures, and take advantage of the subscripting capacities of R:

```
> semanticvars = c("Vf", "Dent", "NsyC", "NsyS", "CelS", "Fdif",
+ "NVratio", "Ient")
> plot(lexicalMeasures.scale[,c(1,2)],type="n")
> text(lexicalMeasures.scale[,c(1,2)], rownames(lexicalMeasures.scale),
```

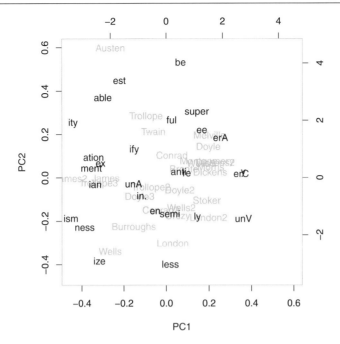

Figure A.9. *Biplot for texts and affixes, the second principal component captures year of birth.*

```
+ col=c("red","blue")[(rownames(lexicalMeasures.scale) %in% semanticvars)+
+ 1])
```

The result is shown in Figure A. 10.

5.3

```
> finalDevoicing[1:3,]
       Word Onset1Type Onset2Type VowelType ConsonantType
1 madelief       None  Sonorant       iuy          None
2     boes       None Obstruent       iuy          None
3 accuraat       None  Sonorant      long          None
  Obstruent Nsyll Stress     Voice
1         F     3      F    voiced
2         S     1      F    voiced
3         T     3      F voiceless
```

A CART tree is fitted to the data with,

```
> finalDevoicing.rp = rpart(Voice ~ ., data = finalDevoicing[ , -1])
```

where we exclude the column labeling the words. We examine the cross-validation error scores by plotting the object, select `cp = 0.021` and prune accordingly:

```
> plotcp(finalDevoicing.rp)
> finalDevoicing.rp1 = prune(finalDevoicing.rp, cp = 0.021)
```

Finally, we plot the cross-validated tree, shown in Figure A.11:

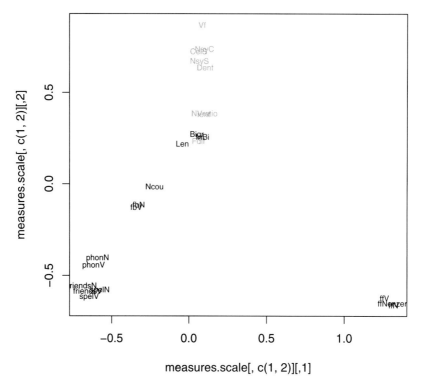

Figure A.10. *Multidimensional scaling for the correlation matrix of lexical measures for 2233 English monomorphemic and monosyllabic words. Semantic measures are shown in grey, non-semantic measures are depicted in black.*

```
> plot(finalDevoicing.rp1, margin = 0.1, compress = T)
> text(finalDevoicing.rp1, use.n = T, pretty = 0)
```

The main split is on the type of obstruent: labiodental and velar fricatives (F, X), as opposed to alveolar fricatives (S) and plosives (P, T). The latter subset is partitioned by vowel type (phonologically long vowels, including phonetically short high vowels) versus short vowels. The phonologically long vowels are in turn partitioned by whether the obstruent is an alveolar fricative or a plosive. Final splits are by sonorant type. Note that, not surprisingly, the characteristics of the onset (Onset1Type, Onset2Type) are not predictive. We cross-tabulate observed and expected voicing,

```
> xtab = xtabs(~ finalDevoicing$Voice +
+ predict(finalDevoicing.rp1, finalDevoicing, type="class"))
> xtab
           predict(finalDevoicing.rp1, finalDevoicing, type = "class")
finalDevoicing$Voice voiced voiceless
           voiced      387       205
           voiceless   104      1001
```

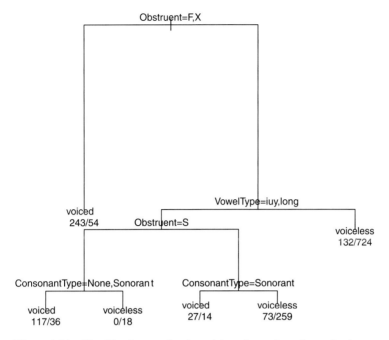

Figure A.11. *Classification tree for the voicing alternation of stem-final obstruents in Dutch monomorphemic verbs.*

and observe a classification accuracy of 82% that is a significant improvement on the classification accuracy of a baseline model that always selects `voiceless`:

```
> xtabs(~finalDevoicing$Voice)
finalDevoicing$Voice
   voiced voiceless
      592      1105
> prop.test(c(387+1001, 1105), rep(nrow(finalDevoicing), 2))
...
X-squared = 120.1608, df = 1, p-value < 2.2e-16
   prop 1    prop 2
...
0.8179140 0.6511491
```

5.4 We follow exactly the same steps as in the analysis of the tag trigrams:

```
> spanishFunctionWords.t = t(spanishFunctionWords)
> spanishFunctionWords.t =
+   spanishFunctionWords.t[order(rownames(spanishFunctionWords.t)), ]
> spanishFunctionWords.pca =
+   prcomp(spanishFunctionWords.t, center = T, scale = T)
```

The number of orthogonal dimensions to be considered in what follows is:

```
> sdevs = spanishFunctionWords.pca$sdev^2
> n = sum(sdevs/sum(sdevs)> 0.05)
> n
[1] 8
```

The cross-validation `for loop` is,

```
> predictedClasses = rep("", 15)
> for (i in 1:15) {
+    training = spanishFunctionWords.t[-i,]
+    trainingAuthor = spanishMeta[-i,]$Author
+    training.pca = prcomp(training, center = T, scale = T)
+    training.x = data.frame(training.pca$x)
+    training.x = training.x[order(rownames(training.x)), ]
+    training.pca.lda = lda(training[ , 1:n], trainingAuthor)
+    cl=predict(training.pca.lda,spanishFunctionWords.t[,1:n])$class[i]
+    predictedClasses[i] = as.character(cl)
+ }
```

and the number of correctly attributed texts is,

```
> sum(predictedClasses==spanishMeta$Author)
[1] 8
```

which fails to reach significance:

```
> sum(dbinom(8:15, 15, 1/3))
[1] 0.0882316
```

As is often found, trigram probabilities emerge as superior to the probabilities of function words.

5.5

```
> regularity.svm = svm(regularity[, -c(1, 8, 10)],
+ regularity$Regularity, cross=10)
> summary(regularity.svm)
10-fold cross-validation on training data:

Total Accuracy: 81.85714
Single Accuracies:
 80 72.85714 82.85714 87.14286 78.57143 84.28571 80 87.14286 ...
```

The cross-validated number of correct classifications is,

```
> round(0.81857*nrow(regularity),1)
[1] 573
```

and given that selecting the majority option would result in 541 correct classifications,

```
> xtabs(~regularity$Regularity)
regularity$Regularity
irregular    regular
      159        541
```

we apply a proportions test,

```
> prop.test(c(541, 573), rep(nrow(regularity),2))
X-squared = 4.2228, df = 1, p-value = 0.03988
alternative hypothesis: two.sided
```

```
95 percent confidence interval:
 -0.08931373 -0.00211484
sample estimates:
   prop 1    prop 2
0.7728571 0.8185714
```

and observe we have achieved a small but significant gain in classification accuracy with the support vector machine.

6.1 Running the examples for the `english` data set with,

```
> example(english)
```

will add the PCs to the data frame. A model which takes `PC1` to have a linear effect on naming latency,

```
> naming.ols = ols(RTnaming ~ AgeSubject + rcs(WrittenFrequency, 3) +
+ rcs(WrittenFrequency,3) :  AgeSubject + PC1,
+ data = english, x = T, y = T)
> naming.ols
Coefficients:
                              Value Std. Error        t  Pr(>|t|)
Intercept                 6.565e+00  0.0050947 1288.5788 0.000e+00
AgeSubject=young         -3.753e-01  0.0071771  -52.2845 0.000e+00
WrittenFrequency         -1.536e-02  0.0013106  -11.7213 0.000e+00
WrittenFrequency'         5.160e-03  0.0016263    3.1731 1.518e-03
PC1                      -5.792e-05  0.0003473   -0.1668 8.676e-01
Age=young * WrittenFreq   7.497e-03  0.0018488    4.0552 5.092e-05
Age=young * WrittenFreq' -3.937e-03  0.0022998   -1.7120 8.696e-02
```

suggests that it is not significant, its slope is very small and indistinguishable from a zero slope. However, models that allow `PC1` to have a nonlinear effect,

```
> naming.ols = ols(RTnaming ~ AgeSubject + rcs(WrittenFrequency, 3) +
+ rcs(WrittenFrequency, 3) :  AgeSubject + rcs(PC1, 3),
+ data = english, x = T, y = T)
> naming.ols
Coefficients:
                             Value Std. Error        t  Pr(>|t|)
Intercept                 6.554979  0.0052809 1241.260 0.000e+00
AgeSubject=young         -0.375250  0.0071427  -52.536 0.000e+00
WrittenFrequency         -0.014801  0.0013070  -11.325 0.000e+00
WrittenFrequency'         0.004611  0.0016206    2.845 4.455e-03
PC1                      -0.004213  0.0007091   -5.941 3.039e-09
PC1'                      0.005685  0.0008471    6.711 2.173e-11
Age=young * WrittenFreq   0.007497  0.0018399    4.075 4.685e-05
Age=young * WrittenFreq' -0.003937  0.0022888   -1.720 8.545e-02
```

suggest it is a significant predictor. Figure A.12,

```
> plot(naming.ols, PC1 = NA)
```

reveals initial facilitation followed by inhibition. A linear model averages over these opposite trends, unsurprisingly resulting in a null effect.

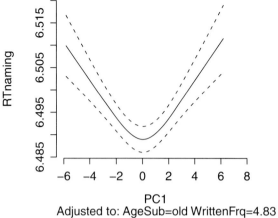

Figure A.12. *The partial effect of PC1 on the naming latencies in the*
english data set.

6.2 We first create the data distribution object:

```
> finalDevoicing.dd = datadist(finalDevoicing)
> options(datadist = "finalDevoicing.dd")
```

We then fit a logistic regression model to the data with `lrm()`,

```
> finalDevoicing.lrm = lrm(Voice ~ VowelType+ConsonantType+
+ Obstruent+Nsyll+Stress+Onset1Type+Onset2Type, data=finalDevoicing)
```

and inspect the significance of the predictors with an ANOVA table:

```
> anova(finalDevoicing.lrm)
                Wald Statistics           Response: Voice

 Factor        Chi-Square d.f.  P
 VowelType       130.65     2   <.0001
 ConsonantType   103.40     2   <.0001
 Obstruent       194.87     4   <.0001
 Nsyll            20.77     1   <.0001
 Stress            5.67     2    0.0586
 Onset1Type        0.77     2    0.6811
 Onset2Type        6.06     2    0.0483
 TOTAL           351.37    15   <.0001
```

The relevance of the last three variables is questionable, unsurprisingly, they are
removed by `fastbw()`:

```
> fastbw(finalDevoicing.lrm)

 Deleted    Chi-Sq d.f.  P       Residual d.f.  P       AIC
 Onset1Type 0.77   2     0.6811   0.77    2      0.6811  -3.23
 Onset2Type 5.30   2     0.0707   6.07    4      0.1942  -1.93
 Stress     5.38   2     0.0678  11.45    6      0.0755  -0.55
 ...
```

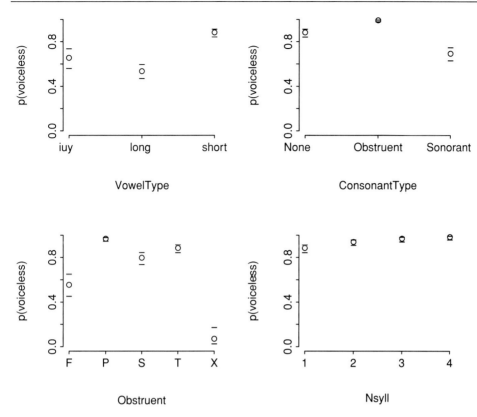

Figure A.13. *Partial effects of the predictors in a logistic regression model for the probability of a Dutch word having a non-alternating final obstruent.*

We redo the simplified model by hand,

```
> finalDevoicing.lrm = lrm(Voice ~ VowelType + ConsonantType +
+ Obstruent + Nsyll, data = finalDevoicing, x = T, y = T)
> anova(finalDevoicing.lrm)
                    Wald Statistics          Response: Voice

     Factor        Chi-Square d.f. P
     VowelType       128.24    2     <.0001
     ConsonantType   100.25    2     <.0001
     Obstruent       196.45    4     <.0001
     Nsyll            18.01    1     <.0001
     TOTAL           348.07    9     <.0001
```

and plot the partial effects, as shown in Figure A.13.

```
> plot(finalDevoicing.lrm, fun = plogis, ylim = c(0, 1),
+ ylab = "p(voiceless)")
```

Finally, we validate the model with 200 bootstrap runs:

```
> validate(finalDevoicing.lrm, B = 200)
...
```

```
           index.orig     training         test      optimism
Dxy        0.755124129  0.752633653 0.7493642840  0.003269369
R2         0.517717019  0.520005018 0.5126806067  0.007324411
Intercept  0.000000000  0.000000000 0.0017320605 -0.001732060
Slope      1.000000000  1.000000000 0.9764758156  0.023524184
...
           index.corrected    n
Dxy          0.7518547594 200
R2           0.5103926079 200
Intercept    0.0017320605 200
Slope        0.9764758156 200
...
```

The small values for the optimism show that the model validates well.

6.3

```
> validate(dutch.lrm.pen, B = 200)
           index.orig     training         test      optimism
Dxy        0.686301864  0.695511136 0.6717651914  0.023745944
R2         0.397411938  0.407178229 0.3842901407  0.022888089
Intercept  0.000000000  0.000000000 0.0347286565 -0.034728656
Slope      1.000000000  1.000000000 0.9615599722  0.038440028
           index.corrected
Dxy          0.6625559192
R2           0.3745238493
Intercept    0.0347286565
Slope        0.9615599722
```

The slope is closer to one, and the intercept closer to zero, so the danger of overfitting has indeed been reduced.

6.4 We rerun the model,

```
> etym.lrm = lrm(formula = Regularity ~ rcs(WrittenFrequency, 3) +
+ rcs(FamilySize, 3) + NcountStem + InflectionalEntropy + Auxiliary +
+ Valency + NVratio + WrittenSpokenRatio + EtymAge, data = etym,
+ x = T, y = T)
> anova(etym.lrm)
                Wald Statistics         Response: Regularity

Factor                Chi-Square d.f.  P
WrittenFrequency       18.15      2    0.0001
 Nonlinear             15.67      1    0.0001
FamilySize              7.28      2    0.0262
 Nonlinear              6.46      1    0.0110
NcountStem             10.23      1    0.0014
InflectionalEntropy     4.53      1    0.0334
Auxiliary               6.64      2    0.0362
Valency                 6.67      1    0.0098
NVratio                 4.97      1    0.0257
WrittenSpokenRatio      4.18      1    0.0408
EtymAge                12.96      4    0.0115
TOTAL NONLINEAR        18.50      2    0.0001
TOTAL                  55.77     15    <.0001
```

but before we accept it, we should validate it:

```
> validate(etym.lrm, bw = T, B = 200)
...
          Frequencies of Numbers of Factors Retained

  2   3   4   5   6   7   8   9
  1   1  14  28  39  39  41  37
                index.orig      training        test      optimism
Dxy           0.621491185  0.639033808 0.549117995  0.089915814
R2            0.382722800  0.404198572 0.300891734  0.103306838
Intercept     0.000000000  0.000000000 0.004753967 -0.004753967
Slope         1.000000000  1.000000000 0.749752658  0.250247342
          index.corrected
Dxy           0.531575371
R2            0.279415962
Intercept     0.004753967
Slope         0.749752658
...
```

There is substantial optimism and a large change in the slope, so it makes sense to shrink the estimated coefficients:

```
> pentrace(etym.lrm, seq(0, 0.8, by = 0.05))

Best penalty:

 penalty       df
    0.65 13.76719
...

> etym.lrm2 = update(etym.lrm, penalty = 0.65, x = T, y = T)
> anova(etym.lrm2)
                  Wald Statistics          Response: Regularity

 Factor                   Chi-Square d.f.  P
 WrittenFrequency         15.99       2    0.0003
  Nonlinear               13.57       1    0.0002
 FamilySize                5.92       2    0.0518
  Nonlinear                5.25       1    0.0219
 NcountStem                9.62       1    0.0019
 InflectionalEntropy       4.39       1    0.0362
 Auxiliary                 6.17       2    0.0458
 Valency                   6.73       1    0.0095
 NVratio                   5.01       1    0.0251
 WrittenSpokenRatio        3.53       1    0.0601
 EtymAge                  11.58       4    0.0207
 TOTAL NONLINEAR          16.36       2    0.0003
 TOTAL                    57.42      15    <.0001
> plot(etym.lrm2, EtymAge = NA, fun = plogis, ylab = "p(regular)",
+ ylim = c(0,1))
```

The partial effects of the predictors are shown in Figure A.14. The lower right panel shows the effect of etymological age. Only two of the labels for the tick marks are shown. As the labels are ordered by the ordering of the factor levels,

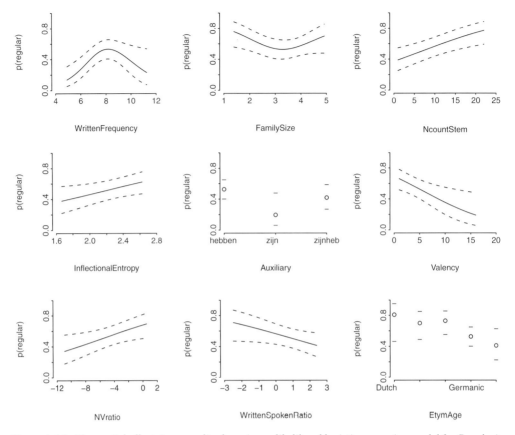

Figure A.14. *The partial effects in a penalized maximum likelihood logistic regression model for Regularity for a data set of* 285 *Dutch verbs.*

etymological age increases from left to right. Hence, we see that the probability of being regular decreases with increasing etymological age.

The nonlinear effect of frequency in the upper left panel is an artefact of the selection of the data. The present subset of verbs was selected such that the mean written frequency for regulars and irregulars was approximately matched. As there are approximately the same number of regular and irregular verbs in the sample, and as low-frequency irregular verbs are infrequent, the composition of the sample is such that low-frequency regular verbs are underrepresented compared to the population.

6.5 The second correct model formulation specifies the slope for the second part of the data as an adjustment to the slope for the first part. The model with both main effects includes two intercepts, one for the regression line to the left of the vertical axis, and a second intercept for the regression line to its right. For our breakpoint analysis, we want a model with a single intercept that is shared by both lines. The anova test shows that this additional intercept is indeed superfluous:

```
> faz.both  = lm(LogFrequency ~ ShiftedLogDistance : PastBreakPoint,
+ data = faz)
> faz.bothB = lm(LogFrequency ~ ShiftedLogDistance * PastBreakPoint,
+ data = faz)
> anova(faz.both, faz.bothB)
Analysis of Variance Table

Model 1: LogFrequency ~ ShiftedLogDistance:PastBreakPoint
Model 2: LogFrequency ~ ShiftedLogDistance * PastBreakPoint
  Res.Df     RSS  Df Sum of Sq      F Pr(>F)
1    797 259.430
2    796 259.429   1     0.001 0.0033 0.9544
```

6.6 We convert words to lower case with `tolower()` for each text:

```
> alice = tolower(alice)
> through = tolower(through)
> oz = tolower(oz)
> moby = tolower(moby)
```

We base our comparisons on the first 27269 words in each text:

```
> compare.richness.fnc(alice, through[1:27269])
                Tokens Types HapaxLegomena GrowthRate
alice            27269  2615          1166    0.04276
through[1:27269] 27269  2727          1208    0.04430

two-tailed tests:
                          Z      p
Vocabulary Size      -2.7041 0.0068
Vocabulary Growth Rate -1.0113 0.3119
```

Apparently, there is a small difference in lexical richness between the two novels by Carroll. *The Wonderful Wizard of Oz*, on the other hand, has a substantially smaller lexical richness than *Alice's Adventures in Wonderland*.

```
> compare.richness.fnc(alice, oz[1:27269])
            Tokens Types HapaxLegomena GrowthRate
alice        27269  2615          1166    0.04276
oz[1:27269]  27269  2383          1003    0.03678

two-tailed tests:
                        Z p
Vocabulary Size      5.8457 0
Vocabulary Growth Rate 4.0938 0
```

The lexical richness of *Moby Dick* is substantially greater, as expected for a novel aimed at an adult audience:

```
> compare.richness.fnc(alice, moby[1:27269])
                Tokens Types HapaxLegomena GrowthRate
alice            27269  2615          1166    0.04276
moby[1:27269]    27269  5405          3314    0.12153
```

```
two-tailed tests:
                                Z p
Vocabulary Size          -47.2373 0
Vocabulary Growth Rate -36.9145 0
```

6.7

```
> nesscg.spc = spc(m = nesscg$m, Vm = nesscg$Vm)
> nessw.spc = spc(m = nessw$m, Vm = nessw$Vm)
> nessdemog.spc = spc(m = nessdemog$m, Vm = nessdemog$Vm)
```

A model for context-governed spoken English with an excellent fit is obtained with:

```
> nesscg.fzm = lnre("fzm", nesscg.spc)
> nesscg.fzm
finite Zipf-Mandelbrot LNRE model.
...
Population size: S = 810.356
...
Goodness-of-fit (multivariate chi-squared test):
        X2 df         p
   6.811325   4 0.1462011
```

A very similar model for the demographic sample of spoken English is:

```
> nessdemog.fzm = lnre("fzm", nessdemog.spc)
> nessdemog.fzm
...
Population size: S = 839.2886
...
Goodness-of-fit (multivariate chi-squared test):
        X2 df         p
   4.157912   3 0.2449096
```

A finite Zipf-Mandelbrot model,

```
> nessw.fzm = lnre("fzm", nessw.spc)
> nessw.fzm
finite Zipf-Mandelbrot LNRE model.
...
Population size: S = 4867.91
...
Goodness-of-fit (multivariate chi-squared test):
        X2 df         p
   31.76712 13 0.002600682
```

turns out to be inferior to a Generalized Inverse Gauss-Poisson model:

```
> nessw.gigp = lnre("gigp", nessw.spc)
> nessw.gigp
Generalized Inverse Gauss-Poisson (GIGP) LNRE model.
...
Population size: S = 5974.933
...
Goodness-of-fit (multivariate chi-squared test):
        X2 df         p
   22.62322 13 0.04642629
```

We plot the growth curves for 40 equally sized intervals between 0 and 106957, the number of tokens sampled for -*ness* in the written subcorpus, the largest subcorpus of the BNC. After calculating the vocabulary growth curves with `lnre.vgc()`,

```
> nessw.vgc = lnre.vgc(nessw.gigp, seq(0, N(nessw.spc), length = 40))
> nessdemog.vgc = lnre.vgc(nessdemog.fzm, seq(0, N(nessw.spc),
+ length = 40))
> nesscg.vgc = lnre.vgc(nesscg.fzm, seq(0, N(nessw.spc), length = 40))
```

we graph them with `plot()`, adding a legend (see Figure A.15):

```
> plot(nessw.vgc, nessdemog.vgc, nesscg.vgc, lwd = rep(1, 3),
+ lty=c(1,1,2), col=c("black", "grey", "black"),
+ legend=c("written", "spoken:demographic", "spoken:context-governed"))
```

The population number of types estimated for the demographic and context-governed subcorpora are 839 and 810 respectively. We add these horizontal asymptotes to the plot:

```
> abline(h = 839, col = "grey")
> abline(h = 810, col = "black")
```

Note that both curves for spoken language have almost reached their asymptotic values within the range of sample sizes shown. By contrast, -*ness* in written English is nowhere near reaching its asymptote, which is estimated at 5975 types. This difference between morphological productivity between spoken and written registers of English is also apparent from the growth rates of the vocabulary, which we calculate here for the sample size of the sample with the largest number of tokens:

```
> nessw.lnre.spc = lnre.spc(nessw.gigp, N(nessw.spc), m.max = 1)
> Vm(nessw.lnre.spc, 1)/N(nessw.lnre.spc)
[1] 0.008786915
> nessdemog.lnre.spc = lnre.spc(nessdemog.fzm, N(nessw.spc),
+ m.max = 1)
> Vm(nessdemog.lnre.spc, 1)/N(nessdemog.lnre.spc)
[1] 0.0003230424
> nesscg.lnre.spc = lnre.spc(nesscg.fzm, N(nessw.spc),m.max=1)
> Vm(nesscg.lnre.spc, 1)/N(nesscg.lnre.spc)
[1] 0.0002389207
```

At this large sample size, the differences in productivity are even more pronounced than for a comparison based on the smallest sample size, the demographic sub-corpus:

```
> nessw.lnre.spc = lnre.spc(nessw.gigp, N(nessdemog.spc), m.max = 1)
> Vm(nessw.lnre.spc, 1)/N(nessw.lnre.spc)
[1] 0.1544806
> nessdemog.lnre.spc=lnre.spc(nessdemog.fzm,N(nessdemog.spc),m.max=1)
> Vm(nessdemog.lnre.spc, 1)/N(nessdemog.lnre.spc)
[1] 0.08195576
> nesscg.lnre.spc = lnre.spc(nesscg.fzm, N(nessdemog.spc),m.max=1)
> Vm(nesscg.lnre.spc, 1)/N(nesscg.lnre.spc)
[1] 0.08755167
```

Vocabulary Growth

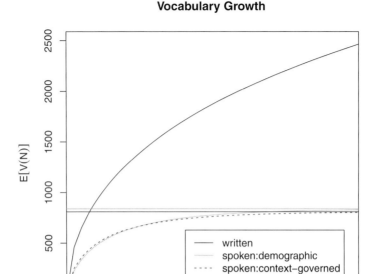

Figure A.15. *The growth curve of the vocabulary for the English suffix -ness in the three main subcorpora of the British National Corpus.*

6.8 We fit a first covariance model:

```
> imaging.lm=lm(FilteredSignal~BehavioralScore*Condition,data=imaging)
> summary(imaging.lm)
Residuals:
      Min       1Q   Median       3Q      Max
 -22.5836  -2.7216  -0.7092   3.7008  10.1119

Coefficients:
                                   Estimate Std. Error t value Pr(>|t|)
(Intercept)                         69.5804     4.2089  16.532  < 2e-16
BehavioralScore                     -0.2606     0.2147  -1.214  0.23405
Conditionsemantics                 -10.2184     4.6626  -2.192  0.03605
BehavioralScore:Conditionsemantics   0.7787     0.2498   3.118  0.00392

Residual standard error: 5.926 on 31 degrees of freedom
Multiple R-Squared: 0.3674,    Adjusted R-squared: 0.3061
F-statistic: 6.001 on 3 and 31 DF,  p-value: 0.002396
```

The residuals of this model are clearly asymmetrical, not surprising given the marked outlier structure visible in Figure 6.20, so model criticism is called for. A plot of the model provides a series of diagnostic plots, from which data points with row numbers 1 and 19 emerge as outliers with high leverage (see Figure A.16):

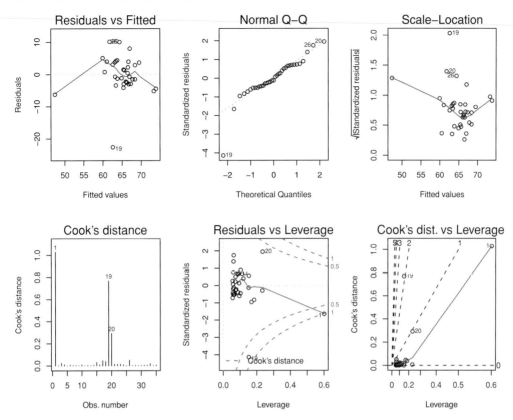

Figure A.16. *Diagnostic plots for the linear model fit to the reconstructed patient data from Tyler* et al. (2005).

```
> par(mfrow=c(2,3))
> plot(imaging.lm, which = 1:6)
> par(mfrow=c(1,1))
```

After removal of these two outliers, there are no significant effects:

```
> imaging.lm = lm(FilteredSignal ~ BehavioralScore * Condition,
+    data = imaging[-c(1,19), ])
> summary(imaging.lm)

Residuals:
    Min     1Q  Median     3Q     Max
-6.525 -2.525   0.140  1.685   7.980

Coefficients:
                                    Estimate Std. Error t value Pr(>|t|)
(Intercept)                          65.71994    2.67193  24.596   <2e-16
BehavioralScore                       0.03398    0.14019   0.242    0.810
Conditionsemantics                   -2.71410    3.24800  -0.836    0.410
BehavioralScore:Conditionsemantics    0.23757    0.18560   1.280    0.211

Residual standard error: 3.673 on 29 degrees of freedom
```

```
Multiple R-Squared: 0.1494,     Adjusted R-squared: 0.06145
F-statistic: 1.698 on 3 and 29 DF,  p-value: 0.1892
```

The correlation of 0.82 reported by Tyler and colleagues for the semantic condition depends on the presence of a single outlier, and reduces to 0.52 after removal of this outlier. We conclude that it cannot be claimed for this data set that the priming scores for the semantic condition are predictive for the intensity of the filtered signal.

7.1 We first rebuild `lexdec3.lmerE`:

```
> lexdec2 = lexdec[lexdec$RT < 7 , ]
> lexdec3 = lexdec2[lexdec2$Correct == "correct", ]
> lexdec3$cTrial = lexdec3$Trial - mean(lexdec3$Trial)
> lexdec3$cLength = lexdec3$Length - mean(lexdec3$Length)
> lexdec3.lmerE = lmer(RT ~ cTrial + Frequency +
+ NativeLanguage * cLength + meanWeight +
+ (1|Subject) + (0+cTrial|Subject) + (1|Word), lexdec3)
```

Next, we add `cLength` to the random-effects specification for `Subject`:

```
> lexdec3.lmerE1 = lmer(RT ~ cTrial + Frequency + meanWeight +
+ NativeLanguage*cLength + (1|Word) + (1|Subject) +
+ (0+cTrial|Subject) + (0+cLength|Subject), data = lexdec3)
> lexdec3.lmerE2 = lmer(RT ~ cTrial + Frequency + meanWeight +
+ NativeLanguage*cLength + (1|Word) + (1+cLength|Subject) +
+ (0+cTrial|Subject), data = lexdec3)
```

Finally, we compare the models with the `anova()` function,

```
> anova(lexdec3.lmerE, lexdec3.lmerE1)
               Df      AIC       BIC    logLik  Chisq Chi Df Pr(>Chisq)
lexdec3.lmerE  10 -1370.90 -1317.39   695.45
lexdec3.lmerE1 11 -1374.59 -1315.73   698.29 5.6933      1    0.01703
> anova(lexdec3.lmerE1, lexdec3.lmerE2)
               Df      AIC       BIC    logLik  Chisq Chi Df Pr(>Chisq)
lexdec3.lmerE1 11 -1374.59 -1315.73   698.29
lexdec3.lmerE2 12 -1379.12 -1314.92   701.56 6.5351      1    0.01058
```

and find that the correlation parameter for the by-subject slopes for length and intercepts is justified. The table of coefficients shows that the interaction of NativeLanguage by Length survives the subject variability for length:

```
> pvals.fnc(lexdec3.lmerE2, nsim=10000)$fixed
                Estimate HPD95lower HPD95upper   pMCMC Pr(>|t|)
(Intercept)    6.4485380   6.356195  6.5442545  0.0001   0.0000
cTrial        -0.0002073  -0.000551  0.0001224  0.2130   0.2098
Frequency     -0.0404660  -0.051234 -0.0290932  0.0001   0.0000
meanWeight     0.0236185   0.009854  0.0360040  0.0004   0.0003
NatLanOth      0.1377618   0.022278  0.2629398  0.0278   0.0120
cLength        0.0026727  -0.007001  0.0125276  0.5776   0.5850
NatLanOth:cLen 0.0189074   0.006944  0.0308654  0.0038   0.0015
```

7.2 We fit models with and without `Word` as random effect to the data,

```
> beginningReaders.lmer4 = lmer(LogRT ~ PC1+PC2+PC3 + ReadingScore +
+ OrthLength + I(OrthLength^2) + LogFrequency + LogFamilySize +
+ (1|Word) + (1|Subject)+(0+OrthLength|Subject) +
+ (0+LogFrequency|Subject), data = beginningReaders)
> beginningReaders.lmer4w = lmer(LogRT ~ PC1+PC2+PC3 + ReadingScore +
+ OrthLength + I(OrthLength^2) + LogFrequency + LogFamilySize +
+ (1|Subject)+(0+OrthLength|Subject) + (0+LogFrequency|Subject),
+ data = beginningReaders)
```

and compare the two models with `anova()`:

```
> anova(beginningReaders.lmer4, beginningReaders.lmer4w)
                   Df     AIC      BIC   logLik   Chisq Chi Df Pr(>Chisq)
begReaders.lmer4w  12  6059.5   6143.2  -3017.8
begReaders.lmer4   13  5961.1   6051.8  -2967.6  100.40      1   < 2.2e-16
```

The likelihood ratio test clearly provides ample justification for including `Word` as random effect. Next, we add random slopes for `PC1`,

```
> beginningReaders.lmer4pc1 = lmer(LogRT ~ PC1+PC2+PC3 + ReadingScore +
+ OrthLength + I(OrthLength^2) + LogFrequency + LogFamilySize +
+ (1|Word) +  (1|Subject) + (0+LogFrequency|Subject) +
+ (0+OrthLength|Subject) + (0+PC1|Subject), data = beginningReaders)
```

and carry out a likelihood ratio test to ascertain whether these random slopes are justified:

```
> anova(beginningReaders.lmer4, beginningReaders.lmer4pc1)
                    Df    AIC      BIC   logLik Chisq Chi Df Pr(>Chisq)
begReaders.lmer4    13  5961.1   6051.8  -2967.6
begReaders.lmer4pc1 14  5778.3   5876.0  -2875.2 184.8      1   < 2.2e-16
```

We check that the confidence intervals of the random effects are all properly bounded:

```
> x = pvals.fnc(beginningReaders.lmer4pc1, nsim=10000)
> x$random
            MCMCmean HPD95lower HPD95upper
sigma        0.33694    0.33167    0.34248
Word.(In)    0.06244    0.05412    0.07303
Sbjc.(In)    0.06304    0.05027    0.07901
Sbjc.LgFr    0.05190    0.04085    0.06596
Sbjc.OrtL    0.05307    0.04182    0.06773
Sbjc.PC1     0.06127    0.04853    0.07745
```

7.3

```
> reading.lmer = lmer(RT ~ RTtoPrime + PC1 * Condition +
+ Rating + LengthInLetters + NumberOfSynsets +
+ (1|Subject) + (1|Word), data = selfPacedReadingHeid)
> pvals.fnc(reading.lmer, nsim=10000)$fixed
                  Estimate  HPD95lower HPD95upper   pMCMC  Pr(>|t|)
(Intercept)       5.005005    4.646787   5.364812  0.0001    0.0000
RTtoPrime         0.094166    0.051356   0.139342  0.0002    0.0000
PC1               0.153690    0.133163   0.174926  0.0001    0.0000
Conditnheidheid  -0.005611   -0.043819   0.028946  0.7524    0.7629
```

```
Rating            0.028568   -0.018961    0.079343 0.2560    0.2514
LengthInLetters   0.029624    0.001995    0.058489 0.0378    0.0362
NumberOfSynsets   0.011431   -0.012116    0.034077 0.3280    0.3335
PC1:Condheidheid -0.025404 - -0.049701   -0.001355 0.0422    0.0415
```

Only word length is relevant as additional predictor.

7.4 The desired initial model is,

```
> writtenVariationLijk.lmer = lmer(log(Count) ~ Country * Register +
+ (Country|Word), data = writtenVariationLijk)
> aovlmer.fnc(writtenVariationLijk.lmer, noMCMC=TRUE)
Analysis of Variance Table
                 Df Sum Sq Mean Sq       F     Df2         p
Country           1   0.98    0.98  6.7945  554.00      0.01
Register          2   2.70    1.35  9.3265  554.00 1.038e-04
Country:Register  2   3.79    1.89 13.0942  554.00 2.777e-06
```

but its residuals are weirdly distributed, as shown in the left panel of Figure A.17:

```
> qqnorm(resid(writtenVariationLijk.lmer))
```

We therefore consider a trimmed model with the offending data points excluded:

```
> writtenVariationLijk.lmerA = lmer(log(Count) ~ Country * Register +
+ (Country|Word), data = writtenVariationLijk,
+ subset = resid(writtenVariationLijk.lmer) > -0.5)
> aovlmer.fnc(writtenVariationLijk.lmerA, noMCMC=TRUE)
                 Df Sum Sq Mean Sq       F     Df2         p
Country           1   0.67    0.67  7.4609  524.00      0.01
Register          2   1.07    0.53  5.9767  524.00 2.713e-03
Country:Register  2   1.97    0.99 11.0275  524.00 2.036e-05
```

The residuals of this trimmed model are well-behaved, as shown in the right panel of Figure A.17. Note that 30 outliers (the difference in `Df2`) gave rise to *p*-values for the untrimmed model that are too small.

7.5

```
> warlpiri.lmer = lmer(CaseMarking ~ WordOrder + AgeGroup +
+ AnimacyOfSubject + OvertnessOfObject + AnimacyOfObject +
+ (1|Text) + (1|Speaker), family = "binomial", data = warlpiri)
```

Inspection of the model summary shows that the two predictors relating specifically to the `Object` are irrelevant. We refit the model without them, and now include the interaction of `AgeGroup` by `WordOrder` that emerged from the mosaic plot of this data set that we made earlier:

```
> warlpiri.lmer = lmer(CaseMarking ~ WordOrder * AgeGroup +
+ AnimacyOfSubject + (1|Text) + (1|Speaker),
+ family = "binomial", data = warlpiri)
> warlpiri.lmer
Random effects:
 Groups  Name        Variance Std.Dev.
 Speaker (Intercept) 0.454679 0.67430
 Text    (Intercept) 0.019611 0.14004
```

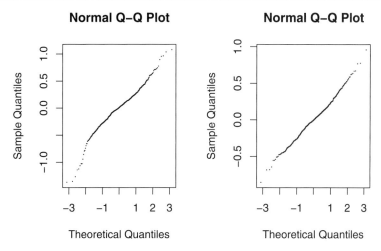

Figure A.17. *Quantile-quantile plots for linear mixed-effects models fit to the* country *data, with log(Count) as dependent variable. Left: untrimmed model, right: trimmed model.*

```
Estimated scale (compare to  1 )  0.948327
Fixed effects:                        Estimate Std. Error z value Pr(>|z|)
 (Intercept)                           -2.4064     0.3816  -6.307 2.85e-10
 WordOrdersubNotInitial                 0.2953     0.4994   0.591  0.55433
 AgeGroupchild                          1.2167     0.4691   2.594  0.00949
 AnimacyOfSubjectinanimate              0.8378     0.3664   2.287  0.02221
 WordOrdersubNotInitial:AgeGrpchild    -1.8501     0.7326  -2.525  0.01156
```

The estimated scale is reasonably close to 1, and the standard deviations for the random effects seem reasonable. Once MCMC sampling is implemented for logistic mixed-effects models, one will also want to check the HPD intervals for the random-effects parameters.

7.6 We fit the requested model:

```
> size.lmer = lmer(Rating ~ Class * Naive + MeanFamiliarity *
+ Language + I(MeanFamiliarity^2) * Language + (1|Subject) +
+ (1|Word), data = sizeRatings)
> pvals.fnc(size.lmer, nsim = 10000)$fixed
```

The coefficients involving the quadratic term for MeanFamiliarity do not reach significance. As we have 6 by-item predictors and fewer than 6 * 15 data points, we run the risk of overfitting, so we remove them without hesitation:

```
> size.lmer = lmer(Rating ~ Class * Naive + MeanFamiliarity *
+ Language + (1|Subject) + (1|Word), data = sizeRatings)
> pvals.fnc(size.lmer, nsim = 10000)$fixed
                   Estimate  HPD95lower HPD95upper  pMCMC  Pr(>|t|)
(Intercept)         3.87498     3.34603    4.37861 0.0001   0.0000
Classplant         -1.78310    -2.35496   -1.22164 0.0001   0.0000
NaivenotNaive      -0.07878    -0.37866    0.20951 0.5924   0.5886
MeanFamiliarity    -0.13910    -0.46626    0.19103 0.3864   0.3963
```

```
LanguagenotEnglish        -0.14275    -0.44275    0.19711 0.3752   0.3616
Clssplnt:NaivenotNaive -0.13866    -0.23985   -0.04267 0.0054   0.0068
MeanFam:LangnotEnglish  0.07486     0.01206    0.13708 0.0178   0.0182
```

We conclude that the effect of lexical familiarity on size ratings appears to be restricted to the non-native speakers of English. Note, furthermore, that a subject's prior knowledge of Class as a predictor leads to a slight increase in the effect of Class.

7.7

```
anova(writtenVariationLijk.lmer1,writtenVariationLijk.lmer2)
                      Df    AIC      BIC    logLik
writtenVariationLijk.lmer2  8  2854.6  2889.2 -1419.3
writtenVariationLijk.lmer1  9  2856.5  2895.5 -1419.3
                      Chisq Chi Df Pr(>Chisq)
writtenVariationLijk.lmer2
writtenVariationLijk.lmer1 0.0246      1      0.8753
```

Appendix B   Overview of R functions

OPERATORS

assignment	to the left: =, <-
	to the right: ->
arithmetic	multiplication * and division /
	addition + and subtraction -
	exponentiation $\wedge$ and remainder %%
logic	AND &, OR |, NOT !
relations	equality ==, inequality !=
	smaller than <, smaller than or equal to <=
	greater than >, greater than or equal to >=
numerical	logarithm `log()`, exponential function `exp()`
	smallest value `min()`, largest value `max()`
	range of values `range()`, sum of values `sum()`

VECTORS

`c(1, 3:5, 7)`	1 3 4 5 7
`seq(1, 10, by=2)`	1 3 5 7 9
`seq(1, 10, length=5)`	1.00 3.25 5.50 7.75 10.00
`1:10`	1 2 3 4 5 6 7 8 9 10
`10:1`	10 9 8 7 6 5 4 3 2 1
`rep(1, 5)`	1 1 1 1 1
`rep(1:3, 2:4)`	1 1 2 2 2 3 3 3 3
`length(rep(1:3,2:4))`	9
`cbind(c(1,2), c(3,4))`	1 3
	2 4
`rbind(c(1,2), c(3,4))`	1 2
	3 4
`sort(c("b", "a"))`	"a" "b"

STRINGS

`tolower("Alice")`	"alice"
`substr("Alice", 2, 5)`	"lice"
`paste("a", "lice", sep="-")`	"a-lice"
`nchar("Alice")`	5

FACTORS

`ordered()`	create ordered factor
`as.factor()`	convert into factor
`as.character()`	convert factor into character vector
`relevel()`	select new reference level
`[drop=TRUE]`	drop unused factor levels

DATA FRAMES

create data frame from vectors	`data.frame(X = x, Y = y)`
add variable to data frame	`mydata$Z = z`
first three rows	`mydata[1:3, ]`
first three columns	`mydata[, 1:3]`
rows where $X < 5$	`mydata[mydata$X < 5,]`
merge data frames	`merge()`
dimensions of data frame	`dim()`
row and column names	`rownames(), colnames()`
initial rows, final rows	`head(), tail()`
sort by column X	`mydata[order(mydata$X),]`

GETTING DATA IN AND OUT OF R

load vector of numbers	`scan("file")`
load vector of strings	`scan("file", what="character")`
load table with column names	`read.table("file", header=TRUE)`
load csv with column names	`read.csv("file", header=TRUE)`
write data frame	`write.table(mydata, "file")`
write data frame in csv format	`write.csv(mydata, "file")`
execute code in file	`source("file")`

SUMMARY STATISTICS

mean	`mean()`
median	`median()`
variance	`var()`
standard deviation	`sd()`
quantiles	`quantile()`
correlation	`cor()`
covariance	`cov()`

TABULATION, GROUPING, AGGREGATING

(cross)tabulation	`table()`, `xtabs()`
table of means	`tapply()`
table of proportions	`prop.table()`
aggregate	`aggregate()`
group	`cut()`

GRAPHICS

scatterplot	`plot()`
adds lines to scatterplot	`lines()`
adds points to scatterplot	`points()`
adds text to scatterplot	`text()`
adds text in margins	`mtext()`
adds regression line	`abline()`
matrix of plots	`par(mfrow=c(x,y))`
histogram	`hist()`
	`truehist()` (MASS package)
boxplot	`boxplot()`
bar plot	`barplot()`
mosaic plot	`mosaicplot()`
scatterplot matrix	`pairs()`
scatterplot matrix with correlations	`pairscor.fnc()`
trellis scatterplots	`xyplot()`, `splom()`
	(lattice package)
trellis boxplot	`bwplot()`
	(lattice package)
trellis scatterplots with smoother	`xylowess.fnc()`
scatterplot matrix with qq-plots	`qqmath()`
scatterplot matrix with densities	`densityplot()`
saving graphics	`postscript()`, `jpeg`, `png()`

DISTRIBUTIONS

normal	`pnorm(x, mean, sd)`
lognormal	`plnorm(x, mean, sd)`
student's *t*	`pt(x, df)`
F-distribution	`pF(x, df1, df2)`
chi-squared	`pchisq(x, df)`
binomial	`pbinom(x, n, p)`
Poisson	`ppois(x, lambda)`

DISTRIBUTION FUNCTIONS

---

density	`dnorm(), dt(), df()` ...
cumulative distribution	`pnorm(), pt(), pf()` ...
quantiles	`qnorm(), qt(), qf()` ...
random numbers	`rnorm(), rt(), rf()` ...

TESTS AND MODELS FOR CONTINUOUS VARIABLES

---

a single vector	`t.test(), wilcox.test()`
	`shapiro.test()` (for normality)
two vectors	`t.test(), wilcox.test()`
	`ks.test()`
	`var.test()`
two paired vectors	`t.test(x, y, paired=T),`
	`wilcox.test(x, y, paired=T)`
	`cor.test(x, y),`
	`cor.test(x, y, method="spearman")`
	`lm(y ~ x)`
multiple regression	`lm(y ~ x1 + x2 + x3)`
	`ols(y ~ x1 + x2 + x3)`
	(`Design` package)
mixed-effects regression	`lmer(y ~ x1 + x2 + x3 +`
	`+ (1|Subject) + (1|Item)),`
	(`lme4` package)

MODELS FOR A CONTINUOUS DEPENDENT VARIABLE AND FACTORS

---

one-way anova	`lm(y ~ f),`
	`aov(y ~ f)`
	`kruskal.test()`
	`ols(y ~ f)` (`Design`)
	`lmer(y ~ f + (1|G))` (`lme4`)
two-way anova	`lm(y ~ f1 + f2)`
	`aov(y ~ f1 + f2)`
	`ols(y ~ f1 + f2)` (`Design`)
	`lmer(y ~ f1 + f2 + (1|G))` (`lme4`)

MODELS FOR A CONTINUOUS VARIABLE AND FACTORS

---

analysis of covariance	`lm(y ~ x1 + x2 + f1 + f2)`, `ols(y ~ x1 + x2 + f1 + f2)` (Design package)
mixed-effects analysis of covariance	`lmer(y ~ x1 + x2 + f1 + f2 + + (1|Subject) + (1|Item))` (lme4 package)

TESTS AND MODELS FOR COUNTS

---

contingency tables	`chisq.test()`, `fisher.test()`
proportions test	`prop.test()`
generalized linear models	`glm(cbind(s, f) ~ x1 + f1, family = "binomial")`
logistic regression	`lrm(y ~ x1 + f1)` (Design package)
mixed-effects logistic regression	`lmer(y ~ x1 + f1 + + (1|Subject) + (1|Item), family = "binomial")` (lme4 package)

MODEL SUMMARIES AND MODEL CRITICISM

---

coefficients	`coef()`
t-tests coefficients	`summary()`
sequential F-tests	`anova() (lm(), aov(), lmer())`
marginal F-tests	`anova() (ols(), lrm())`
multiple comparisons	`TukeyHSD()`
predicted values	`predict()`
fitted values	`fitted()`
residuals	`resid()`
fixed effects	`fixef()` (lme4 package)
random effects	`ranef()` (lme4 package)
p-values for `lmer()`	`pvals.fnc()`, `aovlmer.fnc()`
outliers	`dfbetas()`, `which.influence()`, `dffits()`
collinearity	`kappa()`, `collin.fnc()`
bootstrap validation	`validate()` (Design package)
Markov chain Monte Carlo sampling	`mcmcsamp()`
Highest Posterior Density intervals	`HPDinterval()` (coda package)

WORD FREQUENCY DISTRIBUTIONS

empirical vocabulary growth curve	`growth.fnc()`
rank-frequency distribution	`zipf.fnc()`
load frequency spectrum	`read.spc()` (`zipfR` package)
create spectrum object	`spc()` (`zipfR` package)
load vocabulary growth curve	`read.vgc()` (`zipfR` package)
fit LNRE model	`lnre()` (`zipfR` package)
plot growth curves	`plot.vgc()` (`zipfR` package)

CLUSTERING

principal components analysis	`prcomp()`
factor analysis	`factanal()`
correspondence analysis	`corres.fnc()`
multidimensional scaling	`cmdscale()`
hierarchical cluster analysis	`hclust()` (agglomerative)
	`diana()` (divisive)
	`nj()` (unrooted trees)

CLASSIFICATION

classification trees	`rpart()`
discriminant analysis	`lda()` (MASS package)
support vector machines	`svm()` (e1071 package)

PROGRAMMING

for loop	`for (i in vec)`
define new function	`function()`

References

R. H. Baayen, D. J. Davidson, and D. M. Bates. Mixed-effects Modeling with Crossed Random Effects for Subjects and Items. Forthcoming in *Journal of Memory and Language*.

R. H. Baayen, T. Dijkstra, and R. Schreuder. Singulars and Plurals in Dutch: Evidence for a Parallel Dual Route Model. *Journal of Memory and Language*, 36:94–117, 1997.

R. H. Baayen, L. Feldman, and R. Schreuder. Morphological Influences on the Recognition of Monosyllabic Monomorphemic Words. *Journal of Memory and Language*, 53:496–512, 2006.

R. H. Baayen and R. Lieber. Word Frequency Distributions and Lexical Semantics. *Computers and the Humanities*, 30:281–291, 1997.

R. H. Baayen and F. Moscoso del Prado Martín. Semantic Density and Past-Tense Formation in Three Germanic Languages. *Language*, 81:666–698, 2005.

R. H. Baayen, F. Moscoso del Prado Martín, R. Schreuder, and L. Wurm. When Word Frequencies do NOT Regress Towards the Mean. In R. Harald Baayen and Robert Schreuder, editors, *Morphological Structure in Language Processing*. Mouton de Gruyter, Berlin, pages 463–484, 2003.

R. H. Baayen, R. Piepenbrock, and L. Gulikers. *The CELEX Lexical Database (CD-ROM)*. Linguistic Data Consortium, University of Pennsylvania, Philadelphia, PA, 1995.

R. H. Baayen. Derivational Productivity and Text Typology. *Journal of Quantitative Linguistics*, 1:16–34, 1994.

R. H. Baayen. *Word Frequency Distributions*. Kluwer Academic Publishers, Dordrecht, 2001.

D. Balota, M. Cortese, S. Sergent-Marshall, D. Spieler, and M. Yap. Visual Word Recognition of Single-Syllable Words. *Journal of Experimental Psychology:General*, 133:283–316, 2004.

D. M. Bates. Fitting Linear Mixed Models in R. *R News*, 5:27–30, 2005.

D. M. Bates. Linear Mixed Model Implementation in lme4. URL `http://spider.stat.umn.edu/R/library/lme4/doc/Implementation.pdf`. Department of Statistics, University of Wisconsin – Madison, 2006.

R. A. Becker, J. M. Chambers, and A. R. Wilks. *The New S Language. A Programming Environment for Data Analysis and Graphics*. Wadsworth & Brooks/Cole, Pacific Grove, 1988.

D. A. Belsley, E. Kuh, and R. E. Welsch. *Regression Diagnostics. Identifying Influential Data and Sources of Collinearity*. Wiley Series in Probability and Mathematical Statistics. Wiley, New York, 1980.

D. Biber. *Variation Across Speech and Writing*. Cambridge University Press, Cambridge, 1988.

D. Biber. *Dimensions of Register Variation*. Cambridge University Press, Cambridge, 1995.

W. M. Bolstad. *Introduction to Bayesian Statistics*. John Wiley & Sons, Hoboken, NJ, 2004.

J. Bresnan, A. Cueni, T. Nikitina, and R. H. Baayen. Predicting the Dative Alternation. In G. Bouma, I. Kraemer, and J. Zwarts, editors, *Cognitive Foundations of Interpretation*, pages 69–94. Royal Netherlands Academy of Science, 2007.

J. F. Burrows. Computers and the Study of Literature. In C. S. Butler, editor, *Computers and Written Texts*, pages 167–204. Blackwell, Oxford, 1992.

J. B. Carroll. On Sampling from a Lognormal Model of Word Frequency Distribution. In H. Kučera and W. N. Francis, editors, *Computational Analysis of Present-Day American English*, pages 406–424. Brown University Press, Providence, 1967.

R. J. Chitashvili and E. V Khmaladze. Statistical Analysis of Large Number of Rare Events and Related Problems. *Transactions of the Tbilisi Mathematical Institute*, 92:196–245, 1989.

H. H. Clark. The Language-as-Fixed-Effect Fallacy: A Critique of Language Statistics in Psychological Research. *Journal of Verbal Learning and Verbal Behavior*, 12:335–359, 1973.

W. G. Cochran. Testing a Linear Relation among Variances. *Biometrics*, 7:17–32, 1951.

J. Cohen. The Cost of Dichotomization. *Applied Psychological Measurement*, 7:249–254, 1983.

M. J. Crawley. *Statistical Computing. An Introduction to Data Analysis using S-PLUS*. Wiley, Chichester, 2002.

P. Dalgaard. *Introductory Statistics with R*. Springer, New York, 2002.

L. De Vaan, R. Schreuder, and R. H. Baayen. Regular Morphologically Complex Neologisms Leave Detectable Traces in the Mental Lexicon. *The Mental Lexicon*, 2:1–23, 2007.

M. Dunn, A. Terrill, G. Reesink, R. A. Foley, and S. C. Levinson. Structural Phylogenetics and the Reconstruction of Ancient Language History. *Science*, 309:2072–2075, 2005.

A. Ellegård. *The Auxiliary Do: The Establishment and Regulation of its use in English*. Almquist & Wiksell, Stockholm, 1953.

M. Ernestus and R. H. Baayen. Predicting the Unpredictable: Interpreting Neutralized Segments in Dutch. *Language*, 79:5–38, 2003.

M. Ernestus, M. van Mulken, and R. H. Baayen. Ridders en heiligen in tijd en ruimte: moderne stylometrische technieken toegepast op Oud-Franse teksten (The Syntax of Old-French Knights and Saints in Space and Time). *Taal en Tongval*, 58:70–83, 2007.

B. Everitt and T. Hothorn. *A Handbook of Statistical Analyses using R*. Chapman & Hall/CRC, Boca Raton, FL, 2006.

S. Evert. A simple LNRE Model for Random Character Sequences. In G. Purnelle, C. Fairon, and A. Dister, editors, *Le poids des mots. Proceedings of the 7th International Conference on Textual Data Statistical Analysis*, pages 411–422. Louvain-la-Neuve, UCL, 2004.

S. Evert and M. Baroni. The zipfR Library: Words and Other Rare Events in R. useR! 2006: The Second R User Conference, Vienna, June 2006.

J. J. Faraway. *Extending Linear Models with R: Generalized Linear, Mixed Effects and Nonparametric Regression Models*. Chapman & Hall/CRC, Boca Raton, FL, 2006.

K. I. Forster and R. G. Dickinson. More on the Language-as-Fixed Effect: Monte-Carlo Estimates of Error Rates for F_1, F_2, F', and $minF'$. *Journal of Verbal Learning and Verbal Behavior*, 15:135–142, 1976.

U. H. Frauenfelder, R. H. Baayen, F. M. Hellwig, and R. Schreuder. Neighborhood Density and Frequency across Languages and Modalities. *Journal of Memory and Language*, 32:781–804, 1993.

W. A. Gale and G. Sampson. Good-Turing Frequency Estimation without Tears. *Journal of Quantitative Linguistics*, 2:217–237, 1995.

I. J. Good. The Population Frequencies of Species and the Estimation of Population Parameters. *Biometrika*, 40:237–264, 1953.

S. Grondelaers, K. Deygers, H. Van Aken, V. Van den Heede, and D. Speelman. Het Condiv-Corpus Geschreven Nederlands. *Nederlandse Taalkunde*, 5:356–363, 2000.

H. Guiraud. *Les Caractères Statistiques du Vocabulaire*. Presses Universitaires de France, Paris, 1954.

W. Haerdle. *Smoothing Techniques With Implementation in S*. Springer-Verlag, Berlin, 1991.

F. E. Harrell. *Regression Modeling Strategies*. Springer, Berlin, 2001.

G. Herdan. *Type-Token Mathematics*. Mouton, The Hague, 1960.

D. Hoover. Another perspective on vocabulary richness. *Computers and the Humanities*, 37:151–178, 2003.

P. Juola. The Time Course of Language Change. *Computers and the Humanities*, 37(1):77–96, 2003.

K. Keune, M. Ernestus, R. Van Hout, and R. H. Baayen. Social, Geographical, and Register Variation in Dutch: From Written "mogelijk" to Spoken "mok". *Corpus Linguistics and Linguistic Theory*, 1:183–223, 2005.

A. S. Kroch. Function and Grammar in the History of English: Periphrastic Do. In R. W. Fasold and D. Schiffrin, editors, *Language Change and Variation*, pages 133–172. John Benjamins, Amsterdam, 1989.

H. Kučera and W. N. Francis. *Computational Analysis of Present-Day American English*. Brown University Press, Providence, RI, 1967.

T. K. Landauer and S. T. Dumais. A Solution to Plato's Problem: The Latent Semantic Analysis Theory of Acquisition, Induction and Representation of Knowledge. *Psychological Review*, 104(2):211–240, 1997.

R. F. Lorch and J. L. Myers. Regression Analysis of Repeated Measures Data in Cognitive Research. *Journal of Experimental Psychology: Learning, Memory, and Cognition*, 16:149–157, 1990.

A. Lüdeling and S. Evert. The Emergence of Non-Medical -itis. Corpus Evidence and Qualitative Analysis. In S. Kepser and M. Reis, editors, *Linguistic evidence. Empirical, Theoretical, and Computational Perspectives*, pages 315–333. Mouton de Gruyter, Berlin, 2005.

R. C. MacCallum, S. Zhang, K. J. Preacher, and D. D. Rucker. On the Practice of Dichotomization of Quantitative Variables. *Psychological Methods*, 7(1):19–40, 2002.

S. E. Maxwell and H. D. Delaney. Bivariate Median Splits and Spurious Statistical Significance. *Psychological Bulletin*, 113(1):181–190, 1993.

G. A. Miller. WordNet: An On-Line Lexical Database. *International Journal of Lexicography*, 3:235–312, 1990.

F. Murtagh. *Correspondence Analysis and Data Coding with JAVA and R*. Chapman & Hall/CRC, Boca Raton, FL, 2005.

J. K. Orlov. Dynamik der Häufigkeitsstrukturen. In H. Guiter and M. V. Arapov, editors, *Studies on Zipf's Law*, pages 116–153. Brockmeyer, Bochum, 1983.

E. Paradis. *Analysis of Phylogenetics and Evolution with R*. Springer, New York, 2006.

K. Perdijk, R. Schreuder, L. Verhoeven, and R. H. Baayen. Development of Morphological Relatedness in the Mental Lexicon: a Mixed Model Approach. Manuscript, Radboud University Nijmegen, 2007.

J. C. Pinheiro and D. M. Bates. *Mixed-Effects Models in S and S-PLUS*. Statistics and Computing. Springer, New York, 2000.

I. Plag, C. Dalton-Puffer, and R. H. Baayen. Morphological Productivity across Speech and Writing. *English Language and Linguistics*, 3(2):209–228, 1999.

M. Pluymaekers, M. Ernestus, and R. H. Baayen. Frequency and Acoustic Length: the Case of Derivational Affixes in Dutch. *Journal of the Acoustical Society of America*, 118:2561–2569, 2005.

T. Pollman and R. H. Baayen. Computing Historical Consciousness. A Quantitative Inquiry into the Presence of the Past in Newspaper Texts. *Computers and the Humanities*, 35:237–253, 2001.

H. Quené and H. Van den Bergh. On Multi-Level Modeling of Data from Repeated Measures Designs: A Tutorial. *Speech Communication*, 43:103–121, 2004.

J. G. W. Raaijmakers, J. M. C. Schrijnemakers, and F. Gremmen. How to Deal with "the Language as Fixed Effect Fallacy": Common Misconceptions and Alternative Solutions. *Journal of Memory and Language*, 41:416–426, 1999.

F. E. Satterthwaite. An Approximate Distribution of Estimates of Variance Components. *Biometrics Bulletin*, 2:110–114, 1946.

H. S. Sichel. Word Frequency Distributions and Type-Token Characteristics. *Mathematical Scientist*, 11:45–72, 1986.

M. S. Spassova. Las Marcas Sintácticas de Atribución Forense de Autoría de Textos Escritos en Español. Master's Thesis, Institut Universitari de Lingüística Aplicada, Universitat Pompeu Fabra, Barcelona, May 2006.

R. Sproat. *Morphology and Computation*. The MIT Press, Cambridge, MA, 1992.

W. Tabak, R. Schreuder, and R. H. Baayen. Lexical Statistics and Lexical Processing: Semantic Density, Information Complexity, Sex, and Irregularity in Dutch. In S. Kepser and M. Reis, editors, *Linguistic Evidence — Empirical, Theoretical, and Computational Perspectives*, pages 529–555. Mouton de Gruyter, Berlin, 2005.

F. J. Tweedie and R. H. Baayen. How Variable May a Constant be? Measures of Lexical Richness in Perspective. *Computers and the Humanities*, 32:323–352, 1998.

L. K. Tyler, W. D. Marslen-Wilson, and E. A. Stamatakis. Differentiating Lexical Form, Meaning, and Structure in the Neural Language System. *PNAS*, 102:8375–8380, 2005.

W. N. Venables and B. D. Ripley. *S Programming*. Springer, New York, 2002.

W. N. Venables and B. D. Ripley. *Modern Applied Statistics with S-Plus*. Springer, New York, 4th edition, 2003.

J. Verzani. *Using R for Introductory Statistics*. Chapman & Hall, New York, 2005.

R. Vulanović and R. H. Baayen. Fitting the Development of Periphrastic do in all Sentence Types. In P. Grzybek and R. Koehler, editors, *Festschrift für Gabriel Altmann*, pages 679–688. Walter de Gruyter, Berlin, 2006.

S. N. Wood. *Generalized Additive Models*. Chapman & Hall/CRC, New York, 2006.

G. U. Yule. *The Statistical Study of Literary Vocabulary*. Cambridge University Press, Cambridge, 1944.

G. K. Zipf. *The Psycho-Biology of Language*. Houghton Mifflin, Boston, 1935.

G. K. Zipf. *Human Behavior and the Principle of the Least Effort. An Introduction to Human Ecology*. Hafner, New York, 1949.

Index

Topic index

Author index